Generosity and the Limits of Authority

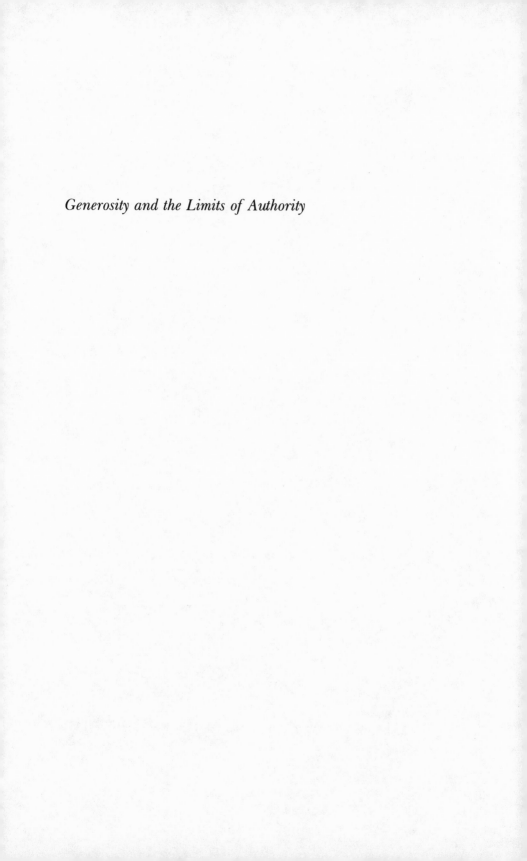

Generosity and the Limits of Authority

Shakespeare, Herbert, Milton

WILLIAM FLESCH

Cornell University Press

ITHACA AND LONDON

International Standard Book Number 0-8014-2642-1
Library of Congress Catalog Card Number 92-52753
Printed in the United States of America
Librarians: Library of Congress cataloging information
appears on the last page of the book.

For Laura Quinney

With thee conversing I forget all time,
All seasons and thir change, all please alike.
(*Paradise Lost*)

Contents

There they are happiest who dissemble best
Their weariness; and they the most polite
Who squander time and treasure with a smile,
Though at their own destruction.

—Cowper

Money, thou bane of bliss, and source of woe,
Whence com'st thou, that thou art so fresh and fine?

—Herbert

Preface

This book treats a common theme in three major literary figures of the English Renaissance too rarely considered together: William Shakespeare, George Herbert, and John Milton. As different as their theological and political commitments are, they share a deep interest in a particular kind of personal authority—the authority that comes from having "a privileged relation to the sources of being" (Clifford Geertz), an inherent right to "heaven's graces" (Shakespeare's sonnet 94)—and all three explore on a fundamental level the question of the relationship of the individual psyche to such a privileged authority. Applying the argument of Marcel Mauss's great book *The Gift*, I see this kind of authority as created and displayed through (often ritualized) acts of generosity. The capacity to give announces the giver's access to the sources of being, and by accepting a gift the beneficiary acknowledges obligation to both the giver and the giver's authority. Herbert describes the experience of the beneficiary and makes palpable the authority that the beneficiary ascribes to the benefactor, who is Christ. Shakespeare describes the experience of the human benefactor, an experience which includes the paradoxical sense that the capacity to be a benefactor is itself a gift. Milton's Satan refuses to be a beneficiary and so to acknowledge obligation, and he attempts to locate the sources of his own being in himself.

I think that the most intense literary power of these writers derives, however, from their exploration of the limits of generosity, from their sense of its ultimate frailty. Herbert's speakers learn to trust themselves—and even the determination of their own wills—entirely to God's generosity. In Herbert's most powerful poems, however, this generosity risks being depleted, as though even God's resources are finite. Christ suffers a loss through being generous to his believers, and it is finally this experience of loss or depletion on a divine scale that Herbert conveys. Shakespeare's greatest tragic figures—Richard II, Lear, Antony—also find their capacity to be generous coming to an end in impoverishment and loss; yet they still somehow attempt a generosity they no longer have the means for, a generosity that can now be expressed only through the grandeur of their language. In *Paradise Lost* the fall of humanity recapitulates the movement that I trace in Herbert and Shakespeare, from abundance—sign and source of generosity—to impoverishment.

These writers place a literary premium on the experience of impoverishment, as though language intensifies in inverse proportion to the resources of its speakers. In *Paradise Lost* abundance finally makes possible and stands for the kind of idolatry and materialism that Milton detested; against it is set the splendor of poetry, a splendor that derives from its spectrality and difference from substance. Milton thus confirms the intensification of language that I treat in Herbert (from the point of view of the beneficiary) and Shakespeare (from the point of view of the benefactor). Herbert's speakers finally share with their God not the absolute beneficence of divinity but the experience of an irretrievable poverty. And Shakespeare's heroes find that when their own privileged access to being is cut off, the only abundance remaining, the only generosity left to them, is the phantasmal generosity of their language.

The disingenuous play of humility and pride—the falsely modest catalog of one's patrons and the equally self-serving display of one's graciousness to others—which is typical of acknowledgments might provide a first example of the double-edged nature of generosity and obligation that Mauss considers. I am only too vividly aware, however, of how true my debts to others are and how little I can express those obligations. Mary Ann Radzinowicz gave me a great deal of careful and tough-minded criticism. Jonathan Culler and Mary Jacobus made extremely useful suggestions. Cynthia Chase read an early version of some of these chapters with much care and acumen. Harold Bloom graciously abided the weakest of my misreadings of his work, while showing me the way to the strongest readings I could achieve of the work of others. He shows in every way the greatness of generosity—and he was just as generous reading my work as he is in reading the great.

Walter Cohen and Paul Morrison read the finished manuscript—or what I kept hoping was the finished manuscript—several times, and each time they made me rethink my argument. Burton Dreben led me to many crucial insights: his resistances and refusals of easy claims have formed a generation of philosophers, but I hope he will not be too ambivalent about being acknowledged in this company of literary critics and theorists. Deborah Gordon made me think. Allen Grossman insisted on rigor and depth throughout and provided a model of strenuous and unyielding thought. John Burt, Ann Cvetkovich, Richard Durocher, Alan Levitan, Christopher Newfield, Vicente Rafael, and Elizabeth Sagaser put me right again and again when I wanted to go wrong. Richard Moran and Thomas Reinert insisted on clarity and accuracy, both by precept and by example. Andrew Garrett made me unafraid to ask everything I needed to know about linguistics. Many conversations with Leslie Kurke and Juliet Fleming have affected this book immeasurably. Moshe Halbertal listened to my ideas with his usual grasp and commented with his usual brilliance and precision. Juliet Floyd, Eli Friedlander, Steven Gerard, and Amélie Rorty helped me see how charming divine philosophy really is. Percy Flesch kept me constant company during the writing. Caroline Burman kept me honest. And in many ways this book could be described as building on the work of Jeff Nunokawa.

In the most fundamental way my parents and grandparents taught me to read and also what to read. I am also more indebted than I am comfortable admitting to Joseph Weiss and Steven Shaviro, who in many ways taught me how to read. Many parts of this book owe much to conversations, which I hope they have forgotten, with them and with Mary Campbell, Scott Derrick, Anne Ferry, Debra Fried, Eugene Goodheart, Kenneth Gross, Neil Hertz, Sally Jordan, Karen Klein, Joseph Kramer, Helena Michie, Christopher Pye, Matthew Rowlinson, David Scobey, Shirley Samuels, Mark Seltzer, Amartya Sen, Joshua Socolar, Susan Staves, Peter Swiggart, Gary Taylor, Gordon Teskey, and Laura Yim. I thank Stanley Cavell, John Mathews, and Timothy Murray as well, for their perpetually intelligent responsiveness.

Beryl-Elis Hoffstein invested a great deal of time and energy in this project. Without her help, and without that of Joseph Koerner, Philip Harper, Teresa Jesionowski, and Andrew Murphy, it's unlikely that I could have completed the book. Bernhard Kendler and two anonymous readers for Cornell University Press also gave me extraordinarily valuable advice.

I owe more than I could ever dream of repaying, least of all by this work, to the dedicatee. Whatever I understand about literature or about life comes from her insight and her example. This book is ultimately about literary vocation, and anything that I know about literary vocation I know from her.

A Sachar Summer Research Grant and a Bernstein Faculty Fellowship, both awarded by Brandeis University, helped immeasurably in the research and writing of this book. An earlier version of part of chapter 3 appeared in *John Milton: Modern Critical Views*, ed. Harold Bloom (New York: Chelsea House, 1986). I gratefully acknowledge James Merrill for permitting me to quote from "The Broken Home" and "In the Dark."

Quotations from Herbert's poetry are from *The Works of George Herbert*, ed. F. E. Hutchinson (Oxford: Oxford University Press, 1941; corrected rpt., 1945); quotations from Shakespeare are from *The Riverside Shakespeare*, ed. G. Blakemore Evans (Boston: Houghton Mifflin, 1974; sixth printing with corrections and additions); occasionally I modify an editorial choice I disagree with, but whenever I do, I discuss my modification; quotations from Milton's poetry are from *John Milton: Complete Poems and Major Prose*, ed. Merritt Y. Hughes (Indianapolis: Odyssey Press, 1957).

WILLIAM FLESCH

Waltham, Mass.

Generosity and the Limits of Authority

Generality and Extremity

The limits of my language . . . *mean* the limits of my world.
—Wittgenstein

Toute exclusion formelle rompt la généralité.
—Rousseau

Skepticism, solitude, mortality: these are three different names for and three different descriptions of the kinds of contingency that the self may perceive in its relation to itself and to the world. Skepticism—by which (following Stanley Cavell) I mean skepticism about the existence of the external world or of other minds—might seem to designate the most radical stance. Skepticism focuses mainly on the relation between the private and particularized self and the more general world; it holds that there is no way to overcome the breach between the internal certainty of selfhood and the unreliable sensory impressions that convey what is other than the self. The skeptical account of the contingency of the self's relation to the world has received a great deal of attention in recent years, whether overtly, as in the work of Cavell, or more indirectly, as in deconstruction. This attention, and its combination of philosophy and psychology, has led to some powerful accounts of the kinds of concerns and uncertainties that may befall human consciousness, and so to some powerful accounts of literary affect. But I shall contend that the focus on skepticism may function to neglect or repress other and deeper apprehensions of contingency: the sorrows of mortality and solitude, or what I will call *extremity*.

This is so because the issue of skepticism offers the ego confronted with contingency a choice of alternatives, and the choice it offers is one by which the ego can't lose. Skepticism demands *proof*, and so it is essentially an intellectual activity. It preserves from the start the realm of the intellect, no matter how much it questions the intellect's suffi-

1

ciency or power. It thus presupposes a distinction between private self and public world, a distinction that guarantees the fundamental autonomy of the self, no matter what happens to the external "world as I found it" (Wittgenstein) or the "Not-me" (Emerson).

On one alternative, then, skepticism preserves a private autonomy, an autonomy which the early Wittgenstein called solipsism. That autonomy may be seen as the refusal of a relation to the world which would be necessarily contingent. But on the other alternative, any effective arguments against skepticism, and in particular the arguments made by the later Wittgenstein, also appear to secure the self against an apprehension of its own contingency by assuring it of its nativity in the world. The later Wittgenstein argues (contrary to the claims of deconstruction) that language is irreducibly public, irreducibly social. There are no private languages. The very language in which the ego might express its skepticism already belongs to the public sphere that skepticism is being used to doubt. As Wittgenstein stresses in *On Certainty*, the use of language *means* a certain kind of life:

126. I am not more certain of the meaning of my words than I am of certain judgments.

158. Can I be making a mistake, for example, in thinking that the words of which this sentence is composed are English words [deutsche Wörter] whose meaning I know?

369. If I wanted to doubt whether this was my hand, how could I avoid doubting whether the word "hand" has any meaning? . . .

370. . . . The fact that I use the word "hand" and all the other words in my sentence without a second thought, indeed that I should stand before the abyss if I wanted so much as to try doubting their meanings—shews that absence of doubt belongs to the essence of the language-games.[1]

The skeptical stance is just that—a stance; and so it is, like every stance, or every linguistic activity, originally learned from others and irreducibly directed toward others. The life of words and the life of human beings hardly differ. "To imagine a language means to imagine a form of life," Wittgenstein argues very early in the *Investigations*,[2] and much later he writes, "What has to be accepted, the given,

---

1. Ludwig Wittgenstein, *On Certainty*, trans. G.E.M. Anscombe and G. H. von Wright (New York: Harper, 1972). All references to *On Certainty* are by section number.
2. Ludwig Wittgenstein, *Philosophical Investigations*, 3d ed., trans. G.E.M. Anscombe (New York: Macmillan, 1968), §19. Following standard practice, I refer to the num-

is—so one could say—*forms of life*" (p. 226). "So you are saying that human agreement decides what is true and false?" challenges Wittgenstein's imaginary interlocutor, to which he answers: "It is what human beings *say* that is true and false; and they agree in the *language* they use. That is not agreement in opinions but in forms of life" (§241). Language is not in itself either a true or a false medium to represent reality; like the life to which it corresponds it is the necessary condition for the very notions of the true and the false.

This account suggests that both alternatives posed by the problem of skepticism may end in denying the contingencies of selfhood, seeing the self either as utterly autonomous and self-reliant or as completely engaged in the world, even or especially when it declares its doubt about that engagement. But—and this is my central claim—given such alternatives, the problem of skepticism might obscure the deeper contingencies and estrangements that I wish to make my subject. Or rather they are not *my* subject; they are the subject of the three writers I treat in this book: Herbert, Shakespeare, and Milton. As I argue in my Herbert chapter, I think that these deeper contingencies are Wittgenstein's subject as well, and that it is one of his signal strengths that in showing how the skeptical problem may be made to pass away, he does not deny the other perils and estrangements to which selfhood is liable. In fact once the issue of skepticism is laid to rest, a sense of these other contingencies is more likely to emerge. If to imagine a language means to imagine a form of life, then the estrangement that I argue Wittgenstein evokes is an estrangement even from language and from all that language confers of personality and life. Such a position goes against much of current interpretation of Wittgenstein, but that interpretation neglects, to my mind, the deep pathos of his most powerful moments.

This book comes out of a Blanchotian perspective, one in which the eerie impersonality and nonworldliness of literary affect, the affect that haunts literary space, loom large. By starting from such a perspective, I may seem in some ways fundamentally opposed to prevailing tendencies in literary criticism. But I aim at something far more modest than challenging these tendencies: I merely wish to undertake the supplementary task of trying to bracket and describe a certain kind of literary affect. There is no reason this project should be irreconcilable with the kinds of inquiry now widely undertaken, and indeed I rely on much recent research. My claims about Wittgenstein are meant partly to underscore the compatibility of my concerns with

bered sections of part 1 of *Philosophical Investigations* by section number and to part 2 by page number.

more extrinsic and contextualizing methods of inquiry. For at his most powerful, Wittgenstein—the champion of anti-essentialism and of the extrinisic—nevertheless sounds more like Blanchot than like Stanley Fish. By focusing on someone as worldly and as antimetaphysical as the late Wittgenstein I hope to show the inevitability of Blanchot's characterization of the unworldliness of solitude.

Thus my argument makes two major moves, which develop as I turn from Herbert to Shakespeare to Milton. In the chapter on Herbert I claim that skepticism may be a symptom of and so displace a deeper kind of solitude. In Herbert this solitude might be called the experience of abandonment. Many of Herbert's speakers describe, with more or less anguish varying with the self-confidence they assert, a skeptical relationship to God and to the community of the saved. Although these moments of skepticism are very serious in Herbert, I argue that they are best read as reaction-formations to or psychic defenses against the anguish of feeling not the nonexistence of God or of the community of the saved, but a deep exclusion from this community. The term *reaction-formation* is Freud's, but I think it describes Cavell's Wittgensteinian diagnosis of skepticism as a refusal of knowledge, a refusal motivated by something other than a purely intellectual problem. Herbert's speakers seem to attain genuine insight when they give up couching the problem of contingency in terms of skepticism, when they recognize the real anguish of abandonment that the question of skepticism risks obscuring.

In a religious context, of course, nonbelief and abandonment are not so easily separable; but the work of Herbert's poetry, like the work of much of Wittgenstein, goes into separating them. I argue that Herbert uses the discovery that abandonment is the real psychic concern of his autobiographical speakers to read that sense of abandonment as a paradoxical sign of salvation. If skepticism betrays the sense of abandonment it attempts to defend against, and if that sense can arise only from a desire for God's presence, then what at first looks like unbelief, or the risk of unbelief, turns out to signify belief, or desire for God's grace. This recognition is in some sense its own reward, since for Herbert the confidence thus achieved that one actually does believe in God or desires his grace can come only from God through his grace. Thus Herbert makes the sense of abandonment do the same work as the focus on skepticism: it finally ratifies selfhood and community rather than undercutting them.

That is my first point: skepticism preserves the coherences it seems to doubt (most important, the coherence of language, or the self's involvement in language). For Herbert the anguish of religious skepticism becomes an earnest of his own faith. Skepticism is a response to the real experience of abandonment, and abandonment implies the reality of the person abandoning. Abandonment itself is read as a source of comfort. (Compare Christ's words in John 16:7: "It is expedient for you that I go away; for if I go not away, the Comforter will not come unto you.")

But this comfort is possible only because Herbert does in fact have faith: faith that those whose despair is genuine enough, whose sense of abandonment is powerful enough, will be comforted. Nevertheless— and this is the second part of my argument and my major concern— even in Herbert there is a sense of another kind of solitude, of loss that does not imply its own recuperation. It is this solitude and loss that I want to bring out. I think it telling that this solitude surfaces even in Herbert and just as telling that it surfaces in Wittgenstein. In the last part of my Herbert chapter I look at the ways even his poetry can evoke a comfortless loss, a deeper and irrecuperable sense of abandonment or estrangement. This loss is not the experience of any of his autobiographical speakers. It is, strangely enough, the experience described by his divine speakers—Christ in "The Sacrifice," God in "The Pulley"—and described of them, as in "Redemption." Herbert's speakers typically begin skeptical of true community but end up recognizing their membership in such a community (cf. "Love" [III]). But in his most powerful poems, that community is ultimately understood as a community of loss.

That experience of loss and abandonment may be described, in terms I derive from Wittgenstein, as an estrangement from the immediacy of life and consequently as an estrangement from the immediacy even of selfhood. Skepticism separates a fully formed and coherent self from the world, but the estrangement I want to evoke is one in which even the most intimate experience takes the form of loss and alterity. As in Freud's account of the painfulness of mourning, loss may consist in a solitude so internalized as to mean an estrangement even from language as a form of life.[3] An estranged relation to language remains, and so also an estranged relation to selfhood. Language is no longer felt as the life shared by both the self and the world, but as a dark alterity, foreign and opaque. Rather than being the site of community, this estranged language becomes in its estrangement the site of loss and solitude, of what Georges Bataille calls "the negative community: the community of those who have no com-

3. See addendum C to *Inhibitions, Symptoms, and Anxiety*, in *The Standard Edition of the Complete Psychological Works of Sigmund Freud*, trans. James Strachey (London: Hogarth Press, 1953–74), 20:169–72.

munity." This, as I hope to show in the chapters that follow, is a way of characterizing one type of literary language.

This deeper contingency or experience of loss or solitude or mortality—which I call extremity—is the central subject of this book, rather than the skepticism that can obscure it. Herbert, who is not primarily a despairing poet, manages on the whole to quell his apprehension of extremity, and in emphasizing it I am reading somewhat against the grain of his work. Still I think its presence is what makes his work so powerful. Shakespeare, I argue, makes extremity one of his major themes, at least in the sonnets and in the plays that I treat at length: *Richard II*, *King Lear*, and *Antony and Cleopatra*. I focus on this theme, not on the question of skepticism, in the chapter about Shakespeare. These plays all depict a fall from power. Such a fall would seem to mean a fall from the heights of the public sphere into the restricted space of the private; at least that is what Richard, Lear, and Antony think. Richard imagines himself a subject and an almsman; Lear wants to live out his old age in peaceful retirement; and Antony sues Octavius Caesar to be allowed to live "a private man in Athens." The fall from public to private would recapitulate the distinction erected by skepticism, but Shakespeare is interested in exploring a fall into a region far more extreme than privacy, the region I am calling extremity. Richard, Lear, and Antony represent different modes of interminable loss, of a loss which goes infinitely beyond that of their public personae. Yet corresponding to their loss of all worldly substance, even of their own self-presence, they experience a gain in the intensity of their language. But this gain is really only the shadow of a gain, since it does them no good at all in the world and does not even enrich their inner lives. The nature of this shadowy gain is what I want to characterize.

The idea that real loss can lead to a shadowy gain is first fully and explicitly articulated by Marcel Mauss in his great essay *The Gift*. Mauss shows that the paradoxical practice of gift giving, sometimes carried to the extreme of destruction rather than conveyance, is a widespread and important feature of human culture. Bataille's brilliant reading of Mauss emphasizes the estrangement that the principle of loss embodied in the gift can lead to and the way that the difference between gain and loss can come undone. In my Shakespeare chapter I look at the prevalence and fate of gift giving in Shakespeare's work. In Shakespeare—as Mauss says is the case in most societies—gift-giving represents a manifestation and exercise of power. To give a person a gift is to oblige that person, at least to oblige his or her gratitude. As Marshall Sahlins points out, Hobbes made this one of his natural laws of social cohesion:

> As Justice dependeth on Antecedent Covenenant; so does GRATITUDE depend on Antecedent Grace, that is to say, Antecedent Free-gift: and it is the fourth Law of Nature; which may be conceived in this forme, *That a man which receiveth Benefit from another of meer Grace, Endeavour that he which giveth it, have no reasonable cause to repent him of his good will.* For no man giveth, but with intention of Good to himself; because Gift is Voluntary; and of all Voluntary Acts, the Object is to every man his own Good.[4]

Whoever is most extravagant in gifts has the greatest claim to power and to loyalty. This expectation, at least, features greatly in pre-bourgeois economic orders. Shakespeare's characters, however, consistently suffer the transition to a nascent capitalism, and one way they suffer this is to see all their extravagance come to grief. In *Power and Civility* Norbert Elias describes how the ruin of aristocratic families in France results from a requirement of generosity, of what Bataille calls *dépense*, and particularly how the king is drawn into the expensive ritual of power he appears to control.[5] As I argue, this is a perfect description of Shakespeare's extravagant kings. Generosity in Shakespeare intends a return in power and obligation (what else can Lear be expecting?), but in the new order it consistently meets only with its own exhaustion. Shakespeare's great tragic figures experience, and describe the experience of, an exhaustion of the generosity of being that they imagined they had embodied.

Pierre Bourdieu quotes La Rochefoucauld: "Overmuch eagerness to discharge one's obligations is a form of ingratitude." This means that obligation in the gift economy has something incorporeally temporal about it, something beyond the value of the corporeal gift.[6] You must wait before you repay; thus with the gift comes an imposition of obligation, not only to repay, but to be in a state of obligation to repay. The gift obliges obligation, and it obliges the duration of obligation. Jean Baudrillard argues on this basis that gifts count more in the

4. *Leviathan*, pt. 1, chap. 15, quoted by Marshall Sahlins in *Stone Age Economics* (Chicago: Aldine-Atherton, 1972), p. 178. Lewis Hyde, in his idealizing book *The Gift* (New York: Random House, 1983), sees the work of art as an instance of erotic generosity. He is less concerned with the onus of obligation and gratitude that generosity imposes, an onus felt even in Herbert.

5. Norbert Elias, *Power and Civility*, trans. Edmond Jephcott (New York: Pantheon, 1982).

6. Pierre Bourdieu, *Outline of a Theory of Practice*, trans. Richard Nice (New York: Cambridge University Press, 1977), p. 6.

realm of signs than in the realm of substance. The power that gifts confer moves counter to their substance, and a loss in substance means a semiotic gain in power. Under certain circumstances, however, such a gain in power may be purely notional. Gifts bring an insubstantial return, a return that inheres only in language.[7] (The actual, later moment of substantial reciprocation, if it comes, is in fact an undoing or a reversal of the gift relation.) It is the great achievement of the Shakespearean plays I am considering that the return their characters fail to obtain in loyalty or obligation or indebtedness they make up for in their language, when that language is no longer the manifestation of their presence in the world, when it has become extreme. According to Hazlitt's famous stricture on Shakespeare, "The language of poetry falls in naturally with the language of power. The principle of poetry is a very anti-leveling principle." I think rather that the language of poetry in Shakespeare reaches its greatest intensity in that extreme region where the generosity of language fails to guarantee a relationship to the world, either public or private. Language becomes simultaneously generous and impotent, and its spectral generosity exceeds all bounds as it attempts the impossible compensation for its own impotent spectrality.

The chapter on Shakespeare makes up about half of this book, not just because Shakespeare provides the most extended evocation of extremity, but also because the three plays I examine treat extremity in three different ways. My last chapter addresses Milton's *Paradise Lost* and is meant as a recapitulation of my argument. Like Herbert, Milton is interested in the strategies by which the self attempts to maintain its own boundaries, but like Shakespeare he is ultimately concerned with extremity and not selfhood. I try to show that both the fallen and the unfallen angels see the Fall as preserving intact the boundaries of selfhood. Skepticism too might have as its motto Satan's sublime question, "What matter where, if I be still the same . . . ?" But Adam and Eve, as well as the Son, learn another understanding of the Fall: a fall into extremity and loss of the sort that is also Shakespeare's theme.

For Milton as for Shakespeare the language of poetry and the language of power seem irreconcilable. Readers of Milton have always felt that his Satan is a being far superior to his God. I believe that Milton's obvious commitment to Christianity (no matter how heretical his doctrine) can be reconciled with the sheerly poetic power of a

7. Jean Baudrillard, *For a Critique of the Political Economy of the Sign*, trans. Charles Levin (St. Louis, Mo.: Telos Press, 1981).

disempowered entity like Satan through observation of the moments where Satan fails to understand the notion of powerlessness, where Satan becomes more enamored of tyrannical power than the apparently tyrannical God he rebels against. To make this claim, I try to demonstrate that the angelic understanding of theology in *Paradise Lost* is just as misguided as Satan's, and that the Fall was a happy one (*felix culpa*) only because it conferred on Adam and Eve the ability to feel the poetry of exclusion and of mortality and so to belong to "the negative community" of mortality, a community to which the Son also consents to belong.

I now begin to flesh out the argument I have so far sketched. I hope to show that the possibility of extremity is an almost inevitable concomitant to the antiskeptical moves made by Herbert or by Wittgenstein, and that it is their strength to recognize the inevitability of this concomitant.

Because the child's relation to the world is necessarily preskeptical, the burden of persuasion is on the skepticism that would doubt the existence of the external world or of other minds. Skepticism asks what grounds one has for one's beliefs, but our relations to the world and to others are not, properly speaking, based on any *beliefs*. That is to say, other people and the outside world are not, in the first instance, things that language—whether truthfully or falsely—*represents*. Rather, they are what language is *for*, and to know a language is already to interact with the world: "absence of doubt belongs to the essence of the language-games." Through language, and through the linguistic interaction that Wittgenstein calls "language-games," the child learns what the world *is like*, or what things in the world are like; it does not learn *that* things in the world exist. The child learns things in a *general* way: the very idea of individuation comes late. And even when it does come, the condition of any particular reference is the generality to which the particular belongs.[8]

8. The topic of generality has not often been treated as such in literary criticism or literary theory. Two major exceptions explore it in ways somewhat different from my own. William Wimsatt's essay "The Structure of the 'Concrete Universal' in Literature" (*PMLA* 62 [1947]: 262–80; an abbreviated version of the essay appears in *The Verbal Icon* [Lexington: University of Kentucky Press, 1954], pp. 68–83) argues that poems are both concrete and universal and that poetry presents "an object . . . which is both highly general and highly particular." Wimsatt argues that literature can be distinguished from other kinds of writing by the fact that the particulars it mentions are "more than usually relevant" to the universalizing claims that it is making. He goes on to say, perhaps unconsciously echoing Wittgenstein's central show/say distinction, "The poetic character of details consists not in what they say directly and explicitly (as if roses and moonlight were poetic) but in what by their arrangement they *show* implicitly" (p.

The child comes to know what the world is like by *practicing* interactions with it. This word *practice* should retain its sense of the nonserious: skepticism is very serious, but the child learns about the world through games. To use the ontological vocabulary that Wittgenstein would eschew, the world consists of language games, not of objects. One can always be skeptical as to the existence of any *particular* object. The chess piece may be an illusion. But its correspondence to a certain kind of move can't be. The bishop isn't a piece of wood; it's a piece that moves diagonally (a piece of—characterized by—diagonal movement).

As Cavell argues, the mistake is to think of the world as an object or a super-object, the object par excellence. Rather, and again I use the vocabulary that Wittgenstein would have us outgrow, the existence of the world means for the later Wittgenstein the playing of language games and not the existence of the counters with which they are played. And the existence of others means the players that these games require and necessarily imply. This implication is stronger than presupposition. To play a language game is not to *presuppose* that there are other players. Presupposition implies doubt, but in most language games doubt of this sort simply does not arise, just as one doesn't *presuppose* that there isn't a chasm outside the front door when one steps outside.[9]

To generalize means to *characterize* the world or to discover that the world does not consist in the sum of objects, nor yet in the totality of facts, but in its having a certain *coherence*, a coherence whose *character* we can recognize.[10] As Peirce puts it, knowledge of the world implies

270). Familiar new critical concerns are obvious here; but I am still interested in Wimsatt's argument for something like W. V. Quine's doctrine of "meaning holism," whereby meanings are not built up from words and sentences but are derived from utterances taken as a whole, with the meanings of individual words and sentences put to correspond to the meaning of the whole. The particular doesn't matter in itself; what counts is the generality derived from the relations established with other particulars.

Scott Elledge provides a useful account of the topic in "The Background and Development in English Criticism of the Theories of Generality and Particularity" (*PMLA* 62 [1947], 147–82). He traces these themes from eighteenth-century views through Eliot's strictures against Milton that he lacked sufficient attention to the particular in "L'Allegro" and "Il Penseroso," where "the imagery . . . is all general" ("A Note on the Verse of John Milton," quoted by Elledge on p. 181).

9. On presupposition, see *Philosophical Investigations*, pp. 179–80.

10. The early Wittgenstein thought that the world did consist in the totality of facts: "The world is all that is the case, . . . the totality of facts, not the totality of things" (*Tractatus Logico-Philosophicus*, trans. D. F. Pears and B. F. McGuinness [New York: Humanities Press, 1972], p. 7). On coherence, see Quine on meaning holism, e.g., *From a Logical Point of View* [Cambridge, Mass.: Harvard University Press, 1980]. Quine, Donald Davidson, and Wittgenstein argue that meaning inheres not in individual prop-

something other than an inventory of its contents: it implies knowledge of its general patterns. But such knowledge is partly a literary question since coherent characterization—of people and of situations or contexts—is a literary activity (not only for writers but also for readers).

In the Herbert chapter I try to describe in detail the consolations that the viewpoint of generality can afford—the consolations of seeing the characteristic and the public as prior to the private or particular. Herbert's fear of being isolated from the ways of salvation is a fear that itself *belongs* to the universe he is afraid of being isolated from. Herbert's proposed consolation is remarkably similar to Wittgenstein's argument that skepticism is itself a language game or can only arise in a language game; it is part of the public world it denies. To belong to this more general world of which skepticism is a part thus means: not to be isolated within skepticism.

The generality and the priority of the *public* categories that alone allow one to think oneself isolated from the public make for a kind of generosity of being (for Herbert) or of language (for Wittgenstein). The solipsist might be understood to wish to destroy the world, but the world's generosity consists in its being able to absorb all skepticism about its objects and still promise the plenitude of its generality. This is not the Cartesian or Heideggerian generosity that *gives* being; it is rather a generosity that *assures* being. The generosity of generality Herbert names grace: the sense that God will console him even for what he takes to be his isolation-imposing disbelief in God.

The theory of generality is a theory of consolation. Generality's consoling force consists in the generous and gracious inclusiveness that it manifests, for both Herbert and Wittgenstein. For Herbert, belonging to the general can take the form of being part of a typological relationship, even without knowing it or sometimes necessarily without knowing it. For Wittgenstein it would mean engaging in a language game. At any rate, generality means interacting with the world on the level of character, not of objects.

But Herbert can ultimately recognize his own childlike belonging to God's world, the realm of grace or of generality, only through its contrast to the terrible emptying of divinity that God's sacrifice of himself for humanity means. The real anguish and power of Herbert's poetry come from his evocation not of the consoling generosity

---

ositions (which could be true or false) but in systems of propositions. They make for a certain coherence, and that coherence has a certain character.

of generality, but of the way generality can encounter a limit beyond which the generosity of being comes to an end. Herbert sees Christ as having passed this limit. And if Christ has passed beyond the guarantees of the general, then the generosity he offers may itself fail— or, rather, all that he can offer is the comfort of their shared comfortlessness.

As I shall argue, in contrast to the austere security of skepticism, the later Wittgenstein sees self and world as inherently fragile, made up of a heterogeneous multitude of diverse, ad hoc, local language games consisting ultimately of ungrounded actions. Fragility and generality go together, since the life of the general can be no more than the fragile life of the language that names and constitutes general terms: "You must bear in mind that the language-game is so to say something unpredictable. I mean: it is not based on grounds. It is not reasonable (or unreasonable). / It is there—like our life" (*On Certainty*, §559). Wittgenstein owes his literary power to his sense of the transience of language or of human participation in language: that is, the transience of human life. It is important that this fragility characterizes not only the self, and not only the relation of self to world, but the world as well, since, as Wallace Stevens says, "it is a world of words to the end of it." Thus a paradoxical formulation can arise: the self shares with the world an inalienable fragility—the fragility of the ever-mutable language games that constitute both. This formulation may make of fragility its own unshakable consolation, but the reflux of such a view would be the endless fragility of all consolation. Everything depends on whether the stress is put on the fact of sharing or on the fragility of what is shared.

Extremity names the endlessness of that fragility and the endlessness of the process by which community and selfhood can be lost. Extremity is a kind of inevitable shadow of generality, a communion among those excluded from the community of the saved, a general failure of the general. This exclusion is different from the self-imposed and self-dramatizing isolation of skepticism but can best be made visible by contrast to skepticism. "The negative community: the community of those who have no community" can be evoked only in the quasi-fictional, shadowy world opened by literature. Literature may consist largely in the process of characterization, but it can rise to its most intense plangency when it passes beyond the limits of relatively stable characterization, beyond the personal and the social, into an evocation of extremity.

I think that the moments in *Paradise Lost* that Geoffrey Hartman

calls "Milton's Counterplots"[11] evoke this negative community—
moments in which Milton alludes to far less important, more contingent figures than his main characters: often they are fictional, like
Proserpin gathering flowers; sometimes they are utterly unremarkable, like the pilot of the skiff on the Norway foam. They too are at
issue and at risk; they too belong to the world, but it is the world into
which a world of woe has been brought. They belong to a general
fragility, or a fragile generality.

So also, it turns out, do Adam and Eve, even in Eden. This version
of the negative community is especially evident in the strange praise
that the narrator of *Paradise Lost* confers on them when they are
described as at once more a part of humanity in general and more
isolated from that humanity than seems appropriate to a situation in
which they as yet constitute the whole of humanity:

> So hand in hand they pass'd, the loveliest pair
> That ever since in love's imbraces met,
> *Adam* the goodliest man of men since born
> His Sons, the fairest of her Daughters *Eve.*
>
> (4.321–24)

There are two Adams here, and two Eves. Or are there? I think,
rather, that Adam and Eve here show their belonging fragility (or
frailty). They show their humanity: though peerless they live in a
world of peers—the world of men born since Adam, the world of
Eve's daughters—to whose community they belong. There is something reassuring about this shared community even in Paradise, since
there is something dimly troubling about their state of parentlessness
in Eden. In this passage they are represented as paradisal orphans no
longer: like all other humans they have parents, namely Eve and
Adam ("our general sire"). This description has the effect not of
rendering them helpless but of reassuring us about them. Adam and
Eve become humanized here, because the other Adam and Eve, the
ones from whom they descend, have become generalized terms, just
as his or her parents first appear to the child as generalized terms, as
the parents par excellence.[12] Adam and Eve seem able to depend on
that generality here; it is anterior but still human and still humanly
characterizable.

11. Geoffrey Hartman, *Beyond Formalism* (New Haven, Conn.: Yale University Press,
1970), pp. 113–23.
12. Quine derives an entire account of human learning from this sort of generality.
See *Word and Object* (Cambridge, Mass.: MIT Press, 1960).

Since the later Adam and Eve are the progenitors of all humanity—
are, in fact, the generalized Adam and Eve from whom they descend—
these later children can be said to achieve for us their own generality.
Adam and Eve are at once parents and children. They are children
who can successfully and completely identify with their parents, since
they are descended from themselves. The parental otherness—the
most anguishing discovery of the child—here ceases to be an otherness.
The usual arc toward solipsism reverses. Or, rather, this passage describes a transient but perfectly successful recovery. Adam and Eve now
utterly identify with the generalized parents from whom they descend;
they are instances of that generality.[13] This coincidence of general and
particular serves as a consoling vision of their humanity. It is consoling
because in it they become fully human—children of human parents as
well as of God. Because of this humanity they are as liable as any of their
peers to fall. But they are also humanly susceptible to forgiveness—
ours (as victims of their sins) and God's. Even when they do fall, it will
still be hand in hand that they take their solitary way. Their humanity
and fragility go together. Since we are descended from this human
fragility, we too participate in the general world of the fully human and
utterly fragile.[14]

Is this consolation enough? Can the sense of a breach between self
and world, or self and other, or subject and language, be healed in
this way? Can the world ever console completely for its own fragility? I

13. See P. F. Strawson's argument that particulars are "individual instances" of the
general, in "Particular and General" in his *Logico-Linguistic Papers* (London: Methuen,
1971), pp. 28–52.
14. After the Fall a kind of countergenerality may inhere in the description of the
stories that may derive from it:

> However some tradition they dispers'd
> Among the Heathen of their purchase got,
> And Fabl'd how the Serpent, whom they call'd
> *Ophion* with *Eurynome*, the wide-
> Encroaching *Eve* perhaps, had first the rule
> Of high *Olympus*, thence by *Saturn* driv'n
> And *Ops*, ere yet *Dictaean* Jove was born.   (10.578–84)

Milton is suggesting that Eurynome (whose name means "wide-encroaching") may be
based on Eve. The punctuation (which I support) suggests that she gets the name
because Eve herself was wide-encroaching. If *encroaching* is taken to mean "transgress-
ing," this is true enough. But the range of Eve's transgressions is not at issue here, and
"wide-encroaching" must also mean that the story of Eve is as "dispers'd" through the
world as the tradition that mentions her. This is not the Eve of *Paradise Lost*, however,
whom we don't imagine now traveling throughout the world, but a more general Eve—
a mythic or literary figure like all the others in Milton's counterplots—and with "wide-
encroaching" as a kind of Homeric epithet which completely identifies her for the
reader.

think the answer that a philosophy like Wittgenstein's or Cavell's will give can finally lead to literary insight similar, perhaps surprisingly, to Maurice Blanchot's.

One of the subsidiary purposes of this book is to show that Wittgenstein and Blanchot have a great deal in common, from the hypnotic severity of their style to their analysis of such states as expectation or grief as being something other than the simple experience of sensation:

> Can only those hope who can talk? Only those who have mastered the use of a language. That is to say, the phenomena of hope are modes of this complicated form of life. (If a concept refers to a character of human handwriting, it has no application to beings that do not write.)
>
> "Grief" describes a pattern which recurs, with different variations, in the weave of our life. If a man's bodily expression of sorrow and of joy alternated, say with the ticking of a clock, here we should not have the characteristic formation of the pattern of sorrow or of the pattern of joy.
>
> "For a second he felt violent pain."—Why does it sound queer to say: "For a second he felt deep grief"? Only because it so seldom happens?
>
> But don't you feel grief *now*? ("But aren't you playing chess *now*?") The answer may be affirmative, but that does not make the concept of grief any more like the concept of a sensation. (*Philosophical Investigations*, p. 174).[15]

The most human of human feelings belong only to human language and inhabit only human language. They do not belong to regions isolated in the self. Grief is not a feeling any more than love is.[16] The criteria for grief are not the presence or absence of some sensation or set of sensations, like pain. Grief names an altered relationship to or in language, not an array of sense-data. The time and personality that are the self's most intimate attributes are parts of a complicated and public language, modes of a certain form of life. A continental philosophical vocabulary would have it that language constitutes these things. But part of Wittgenstein's value lies in his rejection of the dualism of form and matter still inherent in the idea of a

15. Wittgenstein makes a similar argument that expectation is not a mental state in *Philosophical Investigations*, e.g., §§442–45 and 465, and also in *Zettel*, 2d ed., ed. G. E. M. Anscombe and G. H. von Wright, trans. G. E. M. Anscombe (Oxford: Blackwell, 1981), §§53–68; subsequent references to *Zettel* will be by section number. These passages should be compared with Blanchot's account of expectation in *L'attente l'oubli* (Paris: Gallimard, 1962).

16. Cf. *Zettel*, §504: "Love is not a feeling. Love must be put to the test, pain not. We do not say, That was not a real pain, otherwise it wouldn't have passed so quickly."

structured subjectivity.[17] Wittgenstein makes claims deeper and more radical than that, partly because they are less global.[18]

Wittgenstein and Blanchot have in common primarily an unflagging attentiveness to the fragility of human participation in language and life. Literature may be able to urge this fragility as its own cure. The world is *necessarily* fragile, and so fragility takes on the iron irrefutability of necessity. But this also means that there are limits to the ameliorations of generality. Beyond these limits lies the region—or regionlessness—that I call extremity. Blanchot evokes it as "literary space"; Wittgenstein, as the "loss of a paradigm," that is to say, the loss of one or more contacts with the medium of all contact—language games, or the words whose life comes from the fact that they have been "originally heated by the breath of others," as Edmund Burke puts it.

Solitude is the inevitable obverse of generality. Generality, I have argued, is inseparable from the paradoxical fragility that is its essence. The world has a certain character, and in this character we find its essence. But that character may be described as one in which grief, or hope, or love, or expectation are best thought of not as private mental states but as states where the impersonal, the solitary, the phantom come together, states belonging to the language that confers life but that can also distance it. This is how Wittgenstein writes about such states, and this is the way Blanchot's fiction and criticism dramatize them. And this means that a certain anonymous extremity will always haunt generality.

I suggested above that my reading of Wittgenstein would lead to a Blanchotian perspective. This book comes from such a perspective, and so I treat works that describe the limits of generality. Beyond generality or character persists the isolation of a residual and anonymous subjectivity. This is not the subjectivity of skepticism, in which a fully formed self laments its uncertainty about the existence of the world. The residual subjectivity here is other to the self and to the world. The cure for skepticism is the realization that to be an *I* means to be in the world. But the residual is not an I.

17. Bourdieu's critique of structuralism in *Outline of a Theory of Practice* acknowledges itself as Wittgensteinian.
18. The differences between Wittgenstein and the continental tradition are not fully felt, I think, by Henry Staten; in his efforts to negotiate between them, in *Wittgenstein and Derrida* (Oxford: Blackwell, 1985), he tends far too often to assimilate Wittgenstein to Derrida. But Wittgenstein makes even Derrida seem to fall into the trap of a totalizing theory. Difference is close to a master term in Derrida, even though he warns against allowing it to become one. Wittgenstein proceeds far more locally and always avoids giving a general theory.

Blanchot describes the impersonal or the neutral as the space beyond the world. In *L'espace littéraire* he approaches this space through
his discussion of the impersonality of death; but in all his work (especially his fiction) he describes it as indistinguishable from the life it
haunts (just as for Freud, repetition is indistinguishable from the
pleasure principle). Blanchot, somewhat similarly to Wittgenstein and
in some contrast to the formalism of high deconstruction, evokes an
uncanny impersonal affectivity in his description of the impersonal—
the affectivity of unhappiness. As Wittgenstein says, this is not an
affect like pain—it is not a feeling. It is the affectivity of what is
beyond affect. It inhabits and haunts all language, but with the estrangement of language in extremity it takes on the impersonality of
the region beyond the universe of the general. Beyond the limits of
generality, past the boundaries of the characterizable, a kind of anonymity persists. Literary space, as Blanchot evokes it, is the region of
this anonymity. It is a region of anonymous solitude, anonymous unhappiness. The literary voice, "la voix narrative," is the voice of the
neutral, or the other. Recounting Priam's appeal to Achilles for Hec-
tor's body, Blanchot describes "la parole suppliante," the language of
the suppliant: "L'étranger, à qui manque tout langage commun, est
paradoxalement celui qui n'est présent que par sa parole; de même
que lorsqu'il y a défaut de tout, c'est alors que l'homme abîmé dans le
malheur est en mesure de parler, car c'est là sa vraie mesure."[19] This
anonymous unhappiness—whose reiterated positing is the incor-
poreal event that happens over and over again in his novels—
Blanchot describes in *Le pas au-delà*:

> Unhappiness: perhaps we would suffer it if it struck us alone, but it
> always affects the other in us, and affecting us in others, it separates us
> out to an absolutely passive passion where our lost identity no longer
> permits us to suffer it but only to identify ourselves with it, with what is
> beyond the identical, to betake ourselves without identity and without
> the possibility of action, towards the other who is always the unhappy,
> just as the unhappy is always the other.[20]

The alterity of such unhappiness means both that it stands apart
from the élan of human activity or desire or intention and that it

19. Maurice Blanchot, *L'entretien infini* (Paris: Gallimard, 1969), p. 135. ("The
stranger, who lacks the shared language, is paradoxically present only through his
words, in the same way that when nothing is left, it is then that the man plunged into
the abyss of unhappiness has achieved the measure of speech, for that is his true
measure.")
20. Maurice Blanchot, *Le pas au-delà* (Paris: Gallimard, 1973), p. 173.

affects human life and and draws it into its own otherness. The impersonality of grief consists in the way it is irrelevant to the world it mourns, in the way its greatest intimacy goes with its greatest alterity. This intimacy belongs to the fragility that makes up the world, a fragility that inhabits it to the core, while never being simply a presence. This is the great theme in Proust, and it should thus be obvious that I do not mean to restrict the relevance of this argument to seventeenth-century English literature.[21] But it also comes up very clearly in the authors I study.

Shakespeare and Herbert (perhaps influenced by Shakespeare) describe grief in ways anticipating Blanchot. In *Richard II*, the Queen describes the "nameless woe" (ii.ii.40) that forebodes Richard's disasters: "I know no cause / Why I should welcome such a guest as grief, / Save bidding farewell to so sweet a guest / As my sweet Richard" (ii.ii.6–9). Here grief is a third person, an other, inhabiting the first person, and undoing her own personality. Isabel does welcome the guest, despite herself, without wishing to or knowing why she does so, except insofar as she recognizes grief as the anonymous absence—or substitute or representation—both of Richard and of her nonexistent child. Love comes to grief here in the most literal sense.

I think Herbert expresses grief's side of Isabel's act of hospitality in "Love" (iii), but he seems to echo it directly in "Confession:"

> O What a cunning guest
> Is this same grief! within my heart I made
> Closets; and in them many a chest;
> And, like a master in my trade,
> In those chests, boxes; in each box, a till:
> Yet grief knows all, and enters when he will.
>
> (ll. 1–6)

Grief knows him as well as he knows himself; in a sense it is indistinguishable from him, except that it is also other to him. His relation to it is governed by the laws of hospitality, by what in my reading of *King Lear* I call "intimacy without affection." Here it might better be called intimacy without identification, for grief means precisely the end of a happy stability of identity.

I think, to take one more example, that this interplay between the region of the world, which contains all regions, and the anonymous region of sadness, which is beyond all regions, takes place in *Paradise*

21. See my article "Anonymity and Unhappiness in Proust and in Wittgenstein," *Criticism* 29 (1987), 459–76.

Lost. In the invocation to book 7 Milton calls upon Urania to protect him from the Bacchante who killed Orpheus, and yet the fact that he implores immortal aid underscores his own Orphic mortality, a mortality that can only be deferred and not healed.[22] It is Milton who is the guest here:

> Up led by thee,
> Into the Heav'n of Heav'ns I have presum'd,
> An Earthly Guest, and drawn Empyreal Air,
> Thy temp'ring; with like safety guided down
> Return me to my Native Element: . . .
> Standing on Earth, not rapt above the Pole,
> More safe I Sing with mortal voice, unchang'd
> To hoarse or mute, though fall'n on evil days,
> On evil days though fallen, and evil tongues;
> In darkness, and with dangers compast round,
> And solitude; yet not alone, while thou
> Visit'st my slumbers Nightly, or when Morn
> Purples the East: still govern thou my Song,
> *Urania,* and fit audience find, though few.
> But drive far off the barbarous dissonance
> Of *Bacchus* and his Revellers, the Race
> Of that wild Rout that tore the *Thracian* Bard
> In *Rhodope,* where Woods and Rocks had Ears
> To rapture, till the savage clamour drown'd
> Both Harp and Voice; nor could the Muse defend
> Her Son. So fail not thou, who thee implores:
> For thou art Heavn'ly, shee an empty dream.
>
> (7.12–16; 23–39)

Orpheus's voice confers life on everything. Even woods and rocks have ears to rapture. Nothing resists its vivifying power. Nothing remains sheerly material. Milton, on the other hand, gives up in advance this universalizing rapture, "Standing on Earth, not rapt above the pole"; this means he gives up the ambition for a perfected and total world, a world completely animated. He acknowledges the world's frailty, and his own, in exchange for some frail hope that

---

22. See Blanchot's highly paradoxical account of Orpheus in his *L'espace littéraire* (Paris: Gallimard, 1955): "dans le chant seulement, Orphée a pouvoir sur Eurydice, mais, dans le chant aussi, Eurydice est déjà perdue et Orphée lui-même est l'Orphée dispersé, l'«infiniment mort» que la force du chant fait dès maintenant de lui" (pp. 229–30; only in the song does Orpheus have power over Eurydice, but, in the song as well, Eurydice is already lost and Orpheus himself is the scattered Orpheus, the 'infinitely dead' that the force of the song makes of him henceforth).

frailty may be his native element, that frailty may be where he is most at home, and so may also offer a kind of security. He implores Urania not to fail him, as though she *could* fail. He may mean that she might *refuse* him, but the parallel with Calliope matters: "So fail not thou," that is, do not fail in the way that Calliope failed. Calliope fails to defend Orpheus, not because she refuses him, but because she is powerless to protect him. The word *fail* combines the meaning of heavenly denial with the meaning of nonheavenly impotence. That impotence is Calliope's; she fails to defend Orpheus, as the last two lines show, *because* she is an empty dream. Calliope fails to be real enough, to be involved enough with life, to protect Orpheus. Her sorrow—the sorrow of the mother who cannot protect her child— consists in what at first looks as though it should erase that sorrow: her unreality. But Milton stresses her unhappiness, an unhappiness caused by and so figured by her exclusion from all worldly identification.

This may be an unreal sorrow, but in some sense that means that unreality becomes a kind of sorrow. Milton ascribes just this sorrow of unreality to his "late espoused saint," in his twenty-third sonnet: "I wak'd, she fled, and day brought back my night." There too the dream-figure, though one of Eve's daughters, is mournfully unlike the figures endowed with divine reality, such as the unfallen, newly created Eve, when Adam describes how

> She disappear'd, and left me dark, I wak'd
> To find her, or for ever to deplore
> Her loss, and other pleasures all abjure:
> When out of hope, behold her, not far off,
> Such as I saw her in my dream, adorn'd
> With what all Earth or Heaven could bestow
> To make her amiable.
>
> (8.478–84)

Those who turn out to be empty dreams are figures who lose reality, whose reality fades, and not simply fictions like Milton's Eve. Eve disappears in the dream, and so she can be found again, in reality. But by an antithetical movement Catherine Woodcock disappears *after* the dream ends. Milton's awakening does not mean that she has been only a dream. For a moment she hovers in the real world, long enough to show that she is real but spectral. His awakening, unlike Adam's, undoes her presence. What remains instead is their mortal exile from one another. Calliope, I think, has the same spectral and fragile mode of being. She suffers for her own nonexistence, her incapacity to intervene in the world in which her child is dying. Nonrelation has replaced relation, and like the speaker of the twenty-third sonnet, she is exiled into the anonymous region of grief. But what this means is that all mortals share this exile with Calliope.

This exclusion leads to something very different from skepticism. Skepticism disbelieves in the world and so in the existence of other minds or the world grammatically designated by the third-person. But the exclusion from generality means that it is the first-person which is displaced. The disappearance of the general leaves a vanishing residue, in the shape of figures like Calliope. The three authors that I analyze in this book all work toward the limits of the general and to the intimation of that region of impersonal and anonymous extremity beyond those limits. I want to demonstrate that one of the features of literary language is the way it can intimate this anonymous region of extremity.

The world's substance consists in its character and coherence. This idea may be put paradoxically: the world is as believable as a literary work. The believability of a literary work does not consist in its verisimilitude. Rather, belief in the world comes from its conforming to literary coherences. This reversal of the ordinary hierarchy can offer a great deal of reassurance, since it makes of the world a place intended for the self, just as the literary work is intended for the reader.

But the literary work is also haunted by an impersonal alterity and manifests extremity as the failing sign of failure to belong to what Peirce calls the general world of signs. The deepest subject of the authors I study is the evocation of this extremity, both in the literary work and in the world that conforms to the work.[23]

---

23. Jacques Derrida's *Donner le temps* (Paris: Galilée, 1991) came out while this book was in press. I like very much his Blanchotian and Levinasian sense of time as the residuum of giving when there is nothing left to give. I argue for a similar connection between time and extremity.

CHAPTER ONE

"When Griefs Make Thee Tame": Public and Private in Herbert

And God created man in his own image.

—Genesis

What makes my image of him an image of *him*? Not its looking like him.

—Wittgenstein

In undoing the legitimacy of church hierarchy the Reformers also dissolved the reassurance such a hierarchy offered its participants, the reassurance that they *were* participants, assigned their particular place in the general hierarchy. Of course, the removal of all mediation between human beings and the word of God was intended to make God immediate, and Herbert expresses this idea hopefully: "For as thy absence doth excell / All distance known: / So doth thy nearnesse bear the bell, / Making two one" ("The Search," ll. 57–60). But the end of mediation may also be felt, as it is in most of that poem, under the rubric of absence and not nearness. This is the potentially (and purposefully) dismaying side of the Reformation insistence on an unmediated relation to the Bible: now a text, with everything which that implies, substitutes for the synecdochal living presence of the priest. (Thus Herbert's Country Parson is an example for his parishioners; he encourages their understanding, worship, and morals, but he cannot act as a mediator between them and God.)[1]

The Reformation insistence on the authority of an unsupplemented text over the arbitrary and coercive character of some ultimately extrinsic authority has, of course, literary consequences.[2] The text as

1. George Herbert, *A Priest to the Temple, or, The Country Parson*, in *The Works of George Herbert*, ed. F. E. Hutchinson (Oxford: Oxford University Press, 1941; corrected rpt. 1945), pp. 221–90.
2. Barbara Lewalski's *Protestant Poetics and the Seventeenth-Century Religious Lyric* (Princeton, N.J.: Princeton University Press, 1979) treats most fully the consequences of

such is inevitably the first object addressed by anyone who believes in the possibility of even a secular theory of literature. Reformation theology, far from vitiating the literary or poetic claims of the texts it informs, heightens the relevance of these claims. If these literary claims entail any uncertainties, as literary claims tend to do, Reformation theologians must think in literary terms in order to meet these uncertainties.

Protestant theology is haunted by the need for a theory of literature, and so its adherents develop such a theory. It needs this theory because writing *as* writing, or the text *as* text, attempts the impossible task of rendering in the mode of presence an authority whose authority is bound up with its nonpresence. The anxiety Protestant theology responds to can take the form of the question What happens when authority becomes textual rather than charismatic or bureaucratic? Textual authority is the kind of authority most open to skepticism (as the thriving of deconstruction shows). As I claim in my introduction and as I shall show in some detail here, such skepticism can be overcome only by a theory of generality, a theory of the priority of the world to all its contents, both objects and the skeptical subject. Catholic generality is manifestly social; it is provided by the church hierarchy. Protestant generality has a different status and develops, as I say, a literary theory attentive to the life of words and to the individual's inextricable relationship with words.

The usual Protestant answer to the enigma of textual authority, of course, is a denial that textuality implies an authority without presence (implies, I want to say, the nonpresence of "the literary space"). The translations of the Bible were supposed to give immediate access to the word of God in its fullness. Thus Protestant literary practice has been perceived by its defenders as attempting to intimate biblical self-presence. Stanley Fish and Barbara Lewalski, to take the best expositors of diametrically opposing views of Protestant poetry, will agree on the epistemological claims that such a poetry makes, claims for the fullness of divine presence.

For Fish that presence makes Protestant poetry finally irrelevant, a self-consuming artifact that stages "a self-diminishing action in the

---

the difference between Reform and Catholic views of the Bible for seventeenth-century poetry, including Herbert's; she thus enlarges and considerably modifies Louis Martz's argument in *The Poetry of Meditation,* rev. ed. (New Haven, Conn.: Yale University Press, 1964), which did not much consider the relation of a person to a text (and not to another person). The best full-length study of Herbert that treats the consequences of the Reformation insistence on the primacy of the text and not its interpreters is Chana Bloch's *Spelling the Word: George Herbert and the Bible* (Berkeley: University of California Press, 1985). See esp. chap. 1.

course of which the individual lets go, one by one, of all the ways of thinking, seeing, and saying that sustain the illusion of independence, until finally he is absorbed into the deity whose omnipresence he has acknowledged" and so submits to an ineffable word that induces his own expressiveness "finally to stop, to cease to be."[3] For Lewalski the presence of divinity informs and irradiates Protestant poetic practice, which comes out of a new and "overwhelming emphasis on the written word as the embodiment of divine truth"; because of this emphasis, Protestant poets, "far from eschewing aesthetics for a rhetoric of silence or a deliberate anti-aesthetic strategy, . . . committed themselves to forging and employing a Protestant poetics, grounded upon scripture, for the making of Protestant devotional lyrics."[4] Both agree that whatever semiosis is involved is understood to be underwritten and informed by God.[5]

3. Stanley Fish, *Self-Consuming Artifacts: The Experience of the Reader of Seventeenth-Century Literature* (Berkeley: University of California Press, 1972), p. 157; note also, for example, his comment that in "Coloss. 3.3" the speaker simultaneously asserts "the loss of the self and the finding of its greater glory in a union with divinity" (p. 206). In her reading of Herbert, Bloch (*Spelling the Word*, pp. 35–36) strongly disagrees with Fish, insisting on the importance of Herbert's selfhood and personality, of the way he variously gets life from or gives life to the text. Barbara Harman's *Costly Monuments: Representations of the Self in George Herbert's Poetry* (Cambridge, Mass.: Harvard University Press, 1982) is the most extended meditation on the adventures of selfhood in the poetry of Herbert and in many ways concerns itself with the same themes that I discuss in this chapter: the self's fundamental instability and its difficult relations with an authority that has designs on the self, an authority that can never quite be viewed as another self. It is, of course, Helen Vendler's great strength, in *The Poetry of George Herbert* (Cambridge, Mass.: Harvard University Press, 1975), to read Herbert as a poet of experience; but for her, as for Bloch, the self is not as at risk as it is for Harman: Vendler and Bloch share with Fish a sense of Herbert's having some ultimately unified personality (although Bloch regards Vendler and Fish as each telling different halves of the story and not understanding the dialogical relationship between human and God [see pp. 44–45]). Harman's splendid introduction traces the issue of selfhood, and the relation of selfhood to religious and cultural authority, in Herbert's critics from George Herbert Palmer and William Empson through Rosemond Tuve, Joseph Summers, and Arnold Stein to Vendler and Fish and beyond. For a deconstructive reading of Herbert, see Jonathan Goldberg, *Voice Terminal Echo: Postmodernism and English Renaissance Texts* (New York: Methuen, 1986), pp. 101–23.

4. Lewalski, *Protestant Poetics*, pp. 6–7.

5. For a recent, more complex view of Protestant semiotics in Herbert, but one that still depicts him as seeing a divine presence underwriting a textualized world, see Richard Todd's *The Opacity of Signs: Acts of Interpretation in George Herbert's* The Temple (Columbia: University of Missouri Press, 1986), esp. pp. 154–55 on human relation to divine bounty and pp. 193–98 as a useful corrective to Rosemond Tuve's implicit claims (in *A Reading of George Herbert* [Chicago: University of Chicago Press, 1952]) for the transparent significance of Herbert's language for a seventeenth-century reader in a certain context and of the language of the world that such a reader would read and respond to. Heather A. R. Asals is also very alert to the uncertainties that haunt signification, especially human signification in poetry. See *Equivocal Predication: George Herbert's Way to God* (Toronto: University of Toronto Press, 1981), esp. pp. 38–56.

My interest in these questions is epistemological, since I am interested in what could be called literary epistemology. Epistemology is always finally about authority: its central concern is whether there is any authority that can compel unequivocal belief. This concern becomes a theological issue because of the Protestant equation of belief with grace: questions of knowledge and certainty are at the center of questions about salvation. In John Calvin's words, "We do not obtain salvation either because we are prepared to embrace as true whatever the church has prescribed, or because we turn over to it the task of inquiring and knowing. But we do so when we *know* that God is our merciful Father, because of reconciliation effected through Christ . . . , and that Christ has been given to us as righteousness, sanctification, and life. By this *knowledge*, I say, not by submission of our feeling, do we obtain entry into the Kingdom of Heaven."[6]

Protestant epistemology looks to God as an epistemological guarantor of such knowledge. If God grants the grace to have faith, the faith he grants ought not to be susceptible to skepticism. The stakes of this epistemology are terribly high: salvation depends on it. Your lot depended on what you knew, with certain knowledge, and what you knew depended on God. This dilemma leads to the question whose perverse difficulty founds and haunts the Protestant theory of the knowing and willing subject, the question whose intractability signified for Luther God's incomprehensible glory: How can we possibly be culpable for not having faith when the decision as to who has it (and as to who is predestined to salvation) lies with God? Culpability seems to include the notion of the will's responsibility for action, but how can belief or the knowledge Calvin requires be willed? Skepticism about the existence of anything external to the self stems from the apparent recognition that belief and knowledge cannot be willed, that my beliefs about the existence of the external world can in no way depend on my will. But for Luther the great insoluble mystery that signifies God's glory—a mystery only faith, not rationality, can treat with—is that we should be culpable without our wills' being free, that we should be liable to punishment for our wills despite the fact that they are determined by God.

My concern here is not with the morality of this position but with the epistemological theory it implies and with the insight into exclusion and alienation that such a theory can provide. For, I argue, this epistemological theory—which was Herbert's and which it was his

6. John Calvin, *Selections from His Writings*, ed. John Dillenberger (Garden City, N.Y.: Doubleday, 1971), p. 374; my emphasis.

pastoral concern to convey—is on the whole an adequate one. The theory rightly depicts the self as determined and fated by forces outside of it and prior to it. In doing so, however, this scheme makes possible a literary attention to the helplessness of the self so determined and fated; this attention is the burden of Herbert's poetry in its most plangent and uncertain moments.

Protestant Epistemology and Realism

> Blessed be God! and the Father of all mercy! who continueth to pour his benefits upon us. . . . O Lord! thy blessings hang in clusters, they come trooping upon us! they break forth like mighty waters on every side.
> —Herbert, A Prayer after Sermon

God represents certainty, and salvation means access to that certainty. Rescue from the isolation of skepticism would similarly mean an access to certainty about the external world. I propose that both Herbert and Wittgenstein give similar reasons for believing in such access but also that they share a deeply melancholy sense that the access to certainty is itself—in a deeper and more troubling way—intrinsically and necessarily uncertain. I do not mean this as a contradiction of the certainty they champion but as a characterization of certainty and what constitutes being certain. In this context, I argue, uncertainty *means* a desire for reassurance, and so it *means* a desire for a tacitly stipulated external authority to provide reassurance: reassurance that there is an external authority capable of providing such reassurance. Because it assumes the existence and the *authority* of such an authority, uncertainty becomes coincident with the certainty it desires. But counter to this saving formulation is its inevitable inverse: if uncertainty is coincident with certainty, then certainty cannot be anything more solid than uncertainty.

Wittgenstein gives the most cogent and powerful secular account of the self's inextricable relation to the world that constitutes it. Against Kant's resolutely individualistic theory of judgment, Wittgenstein effectively elaborates the pragmaticist definition of Charles Sanders Peirce: "A judgment is an act of consciousness in which we recognize a belief, and a belief is an intelligent habit upon which we shall act when occasion presents itself."[7] Wittgenstein sees judgments as *learned* ac-

7. Charles Sanders Peirce, *Collected Papers*, ed. Paul Weiss (Cambridge, Mass.: Harvard University Press, 1931), 2: §265.

tivities, where learning ultimately means something like inculcating a habit or getting the hang of something. Judgments depend not on "ungrounded presuppositions" but on "ungrounded ways of *acting*" he says in *On Certainty*:[8]

> 139. Not only rules, but also examples are needed for establishing a practice. Our rules leave loop-holes open, and the practice has to speak for itself.

> 140. We do not learn the practice of making empirical judgments by learning rules: we are taught *judgments* and their connexion with other judgments. A *totality* of judgments is made plausible to us.

> 141. When we first begin to *believe* anything, what we believe is not a single proposition, it is a whole system of propositions. (Light dawns gradually over the whole.)

> 160. The child learns by believing the adult. Doubt comes *after* belief.

> 166. The difficulty is to realize the groundlessness of our believing.

> 204. Giving grounds, however, justifying the evidence, comes to an end;—but the end is not certain propositions' striking us immediately as true, i.e. it is not a kind of *seeing* on our part; it is our acting which lies at the bottom [am Grunde] of the language-game.

Wittgenstein grounds all judgment on practice. That a child learns by believing an adult does not mean that the child somehow *assents* to the claims made by the adult. Rather, what later comes to be called belief (to distinguish it from doubt) begins instead as, say, imitation (in its Aristotelian sense: the instinct that makes learning possible). We are competent to make a given set of judgments when (and because) we know how to play the language game in which those judgments can occur.

Thus the self does not consent to (or more melodramatically, suffer the encroachment of) some relationship to the objective world but is *constituted* by the world. The founding category for human beings is the public (or the social or the linguistic), and the private is exactly that: the privative; a special case of public, of *general*, existence; a specifiable move in a subset of the open-ended set of language games.

8. Ludwig Wittgenstein, *On Certainty*, ed. G. E. M. Anscombe and G. H. von Wright, trans. Denis Paul and G. E. M. Anscombe (New York: Harper and Row, 1972), §110, my emphasis; all citations are by section number.

It is this priority of the public that interests me in Herbert's poetry, a priority that has lately drawn some attention. E. Pearlman stresses the subtitle of *The Temple*—"sacred poems and private ejaculations"—and resists the temptation to see these as separable spheres.[9] Like me, Chana Bloch is interested in Herbert as a poet of the general, and some of her formulations seem to me exactly right. She treats Herbert as a writer of "many lyrics whose concerns are public and general" (*Spelling the Word*, p. 171), lyrics that derive their forms from Proverbs and Ecclesiastes. Against Lewalski's contention that the "religious lyric . . . is a private mode" (*Protestant Poetics*, p. 4), Bloch writes, "In talking about Herbert, . . . I think we must finally put aside the distinction between public and private, like that between didactic and expressive. What we may call the 'biblical mode' encompasses these oppositions; Herbert learned from the Bible to write poems at once public and private, didactic and expressive" (*Spelling the Word*, p. 199), and for this reason she disagrees with Vendler's warning against the "peril of generalization for Herbert." Vendler writes that Herbert's "mind is resolutely unphilosophic and wholly restricted to the private case, a turn of temper perplexing to a poet who wishes to address himself to Christians in general" (*Poetry of George Herbert*, p. 151). Against this, Bloch argues that "for Herbert the 'private case' is but an instance of the 'general,' and not unique; his many proverbial sayings draw upon, and contribute to, the fund of common experience" (*Spelling the Word*, p. 197). Of stanzas three and seven of "The Flower" she writes, "In these stanzas of generalized reflection, the poet's 'I' gives way to the 'we' of the human community" (p. 195). For this reason, she would presumably object as well to Vendler's argument that "it is a crushing burden to put on oneself—to reinterpret in a personal, and personally acceptable, way every conventional liturgical and religious act: to make devotion always singular, never simply communal; to particularize, not to merge; to individuate, not to accede" (*Poetry of George Herbert*, p. 148). Richard Strier, in his astonishingly sensitive and useful account of Protestant theology in Herbert's thought, explains Luther's doctrine of assurance as lifting this burden of private responsibility for devotion through the fact of predestination.[10] And Barbara Harman, like Bloch, also reads the New Covenant as meeting personal needs through "a displacement of the

9. E. Pearlman, "George Herbert's God," *English Literary Renaissance* 13 (1983), 89.
10. Richard Strier, *Love Known: Theology and Experience in George Herbert's Poetry* (Chicago: University of Chicago Press, 1983). See also Gene Edward Veith's *Reformation Spirituality: The Religion of George Herbert* (Lewisburg, Pa.: Bucknell University Press, 1985), pp. 83–116.

personal by the collective solution, . . . an exchange of the idiosyn-
cratic for the universal account."[11]

I agree with Vendler. Generality, is not sufficiently saving for Herbert; it does not completely overcome the particular. At any rate,
Bloch is not concerned, as I am, with the theory of the general or the
nature of belongingness to a generalized or pluralized community;
for her this is a given in Herbert. I am glad, however, that someone
making an entirely different argument would use the same vocabulary as I shall be urging. Similarly Claude J. Summers and Ted-Larry
Pebworth write, "What needs to be recognized is that Herbert's poems
are frequently public as well as private, political as well as personal,
and that often the sweet tone of his speakers' voices conceals a passionate engagement in the very issues he seems to avoid. . . . Indeed,
Herbert's rejection of the rhetoric of [ecclesiastical schism] and con-
troversy in favor of a more subtle rhetoric of allusion is itself a political
strategy."[12]

I want to continue characterizing the priority of the public in Wittgensteinian terms. I won't argue here for the adequacy of Wittgenstein's epistemology, but I do want to insist that it *is* an epistemology
(against Richard Rorty, for example). Wittgenstein's philosophy is
deeply antiskeptical: the world can be known, because the world
means the place where we live and act. In this sense Wittgenstein may
be called a realist, since he regards as strictly senseless the denial of
the certain existence of the outside world.[13] Where metaphysics and

11. Harman, *Costly Monuments*, p. 82. (She is commenting on "Redemption.") Bloch,
however, objects to the drama that Harman sees (e.g., pp. 176–77) in Herbert's
speakers' discoveries of their public nature. For Bloch, they've known it all along (p.
142n).

12. Claude J. Summers and Ted-Larry Pebworth, "Herbert, Vaughan, and Public
Concerns in Private Modes," *George Herbert Journal* 3:1 and 2 (1979–80), 1–21.

13. The words *real* and *realism* have many somewhat divergent meanings in philosophy. Peirce called himself a realist, although many historians of philosophy tend to
think of him as a nominalist. But Peirce is closer to the scholastic use of the terms
nominalist and *realist*. He thinks Locke's nominalism a disaster and argues strenuously
for the reality of general terms (but not for the reality of universals). For him, the
coherence of the world is real: it is a semiotic coherence, the coherence of a system of
real signs, each of which is always related to other signs. Reality consists of signs, but
these signs are not representations of the real; they are the real itself. I follow Peirce
here by using the term *realism* to mean a view that regards coherence as an attribute of
the world and not only an attribute imposed by the mind. This leads me, against most
contemporary usage, to call the later Wittgenstein a realist, since he argues for the
coherence of linguistic practice, and to contrast this kind of realism, which ascribes to
linguistic practice an external and coherent existence, to Platonism, which regards
reality as a feature only of an unattainable and incommunicable region of forms. In
contemporary usage the words *Platonism* and *realism* are often used synonymously;
Peirce's polemic insists on undoing this synonymy.

the skepticism that it causes are concerned with the existence of objects, Wittgenstein attributes priority to the existence of *situations*.[14] Existence only has meaning within and with respect to language games: "Our mistake is to look for an explanation where we ought to look at what happens as a 'proto-phenomenon'. That is, where we ought to have said: *this language-game is played.* The question is not one of explaining a language-game by means of our experiences, but of noting a language game."[15] So for something to exist *means* that in a certain language game (the language game in which this meaning is in question) that something makes possible a certain set of moves. And since these language games are not *representations* but *activities*, it makes no sense to ask for any guarantee for the validity of the judgments that arise in a game. The existence of the world means the existence not of objects but of moves or contexts for moves in games. The antiskeptical claim that the world exists is simply a generalization of such statements as that describing how a bishop moves in chess; the existence of the world needs no surer ground than do statements about how games are played.

This claim is not a positivist dismissal of the legitimacy of the category of existence. It is an extremely far-reaching claim for the (legitimate) way language games ground judgments. Thus the extremely moving end of *On Certainty* insists on the ultimate reality of the lived world, even if that world turns out to be a dream:

675. If someone believes that he has flown from America to England in the last few days, then, I believe, he cannot be making a *mistake*.

And just the same if someone says that he is at this moment sitting at a table and writing.

676. "But even if in such cases I can't be mistaken, isn't it possible that I am drugged?" If I am and if the drug has taken away my consciousness, then I am not now really talking and thinking. I cannot seriously suppose that I am at this moment dreaming. Someone who, dreaming, says "I am dreaming", even if he speaks audibly in doing so, is no more right than if he said in his dream "it is raining", while it was in fact raining. Even if his dream were actually connected with the noise of the rain.

14. Stanley Cavell's important reformulation of this claim is that skepticism illegitimately treats the world as an object, as the super-object. But for Cavell and Wittgenstein, the world is the place and sum of games. See *The Claim of Reason: Wittgenstein, Skepticism, Morality, and Tragedy* (New York: Oxford University Press, 1979) and *Disowning Knowledge in Six Plays of Shakespeare* (New York: Cambridge University Press, 1987).

15. Ludwig Wittgenstein, *Philosophical Investigations*, 3d ed., trans. G. E. M. Anscombe (New York: Macmillan, 1968), §§654–55.

It seems important that Wittgenstein wrote this two days before his death, but even without knowing that, this statement sounds like Proust. The elegiac pressure in this formulation comes from the sense it evokes of departure, of leaving. To be aware that being in the world comes to an end (his early formulation was "at death the world does not alter, but comes to an end")[16] does not mean that the world is illusory. The self—fragilely connected with the world though it may be—is nothing without that world. But that apprehension of fragility is also a consoling innocence because it is a manifestation of a pre-epistemological need for comfort, and that need for comfort is the one certitude.

It is true that the reality this passage seems to evoke is not the reality of the dream world but of the world in which the sleeper is lying. The fragility of the world the dreamer lives in (the dream world: the only world there is, the world of traveling from America to England or from Paris to Balbec) is imaged by the world as it appears if the dream were to end (if the world were to end). The world comes to an end, not in the nothingness that the *Tractatus* predicts, but in the dreamer's room. The dreamer, perhaps drugged ("in der Narkose") to ease his pain, is lying in his room on a rainy night with the window open in early spring (this was written April 27, 1951). This fragile tie to the world is all that remains to him. Yet Wittgenstein still maintains that in his dream of life, his claim to know more—to know that it is a dream—is simply wrong. As in Proust, the assertion here is that reality is in the past, that what is in the past is indeed reality, and not that the invalid is stripping himself of all illusions. The touching innocence of this past—belief without doubt—is the characteristic of reality. That innocence is preserved even for the invalid, because his denial of it is corrected as though he's still a child who needs correction because he wrongly thinks that he is not a child anymore. But this wrong thought proves that he is still a child, or an old man like "a child asleep in his own life," as Wallace Stevens puts it.

Being in the world is a fragile affair. But this same fragility is exactly the *characteristic* of the world, so that the more fragile it is, the more worldly it is. To paraphrase Richard Hooker, faith in the world when it is at its strongest is but weak; yet even then when it is at the weakest, so strong that it never utterly fails, not even in those who think it extinguished in themselves. Wittgenstein is arguing against a certain notion of experience as a fall—a fall from the untroubled belief in the

16. Ludwig Wittgenstein, *Tractatus Logico-Philosophicus*, trans. D. F. Pears and B. F. McGuinness (New York: Humanities Press, 1972), proposition 6.4311.

phenomenal world as it is given to the child, into a skepticism as regards that world, a skepticism that might be called the adult's fear of death. Like Freud's, Wittgenstein's consolation is this: that there is really no such thing as the adult fear of death, that what goes under this name is a childhood fear, like any other, and the consolations of the childhood that knew nothing of death ought—at length—to suffice.

Here I want to consider the parallel between Wittgensteinian and Reformation epistemology. Luther's doctrine of assurance—"the comfort of knowing that salvation does not depend on 'free-will'" but on God's faithful grace and mercy[17]—has much in common with Wittgenstein's notion of certainty as the child's unquestioned faith in what the parent says (faith that the actions or moves that the parent makes are *imitable*, able to be legitimately responded to—which is what truth comes down to). Indeed, Luther suggests, the sum of Christian reward and punishment may finally amount to what one's own epistemology affords one under the pressure of mortality. At least in this life, faith really is all there is of grace. (This is Milton's lesson too in *Paradise Regained*, where Jesus has no a priori knowledge of who he is.) To have faith doesn't lead to salvation—it is itself salvation. Belief itself provides the consolation it anticipates:

14. Defective piety or love in a dying person is necessarily accompanied by great fear, which is greatest where the piety or love is least.

15. This fear or horror is sufficient in itself, whatever else might be said, to constitute the pain of purgatory, since it approaches very closely to the horror of despair.

16. There seems to be the same difference between hell, purgatory, and heaven as between despair, uncertainty, and assurance. (Dillenberger, p. 491)

To illustrate how I apply these considerations to Herbert, I turn to the last poem in the sequence of poems making up the body of *The Temple*. "Love" (III), it seems to me, has the same consolatory feeling as the end of "On Certainty." Its speaker is skeptical about his access to the reality of the pleasant scene in Love's inn, skeptical about the sufficiency of his welcome, no matter how grand, to compensate for

17. Martin Luther, *Selections from His Writings*, ed. John Dillenberger (Garden City, N.Y.: Doubleday, 1961), p. 199. I cite this hereafter as Dillenberger.

the nothingness imaged in his dust and sin: surely Love's innocent world is as unavailable to him now as his lost innocence.

> Love bade me welcome: yet my soul drew back,
>   Guiltie of dust and sinne.
> But quick-ey'd Love, observing me grow slack
>   From my first entrance in,
> Drew nearer to me, sweetly questioning,
>   If I lack'd any thing.
>
> A guest, I answer'd, worthy to be here:
>   Love said, You shall be he.
> I the unkinde, ungratefull? Ah my deare,
>   I cannot look on thee.
> Love took my hand, and smiling did reply,
>   Who made the eyes but I?
>
> Truth Lord, but I have marr'd them: let my shame
>   Go where it doth deserve.
> And know you not, sayes Love, who bore the blame?
>   My deare, then I will serve.
> You must sit down, sayes Love, and taste my meat:
>   So I did sit and eat.

The narrator feels embarrassed, too crude for the circle he has ventured upon, but he finds himself magically accepted by that circle. In the midst of guilt, innocence supervenes, the innocence of childhood. What is magical here is that magic is still possible when the speaker has outgrown or become skeptical of magic. As for Wittgenstein, doubt that consolation is possible is really an expression for the need to be consoled.

What does the speaker lack? A guest worthy to be asked such a question: the speaker's ironic (and awkward) answer means that the situation in which such a question would make sense (the situation of the worthy guest who has a right to Love's offer of service) doesn't apply to him.[18] He is so lacking as to lack even the right to articulate a

---

18. Michael Schoenfeldt reads this differently in "Standing on Ceremony: The Comedy of Manners in Herbert's 'Love' (III)" in *Bright Shootes of Everlastingnesse: The Seventeenth Century Religious Lyric*, ed. Claude Summers and Ted-Larry Pebworth (Columbia: University of Missouri Press, 1987), pp. 116–33. He gives the best account of the view that there is a courtesy contest going on here, but I think the grammatical awkwardness implies the speaker as someone who is not courtly, someone who can't engage in a contest of wit.

lack—the guest who would have that right is lacking. But Love can supply even that lack. The speaker's skepticism that he *can* be of any concern is exactly what *is* of concern to the innkeeper here.

But what is most interesting about the poem is this: the assurance Love brings the speaker does not come at the expense of his own wonder that he should receive it. We get that sense, I think, through the awkwardness of the atonement in the last stanza. Critics invariably take it to be the speaker who says, "My deare, then I will serve."[19] But, especially in view of the text from Luke (12:37) to which the poem alludes—"Blessed are those servants, whom the lord when he cometh shall find watching: verily I say unto you, that he shall gird himself, and make them sit down to meat, and will come forth and serve them"—it seems to me that Love is offering to serve not only the meat but to bear the blame. Both Vendler and Bloch quote this passage from Luke. Vendler does not use it to illuminate the word *serve,* however. Bloch argues for some ambiguity and so comes closest to my reading: "Such passages alert us to the density of Herbert's line: 'then I will serve the Lord who serves his servants.' But we realize its full complexity only when we see that the line belongs, in effect, to both speakers: the guest pronounces it, but Love appropriates it by performing the action" (*Spelling the Word,* p. 107)

This seems correct to me, except that I still maintain that Love has as great a claim to having pronounced it as the speaker does. The parallelism of lines 13–14 and 15–16 seems to enforce the sense of a sticomythic dialogue. The speaker says, "Truth Lord, but I have marr'd them: let my shame / Go where it doth deserve." And Love's reply (except for "sayes Love") exactly parallels this: "And know you not, sayes Love, who bore the blame? / My deare, then I will serve." The parallelism is further enforced by the fact that, unlike any other rhymes in the poem, these lines rhyme on the same parts of speech: *shame* and *blame* are both nouns; *deserve* and *serve,* both verbs (unlike the pairings *back/slack, sinne/in, questioning/thing, here/deare, he/thee* [assuming that the difference between nominative and direct object matters], *reply/I,* and *meat/eat*). If Wimsatt is right that such rhymes are either weak or enlisted for special purposes, the parallel seems particularly marked.[20] I agree that bringing out the parallelism as noticeably as this makes it seem a little sing-songy and that this might be a

19. See, for instance, Strier, *Love Known,* p. 77, and Vendler, *Poetry of George Herbert,* p. 276.

20. See William Wimsatt, "One Relation of Rhyme to Reason," in his *The Verbal Icon: Studies in the Meaning of Poetry* (Lexington: University of Kentucky Press, 1954), pp. 152–66.

reason to prefer a typically Herbertian variation (here of voice) within a strict form, as in "Church Monuments," but the speaker seems to me far too abrupt and far too abruptly silenced if he is given the one short line of the last four. Rather, the variation seems to me to consist precisely in the fact that Love goes beyond merely answering the speaker's objection. He does not stop at the word "serve" but continues, "You must sit down, sayes Love, and taste my meat." The repetition of "sayes Love" does not indicate, to my ear, that love is speaking again after the speaker interrupts him with the offer to serve. Rather, it marks the speaker's wonderment at the fact that Love keeps going, keeps adding to the bounty he offers. I cannot make myself believe that the present tense of this last stanza contains yet another objection by the speaker—all those objections are surely in the past. Love is saying, if you are worrying about whether the blame has been borne yet, you needn't be, since I will serve as well as is needed to bear it. A Wittgensteinian might paraphrase: "You are involved in a perilous language game, the game about being excluded from language games; but this is a language game like any other; just as what you really lacked was the knowledge that you didn't lack the right to say what you lacked, so now your situation in this game of needing consolation is one in which you imagine that you are no longer playing it, no longer in the game that can provide consolation; yet this need for consolation is part of the game, and the consolation I can provide is by playing the game with you, and so showing you that you are not excluded from it; I will do—I will serve—to show you that comfort is still available to you." As the present tenses make us feel ("sayes Love"), we are back in the world of childhood: the experience here is of that which escapes the corrosive effects of time which the narrator has suffered. Love is the good mother in Melanie Klein's sense.[21] We already feel this when he asks, "Who made the eyes but I?" Love doesn't permit even the slightest distance between the speaker as seeing eye and the things he sees; Love's intimacy is so unavoidable and so total that he is responsible for the vision that would see him. This arrogation of total responsibility and care is Love's rejoinder to the speaker's total lack, not of this or that thing, but of a guest worthy to be here. Love utterly absorbs the mass of dust and sin

---

21. Bloch notes the feminine feel of the character, but she is more interested in the erotic consequences of this than I am. Pearlman's article "George Herbert's God" describes Herbert's sense of a maternal God. See also Deborah Shuger's fine chapter "Nursing Fathers: Patriarchy as a Cultural Ideal" in her *Habits of Thought in the English Renaissance: Religion, Politics, and the Dominant Culture* (Berkeley: University of California Press, 1990), pp. 218–49.

and guilt whose oppression the child can no longer bear. Love consoles the child who thought in his childish, inconsolable way that he was no longer a child.

Richard Strier rightly sees this poem as the most nearly total expression in Herbert's work of the assurance that goes with irresistible grace.[22] I have been trying to describe the way that assurance feels, in order to assimilate a certain strain of Reformation theology to a philosophical psychology whose affective vocabulary is more resonant for us and, hence, more easily applied to the analysis of the lyric. I argue later for a strand of despair in "Love" (III); now I want to look at the mode of consolation the poem defines a little more closely, to try to extend the analogy between Wittgensteinian and Reformation epistemology.

One of the morals of Wittgenstein's work is that existence can often be necessarily predicated of aspects of the external world, and, as a consequence, at the most fundamental level—the level of pure generality, or of the *fact* of language games—there is no difference between the status of the signified and that of the referent, between type and token. The significance of a move in a language game, or even of a piece or object in the game, depends on the kind of game that is being played, and it makes no sense, within a game, to imagine meaningful but nonexistent pieces or ways of moving. General terms answer the question "What kind of object is that?" While it may make sense to doubt the existence of the referent of an object-name (such as King Louis XXIII), it makes no sense to distinguish the referent from the meaning of a word naming a *kind* of thing: "What kind of object is that?" "A chess piece." "But there's no such thing as chess." For this reason, as P. F. Strawson argues, general terms may be said to come before and *characterize* the particulars that instantiate them—characterize them as being of certain kinds or types.[23] Children learn *about* (the character of) the world they live in, not *that* they live in a world: "Children do not learn that books exist, that armchairs exist, etc. etc.,—they learn to fetch books, sit in armchairs, etc." (Wittgenstein, *On Certainty*, §476). The childhood sense of permanency comes from living in the general. The child believes in a world of what Peirce calls thirdness, a world whose essence is a tendency toward generalization.

The general is always generous: much is guaranteed by each general sign. The generosity of the general underlies what Freud calls the

22. Strier, *Love Known*, pp. 114–17.

23. See P. F. Strawson, "Particular and General," in his *Logico-Linguistic Papers* (London: Methuen, 1971), pp. 28–52. See also his *Individuals: An Essay in Descriptive Metaphysics* (London: Methuen, 1959).

most essential wish of the child, the wish to become an adult, to have
fulfilled the general promise the world makes it. The fall from childhood that real adulthood seems to entail—the fall into time—is a fall
into the specific. The reality principle might be called by Peirce an
antireality principle. It is the moral of the discovery that meaning and
referent are not the same, that reality isn't a guaranteed concomitant
of mental representation, that some things may indeed not exist or
may no longer exist, that irreparable loss is possible.

Wittgenstein's argument, even under the pressure of the most immediate mortality, as at the end of *On Certainty*, provides its consolation through its claim that almost everything we do (all our semiotic
activity) still reposes on the unquestioned, and in practice unquestion-
able, beliefs of childhood. We cannot doubt for long (since life is
activity) the guarantees of the language we learned when we were
children who believed in the magical generality of what adults told us.

That language, as Burke says, is "originally heated by the breath of
others," and we depend on that language even to doubt our dependence. This may be seen in the petulance of a poem like "The Collar."
The way that petulance comes to signify the childishness it attempts to
cut itself off from (because it feels already cut off from it) assimilates
even that poem, in the end, to the consolations of a more general
community:

> I Struck the board and cry'd, No more.
>   I will abroad.
>   What? shall I ever sigh and pine?
> My lines and life are free; free as the rode,
>   Loose as the winde, as large as store.
>   Shall I be still in suit?
>   Have I no harvest but a thorn
>   To let me bloud, and not restore
>   What I have lost with cordiall fruit?
>   Sure there was wine
> Before my sighs did drie it: there was corn
>   Before my tears did drown it.
>   Is the yeare onely lost to me?
>   Have I no bayes to crown it?
> No flowers, no garlands gay? all blasted?
>   All wasted?
>   Not so, my heart: but there is fruit,
>   And thou hast hands.
>   Recover all thy sigh-blown age
> On double pleasures: leave thy cold dispute

> Of what is fit, and not. Forsake thy cage,
>   Thy rope of sands,
> Which pettie thoughts have made, and made to thee
>   Good cable, to enforce and draw,
>   And be thy law,
>   While thou didst wink and wouldst not see.
>   Away; take heed:
>   I will abroad.
> Call in thy death's head there: tie up thy fears.
>   He that forbears
>   To suit and serve his need,
>   Deserves his load.
> But as I rav'd and grew more fierce and wilde
>   At every word,
>   Me thoughts I heard one calling, *Child!*
>   And I reply'd, *My Lord.*

As in so many of Herbert's poems, dialogue, here made explicit by the entry of the second voice (the voice of God), ensures community.[24] But what enables dialogue here is that the speaker's nature is dialogistic anyway. To translate Mintz's formula that "Herbert thought of language as a spiritual instrument, as speech that reaches God because it comes from God" into Wittgensteinian terms, we might say of Herbert that he's playing language games, and language cannot be solitary.[25] Language necessarily implies some community, someone to play with or against. For Herbert the endpoint of community, of dialogue, is always God, the parent who has taught the child to talk and for whose sake the child always talks, even if it plays the game of pretending it is alone, in dialogue only with itself. Herbert is talking to himself like a child, like a child ventriloquizing an adult imperiousness and impatience.

The child cons the part of the adult and convinces himself of his own adulthood. This makes his realization that he is still a child, irresponsible and impotent to make what he wishes of his life, a failure rather than a mode of hope. And yet it is finally because his response to this realization is childish—because it takes the form of a fierce and raving dialogue with himself about how cold are disputes over works (ll. 20–21)—that he turns out not to live in the adult

24. See C. A. Patrides's introduction to *The English Poems of George Herbert* (London: Dent, 1975), p. 17 and Lewalski, *Protestant Poetics*, p. 68.

25. Samuel I. Mintz, "The Motion of Thought: Intellectual and Philosophical Backgrounds," in *The Age of Milton*, ed. C. A. Patrides and Raymond B. Waddington (Totowa, N.J.: Barnes and Noble, 1980), p. 150.

(univocal, nondialogistic) world at all. To the insufficiency of works comes the comfort that such an insufficiency bespeaks a childish relationship to God. The speaker's skepticism about the value of going on turns out to be a completely childlike expression of a desire for the consolation of rebuke. As in a poem like "Dialogue," the speaker finally learns that his childishness is not a matter of will but of fact.

For most of the poem the speaker has to rebuke himself. He has to substitute for the absent parent. The absence of this parent seems to encourage doubt as to his authority, but that doubt conceals and entails a deeper and unquestioned belief in that authority and sees its absence not as its nonexistence but as a rebuke. The existence of the referent—the Father he speaks to—turns out not to be at issue here, since it is the essence of this Father (of any superego) to exist, even if he punishes you by making you feel guilty for doubting his existence. His signification is his reference. Even skepticism about the existence of this signified entails its existence.[26] Skepticism turns out to be a sign for a deeper, nonskeptical need, and this need constitutes belief.

For Herbert, and for Protestant thinkers in general, need modulates into consolation. Thus William Perkins, in "A Graine of Musterd-seede," avouches "that the desire of reconciliation with God in Christ is reconciliation itself: the desire to believe is faith indeed and the desire to repent, repentance itself. . . . The desire of mercy in the want of mercy is the obtaining of mercy; and the desire to believe, in the want of faith, is faith." He goes on in a similar vein: "To see and feel in ourselves the want of any grace pertaining to salvation, and to be grieved therefore, is the grace itself."[27] Similarly Richard Hooker, in his first sermon, sees mourning as hinting at the ineradicability of what is mourned. For believers, no matter how uncertain they are that they do believe, still enjoy God's grace:

> Their faith, when it is at the strongest, is but weak; yet even then when it is at the weakest, so strong, that utterly it never faileth, it never perisheth altogether, no not in them who think it extinguished in themselves. . . .
> For that which dwelleth in their hearts they seek, they make diligent

26. This discussion is a psychological restatement of Todd's argument that "Herbert's speakers . . . learn that what are being experienced in moments of desolation *are* actually apprehensible in terms of their status as signs" (*Opacity of Signs*, p. 45). He goes on to say that when Herbert "interprets the phenomenon [of the hidden God] as a significant response in itself, coming to perceive the essence of this response and consequently coming to interpret his feelings in terms of divine presence, what Herbert has actually been repining over is his own blindness" (ibid., p. 67). I do not think, however, that Todd describes Herbert's self-analysis in terms sufficiently introspective.

27. *The Works of William Perkins*, ed. Ian Breward (Appleford, Berkshire: Sutton Courtenay Press, n.d.), pp. 398–99, 402.

search and inquiry. It abideth, it worketh in them, yet still they ask where; still they lament as for a thing which is past finding; they mourn as Rachel, and refuse to be comforted, as if that were not which indeed is, and as if that which is not were; as if they did not believe when they do, and as if they did despair when they do not.

This sounds like a fair anticipation of the forms of discovery enacted by many of Herbert's poems. His speakers frequently do not know what they believe (even if they think that they do not believe or that they know they do not believe); they frequently do not know what they are thinking, and Herbert anticipates the insights of Wittgenstein and Freud that, although one can know what is going on in other people, one cannot know what is going on in oneself: "It is correct to say 'I know what you are thinking', and wrong to say 'I know what I am thinking'" (*Philosophical Investigations*, p. 222). And, as with Perkins's beautiful claim, "To see and feel in ourselves the want of any grace pertaining to salvation, and to be grieved therefore, is the grace itself," Hooker sounds even more like Herbert in the passage that follows. He continues that the lamentation over the want of belief is itself the surest sign of belief. This is true even if we do not know that we are lamenting, at a time that "'the Spirit groaneth,' and that God heareth when we do not." Thus any grief we are conscious of is an all the more vivid sign of faith:

So there is no doubt, but that our faith may have and hath her privy operations secret to us, in whom, yet known to him by whom they are.
   Tell this to a man that hath a mind deceived by too hard an opinion of himself, and it doth but augment his grief: he hath his answer ready, Will you make me think otherwise than I find, than I feel in myself? I have thoroughly considered and exquisitely sifted all the corners of my heart, and I see what there is; never seek to persuade me against my knowledge; "I do not, I know I do not believe."
   Well, to favour them a little in their weakness; let that be granted which they do imagine; be it that they are faithless and without belief. But are they not grieved for their unbelief? They are. Do they not wish it might, and also strive that it may, be otherwise? We know they do. Whence cometh this, but from a secret love and liking which they have of those things that are believed? No man can love things which in his own opinion are not. And if they think those things to be, which they shew that they love when they desire to believe them; then must it needs be, that by desiring to believe they prove themselves true believers. For without faith, no man thinketh that things believed are.[28]

28. Richard Hooker, "A Learned and Comfortable Sermon of the Certainty and Perpetuity of Faith in the Elect: Especially of the Prophet Habakkuk's Faith," in *Of the*

For the Reformers, consolation appears as the stability provided by a real entity, an entity that becomes a consoling assurance of our salvation because of our ultimate inability to question seriously its existence, even if we think that we do. The Protestant sense of Providence conveys the reassuring nature of its epistemology. What Providence provides is also the faith (the grace) to believe that is providential. (Herbert, in the *Country Parson*, calls it distrust for successful laborers to "doubt Gods providence, thinking that their own labour is the cause of their thriving" [p. 247]). The rejection of works for faith means to deny the existence of a preexistent subject free to accept or reject the proposition that God exists. Jaroslav Pelikan has described the Lutheran rejection of dualism succinctly: "The distinction between the knowing subject and the known object, drawn from common sense and Greek philosophy, becomes worse than meaningless when I make myself the subject and God the object."[29] Luther argues against free will that everything depends on God and that it is a mistake to imagine a dualistic contractual situation in which a private self acts on a footing equal to God's. Cavell's Wittgensteinian refutation of Hume's argument that the social contract is coercive recalls the orthodox refutation of the claims of covenant theology, which regards God and humanity as originally free agents contractually bound to each other.[30] For Cavell the social contract actually constitutes those who agree to it, rather than being contracted by them as preexistent agents, and in the same way the irresistibility of grace constitutes both those it saves and those it passes over. These refutations reject the terms of a model that sees an unencumbered subject, willingly or unwillingly, charged with a contract the fulfillment of whose terms on the subject's part will oblige the author and offerer of the contract (society or God) to save the subject harmless. This is the lesson of a poem like "Dialogue," where it is "Sinne" who is thinking in contractual terms and who leads the speaker to "disclaim the whole designe" (ll. 22–23). But even the speaker's resignation to the terms of the covenant—"Sinne disclaims and I resigne" (l. 24)—is too much the act of a contracting will. Even the willed resignation of the will isn't sufficient. What is sufficient is a real reaction, a real and not willful resignation to a pain that imitates Christ's:

Laws of Ecclesiastical Polity, ed. Christopher Morris (New York: Dutton, 1907), 1:5–7. The whole sermon is highly relevant to the issue of consolation arising from its own absence.

29. Jaroslav Pelikan, *From Luther to Kierkegaard* (St. Louis, Mo.: Concordia Publishing House, 1963), p. 17.

30. See Cavell, *Claim of Reason*, pp. 22–24, and compare Strier's fine account of how Herbert rejects covenant theology, in *Love Known*, pp. 84–113.

> That is all, if that I could
>   Get without repining;
> And my clay, my creature, would
>   Follow my resigning:
> That as I did freely part
> With my glorie and desert,
> Left all joyes to feel all smart— —
>   Ah! no more: thou break'st my heart.
>   (ll. 25–32)

The speaker's pain is caused by Christ but also by his capacity at last to receive Christ and to resign himself to the capacity to feel this pain. Resignation ceases being the detachment of a separate and sovereign ego. It becomes instead the most intense form of a community with the pain to which Christ has resigned himself in order to enter into community with humanity.

As Perry Miller implies, the model of contract would reemphasize works;[31] as in Kant, it makes faith an obligation and so a work. Conversely the orthodox emphasis on faith is a repudiation of the independent existence of an independent subject for whom doubt and belief are equally valid modalities of will. This rejection of the will as an independent faculty anticipates Wittgenstein's. The point is to resist the mistake of imagining that there can be an intention without an object, a private act of will (obligated by God or by the categorical imperative) that only hooks on to the world secondarily:

"For a moment I meant to. . . ." That is, I had a particular feeling, an inner experience; and I remember it.—And now remember *quite precisely*! Then the 'inner experience' of intending seems to vanish again. Instead one remembers thoughts, feelings, movements, and also connexions with earlier situations. . . . But suppose that . . . I did remember a *single* sensation; how have I the right to say that it is what I call the "intention"? It might be that (for example) a particular tickle accompanied every one of my intentions.

What is the natural expression of an intention?—Look at a cat when it stalks a bird; or a beast when it wants to escape. (*Philosophical Investigations*, §645–47)

Wittgenstein's deprivatizing of the individual will, as one might call it, is a secular version of the claims made by the Lutheran argument against its freedom. The world depends entirely on God's will. Hu-

31. See Perry Miller, "The Marrow of Puritan Divinity," in his *Errand into the Wilderness* (New York: Harper and Row, 1964), pp. 48–98.

man activity is part of the world, and because the natural expression of willing is activity, the will too is part of the world. Now, the source for all activity is God, so every human act of will is determined by God, even (although in a privative manner) sinfulness: "For I say, that man without the grace of God remains, nevertheless, under the *general* Omnipotence of an acting God, who moves and carries along all things, of necessity, in the course of His infallible motion; but that the man's being thus carried along, is nothing; that is, avails nothing in the sight of God, nor is considered any thing else but sin."[32]

I think this argument can be pushed into asserting the kind of compatibilism of free will and external determination that a dualistic reading of Wittgenstein would see operative in his philosophy. Being and responsibility are two names for the same state. Every entity along the great chain of being, because of what it is, naturally wills its own existence where it is on the chain.[33] Luther ventriloquizes God's considerations in hardening Pharaoh's heart in Exodus: God does not enter Pharaoh to make him will otherwise than he might; rather, God knows that "he, being evil, cannot but will evil as I move him by the power of omnipotence" to will *something*, because it is a quality of sentience to will (i.e., to act according to its interests). And having been moved to will, Pharaoh can be expected to will evil.

If you ask, "Why then does He not alter those evil wills which He moves?" you're playing with fire: "This question touches on the secrets of His Majesty. . . . It is not for us to inquire into these mysteries, but to adore them" (Dillenberger, p. 195). "It is not for us . . ." means that even here we should yield up our will to know why our wills are not our own. But this yielding relieves the burden of elaborating an epistemology, relieves the burden of knowing. The inextricability of my will with the world, and with God's will as the cause of the world, means I do not have to overcome my own skepticism. It is automatically true that I can be skeptical of any argument that would militate against skepticism, but if my will and belief are determined elsewhere, I no longer have to worry about skepticism's resilience. My actions are determined by God, and for both Herbert and Wittgenstein, knowledge is an epiphenomenon of action. We will "*know* that God is our merciful father," as Calvin requires us, through out actions. Herbert asks for simplicity "that I may live, / So live and like, that I may *know*, thy wayes" ("A Wreath," ll. 9–10), and he recommends to the parson

32. Martin Luther, *The Bondage of the Will*, trans. Henry Cole (Grand Rapids, Mich.: Baker House Books, 1976), p. 314, my emphasis.
33. The great chain of being is a concept that would probably still have currency for Luther, who thought he saw Old Testament influences in the *Timaeus*.

for the cultivation of his understanding "a holy Life, remembering what his Master saith, that *if any do Gods will, he shall know of the Doctrine, John 7[:17]*" (*The Country Parson,* p. 228).

The denial of dualism is a denial of the possibility of a pure skepticism, and even in Protestantism this has its consolatory dimensions:

> I frankly confess that, for myself, even if it could be, I should not want 'free-will' to be given me, nor anything to be left in my own hands to enable me to endeavour after salvation . . . because, even were there no dangers, adversities, or devils, I should still be forced to labour with no guarantee of success, and to beat my fists in the air. If I lived and worked to all eternity, my conscience would never reach comfortable certainty as to how much it must do to satisfy God. . . . But now that God has taken my salvation out of the control of my own will, and put it under the control of His, and promised to save me, not according to my working or running, but according to His own grace and mercy, I have the comfortable certainty that He is faithful and will not lie to me. . . .
>
> Furthermore, I have the comfortable certainty that I please God, not by reason of the merit of my works, but by reason of His merciful favour promised to me; so that if I work too little, or badly, He does not impute it to me, but with fatherly compassion pardons me and makes me better. (Dillenberger, pp. 199–200)

This abandonment of free will is a consolation then, because it removes from the self the Kantian burden of having freely to will its own belief. Instead, belief has priority over the will. The child is saved by believing the father, and if the father causes the child to believe, the question of doubt cannot seriously arise. This is the consolation that Lutheran determinism offers, a consolation present even in Hooker's far less predeterminist account of election. It comes from the recognition of an inability to doubt. You cannot doubt your own substance, whether that substance is called language games or the motion of God. If you really do doubt, according to Luther, you doubt not from some legitimate skepticism or uncertainty but from pride; your doubt is perverse and evil, and you will be damned for it.

Now, such a concession to God's power needs to be distinguished not only from the covenant theologian's re-introduction of the will's privilege, but also from the radical antinomian claim that would obviate any necessity to consider the will at all. Both positions—the contractual and the antinomian—imply an epistemological dualism. In the former an independent self, free to do as it likes, enters into an agreement with God; in the latter an independent self relinquishes (or is understood to have relinquished) all control to God. In each the autonomy of the subject is assumed. Whether burdened with well-nigh crushing responsibilities or completely relieved of all responsibility, the subject considers itself an independent entity. Samuel Rutherford (Milton's enemy) argued against both versions of the believer's independence. He calls it a doctrine of the devil to say "the adultery of a beleever is a sin, that actually condemnes for ever to hell, and argueth the committer thereof to bee in nature, not in Christ, which is a lye, both in the matter, and specially in the end, to cause a beleever despaire." But the antinomian error is just as great: "The *sense* and apprehension of a beleever, that saith adultery in him is no sin, because it was pardoned before it was committed, is as false as the Devill. Now the light of faith saith the contrary, the Word of God saith, adultery in justified *David* is sin, but the inference and logick of the flesh is not to be beleeved, [that] therfore *David* is not in Christ."[34] The orthodox response to the radical position—elaborating a difficult, antidualistic epistemology—anticipates Wittgenstein's rejection of a behavioristic interpretation of his claims. For Wittgenstein it makes no sense to deny the operation of the will:

> "Willing too is merely an experience," one would like to say (the 'will' too only an 'idea'). It comes when it comes,and I cannot bring it about.
> Not bring it about?—Like *what*? What can I bring about, then? What am I comparing willing with when I say this? (*Philosophical Investigations*, §611)

Willing is for Wittgenstein a special case of belief, but belief without the kind of gap between subject and object that the Tractarian interlocutor's term "experience" implies.[35] It is a mistake to imagine that a static and isolated subject comes at some point either to assume activity or to have activity thrust upon it, as though it existed prior to and independently from its own activity. Once the subject is seen as primarily an actor, and not originally a knower, the solution of the transcendental problem of responsibility for the will is seen in the vanishing of the problem. To the extent that I can analyze what goes on in willing, I see that I cannot separate it from myself. Willing is the name I give to my agreement with my own action, and it is not an inaccurate name. I don't do anything that I haven't willed. Thus Witt-

34. Samuel Rutherford, *Luther against Antinomians*, in *A Survey of the Spirituall Antichrist . . .* (London: 1648), p. 154.
35. See Wittgenstein's *Tractatus Logico-Philosophicus*, trans. D. F. Pears and B. F. McGuinness (New York: Humanities Press, 1972), proposition 6.423, where Wittgenstein speaks of "the will as a phenomenon."

genstein defines volition in a nondualistic way: "So one might say: voluntary movement is marked by the absence of surprise" (§628).

People like Rutherford, who has been taken to be a fair representative of the opponents of the radicals, urged precisely this conception of voluntarism against the antinomian idea that the operation of grace supplanted any need even to think about the will.[36] Rutherford follows Luther by insisting on the concurrence of the will with grace (a concurrence made possible by grace); he refuses to consider the operation of the will a dead issue. Thus Rutherford, like Wittgenstein, wants to elaborate a doctrine of the will that sees our own deepest and most original role in willing as a passive acquiescence (William James calls it "consent") to our being what we are (to our doing what we do).[37] This is a vanishing passivity, however, since even that passive being is of the world—is active in the world.

36. Hooker distinguishes the will, as a free and rational faculty oriented toward goodness, from the appetites, which pertain to action in the world and the impulses of which are not voluntary, though under the control of the will (*Laws*, 1:170).

37. Shuger's *Habits of Thought* contains a fine account of passivity and grace in Herbert, in many ways compatible with my argument (pp. 92–119). See also Goldberg's *Voice Terminal Echo*, which gives a Derridean account of the priority of an exterior writing to the selfhood it founds. I differ from Veith, who sees "the irresistible power of grace" as determining a spark of love against "the depravity of the human will" (*Reformation Spirituality*, p. 109). I argue that, for Herbert, the human will (of the saved), always turns out to be fundamentally innocent, even when it is unaware of its innocence. Harman, writing about Lewalski, addresses a similar issue in terms similar to Shuger's and Goldberg's: "The Bible may sanction literary productivity, but what it also sponsors (in this view) is a writer whose agency is immediately subverted by the discovery that he is not only the writer but the written-upon. Lewalski takes both points as evidence of the fact that Protestant poetics personalize scripture—they take *up* writing and they take writing *to* themselves—but she might easily have seen them as evidence of the fact that the Bible provides a model for activity only to subvert activity, that it transforms subjects into objects, embodiers into embodiments" (*Costly Monuments*, p. 27). This is always the risk of the kind of passivity that Rutherford and Luther advocate, and it may be seen, perhaps in "The Holdfast," where no acknowledgment of passivity is sufficiently passive. "Nay, ev'n to trust in him, was also his" (l. 6) the speaker learns, but he goes too far even to confess his own neediness: "But to have nought is ours, not to confess / That we have nought" (ll. 8–9). He risks losing all subjectivity, as Fish notes (*Self-Consuming Artifacts*, pp. 175–76). In this way, it turns out, all things are more ours, but this is because of Christ, "who cannot fail or fall" (l. 14). It is Christ, here, who harmonizes predestination—he cannot fail or fall—with free will; Christ who represents the compatibilist position, rather than any other human beings (except insofar as we are allowed to share Christ's nature). Harman regards this poem (against Fish) as securing the self's representation through that representation's being "turned over to another for safe-keeping" (*Costly Monuments*, p. 56); for her this is the happy version of divine sponsorship of an authentic selfhood. The unhappy versions, in which selves are objectified, collapse, or dissolve (as in "Church Monuments"), she describes very powerfully, and I differ from her mainly in the progression of my exposition, ending at what for her is an intermediate stage and seeing her own endpoint as intermediate for my argument.

See also William H. Pahlka's *Saint Augustine's Meter and George Herbert's Will* (Kent,

When eventually I come to speak about the ways in which this epistemology implies the deep alienation belonging to what might be called the inconsolable, I will return to this question of passivity. I will want to argue that while passivity may occur only at a vanishing point, it can never be said to have entirely vanished. All activity, all willing, is indeed of the world, and its primary grammatical form is the active; but in the passive is suffering, the helpless inability to consent to activity, which is to say, the helpless inability to refuse to consent to activity. And suffering will mean, finally, to have to bear the unbearable.

For the present, though, I want to look at the volitional experience of those who are saved through their assurance of the real (which for the Protestants is God and for Wittgenstein the world, the field of language games). The epistemological account I have been trying to articulate through a comparison of Reformation theology and Wittgensteinian philosophy elides the difference between active and passive. Being (which in any individual means "being carried along by the real") and activity are the same thing. We experience the activity of what we will, and that is the total experience of willing.[38] Such a conception, even if it subscribes to the Reformation theory of grace, will not throw out the experience of willing something. Against the

---

Ohio: Kent State University Press, 1987), esp. pp. 173–208. Pahlka's fascinating and original book uses the notion of meter as determining the will through time to a pattern, even though the will, at any instant, is utterly free. Commenting on "A true Hymn," ll. 9–10—"The finenesse which a hymne or psalm affords, / Is, when the soul unto the line accords"—Pahlka writes: "Soul and lines may literally be in or out of accord with each other because, according to Augustine, both are constituted by number. The lines of verse achieve fineness when they are a faithful creation of a soul whose *rhythms* are in harmony with God's creative patterning. Poetic art is born when the lines reflect the rhythms of the soul, as long as the soul is itself rhythmed by God. . . . A heart that is 'moved' is not merely in a state of aroused emotion; it is a heart whose *motions* are supplied by God, a heart that in turn supplies those motions to its words" (p. 186). Pahlka argues that the tendency to meter is a tendency to a conformity with a nonphenomenal determination of any phenomenal will. Though he doesn't mention Freud, his account is consonant with Freud's in *Beyond the Pleasure Principle*. But where Pahlka sees a rhythmical third-person agency at the heart of the first person determining the human toward God, Freud sees that agency as the death drive. Read in light of Freud, I think Pahlka's book is even better.

38. See *Philosophical Investigations*, §621, and William James's *Principles of Psychology* (New York: Dover, 1950), 2:486–592, e.g., p. 487: "No creature not endowed with divinatory power can perform an act voluntarily for the first time," and p. 505: "The consciousness of muscular exertion [which is what the consciousness of willing comes down to], being impossible without movement *effected somewhere*, must be an afferent [i.e., moving from world to brain] and not an efferent sensation [i.e., moving from brain to world, which would be the characteristic of a pre-kinetic intention or act of the will]; a consequence, and not an antecedent, of the movement itself."

antinomians, Rutherford argues that *"Luther* speaketh pathetickly of the slavery and impotency of our free-will by nature, but no wayes to favour *Antinomians* and *Familists*, who would have us blocks and stones in all wee doe" (*Luther*, p. 155). Rather, we should think of ourselves as being like a saw, which does act, although it is a "patient" of the activity that causes it to act:

> The subjective power of doing good that *Luther* calleth a passive power, and which was in man before the fall, in the renewed man is not simply passive, for in regard to it, saith *Luther*, . . . the will rather is drawen, then it doth draw and act, but inclineth more to bee drawen; but it is passive, because free will in pure naturalls, before the fall or after re-generation, is a subject receiving a holy sanctified rectitude of will: and before the fall, that rectitude was that concreated and naturall Image of God in the *first Adam*, in regeneration it is the supernaturall image of the *second Adam*, which we call the *new heart*, and before the fall *Adam* did not love and serve God by free will simply, but by free will gifted with that naturall accident of concreated sanctity and holinesse added to the will as a connaturall gift to make the will compleat in its operations. Now the will is a mere patient in receiving a supernaturall active power to will according to Christ, and in this regard the will is patient and must bee elevated in its naturall activity, by receiving a new infused heart. . . . And because free-will acts according to Christ in beleeving, hopeing, loving out of faith, all by the strength of new supernaturall habits, therefore doth *Luther* call the renewed man a patient, and his supernaturall works like the drawing of a Saw which yet hath its own activity of cutting the tree and hath teeth by art for that effect, yet tis called a patient in sawing the tree, because it is moved in its motion by him that draweth the saw. . . . In the receiving the active determination of actuall assisting grace, the will is a patient in the reception and subjective and passive lying under the actuall motion of him who workes in us to will and to doe, for wee can do nothing more than clay, when God infuseth a spirit in it, to move the predeterminating wind of the spirit, to blow right on us, in regard of both these, though being acted by habituall grace, and by actuall assisting grace being drawen . . . we doe and have our own subor-dinate active influence in all the workes wee doe toward Heaven, and life eternall, yet *Luther saith*, wee are patients. (Pp. 157–58)

For Rutherford, consolation comes of this determination of the will (this passivity of the active): "Free-will's Sabbath and rest is to lye quietly and contentedly under the sweet actings of grace. . . . Man chooseth God, because he is chosen. And marrieth Christ, because he was first married against his will, for without consent, the consent is conquered to Christ. . . . It was a depth that our wise Lord would create such timber or metall, as free-will, that Christ might ingrave on it the artifice and elaborate skill of never-enough admired free-grace" (pp. 162–63).

This idea that will and fate run concurrently implies, as we have seen, the saving consolation that we cannot help willing our own belief (unlike the Kantian obligation to will our own belief). Such a disinclination to distinguish between will and activity has consequences for a theory of language, since the effect is to deny the dualistic conception of a private, preexistent self (thinking a private language) come face to face with the world (or with God). Rutherford sees that the idea of an independent subject inevitably implies justification by works, rather than by faith, even for the antinomians: "*Antinomians* hold *that a justified man is perfect and free from sin both in person and in works, as if he were in heaven, and that the naturall, civill, and religious works of beleevers are made perfect in the sight of God*. Then must they perfectly keep the Law, and Christ must make our good works exactly conforme to the Law, what can hinder us then to be justified by works?" (p. 143).

One consequence of a theory of the private self would be a rigorous insistence on the difference between signified and referent; the signified stands to the referent as the private to the public or the representational to the real.[39] Such a theory puts will prior to belief, in its account of conformity to law (to use the Kantian terminology) or of following rules (to use the Wittgensteinian expression). Legislative language *signifies* a situation or state of affairs, and it is up to the subject of legislation to bring the referential world into conformity with what the legislation has signified. On this account, to follow a rule is to change its grammatical voice from the jussive subjunctive to the indicative and to make that indicative a true statement. The rule signifies, the world is a referent, and so to conform to a rule is successfully to will an adequation between signified and referent or to make two independent spheres correspond. To follow an order would mean to represent, privately, exactly what the order contemplates and then to bring the world, publicly, into agreement with the private representation. The mode of prescription is signification; the mode of description, reference.

It is already clear, I hope, that Wittgenstein rejects this account of legislation (for example, by saying that we do not learn rules but judgments). His response would be that to give an order is to make a

---

39. The strength of a deconstructive theory of language lies in its ability to reverse these terms, to see reference as private and arbitrary and signification as determined by public conventions; but it still insists on the difference.

move in a language game; this move would ordinarily (i.e., in most language games) set up a situation in which the recipient's ensuing activity would count as following or not following the order. But such a situation implies that you already know the rules of the game—that is, that you can already follow a set of rules before you need to learn the *procedure* for following a rule. A Lutheran Wittgensteinian might call justification by grace a willingness on the bank's (or on God's) part to treat leniently a lot of losing moves (moves that wouldn't count as following God's orders—moves that would end the game, that is); with this leniency would come a concomitant gratefulness on your part for the grace that allows you to keep playing and, indeed, a consequent willingness to keep playing instead of upsetting the board in a childish fit of pique (which itself would be a bad move, but still a move).

Here too, then, the Wittgensteinian account insists on an adequation between signified and referent, since once you're playing a language game, *anything* counts as a move. The order is a move, and the response is a move. And in an act of willing, there is no distinction between what would be the subjunctive intention and the indicative action. Both are moves within the game. For Rutherford, then, rejecting justification by works means that what matters is not the ascertainment of an adequation between the prescriptive signified and the descriptive referent, whether it is the self or God who is charged with maintaining that adequation; what matters is the willingness to see the *inevitable* adequation between signified and referent (faith), a willingness granted to you by God (grace), this willingness itself thus both signifying and referring to such an adequation.

Indeed, Rutherford uses similar terms. He will not permit the idea that holiness is a pure referent indifferent to all signs. To get rid of the "ought" in this system, to get rid of justification by works, is not to get rid of the obliged activity but rather of the epistemology that describes a subject as first representing an activity in the subjunctive (through an understanding of the law) and then fulfilling (or not) that activity in the indicative. Rutherford quotes Luther—"The Law of the letter and the law of the Spirit differ, as the signe and the thing signified: as the word and the thing, then when the thing is obtained, there is no need of the signe. So there is no law to the just man, but having only the signe, we are taught to seek the thing itself"—and comments:

> This expression of *Luther*, with another in the same Tome, to wit, *The justified man ought not to live holily, but hee doth live holily:* gave occasion to

Antinomians to dream (but its but a dream) that *Luther* is theirs, as if *Luther*
had been of their minde, that the justified is under no commanding
power of the law, and that being once justified, and having obtained the
Spirit, they are not obliged by any obligation of a command involving sin
in case of disobedience, to either read, heare, or meditate in the Scriptures, but are so freed from the signe, having obtained the thing, that
they are not under the letter of the law or Gospel written or preached, or
under any outward command, or Ordinance, or Law, or Sacrament, or
sin, or obligation at all, but are led by a free arbitrary Spirit separated
from all letter of the word. A vain dream. For *Luther* holdeth the letter of
the Law, to be an erroneous, false, and wicked seeking of righteousnesse
by the works of the Law, and a living to sin, and from the oldnesse of the
letter in this sense are we freed by the Spirit of faith; and *Luther* explaineth himselfe, when he saith, . . . having obtained the Spirit, we
need not the letter. He meaneth nothing lesse than when we have received the Spirit, we need not the written Scriptures or the Commandment or any outward Ordinances, nor any commanding. Sure *Sathan*
devised that sense, it came never in *Luther*, never in *Pauls* mind; but he
meaneth having obtained the thing, that is, the Spirit, we need not the
signe, that is the letter of the Law only, without the Spirit: now the letter
of the Law only commandeth perfect and exactly absolute obedience
under the paine of eternall damnation. But *Luther* explaineth himself in
the very next words. . . . He so liveth that hee hath not need of the Law
to teach and command without Christ that he must performe absolutely
perfect obedience to the Law, otherwise he is eternally condemned; this
is the letter of the Law, for the just man is in Christ. . . . The law cannot
accuse and condemne beleevers in Christ: in the same sense, saith
Luther . . . the justified man ought not to live holily, according to the
letter of the absolute commanding Law enjoyning obedience under
paine of eternall condemnation; for faith looseth him from this . . . Law
debt yet . . . hee liveth holily, and he ought to live holily in an Evangelick
sense. (Pp. 141–42)

In his second sermon Hooker similarly argues that the result of
imputed or habitual holiness is actual holiness.[40] Now, from the
central Protestant idea of an adequation between sign and referent
under the aegis of faith (or grace) springs the Protestant hermeneutic,
with its insistence on the literality of the Bible. As William Madsen has
taught us, the typological was the only principle of (quasi-) allegorical
figuration that Reformation interpreters considered operative, since
it was a principle enunciated by Paul.[41] The Reformers insisted, how-

40. *The Works of . . . Richard Hooker*, 7th ed., ed. John Keble (New York: Burt Frank-
lin, 1970), 3:507.
41. William G. Madsen, *From Shadowy Type to Truth: Studies in Milton's Symbolism* (New
Haven, Conn.: Yale University Press, 1968).

ever, that typological interpretation took place in the realm of the literal, not the figurative (the place of the allegorical and anagogical), and justified this claim by an expanded conception of the literal. William Whitaker is usually taken to be a representative English theorist of typology (by Madsen and Lewalski, for example), and his definition of literal meaning anticipates Rutherford's claims for an adequation of signified and referent. Whitaker insists that any interpretation of a biblical passage must be "concluded from the very words themselves" and then extends this principle of contextual reading to a typological realm that would seem noncontextual:

> We should form a like judgment of the type or anagoge. In psalm xcv. God says, "I sware in my wrath, that they should not enter into my rest." There the rest may be understood both of the land of Canaan, and typically also of the kingdom of heaven. Yet this is not a twofold sense: but, when the sign is referred to the thing signified, that which was hidden in the sign is more openly expressed. When we proceed from the sign to the thing signified, we bring no new sense, but only bring out into light what was before concealed in the sign. When we speak of the sign by itself, we express only part of its meaning; and so also when we mention the thing signified: but when the mutual relation between sign and the thing signified is brought out, then the whole complete sense, which is founded upon this similitude and agreement, is set forth.[42]

In this way a typological theory of literal meaning ensures an adequation between signified and referent (Whitaker's "thing signified"), an adequation that itself might be called the "rest" that full participation in the kingdom of heaven vouchsafes (and the rest too of Wittgenstein's sleeper, whose dreams carry their own referents): "The sense is one only, namely the literal or grammatical. However, the whole entire sense is not in the words taken strictly, but part in the type, part in the transaction itself. In either of these considered separately and by itself part only of the meaning is contained; and by both taken together the full and perfect meaning is completed" (*A Disputation*, p. 406). This principle of interpretation becomes, as we have seen, a principle of living when human life, "living holily," is a concomitant of believing the literal word of God: when humans are themselves absorbed into a typological reality in which they serve as either antitypes or correlative types.[43]

---

42. William Whitaker, *A Disputation on Holy Scripture against the Papists, especially Bellarmine and Stapleton*, trans. William Fitzgerald (New York: Johnson Reprint Corp., 1968), p. 407.

43. Lewalski argues that Protestant poets represent themselves sometimes as antitypes and sometimes as correlative types of biblical figures.

A conception of the world informed by typological thinking, then, is realist in a way that the Catholic Platonic or Neoplatonic world view is not. Modern scholarship has shown that the Puritans saw history, their own included, in typological terms and so believed that their own political activity was valuable not only as a sign—allegorically or ana- gogically representing spiritual improvement—but in and of itself, that is, literally. Lewalski analyzes in detail how the personal too is considered to have its own intrinsic value—a value underwritten by typology. She opposes Protestant typologizing to the Catholic notion that the Bible presents standards (of action, of truth, of virtue, etc.) to which as private subjects we are commanded to conform. Typologists, seeing themselves as already implicated in the scriptural system, as (always already) antitypes or correlative types, take themselves to be in the same inescapable position with respect to grace as are the types they reflect. Against Madsen's dualistic claim that there is a distinction between the material (the preexistent and private self or subject who becomes typical) and the typological function (*From Shadowy Type*, p. 5), and in the spirit of Auerbach's great essay on the original merging of form and matter in the concept of figura,[44] Lewalski shows that according to Protestant typology the Old Testament types knew them- selves to be types (*Protestant Poetics*, pp. 124–44) and so were really saved in themselves instead of merely signifying salvation. A major consequence of this argument is the denial of the notion of a private self called upon to an *imitatio Christi* (called upon to become public). Rather, any self is constituted by a preexistent reality, of which it is a part:

> Instead of an application of the self to the subject [Protestant meditation] calls for the application of the subject to the self—indeed for the sub- ject's location in the self. . . . To be sure Protestant meditation did not stimulate the senses to recreate and imagine biblical scenes in vivid de- tail; it would not therefore give rise to poetry based upon visual imagery and sensuous immediacy. But Protestant meditation did engage the mind in an effort to penetrate deeply into the motives and motions of the psyche, and also to understand the self as the very embodiment of the subject meditated on. The Word was still to be made flesh, though now in the self of the meditator. . . . This emphasis contributed to the creation of poetry with a new depth and sophistication of psychological insight, and a new focus upon the symbolic significance of the individual. (*Protestant Poetics*, pp. 149–50)[45]

44. Erich Auerbach, "Figura," in his *Scenes from the Drama of European Literature* (Minneapolis: University of Minnesota Press, 1984), pp. 11–76.

45. Similarly Bloch writes of Herbert's "recognition that the text means him" (*Spell- ing the Word*, p. 30), or as Herbert puts it about the Israelites, "Their storie pennes and

The Protestant insistence on the original reality of the psyche's participation in divine reality—rather than its legislative obligation to participate, an obligation it will either meet or not meet—is a direct result of the rejection of legislative authority. Like Calvin, Whitaker discovers tyranny in the Catholic claim that it belongs to Holy Mother Church "to judge of the true sense and interpretation of scriptures." He rejects the assertion that it is finally impermissible to ask for the grounds of the Church's authority, impermissible because the Church has the authority to authorize the interpretation that will justify its authority (*A Disputation*, pp. 402–10). Catholicism posits the Church as a transcendental "ground of truth" (p. 503) and hence as the ultimate authority to which all judgments are to be referred. However, the Protestant, typological theory of judgment sees judgment as referring to Scripture itself. And Scripture is taken not merely as a standard (in which case the question would be: Who is to judge whether my judgment conforms to a scriptural standard, and whence comes the standard for that judgment about my judgment, and who is to judge whether that judgment conforms to that second standard, etc.?) It is also a way of life, a historical event that governs, through the universalizing mode of typology, the history to which I passively belong and that governs me as a being without free will.[46]

Protestant epistemology makes the paradoxical claim that the interpretive richness of Catholic Platonism and Neoplatonism is fundamentally antirealist and that the literalizing refusal of such a richly elaborated organic connectedness is in fact a realist position. Malcolm Ross argues that the denial of transubstantiation led to the dissociation of sensibility and the attendant fragmentation of modern life, but a Protestant epistemologist would argue that transubstantiation symp-

---

sets us down" ("The Bunch of Grapes," l. 11). Bloch writes of the active/passive relation of Herbert to the Bible: "When we start with a movement of self-definition in the speaker's life, we find him reaching for a biblical text for support; when we start, on the other hand, with a biblical text, we are thrust at once into the life of the man who identifies with it" (p. 12).

46. My argument here is diametrically opposed to the brilliant Weberian argument that John Guillory makes in "The Father's House: *Samson Agonistes* in Its Historical Moment" in *Re-membering Milton: Essays on the Texts and Traditions*, ed. Mary Nyquist and Margaret W. Ferguson (New York: Methuen, 1987), pp. 148–76. Guillory argues that since works are public but vocation is personal, Catholicism would be the public religion but Calvinism would stress the coherence of the private individual. Ultimately, however, I think we are not entirely at odds; Guillory would agree, I think, that the private turns out to be a special case of a prior publicity. I would simply add that Catholic publicity was conceived, at least by Luther and Calvin (as both Strier and Veith make clear), as producing tremendous pressure on the private person to conform at every possible moment, a conformity resting entirely on the will of the individual.

tomizes precisely the antirealist distinction between the divine and the worldly (as though there could be an occult and mystical substance differing utterly from any of its attributes.)[47] The doctrine of transubstantiation sees the worldly as nullified by the divine, but Protestants like Herbert saw the bread as symbolizing Christ's surrender of his divinity, his kenosis. This surrender is precisely God's grace—his gracious bestowal of life, even at his own cost. Hooker argues against theological subtlety and for the symbolic view in terms that Herbert shares:

> The real presence of Christ's most blessed body and blood is not therefore to be sought for in the sacrament, but in the worthy receiver of the sacrament.
>
> And with this the very order of our Saviour's words agreeth, first "take and eat;" then "this is my Body which was broken for you:" first "drink ye all of this;" then followeth "this is my Blood of the New Testament which is shed for many for the remission of sins." I see not which way it should be gathered by the words of Christ, when and where the bread is His body or the cup His blood, but only in the very heart and soul of him which receiveth them. As for the sacraments, they really exhibit, but for aught we can gather out of that which is written of them, they are not really nor do really contain in themselves that grace which with them or by them it pleaseth God to bestow. (*Laws*, 2:323)

Such a symbolic relation is similar to the typological and preserves its coherence by uniting tenor and vehicle or type and antitype: "Because the sacrament being of itself but a corruptible and earthly creature must needs be thought an unlikely instrument to work so admirable effects in man, we are therefore to rest ourselves altogether upon *the strength of his glorious power* who is able and will bring to pass that the bread and cup which he giveth us shall truly be the thing he promiseth" (*Laws*, 2:325). The food that sustains us in our physical life is a type for the mystical sustenance of God's grace (2:318–19); as physical food sustains the physical body, Christ's presence sustains the soul (2:320). Hooker interprets Christ as saying "this hallowed food, through concurrence of divine power, is in verity and truth, unto faithful receivers, instrumentally a cause of that mystical participation, whereby as I make myself wholly theirs, so I give them in hand an actual possession of all such saving grace as my sacrificed body can yield, and as their souls do presently need, this is *to them and in them* my

---

47. See Malcolm Ross, *Poetry and Dogma: The Transfiguration of Eucharistic Symbols in Seventeenth Century English Poetry* (New Brunswick, N.J.: Rutgers University Press, 1954).

body" (2:329; italics reversed). Thus the eucharist brings together the earthly and the divine by hallowing the earthly and making it symbolic of the divine rather than by destroying earthly substance and replacing it with the real presence of the divine.

Indeed, the Eucharist itself may be seen in Hooker as embodying the principle of typology in its purest form, almost as an antitype answering to the principle of typology: "With touching it sanctifieth, it enlighteneth with belief, it truly conformeth us unto the image of Jesus Christ; what these elements are in themselves it skilleth not, it is enough that to me which take them they are the body and blood of Christ, his promise in witness hereof sufficeth, his word he knoweth which way to accomplish" (2:331). The Eucharist—the thanksgiving for God's grace—symbolizes that grace: "In the Eucharist we so receive the gift of God, that we know by grace what the grace is which God giveth us" (2:319).

For Herbert the Eucharist signifies both God's bounty and the cost of that bounty. In the version of "The H. Communion" that he did not include in "The Temple" he asks,

> O Gratious Lord, how shall I know
> Whether in these gifts thou bee so
>   As thou art evry-where;
> Or rather so, as thou alone
> Tak'st all the Lodging, leaving none
>   ffor thy poore creature there?
>   (ll. 1–6)

The rest of the poem urges that Christ's kenosis consisted in his willingness to become flesh. The Eucharist symbolizes Christ's care and generosity for the fallen. The point is that Christ does not deprive the poor, fallen creature of his lodging but comes to aid that creature:

> Then of this also I am sure
> That thou didst all those pains endure
>   To'abolish Sinn, not Wheat.
> Creatures are good, & have their place;
> Sinn onely, which did all deface,
>   Thou drivest from his seat.
>   (ll. 19–24)

The poem stresses, then, the philosophically realist position that the Eucharist represents the ubiquity of God because it participates in that ubiquity. This poem has a suggestion of the Lutheran argument that with participation comes consubstantiation: "In these gifts thou bee so / As thou art evry-where." What matters is that the same anti-dualism informs the less militant, more Anglican poem of the same title in "The Temple," where Herbert conforms more closely to Hooker's view:

> Not in rich furniture, or fine aray,
>> Nor in a wedge of gold,
>> Thou, who for me wast sold,
> To me dost now thy self convey;
> For so thou should'st without me still have been,
>> Leaving within me sinne:
>
> But by the way of nourishment and strength
>> Thou creep'st into my breast;
>> Making thy way my rest,
> And thy small quantities my length;
> Which spread their forces into every part,
> Meeting sinnes force and art.
>
> Yet can these not get over to my soul,
>> Leaping the wall that parts
>> Our souls and fleshy hearts;
> But as th'outworks, they may controll
> My rebel-flesh, and carrying thy name,
>> Affright both sinne and shame.
>
> Onely thy grace, which with these elements comes,
>> Knoweth the ready way,
>> And hath the privie key,
> Op'ning the souls most subtile rooms;
> While those to spirits refin'd, at doore attend
>> Dispatches from their friend.

The bread is refined to (human) spirit through the human/divine process of digestion; the body is no longer shameful, since it is seen to be made of the Eucharist that nourishes it; and the person thus nourished—not by the actual body of Christ, but (as grace would enable him to recognize) by the friendly providence that provides food for its creatures—now has the strength to await faithfully the friendly operation of grace. This system again stresses the concurrence of will and predetermination because grace means the tranquil willingness to await the dispatches from grace. Grace is the recognition that grace is a friend.

The community of communion is intimated here. The elements of the communion absorb the partaker into a reassuring plurality.[48] The waiting is done by a group. The elements of the communion have been refined to spirits who act out within the speaker's body their adult, assured roles. These spirits might seem threatening—knowing so much about him and taking over his body as they do—but they are made to seem friends instead. In spite of their efficiency, and his wary obstinacy, they do more than tolerate him; they accept him fully. The speaker can belong to this group because he is a friend of their friend—the friend mentioned in the last word of the poem. The elements of the Eucharist witness through their patient faithfulness the generosity of the grace now at work in the speaker's soul, and it is as though the speaker waits with these faithful and reassuring spirits. The speaker somehow belongs to the group of those who can await dispatches patiently, adults who don't rebel and chafe (as he has) because of the long wait. His final belongingness is now registered as the absence of anxiety. He is accepted and accepting.

What is given with the Eucharist is not a magical substance but the reassurance that a gift is being made. The gift consists of the reassurance of the giver's generosity, and it is to this atmosphere of communal generosity that the speaker can belong. William Nestrick argues for the centrality of a similar notion of generosity in Herbert; I find many of his formulations congenial. He sees a dense communion of grace in the Eucharist and prayer as the human reciprocation to God: "In this sacramental act of giving and receiving [which is the subject of "The Priesthood"], Herbert returns to the most archaic and only total form of gift-giving, one that involves the entire community of indebted creditors and God in a completely inward reciprocity."[49] Nestrick argues for human passivity in a vocabulary that I agree with: "Even gratitude, once all motions are allowed to be God's, must be considered as a gift" ("The Giver and the Gift," p. 191; cf. also "The Holdfast") so that "the return must be man's identity as recipient" ("The Giver and the Gift," p. 204).[50]

It is not the physical gifts themselves that count; they are merely

48. Compare Bloch's comments on typology in Herbert: "Because he assumes that Aaron or Exodus is as much a part of the reader's past as of his own, his references to biblical history are intended to convey a sense of shared experience" (*Spelling the Word*, p. 128).

49. William Nestrick, "George Herbert: The Giver and the Gift," *Ploughshares* 2 (1975), 203.

50. Nestrick, with Michael Schoenfeldt, also stresses the artfulness of gift giving and the competition such artfulness conceals. Schoenfeldt, like Nestrick, does say that there

signs. What counts is the aura of giving, the calm expectation that dispatches from the friend will come. And yet the signs carry their own referents, since this calm faith in the generosity of grace is grace. As Hooker says, the promise of the gift is the gift itself. In the chapter "The Parson in Sacraments" in *The Country Parson* Herbert says of God: "Thou art not only the feast, but the way to it" (pp. 257–58).

As in "Love" (III) the fact that the speaker responds to love allows him to experience love: "All may certainly conclude, that God loves them, till either they despise that Love, or despair of his Mercy: not any sin else, but is within his Love; but the despising of Love must needs be without it. The thrusting away of his arme makes us onely not embraced" (*Country Parson*, p. 283). Here, because the speaker recognizes the attestation of generosity that it makes, the bread confers the loving power to wait for the love that the bread attests and will continue to attest in future communions. Grace manifests itself as love of grace and as a calm trust that it will send its dispatches. This is Protestant realism, in which grace and faith are the same, in which love and the desire for love are one. As in "Love" (III), a faith in the adequation of sign and referent comes through grace. As Arnold Stein notes, Love's "You shall be he" "makes the guest who is unworthy of love worthy of love." If the speaker responds to it, "the transforming power of love can do this, can make the unworthy worthy."[51] We see this transformation enacted in "Love" (III), marked when the speaker sits and eats, as he sits and eats also for communion, worthy of love because he believes that God loves him despite his unworthiness.

Elegy and Exclusion from Community

> Il y a le don par lequel on oblige celui qui le reçoit à rendre un surplus de pouvoir ou de prestige à celui qui donne—ainsi, on ne donne jamais. Le don qui est abandon voue l'être abandonné à perdre sans esprit de retour, sans calcul et sans sauvegarde jusqu'à son être qui donne: d'où l'exigence d'infini qui est dans le silence de l'abandon.
>
> —Maurice Blanchot

The generosity of the general is the generosity of being vouch-safed membership in the community of generosity. In my Shake-

---

is ultimately no possibility of reciprocating God's gifts ("Standing on Ceremony," p. 132). Such modes of competition are the subject of the next chapter, where I examine the ambivalence of gifts in Shakespeare.

51. Arnold Stein, *George Herbert's Lyrics* (Baltimore: Johns Hopkins University Press, 1968), pp. 192–93.

speare chapter I will argue the darker side of this self-endowing generosity; yet even there I will argue that it *is* generosity. But here I wish to show its limits in Herbert.[52]

The end of "The H. Communion" illustrates an important component of realist consolation—its third-person quality. The consoling reassurance of language games is that you begin and continue a third person. Nostalgia is always nostalgia for the third person, the innocent player of a language game, one of a community of innocent players. Mark Strand catches this in his brave lie, "I am still the boy my mother used to kiss": in other words, I am still the third person whose young, attentive (i.e.,: game-playing) mother hasn't been forced to undergo the ravages of time that the mother I know now has. In "The H. Communion" the poem's first three stanzas are about the speaker, in the first-person singular, to whom Christ is conveyed, for whom he was sold, and for whose salvation wealthy appointments do not suffice. The eucharist brings peace to the speaker, and "Yet can these not get over to my soul." The third stanza then widens the perspective, moving to the first-person plural, and in the last stanza the first person drops out altogether.[53] God's grace opens "*the* souls most subtile rooms; / While those to spirits refin'd, at doore attend / Dispatches from their friend." Why not "*my* soul's" rooms? Because when salvation comes through grace, I the unkind, ungrateful no longer count. Instead I am unself-consciously (impersonally) present. The feeling here is complex but can be explicated. The speaker belongs to a group whose acceptance of him he discovers through the fact that they consider his being there natural; if he were a child, he'd be a little proud to be considered unremarkable by this group of adults, proud also that they should consider unremarkable their attentive care for the state of his soul, as though he were as ordinarily worthy of their attention as any of the adults they from time to time visit. He'd be self-conscious about the fact that no one seems to realize that he's self-conscious, since no one regards his presence as extraordinary. But this would be a contented and residual self-consciousness, giving way to the speaker's feeling of being part of a plurality. The expansion to the

52. I conceive these limits somewhat differently from the way that Michael Schoenfeldt does when he argues for the coercive effects of generosity in Herbert in "Standing on Ceremony" and in " 'Subject to Ev'ry Mounters Bended Knee': Herbert and Authority," in *The Historical Renaissance*, ed. Richard Strier and Heather Dubrow (Chicago: University of Chicago Press, 1989), pp. 242–69. But I will make an argument similar to his about Shakespeare.

53. Compare Bloch's analysis of "The Flower" (*Spelling the Word*, p. 195); the plurality that she sees developing in that poem is a plurality of sinners, not of the gracious community, membership in which implies salvation.

plural takes place in the third stanza: it is not only the speaker who looks to be saved, but his whole group (a group that feels like an extended family). The tone of the last stanza is that of a child who belongs to a group anxious for news (dispatches) but whom the adults have soothed with their assurance that news will come. I don't mean to make this poem an allegory.[54] I want to pin down the odd effect of the dropping away of the first person. Once the poem goes into the plural, its tone seems that of a child who has been assured that things are under a control he need not be responsible for. He considers himself and his family and ventriloquizes someone else saying of them—of the grown-ups, whose ranks he's considered to be part of—that they waited patiently for news from their friend. Children love to be referred to in the third person because they take this as a sign that they belong to what they understand as the adult community—the community of third persons. Thus adult nostalgia for the third person is nostalgia for this most childlike feeling of belongingness, belongingness to an adult world tinged with the childishness of the child who imagines it. Leah Marcus writes accurately that "Herbert's sustained self-portrayal [is] as child and servant in the house of a mighty Lord," but the child here is much more modern, much less oppressed, than she wants to claim.[55] He knows that the adults around him are still God's children, since they still attend dispatches from him, and this alleviates his own fear that he's an adult. It turns out that even the adults who surround him and define his community are or can be children—adult children, unanxious children, children unharassed by the adult worry that they will become adults.

The switch to the third person is consoling, and it recurs often in Herbert's poetry. A similar shift seems to occur in "The Forerunners," for example. There the speaker fears first-person solitude, the loss of all the company that had inhabited the rooms of his soul (l. 7), as they inhabit the soul's rooms in "The H. Communion." But this fear is alleviated through the generosity of those who reassure the speaker that winter will not abolish—but will intensify—gregariousness: "Go birds of spring: let winter have his fee; / Let a bleak palenesse chalk the doore, / So all within be livelier then before" (ll. 34–36). A similar switch of person occurs, I think, in "The Flower," when

54. Compare "The Familie," about the caretaker family that dwells within its speaker's heart (the Lord's house). That poem would itself seem a more explicitly allegorical avatar of "The H. Communion"; in it one of the family members, Humble Obedience, "neare the door doth stand, / Expecting a command" (ll. 13–14).

55. Leah S. Marcus, *Childhood and Cultural Despair* (Pittsburgh, Pa.: University of Pittsburgh Press, 1978), p. 112.

the speaker recognizes that he is relieved of responsibility for his own happiness: "It cannot be / That I am he / On whom thy tempests fell all night" (ll. 40–42): it turns out that my decline into decrepitude was only your chastisement of the delicately growing, childlike flower I continued to be, and took the form of making me believe that I was no longer such a flower. "Now in age" I realize that this belief was mistaken:

> These are thy wonders, Lord of love,
> To make us see we are but flowers that glide:
> Which when we once can finde and prove,
> Thou hast a garden for us, where to bide.
>
> (ll. 43–46)

In "The Collar," as we have seen, he is surprised by the address "Child!" and by its implication that he is still the child he used to be. In "H. Baptisme" (II)—the poem where he declares for childhood—the healthy child is described in the third person, doubly distanced by the change in sex:

> Although by stealth
> My flesh get on, yet let her sister
> My soul bid nothing, but preserve her wealth:
> The growth of flesh is but a blister;
> Childhood is health.
>
> (ll. 11–15)

And in "Love" (III) the third-person consolation begins when Love says "You shall be he"; that is, he'll be the third-person child that they (those magical third persons of childhood) called him.[56]

The third-person quality of this pastoral vision of childhood is an example, perhaps, of Barbara Harman's revision of Lewalski's account of typology in Herbert: "Typology does not 'personalize theol-

---

56. Chana Bloch also stresses how the childishness of Herbert's speaker manifests itself as despair but becomes a saving formulation: "Herbert's poems of discovery focus on either the narrator's misguided zeal or his stubborn resistance. In 'Redemption,' 'The Thanksgiving,' 'Jordan,' II' and 'The Holdfast,' he is like an earnest child, trying almost too hard to please; in 'Affliction, I,' 'The Crosse' and 'The Collar,' tired of trying, he bangs on the table in a rage" (*Spelling the Word*, p. 148). Of the last of these poems, she writes that God's vocative "offers both rebuke and comfort. . . . The word *child* epitomizes the spiritual condition of Herbert's naive personae: as 'children of the understanding' [1 Cor. 14:20], they are deficient, retrograde; as 'children of God' [Rom. 8:16], they are received with love in a new order of being" (pp. 166–67). Bloch does not give this the interior and psychological account that I am attempting, however.

ogy'; it theologizes the personal, and makes unavailable the very notion of a 'radically personal' account. In Herbert's typological poems
persons do not appropriate and rewrite Scripture: Scripture appropriates and rewrites them" (*Costly Monuments*, p. 189). For an antidualistic epistemology, this is or should be a distinction without a
difference (and indeed Harman immediately goes on to argue "that
the competition between personal and scriptural stories is eliminated
and that their unity is stressed in its place"). But her formula does
emphasize the willessness (or childlike innocence) implied in this theory of typology as consolation and reassurance (although here I am
parting with her argument that the typological involves humans in a
loss of their individuality). In fact the performative/constative utterance "You shall be he" exemplifies this entire argument, since what
Love legislates it does through its constative assurance that the speaker is still, and will continue to be, the child he was. Indeed, the slight
hint of constraint and awkwardness in the last line of "Love" (III)—as
though the speaker is utterly unused to first-person declarative statements of such simplicity—feels like the constraint and awkwardness
of a child unsure how to respond to the surprisingly serious and
sustained ministrations of an adult. It is as though the child had
thought he'd escape notice, would not be a problem, but now discovers that he's the center of an attention that he didn't seek. Love's
Calvinist requirement that he sit and eat emphasizes the strangeness
of this attention; compare the chapter in *The Country Parson* on the
sacraments: "The Feast indeed requires sitting, because it is a Feast;
but man's unpreparednesse asks kneeling. Hee that comes to the Sacrament, hath the confidence of a Guest, and hee that kneels, con-
fesseth himself an unworthy one, and therefore differs from other
Feasters: but hee that sits, or lies, puts up to an Apostle" (p. 259), so
that when at the end the speaker is made to sit, he's like a child at the
adult's table, sitting because he's too humble even to insist on his
humility by kneeling.[57]

The "I" in "I did sit and eat" should be seen as referring to a child, a
child embarrassed that this "I" should correspond to what he considers an adult "he," as though he's putting up to an apostle and does
not differ from the worthy feasters. The adulthood the child is embarrassed about, though, is in fact refracted through the eyes of a

57. This point has received some attention. Schoenfeldt's argument is similar to
mine; although he sees more witty competition between the speaker and Love than I
do, he concludes that the speaker ends in confusion and real surrender ("Standing on
Ceremony," pp. 130–31). Because the speaker sits, Strier concludes that communion
isn't being referred to here.

child, and so the whole line of thought remains childish and innocent, even at the point when the child appears to be granted adulthood.

To summarize this reading thus far: the adult speaker (who thought himself above these kinds of anxieties, just as the speaker in "The Collar" did) discovers that Love's gesture apparently ascribing adulthood to him in fact inspires him with childish hopes and fears. He is made to feel that his unkindness and ungratefulness come not from adult disillusionment but childish petulance, and so he sees the consequence of his sins not as a foreclosure from childhood, now, but as a foreclosure from that childish version of utopian childhood—adulthood. Half the battle is won because the speaker is imagining himself, now, as a child again. And even if he's a bad child, childhood is health. Thus when he's told he's an adult, he responds to the news as a child would; and so he can feel that he is a child, a child who has fulfilled his deepest wish—to become an adult: to be himself (a child) still and to be an adult. And so the poem gives its adult speaker childhood again; he becomes a child who is encouraged to imagine that he's part of the company, not of adults really, but of grown-ups. Herbert suggests a similar correction in *The Country Parson*. To convince those the parson sees near desperation,

> He hath one argument unanswerable. If God hate them, either he doth it as they are Creatures, dust and ashes; or as they are sinfull. As Creatures, he must needs love them; for no perfect Artist ever yet hated his owne worke. As sinfull, he must much more love them; because notwithstanding his infinite hate of sinne, his Love overcame that hate; and with an exceeding great victory, which in the Creation needed not, gave them love for love, even the son of his love out of his bosome of love. (P. 283)

But this is not the whole story, I suggested earlier that there is a darker side to "Love" (III). Indeed, in some ways I think it is a despairing poem. The nature of this despair lurks in the self-undoing quality of the wish to become an adult, since the fulfillment of any child's wish to become an adult manifests itself as disillusionment with a wish so childish and ignorant: only a child would wish something as painful as to be an adult. Any sense that such a wish can only come from ignorance marks the distance traveled from that ignorant state. What's striking about "So I did sit and eat" is its insistent past tense. "Did" may be joining its aid to fill out a line and preserve the rhyme *meat/eat*, but if Herbert did not want to emphasize the past, he would not have put the rest of the third stanza into the present. This shift from "Love said" (l. 8) to "sayes love" (ll. 15 and 17) is analogous to the shift into the third person. I admit that its immediate effect is to tinge "I did sit and eat" with a timeless, epiphanous quality, so that even the speaker telling us (or his friend) the story, in thinking of the scene, is thinking something like "He is sitting and eating." Still, while he may take bread at Love's hand, this epiphanous child nevertheless owes his timelessness to his pastness.

This poem, I think, illustrates Richard Sennett's insight that the ascription of authority (to person or to poem) is an interpretive attempt to understand power as possessing a solacing integrity immune to the ravages of time.[58] Thus Love speaks in the present tense: "You must sit down, sayes Love." Such an authority and such a present tense, however, are by their nature in the past: they belong to a time before the fall into time, before the fall into the discrimination between before and after. What grace grants is invulnerability from this fall. It grants the *presence* of authority's present tense.

This all-engrossing present tense leaves nothing behind when it becomes nonpresent, when it becomes conceived only in the tense of what excludes all presence: the past. Love's authority in "Love" (III) is invulnerable, but the inflexible past tense with which the poem ends threatens the speaker with exclusion from this present-tense timelessness—a timelessness that nevertheless subsists only in the past.[59]

I began by arguing that the Reformation replaced the living authority of the priest with the absolutely non-present authority of a text. Such a replacement gains on the side of authority only by a corresponding loss on the side of presence. In effect, I have been trying to show how Reformation theology sought to compensate for the textuality of the manifestation of God by emphasizing the authority of this manifestation, an authority in which sense and referent would coincide, so that biblical language itself would be the presence such language referred to when it signified authority. The attestation of such a coincidence I have been calling epistemological reassurance and have urged its Wittgensteinian version and the consolations of Wittgenstein's philosophy (so close to Bacon's essay "On Death").

58. Richard Sennett, *Authority* (New York: Knopf, 1980), pp. 18–19.
59. Vendler notes what should be both obvious and problematic: that the poem is spoken *after* the experience it describes. She writes of Herbert's "daring" in this regard and sees the speaker as one of the blessed in heaven (*Poetry of George Herbert*, pp. 275–76). "Daring" that would be indeed, and yet (as Vendler says) the feel of this poem is of a delicate hesitancy, not daring. This is why I prefer to argue that the voice is that of the *once*-blessed, marveling at a moment of inherent excellence, but a moment that belongs to the past.

But is there for Herbert such a thing as despair? What does despair consist in, then? If reality (simultaneous sense and referent of a realist epistemology) is its own consolation—if God's assurance of salvation comes without conditions and without the corresponding conditionals whose senses may not coincide with their referents—then the despair of Luther's sixteenth thesis—the despair, in theological terms, of an exclusion from grace—must be understood (in the terms of a Wittgensteinian philosophical psychology) as an exclusion from the real. The stakes of this anti-Platonic formulation are considerable. The Platonic theory of authority—Hannah Arendt's—sees authority as a function of an implied contractual acceptance by originally free and responsible agents (both the governors and the governed) of the parameters dictated by a hierarchical chain of being. Since such a chain, even in its Neoplatonic, materialistic avatars, is based on the idealism of the theory of forms (an idealism masquerading as realism), it implies a dualistic account of subject and world (cave dweller and sunlight). Exclusion or exile from the real, in such an account, is equivalent to the state of affairs that obtained before the subject's contact with reality. The status of the subject is not put at risk either way. The person is the same whether he squats in the cave or celebrates in the sun, whether she accepts the authority of a more highly placed figure or refuses it.

A genuinely realist epistemology would reject such a contractual conception of social or religious obligation or knowledge. Wittgenstein would deny the meaningfulness of speaking of a subject who was not an actor in the world, a participator in reality, a player of language games. The refutation of private languages may be seen as the refutation of the radical separation between subject and world imaged by the cave (skull). But the consequence of Wittgenstein's all-embracing view of the ubiquity of reality (in which the world is not the moving image of eternity but is eternity itself) is weighty: while it is hard to fall, once fallen there are no resources with which to rise again. All hope of resource is with the irretrievable real. This is the hell of Protestant despair.

This despair appears in very muted form in "Love" (III), but I think it is there. There is an irrecuperable sadness in Herbert, a sadness that persists even after the immensely flexible arguments for consolation have been applied. "Love" (III) is perhaps the most deeply consolatory of Herbert's poems, but a hopelessness can nevertheless be registered in the intense and free-floating elegiac feeling of the poem. What's being described is in the past. It's all over. It's hard to separate out ex post facto elegy (the kind of sadness that suffuses old photographs, especially if they're of happy people) from an elegiac intention, in reading such poems. A speaker we know is dead claims to have achieved a privileged and timeless moment, to have forgotten need's golden hand and escaped the assaults of time; but we know this is not so. Did Herbert feel the elegy in the poem, the real fragility of its consolation? I think he did, partly because the poem does not entirely suppress openness to a cannibalistic interpretation ("my meat" echoing "This is my body"—sadness often takes baroquely grotesque forms in Herbert), but also because the poem still views eating (and not just the tasting Love suggested) as a boon, implying that the speaker is recalling a time when he was hungry (dusty, sinful, hesitant to come out of the dark) and was afforded sustenance; this recollection feels wishful, as though those salad days are over and as though he's hungry now but, as in "The Glimpse," is not being bid to eat. The revelation of grace and its consolations are in the past, and the poem ends with the sense of a fall from an abundance that was once spread around him like a sea.

What would such a fall from reality's graciousness look like to a realist epistemology? It is the other side of the situation at the end of *On Certainty*. For if the sleeper would be wrong to assert that he is dreaming, he is, nevertheless, dreaming. It is certainly a vain dream (as Rutherford says) if he thinks his dreams can be permanently reassuring, for the dreamer hears the small rain of his own mortality. From his dream of reality he will wake to die. Childhood is health, but old age is disease, and his dream of health is about to end.

For Wittgenstein does describe the possibility of exclusion from language in *Philosophical Investigations*—the possibility not only that the referent will decay but, more unnervingly, that both signified and referent will vanish. One might think that the name of a simple would imply the existence of the simple; otherwise the simple would be as unimaginable as another dimension. Wittgenstein's interlocutor tries to specify this linguistic adequation of signified and referent: "I want to restrict the term '*name*' to what cannot occur in the combination 'X exists'.—Thus one cannot say 'Red exists', because if there were no red it could not be spoken of at all." Wittgenstein comments that this looks like "a metaphysical statement about red" which "finds expression again when we say such a thing as that red is timeless, and perhaps still more strongly in the word 'indestructible'" (§58). Nevertheless Wittgenstein doubts not the adequacy of sense and referent but the assurance that this would seem to provide. As long as we are in language, we can count on the world really constituted by language. That most robust of substances is also the most fragile, however, and even the timelessness of red can be submitted to the corrosive effects of time:

> "Something red can be destroyed, but red cannot be destroyed, and that is why the meaning of the word 'red' is independent of the existence of a red thing," [says the Platonic interlocutor].—Certainly it makes no sense to say that the colour red is torn up or pounded to bits. But don't we say "The red is vanishing?" And don't clutch at the idea of our always being able to bring red before our mind's eye even when there is nothing red any more. That is just as if you chose to say that there would still always be a chemical reaction producing a red flame.—For suppose you cannot remember the colour any more?—When we forget which colour this is the name of, it loses its meaning for us; that is, we are no longer able to play a particular language game with it. And the situation then is comparable with that in which we have lost a paradigm which was an instrument in our language. (§57)

At the vanishing point of belonging to a world, one loses every paradigm. This does not leave an unencumbered subject—a subject unencumbered by language—but a nonsubjective *instance* of loss.

Loss usually means loss of a position within a language game. The all-encompassing purview of language games recuperates the losing of a game into a situation within the game, and not the game's disastrous disappearance. But there is also the loss of the possibility of continuing to play the game—the loss of all access to the consolations of access, to the authoritative grace which "knows the steady way." In Wittgenstein and in Freud, pain (or insomnia or fatigue) is the name of the exclusion from language, of the loss of a paradigm.[60] This is disaster as an exclusion from a relation to reality, disaster not as a relation to malignant stars but as the termination of any relation to stars at all.[61] To lose subjectivity is to lose the capacity to act, but it is not necessarily to lose the capacity to suffer that endless loss.

This strange fashion of forsaking—by love, as earlier, but less disastrously by hope (since the speaker of "Hope" is sent a telescope with which he might look at the stars)—seems to me to occur even in "Love" (III). I do not want to urge a counterintuitive reading of Herbert that would claim him as a bitterly despairing poet. Rather, it seems to me that in his best poems he registers the necessity of choosing between two competing claims—between the claim of a realistic, ubiquitous, living, omnipresent, all-assuring, all-controlling authority,

---

60. See J.-B. Pontalis, *Entre le rêve et la douleur psychic* (Paris: Gallimard, 1977).
61. This is Maurice Blanchot's formulation in *L'écriture du désastre* (Paris: Gallimard, 1980).

imaged in the symbols of ceremony and sacrament, and the phantom, spectral, powerless, aphasic, impossible claim of a capacity to suffer, without a capacity to act, without a capacity to make suffering activity—the claim of something so entirely preterite (past tense and unsaved) as to be wholly nonpresent. The first is the claim *in* the Bible, the claim of God's omnipresence; the second, the claim *of* the Bible, the ungrounded pastness, preterition—textuality—of what has no presence.

I do not want to say that the Protestant (or more accurately, Hebrew) insistence on the Bible as a book and not as a presence inaugurated the nonphenomenal experience of loss that I am trying to describe, but that the centrality of the Bible's *writtenness* to the Hebrews and the Protestants came from the former's insight into the nature of all experience and the latter's refusal to accept the easy authoritarian assurances of a Platonic Christianity.

Thus I agree with Vendler's principle that Herbert's is a poetry of experience. The experience I want to assert for Herbert's poetry is the strange experience of forsakenness, whose decentered centrality to Herbert's thought is a version of an intense kind of literary experience, of what Blanchot calls "the essential solitude." Having faith in an Augustinian plenitude is a way of securing yourself against this solitude, but if this faith is replaced by an attempted faith in a preterite text, the experience of solitude is confirmed and not overcome.

Forsakenness is the deepest sorrow in Herbert's poetry and is the common element that binds together what Bataille calls "the negative community: the community of those who have no community."[62] Herbert's most usual name for this experience is grief, which is for him, as for Freud, the name of an exclusion from a stably elaborated reality. In "Grief," as in "Denial," this exclusion is allegorized as a poetic failure—a failure to rhyme. This failure is the obverse of the repudiation of rhyme in "Home" and shows how easily such repudiation can come to grief, even as grief makes possible the acknowledgment of God. The five "Affliction" poems describe grief's strange and hopeless cunning, as Herbert's delighted trust in the abundance of God is undeceived by the relentless claims of reality:

> At first thou gav'st me milk and sweetnesses;
> I had my wish and way:
> My days were straw'd with flow'rs and happinesse;
> There was no moneth but May.

62. From an unpublished manuscript by Bataille, quoted by Maurice Blanchot in his *La communauté inavouable* (Paris: Minuit, 1983), p. 45.

> But with my yeares sorrow did twist and grow,
> And made a partie unawares for wo.
>> ("Affliction" (1), ll. 19–24)

At some basic level, Herbert's poetry is about the solitary/universal experience of the loss of assurance, a loss here called aging. Sorrow itself—deeply and inherently excluded from consolation, like Spenser's Despayre who despairs himself (and also like the "cunning guest" that grief is called in "Confession")—suffers the grief it represents. Sorrow is here embarked upon its sorrowful destiny "unawares"; it is not the realization of an intention or move in a language game. The intent to see grief as intentional, to justify it by making the void a purpose, gets crossed up:

> Yet lest perchance I should too happie be
>> In my unhappinesse,
> Turning my purge to food, thou throwest me
>> Into more sicknesses.
> Thus doth thy power crosse-bias me, not making
> Thine own gift good, yet me from my wayes taking.
>> (ll. 49–54)

True, affliction, in the first poem of the series, is something the speaker experiences, and its relief might still consist in the ascertainment of a consoling (graceful) faith: "Ah my deare God! though I am clean forgot, / Let me not love thee, if I love thee not" (ll. 65–66). In the other poems, however, affliction comes not primarily to Herbert but to Christ, and this changes things considerably.

Christ represents in these poems less the promise of a universal realm than the possibility of endless exclusion and loss. He is seen, there as elsewhere (for instance, in "The Thanksgiving"), as having suffered more than the afflicted speaker. In "Dialogue" the human speaker cannot stand even a description of Christ's suffering: "Ah! no more: thou break'st my heart" (l. 32). Thus the speaker is joined with Christ in a community of suffering but also is shown how infinitely greater, how incommensurable, Christ's suffering is. Indeed Herbert's suffering always seems recuperable to a representational (typological) scheme, and for this reason its correspondence to Christ's suffering is inadequate, since Christ's suffering can never be recuperated. Herbert suffers the pain of this inadequacy, and that pain is the inadequate correlative of Christ's pain. The inadequacy of the correspondence enables the correspondence, which means that the correspondence is inherently dysfunctional. "Affliction" (III) describes such a self-discrepant typological relation:

> My heart did heave, and there came forth, *O God!*
> By that I knew that thou wast in the grief,
> To guide and govern it to my relief,
>   Making a scepter of the rod:
>   Hadst thou not had thy part,
> Sure the unruly sigh had broke my heart.
>
> But since thy breath gave me both life and shape,
> Thou knowst my tallies; and when there's assign'd
> So much breath to a sigh, what's then behinde?
>   Or if some yeares with it escape,
>   The sigh then onely is
> A gale to bring me sooner to my blisse.
>
> Thy life on earth was grief, and thou art still
> Constant unto it, making it to be
> A point of honour, now to grieve in me,
>   And in thy members suffer ill.
>   They who lament one crosse,
> Thou dying dayly, praise thee to thy losse.

The witty paradoxes here approach grotesquery, but the poem's movement toward grotesque wit is almost the point. The poem begins with a realist theory of grief: the speaker's apparently unmotivated sadness must somehow be about Christ because his heart is not broken by the heartbreaking depth of that sadness, and this depth confirms that Christ is in the grief because (as the speaker wants the consolation of claiming) the unknown object of such depth can only be Christ crucified. Only God could make such grief not its own fall but the pedagogic tool of a parental figure. The discovery that the situation is pedagogic means that, even had the speaker not discovered the source of his grief, this grief would stand not for God's despair-producing absence but for his rebuking sternness, for his displeasure. Thus do sense and referent coincide so that "O God!" literally implies that God is in the otherwise heartbreaking sigh. Perkins makes a similar pun in "A Graine of Musterd-Seede," elaborating Romans 8:26, "Likewise the Spirit also helpeth our infirmities: for we know not what we should pray for as we ought: but the Spirit itself maketh intercession for us with groanings that cannot be uttered." Perkins takes literally the root meaning of spirit as breath—the breath of a sob or a sigh—when he writes that these words afford a comfortable instruction to the children of God, namely, that being in distress, whether in life or death, if we can but sigh or sob unto God, though it be weak and feeble like the faint pulse in the time of death, we or the Spirit of God in us do indeed make request unto God that shall be heard. Yea, as the words are, we do more than make request: and though we do not always see what God's Spirit makes us to sigh after, yet God doth. (P. 400)

The second stanza of "Affliction" (III) asserts the unity of God's breath with the speaker's, whose life was breathed into him by God. The unity of breath—the union of speaker and God—is figured in the speaker's Cratylian theory that his breath is what it names. This figurative unity is brought closer to literality by either of two alternatives: since he breathed so much out he must be substantially breathed out of his body himself (since breath is life), and so closer to pure spirit (pure breath); or if he stays with his body, he is that much bated of breath—that much closer to death, and salvation. Expiration would mean a full union with spirit. (This is a late poem, not in the Williams manuscript, and there may be a chilling suggestion of Herbert's consumption in its description of limitedness or shortness of breath.)

The last stanza, though, describes the opposite union: not the speaker's with a state of bliss, but Christ's with the mortality the speaker is seeking a way out of.[63] This union is also described in "Affliction" (v):

> At first we liv'd in pleasure;
> Thine own delights thou didst to us impart:
> When we grew wanton, thou didst use displeasure
> To make us thine: yet that we might not part,
>   As we at first did board with thee,
>   Now thou wouldst taste our miserie.
>   (ll. 7–12)

In "Affliction" (III) the tasting of misery is grotesque indeed. At first Herbert merely develops the association of Christ with the grievous sigh, this time, though, under the rubric of the sigh. The discovery of the last stanza is that Christ is still grieving, as he grieved on the

---

63. Discussing several poems, including this one, Vendler judges that "in Herbert's finest poems, Jesus is seen as a fellow-sufferer rather than as a judge or remote deity. . . . The phenomenon of Christ as permanent sufferer . . . takes on more and more importance in Herbert" (*Poetry of George Herbert*, p. 238; see pp. 238–41). Nevertheless, Vendler regards even these poems as enabling a kind of "serenity following on pain" (p. 239) and assuring "the confidence of ultimate relief" (p. 238).

cross. The nature of God's communion with humanity is grief.[64] This is first expressed wittily, as though the metaphor is a useful conceit for spinning a sermon, and the wittiness is underlined by the grief's being called "a point of honour." And in this conceitful vein the poem would seem to continue, as a rebuke to complaint, with Christ's willingness to suffer the ill that his followers (the Church's "members") suffer.

But the gruesome pun of the last three lines emphasizes the irrecuperably grotesque literalness of the crucifixion (in which a point of honor becomes one of the nails): Christ's members suffer ill in being nailed to the cross. Christ suffers daily because he is identified with the speaker's daily sighs. Every day Christ again suffers human griefs. Every day the speaker crucifies him, and the cross on which he is crucified every day is literally the speaker's body. Christ suffers ill when a point of honor nails his suffering members to his suffering members, when his limbs are linked or nailed to the suffering bodies of his followers. The last stanza punningly combines a beautiful idealism (the free presence of Christ to sinning humanity) with a macabre materiality. These may be competing meanings, but the competition itself is so macabre that the latter wins. Christ is felt to be not a god but a fly with his legs pulled off, the impotent object of a real human sadism deeply sad at its own inability not to indulge its gruesome humor. The emphasis of this poem is on the overwhelming contamination of culpability; the speaker ends feeling barbarously guilty, not ecstatically saved. Because the burden of all Herbert's poetry is to discover the speaker's innocence, even when he most feels guilt, the gruesomeness of a moment like this is of major importance to an estimation of whether innocence will carry the day. Here—because of the poem's ambivalence and its shock at its own repressed sadism—it does not.

Herbert makes the same grotesque joke (although much suppressed) in the first of the "Affliction" poems. There the reference to the cross occurs punningly when the speaker says that he is cross-biased. Immediately after that stanza (quoted above), he continues:

> Now I am here, what thou wilt do with me
> None of my books will show:
> I reade, and sigh, and wish I were a tree;
> For sure then I should grow

64. See Vendler, *Poetry of George Herbert*, pp. 240–41.

>   To fruit or shade: at least some bird would trust
>   Her household to me, and I should be just.
>
>   (ll. 55–60)

Herbert would want a reader to remember "The Sacrifice," the great poem about Christ's grief that appears several pages earlier:

>   *O all ye who passe by, behold and see;*
>   Man stole the fruit, but I must climbe the tree;
>   The tree of life to all, but onely me:
>   Was ever grief like mine?
>
>   (ll. 201–04)[65]

The stanza from "Affliction" (i) is an ironic rebuke to typological thinking. Its speaker cannot find himself in the religious books that would typologically delineate his story. But, of course, the echo is from Matthew: "The foxes have holes, and the birds of the air have nests; but the Son of man hath not where to lay his head" (8:20). Typologically, the speaker fulfills the exclusion from abundant providence that Christ suffers in Matthew. He fulfills exclusion by failing to find himself included in a typological relationship, by feeling excluded just as (but he doesn't know it's just as) Christ was excluded. His failure to be a tree needs to be visualized: instead of providing a place for the household of the bird of the air, no longer bearing the stolen fruit, and entirely exfoliated, the speaker of the last stanza seems not to be a tree but a tree *sous rature*, crossed out—the last stanza seems spoken by a cross.

Herbert is not, on the whole, a gruesome poet (although anyone doubting his capacity for the grotesque need only read "The Bag"). The point of the gruesomeness here, as I've suggested, is to insist on the brute physicality of Christ's kenosis; the flesh he nailed his essence to corrupts and dies. How one comes to grief, I think, is the final subject of Herbert's poetry; to the extent that it's about Christ it's about a "King of grief," as he's addressed in "The Thanksgiving." The most detailed, sustained treatment of Christ's grief is, of course, "The Sacrifice," a soliloquy spoken by Christ. Here particularly, grief and forsakenness are equated. Each stanza detailing the sufferings of the passion ends with Christ asking, "Was ever grief like mine?"

This grief is especially stressed in the fifty-fourth stanza. The importance of this stanza is marked by the third line's breaking off and

65. William Empson argues that Christ is like a child here, involved in an oedipal drama. See *Seven Types of Ambiguity* (New York: New Directions, 1947), p. 232.

failing to rhyme (a failure that in "Denial" stands for the absence of God) and also by the fact that the question turns into a certainty:

> But, *O my God, my God!* why leav'st thou me,
> The sonne, in whom thou dost delight to be?
> *My God, my God— —*
>
> Never was grief like mine.
>
> (ll. 213–16)

"Never was grief like mine" means that Christ is asserting the irrelevance of the fact that he's quoting someone else's grief (David's in Psalm 22:1: "My God, my God, why hast thou forsaken me?"), just as Herbert's speaker in "Affliction" (1) had not known he was quoting Matthew. But Christ is quoting Psalm 22, when he asserts his unrhymable grief, and indeed the quotation appears in italics. The question is, What is being quoted and who is doing the quoting? Herbert italicizes when his Christ speaks words the biblical Christ has spoken, as in line 23: *"O let this cup passe, if it be thy pleasure"* (quoting Matthew 26:39), and we may feel that he italicizes here because his poem is actually quoting not the psalmist but Christ (Matthew 27:46, where Christ repeats the words of Psalm 22). The italics can mean that Herbert is quoting Christ, or they can mean instead that Christ is quoting David, as he quotes his tormentors in italics (see ll. 97–98, 102, 107, 142, 186, and 221). Here Christ would be citing Psalm 22 as he earlier cites the Old Testament in lines 1 and 201 (*"O all ye who passe by, behold and see;"*), which quote not the biblical Christ but Lamentations 1:12: "Is it nothing to you, all ye that pass by? behold and see if there be any sorrow like unto my sorrow." That the Lamentations quotation should meet its antitype raises a doubt that the previous sorrow *is* like unto the present grief. "Was ever grief like mine?" means that the grief in Lamentations was not like Christ's. The antitype both echoes and rejects the type by echoing its denial that anything like it had ever occurred before. If we say that it is possible that Christ anticipates as an answer "Yes, the grief in Lamentations was like yours," we then get the negative answer that breaks off the community of quotation binding Herbert's Christ to David and to Matthew's Christ: "Never was grief like mine."[66] This conforms to Lancelot Andrewes's typological

---

66. On Herbert as a collator of biblical texts, often dispersed from one another, see Bloch, *Spelling the Word*, pp. 53–79. She emphasizes Herbert's own description (in "The H. Scriptures, II") of biblical verses as forming constellations—patterns among verses that are not necessarily contiguous.

argument in his second Passion sermon that the "party in great extremity" in Lamentations is Christ:

> And to say the truth, to take the words strictly as they lie, they cannot agree, or be verified of any but of Him, and Him only. For though some other, not unfitly, may be allowed to say the same words, it must be in a qualified sense; for in full and perfect propriety of speech, He and none but He. None can say, neither Jeremy, nor any other, *si fuerit dolor meus*, as Christ can; no day of wrath like to His day, no sorrow to be compared to His, all are short of it, nor His to any, it exceedeth them all. . . .
> "My God, my God, why hast thou forsaken me?" at the first uttered by David; yet the same words our Saviour taketh Himself, and that more truly and properly, than ever David could.[67]

Even typologically considered, grief means the exclusion from a universalizing, typological doctrine of assurance. Luther on Psalm 8:5—"Thou wilt let him be forsaken of God for a little while"— describes Christ's experience of this exclusion—"To be forsaken of God is far worse than death"—and says that the verse is an anticipation, not of Psalm 22, but of Matthew: "There is no doubt that in the spirit David is here looking at Christ as he struggles with death in the garden, and cries out on the cross, 'My God, My God, why hast Thou forsaken Me?' . . . And in fact He was forsaken by God."[68] These psalmic verses are typological anticipations of the despair of being excluded from a saving typological structure. In the last line of "The Sacrifice" the question of the relation of quotation to typology comes up again:

> But now I die; now all is finished.
> My wo, mans weal: and now I bow my head.
> Onely let others say, when I am dead,
>   Never was grief like mine.
>   (ll. 249–52)

Empson remarks that it is ambiguous whether the last line is indirect discourse (so that "mine" means Christ's grief) or whether it is a quotation of what the others will say: will each complain of his or her own grief?[69] He sees the latter overtone as a threat: the crucifiers will

---

67. Lancelot Andrewes, *Ninety-Six Sermons* (Oxford: Oxford University Press, 1841), 2:138–39.

68. Martin Luther, *Works*, ed. Jaroslav Pelikan (St. Louis, Mo.: Concordia Publishing House, 1955–86), 13:124, 126.

69. *Seven Types of Ambiguity*, pp. 228–29.

get theirs. But it seems important to add that after Christ's death it is the faithful who will lament him in the most desperate terms. They themselves will quote Christ in order to utter the despair they feel over his absence. In this atypological typology, sense and referent will come together again (as when "O God" is in Herbert's sigh) in the quoted assertion that they cannot come together. In order to assert that they are not quoting, people will quote Christ's quoted assertion that he is not quoting; they will quote the assertion that this claim has never been asserted (or even quoted) legitimately before. The others who say "Never was grief like mine" will be quoting Christ, if not at the end of the poem, then at least when he quotes Psalm 22; and Christ himself, in addition to quoting Psalm 22, is echoing Lamentations throughout (Was there ever any sorrow like mine?). The force of these ubiquitous assertions of unparalleled woe would be to intimate the world of exclusions from the world.[70]

The poems that follow "The Sacrifice"—"The Thanksgiving" and "The Reprisal"—paradoxically confirm this paradoxical community of isolation. In those poems the speaker laments that he cannot come up to Christ in lamentation. However, one of the aspects of his inability to match Christ is, as Michael Schoenfeldt suggests, that he thus insists that he is even more debased than Christ.[71] (By the antithetical movement typical of Herbert's poetry, "The Crosse" seems in part an attempt to recuperate even this exclusion.)

This self-undoing sharing of isolation is, I take it, the other side of typological thinking—the textual side. Christ's words—or biblical words in general (from Lamentations, the Psalms, Matthew)—stand now for the absence of their speakers, whose deaths they memorialize. Here language is backed neither by the presence of any authority nor by the authority of any presence: what it laments it laments in the mode of exclusion, even from a shared and public context of lamentation. Tuve devotes her book on Herbert to denying the speaker of the poem the depth of character necessary for him even to conceive of quoting from the Old Testament; he is supposed to be only a mouthpiece for a religious tradition that automatically imputes all

70. For a reading concerned with some of the same issues, see Pahlka's chapter "Poetry as an Imitation of 'The Sacrifice,'" in *Saint Augustine's Meter*, pp. 100–119; he argues that both imitation and Christ's lamentation are not intended as poetry but that a divine ordering determines them as poetry. It should be clear as well how much greater my allegiance is to Empson's than to Tuve's reading of "The Sacrifice."

71. See "'Subject to Ev'ry Mounters Bended Knee,'" pp. 252–57. Schoenfeldt, here and elsewhere, is vigorously attentive to the deep currents of competitiveness and ambition that flow under the placid surface of the systems of generosity and courtesy in Herbert.

biblical lamentation to Christ in propria persona.[72] Herbert did make enormous efforts—as I've argued—to use typology as a universalizing mode. But the play of quotations in "The Sacrifice" is so densely undecidable that the typology that informs it undoes it; the poem's universalizing strategy threatens a universal dissolution of universality. Christ stands in Herbert for what seems to me a characteristically literary (that is to say, worldless or essentially solitary) affect: exclusion from all presence or preterition (or Walter Benjamin's sorrowful quotation out of context).

"Redemption" seems to me to point up Herbert's insistence on God's worldlessness:

> Having been tenant long to a rich Lord,
>   Not thriving, I resolved to be bold,
>   And make a suit unto him, to afford
> A new small-rented lease, and cancell th' old.
>   In heaven at his manour I him sought:
>   They told me there, that he was lately gone
>   About some land, which he had dearly bought
> Long since on earth, to take possession.
>
> (ll. 1–8)

How is one to make sense of lines 6–8? As Vendler points out (*Poetry of George Herbert*, p. 60), the reader has already been clued into the allegory (with the specification "In heaven at his manour") and knows that the new lease is the Gospel. The speaker wants the grace of the New Dispensation. This is a grace already given, we now realize: his desire for a new lease is cued by the New Testament, which he wants to receive as his own. While we might begin the poem thinking that it is an allegory about the first coming and that Christ comes when the childlike Everyman (desiring to become part of the company of those informative third persons in line 6) calls for him, it turns out that the speaker is postbiblical. Christ has already dearly bought the land that will be leased to the speaker in the New Dispensation; he has already been crucified. In fact, the poem now sounds like a plea for the Second Coming, not the first. Christ has redeemed humanity long since. Now he is coming to take possession, it would seem, of his kingdom on earth.

The speaker seems relieved of the long waiting of the earlier converts. Having decided to sue for the New Dispensation (a decision that

---

72. In *Spelling the Word*, pp. 66–72, Bloch shows the surprising extent to which Tuve refuses to see the New Testament, as opposed to the liturgical tradition, as a direct source for Herbert's language.

grants itself, as the last line of the poem will also confirm), to our vicarious delight he discovers that the new lease is about to turn a profit, since Christ has gone to earth now to dwell among the faithful new lessees. The speaker has jumped aboard at the last second and is relieved of the tedious business of waiting sixteen centuries for the new lease to start thriving. The next line confirms this interpretation of the allegory, when the speaker refers to Christ's "great birth," which must mean that the lord here is not to be taken as the child of the impoverished Joseph and Mary. The second time he comes, Christ comes as a gentleman. But the sestet is a demystification of this wishful allegorical autobiography:

> I straight return'd, and knowing his great birth,
>> Sought him accordingly in great resorts;
>> In cities, theatres, gardens, parks, and courts:
> At length I heard a ragged noise and mirth
>> Of theeves and murderers: there I him espied,
> Who straight, *Your suit is granted*, said, & died.
>
> (ll. 9–14)

His death is of course the crucifixion. (In the Williams manuscript the poem is entitled "The Passion.") In this Lutheran insistence on a *theologia crucis* over a *theologia maiestatis*, Christ's forsakenness, his alienation from the world he has created and should own, is prevented from belonging to a unified narrative. The narrator had thought of his redemption as an event—an act in the world—that had occurred in the past, once and for all. He has linked it in a narrative chain of causality. "& died" should have appeared in line 7, and it should in turn cause the narrator's redemption. Instead, the phrase ends the narrative because it stands for a recurring exclusion. His death is always and continually the condition for salvation, not a price paid and now redeemed. He dies daily. And if this continuing exclusion at least seems counterbalanced by the odd present tense (we expect "your suit *was* granted," "long since"), still, as in "Love" (III), that present tense becomes part of a preterite nonpresence: "said, & died."

Of course the emphasis here is on how extraordinarily much Christ will sacrifice to procure the murmuring and ungrateful speaker a new lease. But the meaningfulness of this sacrifice is exactly the point. The speaker turns out to have mistaken the circumstances not only of his salvation but of his lord's substance. The tenant's implicit complaint was that his lord could well afford to help him. The lord does help him, abundantly, but that abundance, it transpires, is not the lord's overplus but all his substance. He is more like Simone Weil (whose favorite poet, for this reason, I think, was Herbert) than Andrew Carnegie. His generosity, which the speaker expects will not be a very great drag on his resources, requires all he has. It bankrupts him, and it kills him. Christ stands not for a limitless capacity to provide but for an endless exclusion from a provident pastoral abundance. On another level this exclusion from abundance carries over to the speaker, for whom this is all past tense, since "Your suit is granted" seems an ineffectual promise when the promiser dies before he can put it into effect. Who will believe that the landlord who died in circumstances his family might wish to hush up granted this lowborn suitor a new lease as he was dying? His suit *is* granted, but only insofar as he shares with Christ an exclusion from a shared reality. All that is granted to him is the sentence that Christ utters. This sentence represents pure literariness, sense with no reference except its being without referent. It stands for the Bible, the ineffective words that Christ utters. The new lease is the utterance itself, or rather, it is the endlessly repeated nonevent of Christ's death. With the speaker, Christ shares mortality.

What could the language of the "community of those who have no community" be? If language is what a community shares (a totality of language games), then the language of those without community is an impossible language, an ineffectual and sorrowful memorial of exclusion. It is the language of a certain kind of poetry, language on the verge of silence. I claimed earlier as the essence of realist salvation the reassurance and comfort that the ability to ground language on a parent's authority offers. It makes you a child. It relieves you of the responsibility of having to guarantee the meaningfulness of your language yourself. The reverse of this is the unbounded and unbearable preterition—in the Calvinist sense of being passed over for salvation—that the parent's loss of authority would imply.[73] To be preterite or excluded from salvation, even when you have faith, means to have faith in a lord (for Herbert) or parent (for Christ) without authority; to be preterite is to be implied by the language of others without any guarantee that this third-person language has any authority. This is the reason, I think, for the odd absence of God in the heaven described by "Redemption." The rich lord who owns the

---

73. Compare Harman's disagreement with Vendler's reading of "The Collar." Where Vendler argues that the poem enables a "safe return," as Harman (*Costly Monuments*, p. 87) puts it, to a stable selfhood, Harman writes that "to return is to establish a relationship with God, not in a world where order is necessary, but in a vulnerable present where images cannot be secured" (p. 88). See also her account of "dissolving poems," pp. 109–37.

old lease under which the speaker has not thrived must be Yahweh; yet when Christ has gone to earth, there is no lord (no Father) in heaven. The mortality the speaker and Christ share is the mortal discovery that no authority will rescue them from forsakenness. This, it seems to me, is the burdensome, endlessly repeated attestation of Herbert's poetry. The language that wants most—the language of the Bible or of a certain kind of literature—is a language that has nothing.

I have been arguing that ascribing this language to God does not have the effect, when Herbert is thinking most deeply, of lending that language the authority it lacks; instead, preterite language undoes God's authority as well. It undoes the ubiquity of the real, and if the characteristic of reality is gregariousness, preterition's still small voice is the voice of solitude. I think this can be seen in "The Pulley," which seems to me—late in "The Temple" and late in composition—to artic- ulate this solitary language directly. The poem begins with the lan- guage of plenty:

> When God at first made man,
> Having a glasse of blessings standing by;
> Let us (said he) poure on him all we can:
> Let the worlds riches, which dispersed lie,
> Contract into a span.
>
> (ll. 1–5)

This is the same abundant generosity that the speaker of "Afflic- tion" (i) remembers marveling over before his party for grief. The use of the royal we—"Let us . . . poure on him all we can"—alludes to the rare plural form for the Elohim in the Bible. The only place where it is translated as the plural in the Authorized Version is the relevant one: "Let us make man in our own image, after our likeness" (Gen. 1:26). Even without the specific allusions to the Pandora myth, the God of the opening of "The Pulley" seems more a Greek than a monotheistic divinity. The "glasse of blessings standing by" richly ex- tends the context of God's world. We imagine leisure activity in some divine court: the abundance of the kingly household has blessings to spare, standing by casually, for all comers to partake in. The kingdom of heaven is a plural, gregarious kingdom, and the Elohim, or at least the one who proposes to them the game of creation, enjoys the easy, ample providence of the place. And "all we can" underlines the opu- lence, as though the glass were inexhaustible and the limit to pouring not a limit of its content but of the pourer's perseverance.

The second stanza, though, modifies the impression of amplitude considerably:

> So strength first made a way;
> Then beautie flow'd, then wisdome, honour, pleasure:
> When almost all was out, God made a stay,
> Perceiving that alone of all his treasure
> Rest in the bottome lay.
>
> (ll. 6–10)

"Worlds riches" we had taken to mean "riches on a scale with the world," but lines 8–10 imply that the emphasis may be on the entire world's not being able to afford more than a glassful of riches. God does pour nearly all he can, but this no longer means that he pours until he tires of pouring; after only two lines (5–6), he perceives that "almost all was out." This is a surprise, this discovery of limitation and potential exhaustion. The discovery here is like the discovery in "Redemption" that God's opulence costs him "dearly." And indeed, in the third stanza we find that this opulence seems to cost God the abundance of plurality that had been the Elohim's:

> For if I should (said he)
> Bestow this jewell also on my creature,
> He would adore my gifts in stead of me,
> And rest in Nature, not the God of Nature:
> So both should losers be.
>
> (ll. 11–15)

Instead of the plural, "Let us (said he)," God speaks in the singular, "For if I should (said he)." The effect of this surprising singularity is to make us doubt the gregariousness of God's world after all. And our suspicions are confirmed in the last line of the stanza. That "both should losers be" implies that it is not into the already delightful society of heaven that the creature may or may not enter. God risks a loss like human loss, should humanity not come to him.

The line does more though. The overwhelming effect of comparing God to a human loser is to imply that whatever humans lack, God lacks also. The last stanza diagnoses human poverty:

> Yet let him keep the rest,
> But keep them with repining restlesnesse:
> Let him be rich and wearie, that at least,
> If goodnesse leade him not, yet wearinesse
> May tosse him to my breast.
>
> (ll. 16–20)

Man's weariness here is an avatar of his passivity with respect to his will, a passivity that undoes all earthliness. Weariness is not susceptible to a description grounded on the primacy of the will, since it undoes that primacy. The God in the poem shares that passivity and weariness. The speaker of this stanza is entirely solitary. The shelter he offers is love and not rest, a shared solitude and not gregariousness. Once man—light as he is, despite all the blessing poured on him, "a sick toss'd vessel, dashing on each thing" ("Miserie," l. 76)—is tossed to God's breast, tossed to a breast like the breast of the sea, can we imagine that God will "pour" rest on to him (perhaps capsizing him)? Baxter admired Herbert but misread this anti-Augustinian poem: it is not about everlasting rest but about everlasting exile from rest and about the preterite consolationless comfort of sharing that exile. On God's great sea, the speaker is borne darkly, fearfully afar. The comfort God offers here is consoling not saving. What man and God will share is their poverty.

Pearlman argues that Herbert took comfort in imagining God as mother; this was a "confusion of gender, perhaps arising out of the incomplete differentiation of his own identity from that of his mother" ("George Herbert's God," p. 97). Such an analysis recalls Julia Kristeva's psychoanalytic account of what she calls *abjection*—the sense, which I call preterite, that there is no stability of place or world for the self, nor even a stability of self.[74] I think that Herbert's most powerful poetry expresses this sense of abjection.

Schoenfeldt and Nestrick both argue for the persistent humiliation of Herbert's speakers in their repeated discovery of their utterly dependent position in a gift economy. I agree with those arguments, but I want to radicalize them. For Schoenfeldt and Nestrick, the speaker's nothingness is demonstrated by his complete dependence on a largess that reaches even to determining and shaping his powers of gratitude. He is utterly assimilated to, and even constituted by, an alien largess, so that for him "begging and thanking are identical" (Nestrick, "The Giver and the Gift," p. 193). The speaker is grateful for the existence that enables him to beg. But the condition that I call extremity or preterition reverses the valences of this economy so thanking becomes equivalent to begging, and not only the other way around. I think that this can be felt in a poem like "The Crosse," where the speaker gets what he desires and finds it to be impoverishing: "this deare end, / So much desir'd, is giv'n, to take away / My power to serve thee" (ll. 8–

74. See, especially, Julia Kristeva, "L'abjet de l'amour," in *Tel Quel* 91 (Summer 1982): 17–32.

10). In the poem the speaker's impoverishment comes closer and closer to Christ's:

> To have my aim, and yet to be
> Further from it then when I bent my bow;
> To make my hopes my torture, and the fee
>   Of all my woes another wo,
> Is in the midst of delicates to need,
> And ev'n in Paradise to be a weed.
>
>   Ah my deare Father, ease my smart!
> These contrarieties crush me: these crosse actions
> Doe winde a rope about, and cut my heart:
>   And yet since these thy contradictions
> Are properly a crosse felt by thy Sonne,
> With but foure words, my words, *Thy will be done*.
>   (ll. 25–36)

The last stanza is very tricky, but I read "thy Sonne" as referring both to Christ and to the speaker who is addressing his "deare Father." Christ's words and his are the same, and both he and Christ end on the cross, sharing suffering and not largess.

I have been trying to show how Herbert evokes literary space, the space of literary extremity. I think he evokes it as the space of exclusion from all modes of efficacy. The depth of this exclusion can be felt when even the divine figures enter this space, through the extremity of their generosity. For Herbert this is an intermittently but powerfully apprehended possibility. For Shakespeare, to whom I now turn, the poverty and extremity that result from overabundance is a central theme. But both Herbert and Shakespeare share with their impoverished speakers a sense of the ghostly generosity of the language that is left when generality fails.

CHAPTER TWO

Shakespeare's Gifts

'Tis paltry to be Caesar:
Not being Fortune, he's but Fortune's knave,
A minister of her will.
                        —*Antony and Cleopatra*

It is one of the important consolations of viewing the world not as a collection of objects but as a *kind* of place, as a locus of generality, that such generality promises to be inexhaustible. To describe worldliness in general terms means to characterize it, not to inventory its contents. Those contents may be contingent and ephemeral, but the world itself will continue. Generality promises generosity, and that promise is self-fulfilling. The promise means something general: the existence of the external world that promises its own existence and, by promising, fulfills that promise. The self desires the generosity of the world's acknowledgment, the generosity that comes from the attention of that world. The generous promise of attention is self-fulfilling because the promise already signifies that attention.

Yet, as I have claimed even Herbert felt, that self-fulfilling generosity can reach a limit. Blanchot calls the extreme residue that remains when worldliness comes to an end "the essential solitude," and he sees this solitude as the exclusive province of literary language—language brought to its most extreme pitch. The previous chapter has described the exhaustion of generosity, and the resulting intensification of literary language, from the perspective of the beneficiary. Herbert's most powerful poems illustrate the experience of a loss of a whole world of generosity, as though what William Nestrick calls the "only total form of gift-giving, one that involves the entire community of indebted creditors and God in a completely inward reciprocity," has become utterly defeated and phantasmal.[1] In this chapter I examine the same movement from the benefactor's perspective.

1. William Nestrick, "George Herbert: The Giver and the Gift," *Ploughshares* 2 (1975), 203.

If Herbert consistently portrays himself as the humblest of beneficiaries (however complex a maneuver this is), Shakespeare best describes the perspective of the benefactor. I take Shakespeare's knowledge of his own strength as nearly self-evident; his contrast with Herbert is palpable in the audacity of his representation of power. Shakespeare, perhaps more than any other poet, has been thought of as self-originating and self-sufficing.

In this chapter I aim to show how Shakespeare works out the paradoxes of self-origination or charisma. These *are* paradoxes: the opacity and hence the authority of charisma come from our inability to imagine a self-originating consciousness. For the question would still remain: where did the capacity for self-origination originate? In *Paradise Lost* Satan demonstrates a curious moment of weakness when he asserts, "We know no time when we were not as now" (5.859). He means to say that there is no reason for the rebel angels to ascribe their origin to any external source, but he indicates, in fact, his utter lack of knowledge as to his own origin: his powers are a gift from an external source. As Herbert was acutely aware, consciousness is always receptive. It is radically passive, and its *data* originate outside itself, even the data of its own existence. We cannot imagine what any consciousness would be like that was self-originating: this was Nietzsche's disproof of the existence of a conscious divinity. As Richard II says, for any power that we can imagine having, there is nothing in it that we can call our own. It derives from elsewhere, part of what Wittgenstein calls "the world as I found it." For Nietzsche, even a conscious divinity would have to be surprised that it was a divinity; its powers and its divinity would be a fact, a given about the world.[2]

It is the opacity of the unimaginable source of authority—the otherness of charismatic self-origination—that Shakespeare explores. As

2. I think that a similar idea occurs around Milton's time in Spinoza's version of God. True, thought is an attribute of his God, but it doesn't make sense to say that his God thinks, except perhaps insofar as human minds, modes of that attribute, think. See also Martha Nussbaum, *The Fragility of Goodness: Luck and Ethics in Greek Tragedy and Philosophy* (New York: Cambridge University Press, 1986), pp. 1–8. Jonathan Goldberg talks about related issues in *James I and the Politics of Kingship: Jonson, Shakespeare, Donne, and Their Contemporaries* (Baltimore: Johns Hopkins University Press, 1983) when he argues that the king is both an object of sight and a seeing eye, that is, both an object of the consciousness of others and himself a hyperconsciousness (at least he is thought to be a hyperconsciousness). Christopher Pye gives a fascinating Lacanian account of how consciousness can be projected onto the spectacle of the king without effacing the qualitative difference between conscious self and authoritative and transcendent other: the gaze itself is prior to either subject or object, and although it comports the essence of consciousness (always thought of as a kind of seeing), it is not a seeing that belongs as intimately to the self as the self wishfully believes; it is not essentially a first-person affair. See *The Regal Phantasm: Shakespeare and the Politics of Spectacle* (New York: Routledge, 1990). John Rawls's Miltonic view of talents as not being owned by talented individuals is also relevant here.

many people have recently argued, Shakespeare analyzes the theatrical economy that enables the construction of charismatic authority.[3] I argue that Marcel Mauss provides illuminating insight into this theatrical economy, which Mauss sees as nearly a universal of human culture. But Shakespeare is also interested in the *phenomenology* of this authority, the seemingly incoherent internal experience of self-origination. (For I do not wish to claim that Shakespeare thought of this authority as wholly projected by its subjects.)

In Shakespeare's plays self-origination manifests itself most fully under the pressures of loss. When a character (usually male) continues the expenditure of substance when he has no substance left to expend, what he expends can no longer be thought of as originally coming from elsewhere; now his generosity comes from nothing, which means it can come only from the self, since the self is reduced to nothing. This is extremity from the perspective of the benefactor, rather than of the beneficiary, and the solitude that marks it is, if anything, even more intense in Shakespeare than in Herbert.

Lords and Owners

> Authority is inconceivable within the sphere of immanence, or else it can only be thought of as something transitory.
>
> —Kierkegaard

> To give away yourself keeps yourself still.
>
> —Sonnet 16

What is the origin of generosity? Following Marcel Mauss's great book *Essai sur le don*,[4] Georges Bataille sees in the principle of expenditure a founding category for social interaction; indeed he expands

3. On the subversive tendencies of seeing kingship in theatrical terms, see David Scott Kastan, "Proud Majesty Made a Subject: Shakespeare and the Spectacle of Rule," *Shakespeare Quarterly* 37 (1986), 459–75. On the general question of theatricality and power, see Stephen Orgel, *The Illusion of Power: Political Theatre in the English Renaissance* (Berkeley: University of California Press, 1975). Orgel argues that theatricalizing can distance and intimate as well as render familiar; see also, among many other works, Pye, *Regal Phantasm*; Stephen Greenblatt, *Shakespearean Negotiations: The Circulation of Social Energy in Renaissance England* (Berkeley: University of California Press, 1988); Clifford Geertz, *Local Knowledge: Further Essays in Interpretive Anthropology* (New York: Basic, 1983), and *Negara: The Theatre State in Nineteenth Century Bali* (Princeton, N.J.: Princeton University Press, 1980); and Goldberg, *James I.*

4. Reprinted in Marcel Mauss, *Sociologie et anthropologie* (Paris: Presses Universitaires de France, 1950).

the notion of expenditure into a primordial explanation not only of human social structure and history but of natural history as well. In *La part maudite* he argues for a kind of countereconomy and refuses to reason only the need assumed by the classical economics of scarcity. His main principle is that "every system with a certain quantity of energy available to it must expend it."[5] Given the laws of the conservation of energy, it is as pressing for the living to accommodate excess as to accommodate lack:

> The living organism, in the context determined by the play of energy on the surface of the globe, necessarily receives more energy than is necessary to the maintenance of life. The excess energy (or wealth) can be used for the growth of the system (for example, the growth of the organism); if the system can't grow any further, it is necessary to waste it without any profit, to expend it, whether voluntarily or not, gloriously or if not gloriously then catastrophically. (*Oeuvres*, 7:29)

This breathtaking challenge to the conventional economics of energy is Shakespearean in scope. This is a credo as illuminating as it is perverse, a credo that could belong to many of Shakespeare's characters. Like Freud in *Beyond the Pleasure Principle*, Bataille understands energy (Freud's libido) to enable life but also to threaten an excess that life must dissipate in order to avoid destruction. All life forms are only products of the sun ("nous ne sommes au fond qu'un effet du soleil" [*Oeuvres*, 7:10] he writes in the prospectus for *La part maudite*): life dissipates the excess of the solar energy it depends on in the production of more life and in the creation of ever more complicated and ever more wasteful forms of life. Humanity represents both a pinnacle of organization (organization that absorbs excess energy) and an unparalleled mechanism for wastefulness. (Indeed the unexampled wastefulness of human beings is notorious.) The problem of expenditure is thus particularly acute for humans, since onto them is displaced the largest quantity of the excess energy that fueled and that results from the development and evolution of life.

The ambiguity of generosity is felt most intensely by humans, who must dissipate its riches either gloriously or catastrophically. The glory that is available to them is a glory imitative of the sun, whose generosity is absolute and endless: "In practice, from the point of view of wealth, the radiance of the sun is distinguished by its unilateral character: *it wastes itself without calculation and without return*" (7:10). All

5. Georges Bataille, *Oeuvres complètes* (Paris: Gallimard, 1970–), 7:13. All translations from Mauss and from Bataille are my own.

human richness is necessarily secondary; it comes from the sun, to whom alone pure plenitude and generosity could belong: "The source and the essence of our wealth are given in the radiance of the sun, which expends energy—wealth—without return. The sun gives without ever receiving" (7:35). All that consciousness, or life, gives, it has received from elsewhere; only the sun gives without receiving.

Mauss and Bataille see identification with this self-originating plenitude as the mode of social power.[6] Bataille, in his essay on the psychological structure of fascism, argues that the dictator's charisma or mana comes from his representing "unproductive expenditure," "dépense *improductive*" (1:346), which is read as the glory of the state he incarnates: "The chief as chief is in fact nothing but the emanation of a principle which is no other than the glorious existence of a nation brought to the level of a divine force (which, superior to every other conceivable consideration requires not only the passion but the ecstasy of its participants)" (1:363). This is a strange avatar of Rousseau's idea of the sovereign as representing the general will, but the image of divine self-origination is still the mark of the general: the coincidence of signified and referent in a sign that refers to itself.

The origin of absolutist power, at least its psychological power, is an imitative generosity, a theatrical staging of expenditure. This would have been particularly true in England, where the lack of a standing army and the confluence of naval and mercantile interests tended to unite the gentry with the mercantile class. Absolutism, as Perry Anderson writes, was brief and weak in England, outmoded by nascent capitalism. Absolutist power in England had to be theatrical in some sense (as many new historicist critics have argued) because, as Ander-

---

6. Compare Aristotle on magnificence in the *Nichomachean Ethics*; but Aristotle sees magnificence as a mean and contrasts it with wastefulness or prodigality. See also Paul Veyne, *Bread and Circuses: Historical Sociology and Political Pluralism,* abridged by Oswyn Murray, trans. Brian Pearce (London: Penguin, 1990). Veyne quotes Aquinas's highly favorable view of Aristotelian magnificence: "Pride [a virtue] suffices to explain the collective character of munificent expenditure: the proud man wants to do something on a grand scale, but everything individual is petty in comparison with divine worship or public affairs. The munificent man does not think of himself: not because he disdains his own property but because there is nothing there that is great" (p. 17), so that he becomes great by identifying himself with the divine; Veyne also quotes Aquinas on the difference between ostentation toward peers and a generous refusal of ostentation among inferiors, which is a second-order generosity bespeaking the ease of the magnifico's sense of self-origination: "He merely refrains from displaying the whole of his greatness, especially to the huge crowd of lesser men. For as Aristotle further says in that same passage, the role of the magnanimous man is to be lofty towards men of high rank and wealth, but courteous to those of moderate station. The fourth trait is that he cannot associate with others intimately, except with his friends" (p. 61, n.9). I should note that Veyne is in general rather hostile to Mauss and Bataille.

son writes, "The coercive bureaucratic machinery of the monarchy remained very slim compared with political prestige and executive power."[7] In France and Spain power might come from the end of a gun, but in England it was already Foucauldian to some extent.[8] Social energy, and the discipline of self-fashioning, to use Greenblatt's phrases, had to substitute for military power (except, of course, with respect to Ireland).[9] The theatrical display of imitative abundance and glory allows us to see a continuity underlying the contrast between Elizabethan parsimony and Jacobean prodigality: for Elizabeth, generosity was theatrical rather than substantial, as in her royal progresses (all real excess went usefully, indeed necessarily, by her lights, to the Anglo-Spanish War); for James, his own glory reached theatrical levels precisely because of the extent of his lavish prodigality.[10]

Bataille argues that the dictator or ruler displays himself or herself as divine and does this by imitating—by appearing to share—the generosity of being itself (although the dictator's aim, like Elizabeth's, is the accumulation and not the destruction of wealth). The concept of the divine—and its opacity—springs from the sense that generosity is necessarily *intentional* (in the phenomenological sense); if being really is generous, it must itself have some intentionality. Indeed, the idea that there is an intentional generosity to being persists in almost pure form as the inheritance of Husserl and Heidegger. Divinity is one

7. Perry Anderson, *Lineages of the Absolutist State* (London: Verso, 1979), p. 129. On Shakespeare as attempting to reconcile absolutism with bourgeois capitalism and finally seeing their incompatibility, see Walter Cohen's *Drama of a Nation: Public Theatre in England and Spain* (Ithaca, N.Y.: Cornell University Press, 1984).

8. The best Foucauldian account of the Jacobean era, I think, is Jonathan Goldberg's *James I*. Stephen Greenblatt's *Renaissance Self-Fashioning: More to Shakespeare* (Chicago: University of Chicago Press, 1980) is deeply influenced by Foucault as well and provides a splendid and passionate set of readings of the Tudor mode of creating subjects (in all senses of the word).

9. In "Reason and Need: *King Lear* and the 'Crisis' of the Aristocracy" (in *Some Facets of King Lear: Essays in Prismatic Criticism*, ed. Rosalie Colie and F. T. Flahiff [Toronto: University of Toronto Press, 1974], pp. 185–219) Rosalie Colie anticipates some new historicist insights in an essay that reads *King Lear* from the perspective of Lawrence Stone's *The Crisis of the Aristocracy: 1558–1641* (Oxford: Oxford University Press, 1965; rptd. with corrections, 1979). She sees *King Lear* as extremely good supporting evidence for the existence of such a crisis. Like Cohen, she concentrates on the opposition between feudalism and absolutism as well as their incompatibility with capitalism (p. 186). I will return to this opposition when I consider *Richard II*. My own interests are neither new historicist (despite my use of anthropological data) nor about ideological functioning (though the Marxist account, especially Cohen's, seems to me convincing on that score). My far narrower concern is how Shakespeare thought power as excess appeared to its possessors.

10. On progresses and theatricality, see Geertz, *Local Knowledge*, pp. 121–46, and *Negara*. For an acute analysis of the differences between Elizabethan parsimony and Jacobean prodigality, see Stone, *Crisis*, pp. 470–76 and 488–89.

name or, at least, one putative bearer of this intentionality. To ascribe divinity to being is partly to anthropomorphize it, to see it as intentional, and so to see—though not to understand—the possibility of a charismatic human sharing that self-origination. Divinity entails an ascription of a radical ambiguity, as though the divine person *could* be both self-originating and conscious. To believe in divinity (as Nietzsche could not) would necessarily mean, then, not to be able to identify oneself with it (except perhaps at the cost of believing that one is split between self and other, between beneficiary and benefactor, or that one has two bodies, for example).

To be allied with this sort of generosity is to appear as source rather than as beneficiary and so to assert priority and power, or the power of absolute priority. For Mauss any social power not based on the immediate threat of violence consists in this priority: to give a gift is to oblige gratitude, and so it is an assertion of power. Absolute power would accrue to a figure who gives without receiving. This provides an account, I think, of the importance of priority or earliness. For Harold Bloom these terms are ends in themselves; their relation to power is self-evident. But it seems to me that Mauss's and Bataille's analysis of the economy of divinity and imitative generosity can illuminate the indisputable desire for earliness—for self-origination—better than a sheerly oedipal paradigm like Bloom's, since such a paradigm depends much more on a model close to the classic nineteenth-century economics of scarcity than do Mauss's and Bataille's.

Shakespeare's most overt meditation on the theological sociology of gift giving is *Timon of Athens*. Coppélia Kahn combines Mauss with psychoanalysis to read in Timon's seemingly magical generosity a kind of imitation of lost maternal plenty.[11] At the very start of the play the Poet addresses Timon as "magic of bounty" (i.i.6); Timon's sense of himself as source and not merely as recipient and relay comes out in the phrase. Timon doesn't *use* magic (as Prospero will): he is magic itself, and so he is utterly self-sufficient. But, as Kahn suggests, the presence of so magical a bounty can itself feel subjugating and oppressive ("'Magic of Bounty,'" pp. 39–41).

For his ephebes, Shakespeare represents the power and oppressiveness of a self-sufficient generosity, but Shakespeare himself can chafe at such enigmatic self-sufficiency in others. This vexing self-sufficiency can be an especially salient feature of erotic life. There the

11. Coppélia Kahn, "'Magic of Bounty': *Timon of Athens*, Jacobean Patronage, and Maternal Power," *Shakespeare Quarterly* 38 (1987), 34–57.

Freudian opposition between narcissistic and anaclitic love corresponds to the opposition I am trying to draw here between benefactor and beneficiary.[12] For Shakespeare the young man of the sonnets represents this kind of self-sufficient narcissism.[13] He attracts the speaker in exactly the way Freud sees the narcissist attracting what his translators call anaclitic object-choice. The narcissist seems to need no generosity, to be utterly self-sufficient. He provides the anaclitic lover, for whom love is a substitute for a lost narcissistic self-sufficiency, a reminder and wishful displacement of her own original but now blasted self-sufficiency. To love narcissism is invariably painful; it is inevitably to experience the pain of one's own irretrievable removal from narcissism. And the beloved narcissist will be the last person to be able to empathize with and so comfort one for that pain (as the mother once could, before she became separated from the self in the latter's fall from primary narcissism). Thus love directed toward a narcissist can quickly modulate into envy and resentment.

It is obvious that the speaker in many of the sonnets seeks to persuade the young man into a less oppressive form of generosity than narcissistic self-sufficiency—seeks to persuade him into the generosity of action rather than of being. This is the reason for all the speaker's attempts to hammer at "the most touchy point in the narcissistic system, the immortality of the ego, which is so hard pressed by reality" ("On Narcissism," p. 91). Shakespeare continually warns the young man not to try to align himself with the absolute self-sufficiency of being, with its Olympian and careless generosity, warns him that he cannot be entirely self-sufficient since he will die. The sonnets repeatedly try to move the young man away from a *careless* generosity. They urge him to go beyond the ambiguous generosity of his self-sufficing presence in the world, his own "unthrifty loveliness" (Sonnet 4), and to develop a different kind of generosity, one in which he will care for others and so will want their care. He will want, that is, to be beneficiary as well as benefactor. Narcissistic self-sufficiency, according to Freud, *expects* care, but this is not the same as wanting it. The narcissist is beyond any desire.

12. Freud develops this opposition in "On Narcissism: An Introduction," in *The Standard Edition of the Complete Psychological Works of Sigmund Freud*, trans. James Strachey (London: Hogarth Press, 1953–74), 14:73–102.

13. Thomas Greene's fine essay "Pitiful Thrivers: Failed Husbandry in the Sonnets" (in *Shakespeare and the Question of Theory*, ed. Geoffrey Hartman and Patricia Parker [New York: Methuen, 1985], pp. 230–44) analyzes the libidinal economics of the speaker's narcissism in his relations to the young man. See especially p. 234. Although Greene does not mention Mauss, his essay grapples with the great paradox that Mauss analyzes, how "in spending more, verbally, sartorially, and sexually, [one] may get more" (p. 237).

It is this self-sufficiency that makes the narcissist so attractive, even as it motivates the anaclitic lover to attempt to change him. The anaclitic lover does have desires. She desires access to what the narcissist can give her: the stuff of a self-sufficiency beyond desire. She hopes to gain such access by making the narcissist desire her care. Her own generosity, her care for the narcissist, tries to stake a claim to a special intimacy with a generosity whose indifference as to object both attracts and distresses her. She wants the care of someone whose attractiveness consists in his not caring.

The anaclitic person's love for the narcissist is inherently self-contradictory since she seeks the love precisely of an object that will not give love, that is unconscious (of love, at least). She seeks the love of an object whose generosity cannot be relied on as intentional. She attempts to win a love that, if won, will dissipate what made the object attractive to begin with.

At best her relief can only consist in a kind of cruelty: if she can get the narcissist to love her, then she will no longer be tormented by her love for him. If she can win him over with her generosity, she can make him needy enough for her to abandon him. The narcissist's careless generosity can enrage the anaclitic, and her response may be a reciprocal generosity that intends to render the narcissist needy. If this leads to abandonment, the relationship will end, and she will have failed to derive anything from it. The most that can be hoped is that the relationship can continue in the mode of cruelty: the narcissist is still desirable enough for the anaclitic's attention, but she is free enough to make him feel her cruelty. This is the paradox of generosity in erotic life, a paradox inherent to all generosity.

In the sonnets, the young man's painful, anguishing indifference is a sine qua non for the speaker's passion for him, and the speaker's response to this will often modulate into an attempt at just this cruel but still engaged revenge. There is, of course, nothing unusual about this situation. What is unusual are the strategies that some of the sonnets employ to attempt to represent the young man as at once powerfully self-sufficient yet also desperately needy. Sonnet 73, for example, is, I think, less about the vulnerability of its speaker than it is an attempt to use the young man's narcissism against itself and him:

> That time of year thou mayst in me behold
> When yellow leaves, or none, or few, do hang
> Upon those boughs that shake against the cold,
> Bare [ruin'd] choirs, where late the sweet birds sang.
> In me thou seest the twilight of such day

> As after sunset fadeth in the west,
> Which by and by black night doth take away,
> Death's second self, that seals up all in rest.
> In me thou seest the glowing of such fire
> That on the ashes of his youth doth lie,
> As the death-bed whereon it must expire,
> Consum'd with that which it was nourish'd by.
> This thou perceiv'st, which makes thy love more strong,
> To love that well, which thou must leave ere long.

Somewhat peculiarly, the last line makes it the young man who is submitted to the workings of necessity. One expects that it is the aging speaker who will have to "leave ere long." But here the logic is somewhat different: the speaker will die; the young man will, in the strength of his youth, survive him; hence the two will part; and since in any parting two people leave each other, the young man will leave the speaker as the speaker leaves the young man. Of course leaving is not quite the same as parting. If one person leaves, the other person is left behind. They don't both leave. There is no question here that the speaker is regretting the abandonment that he himself will undergo when he dies, when he is left behind in his grave. Still the formulation is very strong, since it is the speaker who seems submitted to necessity, the speaker who *must* die. To apply that "must" to the young man, as the sonnet does, poses a severe challenge to his perfect self-sufficiency.

What is the source of the young man's potential vulnerability? His own power. What disturbs the young man's narcissism is not, on this level, a potential challenge to his immortality, but that the self-sufficiency (the quasi-immortality) that the speaker grants him should force him to be parted from the speaker. Where the speaker is going he cannot follow because he is (still) immortal and the speaker is not.

It is not, of course, completely accurate to claim that the manifest aggressiveness of the poem consists in its imputing invulnerability to its addressee. Aggressivity always seeks to wound, and even here the poem uses the young man's narcissism against him. For, despite the fact that the poem ends unusually, with a sense of the young man's love for the speaker, the young man in this poem remains a narcissist.[14] The play of general and specific makes that narcissism clear, I think. Narcissus cares nothing for others, cares nothing for the gener-

14. This is certainly the case in the continuation in Sonnet 74, where the speaker's death doesn't matter since the important part of him is his poetry, whose value comes from its subject, the young man.

ality of humanity, the Shakespearean general, because he does not know himself. Primary narcissism does not have the internal self-differentiation necessary for self-reflexivity. Secondary narcissism, on the other hand, confronts and attempts to repress its knowledge that the self is like the other and is not special; it attempts to deal with this knowledge by making the self the only other. As Ovid says, Narcissus is safe in his cruelly indifferent primary narcissism until he comes to know himself; then, at last confronted with otherness, he treats himself, his reflection, as the *only* other. He avoids the generality of all others, of otherness, for the specificity of his own reflection.

But it is that generality—the general fate—that the speaker of Sonnet 73 intends the young man to confront. "That time of year thou mayest in me behold" is a warning and not only a lament; it is like those tombstones that say, "Such as I now am you are soon to become." The passage of time is a general phenomenon (the speaker has been warning the young man of this from the opening sonnets); the young man is to behold his own fate in the speaker, or what will be his fate when forty winters shall besiege his brow. This confrontation creates the ambiguity of the last line of the sonnet, in which the young man is praised for loving that which he must leave ere long. What is it that he loves well but must leave ere long? Is it the speaker or is it his own life? To a certain extent they are indistinguishable, because the speaker himself embodies what will finally and inevitably happen to the young man. The oppositions between them are only a different form of connection: the speaker's leaves are dying, while (by a pun) the young man may continue to put forth leaves or to adorn his life with leaves;[15] but that meaning of *leave* will soon decay and fall into the more usual *depart from*. The language used to characterize the narcissist's youth and invulnerability and originating powers will at length characterize his vulnerability to old age and death.

An even deeper, and even more aggressive, meditation on the status of ontological generosity is Sonnet 94. There the progression of the poem, through the internal rhymes *pow'r, flow'r, sourest* (see Booth, *Shakespeare's Sonnets*, p. 307), may be taken to mark the vicissitudes that Shakespeare as beneficiary wishes to see even power submitted to. This poem is striking because the speaker never denies the privileged status of the young man as a source of being. Rather, he insists

15. Stephen Booth notices the possible meaning of *leave* as "to put forth leaves," as in the *OED*, though for him it is merely a dim and excluded alternate haunting the obvious meanings of leave: depart from or give up, forgo. See his commentary in his edition of *Shakespeare's Sonnets* (New Haven, Conn.: Yale University Press, 1977), p. 260.

that the difference between the source of abundance and its recipient
can redound only to the benefit of the latter:

> They that have pow'r to hurt, and will do none,
> That do not do the thing they most do show,
> Who moving others, are themselves as stone,
> Unmoved, cold, and to temptation slow,
> They rightly do inherit heaven's graces,
> And husband nature's riches from expense;
> They are the lords and owners of their faces,
> Others but stewards of their excellence.
> The summer's flow'r is to the summer sweet,
> Though to itself it only live and die,
> But if that flow'r with base infection meet,
> The basest weed outbraves his dignity:
> For sweetest things turn sourest by their deeds;
> Lilies that fester smell far worse than weeds.

Like Spenser (though with a different valence) Shakespeare is alert
to the distinction between being a source of some quality and being
endowed with that quality. Spenser's version of the distinction is desperately wishful, surfacing just as he tries to efface it: Adonis *must*
have life, he claims, "who living gives to all." Here Shakespeare treats
the self-sufficiency of power on its own terms. For Shakespeare it is
the quality of self-sufficiency that it is unmoved by what is moving
(others) in it even as it is moving (them). That this is a resentful
characterization is clear. What moves the young man's admirers can
also move their resentment. The ambivalent nature of the narcissist's
effect on others was Ovid's insight before Freud's. Here the young
man is described, as though in praise, as "unmoved, cold, and to
temptation slow"; the last characterization must indicate some sense
of his resistance to seduction.

The ambiguously laudatory formulations and equations in this
poem are well known, and they are properly taken to express the
poem's bitterness: "a piece of grave irony," Empson calls it.[16] But the
ambiguities that interest me here have more to do with the young
man's status. What does his self-sufficiency mean? Where can it come
from, especially if to come from outside would give the lie to the self-
origination it asserts? I think that this ambiguity is behind the tension
between the image of those that have power as being the husbandmen

---

16. William Empson, *Some Versions of Pastoral* (New York: New Directions, 1974),
p. 89.

of nature's riches and that of their being "the lords and owners of their faces," where others are their stewards.[17] This tension also animates the opposition between the sense of those that have power as inheritors and beneficiaries of heaven's graces and the sense of them as natural objects, or like natural objects—"as stone" or like the "summer's flow'r." Under this description they simply *are* (examples of) nature's riches. They are instances of excellence, not possessors of it.

Here, I think, is the explanation of the peculiarity of the line "They are the lords and owners of their faces." One can, properly speaking, possess only what one can also not possess, what one can alienate. But to be the lord and owner of one's own face is somehow to possess something that is intrinsically inalienable. It is true that there is a suggestion here that others are not the lords and owners of their own faces (as though they were alienable), but I think this suggestion is made because it lays down the possibility of seeing everything that attaches to the self—even one's own face—as having its source elsewhere, of belonging to some agency other than oneself. This possibly would intensify the contrast with those that have power: what others would merely possess, what for others would have its source elsewhere, in nature's riches, they that have power both possess and originate. They are what they possess, unlike other people who only possess what they are not.

The poem, then, articulates the almost self-contradictory self-sufficiency that anaclitic persons ascribe to narcissism. (This is a version of the transference, which is in general marked by a belief in authority as having magical power, that is the power to be its own standard. Authority is always an attribute of the other, since every self will be aware of the contingency of its own claims to authority and their dependence on external authorities: the authority of the other.) The young man who is the sonnet's subject is allowed to appear in the sonnet as genuinely self-possessing—that is, actually instantiating what he possesses rather than being the beneficiary of something the source of whose being is elsewhere. Thus he appears quasi-divine— an unmoved mover who moving others is himself as stone. If he appears to derive his power from elsewhere, if he seems to "inherit heaven's graces," he nevertheless inherits them "rightly," by law, as by the law of primogeniture, since he is hardly susceptible to being called

17. Again, this tension is noted by Booth: "Note that, in keeping with the self-contradictory spirit of the poem, the lords and owners husband riches and thus are characterized by exactly the defining function of the stewards, the group with which they are contrasted; in fact the noun 'husband' was a synonym for 'steward'" (*Shakespeare's Sonnets*, p. 307).

one of the meek. He inherits the graces, but his right to inherit heaven's graces is not itself an inherited right; it originates in his own authority.

Unlike Sonnet 73 there is very little here to challenge this narcissistic scenario of self-origination directly. Though the sonnet does foresee the possibility of the young man's death, or his festering through a base infection, its warning is not of mortality but of the possibility of the young man's ontological generosity going sour. I think the speaker issues this warning because it turns the tables on the young man. If, according to the octet, it is possible to originate rather than merely benefit from wealth, the sestet goes farther and sees such origination as *precluding* benefit: "The summer's flow'r is to the summer sweet, / Though to itself it only live and die." The summer here is a purely passive recipient, a kind of Wildean aesthete. It is, surprisingly, not the source of the riches it possesses and allegorizes. It allegorizes them by enjoying them. Summer here is Will's testament: it stands for the speaker, able in the anaclitic mode to enjoy the narcissism of the narcissist who is unable to enjoy anything.

The aggression in this poem seeks not to wound but to paralyze. The speaker goes so far in his acknowledgment of the fact that riches originate elsewhere than in himself that he is willing to accede to an almost parasitical status, enjoying the sweetness of an object that cannot enjoy that sweetness itself. The moralistic pressure in the poem means to sustain this relationship. The poem is a homily, a goad and guide to action. And yet it is not action but stasis that the poem urges. The ideal is to be one of those "that have pow'r to hurt *and will do none*, that *do not do* the thing they most *do show*." Actually *to do* anything is to be destructive of the state of uprightness the poem urges. The word *do* appears five times in the first five lines, and each time it is either in a negative formulation or in a phrase opposed to the idea of action that the verb *to do* indicates. "Do none," "do not do the thing" are in apposition, not opposition, to the nonactive verbs. That is, they correspond to the verbs of a quasi-middle voice, "do show," and "do inherit."

This explains the peculiarly absolutizing character of the couplet, when the verb *to do* returns in its noun form, *deeds*: "For sweetest things turn sourest by their deeds; / Lilies that fester smell far worse than weeds." One can destroy one's sweetness by engaging in noxious actions, but all action is noxious, at least for sweetest things. The implication here is both that the narcissist will inevitably engage in deeds that are rank and that it is action itself—the relinquishment of the stasis of *being* one of nature's riches—that destroys the pleasantness, for others, of narcissistic self-sufficiency. I think the poem is deeply allusive to the myth of Narcissus. There, the destruction of his self-sufficiency causes Narcissus to pine away into a flower. Here, the vector has a different direction, but the comparison of the young man to a flower that can cheer others but not itself must also look to Narcissus's ability to move love in others when he himself does not love. It must also look to the flower that is at once the emblem of Narcissus's self-divided self-love (Freud's secondary narcissism) and of the destruction that such a self-division from pure and self-sufficient being leads to.

The poem renders pure generosity a paralyzed and self-paralyzing state. It thus projects onto the narcissist the passivity more intuitively associated with the beneficiary, in this case the summer.

That Shakespeare can and should want to do this indicates as well as Mauss that generosity ought not to be understood as an entirely kind thing nor to be taken kindly. The aggressive edge of generosity needs stressing against an argument like Lewis Hyde's or Patricia Fumerton's that would idealize gift exchange.[18] In *Paradise Lost* Satan's chaf-

---

18. Coppélia Kahn stresses the oppressiveness of generosity; cf. her article on *Timon*, p. 39. I think the best use of Mauss for the reading of Elizabethan and Jacobean literature has been made by those critics who see the fundamental ambivalence of the gift relationship, such as Kahn, Karen Newman in "Portia's Ring: Unruly Women and Structures of Exchange in *The Merchant of Venice*," *Shakespeare Quarterly* 38 (1987): 19–33; Lynda Boose in "The Father and the Bride in Shakespeare," *PMLA* 97 (1982), 325–47; Marianne Novy in *Love's Argument: Gender Relations in Shakespeare* (Chapel Hill: University of North Carolina Press, 1984), pp. 63–82; and Lars Engel in "'Thrift Is Blessing': Exchange and Explanation in *The Merchant of Venice*," *Shakespeare Quarterly* 37 (1986), 20–37, and in "Afloat in Thick Deeps: Shakespeare's Sonnets on Certainty," *PMLA* 104 (1989), 832–43. Louis Adrian Montrose, in "Gifts and Reasons: The Contexts of Peele's *Araygnement of Paris*," *ELH* 47 (1980), 433–61, is useful too, although his interests are much more narrowly historical than mine. Along with Novy and Montrose, Patricia Fumerton in "Exchanging Gifts: The Elizabethan Currency of Children and Poetry," *ELH* 53 (1986), 241–78; Ronald Sharp in "Gift Exchange and the Economies of Spirit in *The Merchant of Venice*," *Modern Philology* 83 (1986), 250–65; and John M. Wallace in "*Timon of Athens* and the Three Graces: Shakespeare's Senecan Study," *Modern Philology* 83 (1986), 349–63, develop Edgar Wind's great study of the iconography of the graces, *Pagan Mysteries in the Renaissance* (London: Faber and Faber, 1958), pp. 31–38, to argue the importance of Seneca's *De Beneficiis* to the Renaissance concept of gift giving. Wind traces back to Seneca (and beyond) the history of the iconography of the three graces (employed by Spenser in book 6 of *The Faerie Queene* and in *The Shepeardes Calendar*), who were considered to stand for gracious giving, gracious reception, and gracious return. But Wallace does not make much of the Maussian framework; he sees *Timon* as presenting a kind of Hobbesian critique of Seneca, an argument I disagree with, since it seems to me both Seneca and Hobbes conform to Mauss's descriptions. Fumerton, Sharp, and Wallace share with Lewis Hyde, in *The Gift: Imagination and the Erotic Life of Property* (New York: Random House, 1983), a highly idealizing notion of the gift as mediating communitarian relationships among people. But the thrust of Mauss's argument is to show the opposite, to show that gift giving is not, as Fumerton

ing against gratitude, paradoxically burdensome in proportion as it is light, is one of the primary reasons for his revolt:

> What could be less than to afford him praise,
> The easiest recompense, and pay him thanks,
> How due! yet all his good prov'd ill in me,
> And wrought but malice; lifted up so high
> I sdein'd subjection, and thought one step higher
> Would set me highest, and in a moment quit
> The debt immense of endless gratitude,
> So burdensome, still paying, still to owe;
> Forgetful what from him I still receiv'd,
> And understood not that a grateful mind
> By owing owes not, but still pays, at once
> Indebted and discharg'd; what burden then?
>
> (4.46–57)

The answer to this—the reason that if Satan "could obtain / By Act of Grace my former state; how soon / Would highth recall high thoughts, how soon unsay / What feign'd submission swore" (4.93–96)—is that (as for Herbert) the burden is great because the debt of gratitude consists in endless gratitude for the ease of its discharge. This idea comes from Seneca: "Even so also art thou a verie Churle, if thou on the othersyde, in respect that he accepteth thy good will [alone] for payment, bee not so much the more willingly beholden too him because thou art released."[19] More subtle in its aggressivity than

---

would have it, an end to aggression but simply warfare pursued by other means, with the aggression always latent and sometimes manifest. Cf. Mauss, *Sociologie*: "Le potlatch est une guerre. Il porte ce titre, «danse de guerre», chez le Tlingit" (p. 201n). ("The potlatch is a war. It bears this title, 'War-dance,' among the Tlingit.") Generosity and aggression are not fully extricable from each other, as Montrose, Kahn, and Greene see. Natalie Zemon Davis applies Mauss suggestively in her article "Books as Gifts in Sixteenth Century France" (*Transactions of the Royal Historical Society*, 5th ser. [1983], 33:69–88). I find most interesting her arguments that certain types of books, jokes, fabliaux, folk tales, etc. that might be considered communal property were never dedicated to a patron (which she regards, with Montrose and Kahn, certainly correctly, as one type of gift giving). She suspects that this is because such books were already considered common property; in my terms, I would say that they are already general, prior to the soi-disant originating powers of the gift giver and already part of generality, and are not the province of the particular person.

For a brief account of gift giving and its relation to patronage in the Renaissance, see Werner Gundersheimer, "Patronage in the Renaissance: An Exploratory Approach," in *Patronage in the Renaissance*, ed. Guy Fitch Lytle and Stephen Orgel (Princeton, N.J.: Princeton University Press, 1981), pp. 3–23, esp. pp. 12–16.

19. Seneca, . . . *Concerning Benefyting* . . . , trans. Arthur Golding (London: 1578), pt. 7, chap. 16, pp. 113–14. I think some of Golding's language in these chapters (especially chapters 14–15) may be echoed in *The Merchant of Venice*.

Satan, who merely refuses to submit to the reality principle when his own self-love is challenged by God's superior narcissism, the paradox that the speaker in Sonnet 94 develops represents generosity as paralyzed and overcharged with the stasis of its own being.

But both Milton and Shakespeare are deeply aware of the ambivalent nature of generosity, whether as conscious performance of self-sufficiency and overflow of grace or as unconscious display of the gracious narcissism that compels love in the needy anaclitic.[20] As Sahlins writes, and as I pointed out in my introduction, Hobbes described gratitude as one of the primary passions that hegemony seeks to instill in its objects. Gratefulness is the origin of the tendency to submit to the hegemony of the gracious being:

> As Justice dependeth on Antecedent Covenant; so does GRATITUDE depend on Antecedent Grace, that is to say, Antecedent Freegift: and it is the fourth Law of Nature; which may be conceived in this Forme; *That a man which receiveth Benefit from another of meer Grace, Endeavour that he which giveth it, have no reasonable cause to repent him of his good will.* For no man giveth, but with intention of Good to himselfe; because Gift is Voluntary; and of all Voluntary Acts, the Object is to every man his own Good.[21]

If "a grateful mind / By owing owes not, but still pays" (Seneca makes this point as well), that mind is nevertheless submitted to the burden of gratitude for this situation in which it owes *only* gratitude. Psychological submission, whether to an external parental figure or to the superego, always takes the form of an intangible obligation. It is the intangibility of the obligation that renders it so paradoxically substantial, as though in failed compensation for the impossibility of tangible compensation. To be the recipient of a genuine "Freegift," to be the beneficiary of the generosity of the source of all wealth—what the child is made to feel with respect to its parents—means to be in a position in which one can never be quit of the debt, since the debt can only be paid with wealth derived from that source. What else does Donne's question—"Yet grace, if thou repent, thou canst not lacke; /

---

20. Cf. Deborah Shuger, *Habits of Thought in the English Renaissance: Religion, Politics, and the Dominant Culture* (Berkeley: University of California Press, 1990), especially the chapter "Nursing Fathers," pp. 218–49.

21. *Leviathan*, pt. 1, chap. 15, quoted by Marshall Sahlins, in *Stone Age Economics* (Chicago: Aldine-Atherton, 1972), p. 178. Hobbes can be seen as writing against this Senecan idealization when he sees life as the war of all against all; nevertheless his law of gratitude includes a possibility of social integration that derives from Seneca. Hobbes can be likened to Bourdieu in that he sees gratitude and obligation as symbolic capital, available as symbolic in the practical sphere only because of the repression of the quid pro quo aspect of the interaction.

But who will give thee that grace to beginne?"—imply? Herbert's dedication to *The Temple* makes this paradox vivid and makes vivid its Shakespearean resonance, since it recalls the beginning of *King Lear*:

> Lord, my first fruits present themselves to thee;
> Yet not mine neither: for from thee they came,
> And must return. Accept of them and me,
> And make us strive, who shall sing best thy name.
> Turn their eyes hither, who shall make a gain:
> Theirs, who shall hurt themselves or me, refrain.

Much could be made of the ambivalence of obligation and of the competition to return the richest gifts.[22] Even the enjambment between lines two and three carries the sense that receiving a gift is never final. "From thee they came" seems to come to a colon, but there is another verb for the subject "they": "and must return." No doubt this formula echoes (and tries to mitigate) Genesis, where Adam's eating of the fruit that does not belong to him leads to the judgment: "Cursed is the ground for thy sake; in sorrow shalt thou eat of it all the days of thy life. Thorns and thistles shall it bring forth to thee; and thou shalt eat of the herb of the field. In the sweat of thy face shalt thou eat bread, till thou return unto the ground; for out of it wast thou taken: for dust thou art, and unto dust thou shalt return" (3:17–19).

The resentment that the structure of endless debt imposes is similar to Adam's deep resentment as well, as though he never acceded to the benefit that now has become an endless burden:

> Did I request thee, Maker, from my Clay
> To mould me Man, did I solicit thee
> From darkness to promote me, or here place
> In this delicious Garden? as my Will
> Concurr'd not to my being, it were but right
> And equal to reduce me to my dust,
> Desirous to resign, and render back
> All I receiv'd, unable to perform
> Thy terms too hard, by which I was to hold
> The good I sought not. To the loss of that,
> Sufficient penalty, why hast thou added
> The sense of endless woes?
>   (*Paradise Lost*, 10.743–54).

22. Michael Schoenfeldt writes well on the ambiguities of this dedication in "Submission and Assertion: The 'Double Motion' of Herbert's 'Dedication,'" *John Donne Journal* 2:2 (1983), 39–49, and "'Respective Boldnesse': Herbert and the Art of Submission" in

Where Herbert desires to give up all responsibility for the grace that is so encompassing as to be the source of his gratitude for the free gift of grace, Milton is intent on a conception of character that includes freedom; but with that freedom necessarily goes an endless, because free, obligation to the source of that freedom. And freedom, as God points out, means only the freedom to feel this obligation; not to feel it is to be an ingrate:

> So will fall
> Hee and his faithless Progeny: whose fault?
> Whose but his own? ingrate, he had of mee
> All he could have; I made him just and right,
> Sufficient to have stood, though free to fall.
> Such I created all th'Ethereal Powers
> And Spirits, both them who stood and them who fail'd;
> Freely they stood who stood, and fell who fell.
> Not free, what proof could they have giv'n sincere
> Of true allegiance, constant Faith or Love,
> Where only what they needs must do, appear'd,
> Not what they would? what praise could they receive?
> What pleasure I from such obedience paid,
> When Will and Reason (Reason is also choice)
> Useless and vain, of freedom both despoil'd,
> Made passive both, had serv'd necessity,
> Not mee.
>
> (3.95–111)[23]

Freedom and reason here have the role that power has in Shakespeare: a faculty created elsewhere that nevertheless has as part of its creation the status of self-origination. Thus Adam rebukes himself in book 10 by imagining that had he been free to decide his own creation he would have done so, and thus he cannot see his own freedom as something he had not consented to: "to say truth, too late / I thus contest; then should have been refus'd / Those terms whatever, when they were proposed" (10.755–57). Of course there is a bitter irony here. Had he refused the terms he would have died—been uncreated—and what he complains of now is that he must die. So the terms are already forced upon anyone able to consider them—anyone who exists. But the point is that Adam did not feel this situation as a

---

A Fine Tuning: Studies of the Religious Poetry of Herbert and Milton, ed. Mary Maleski (Binghamton, N.Y., Medieval and Renaissance Texts and Studies, 1989), pp. 77–94.
23. For more on the idea of passivity in this passage, see chapter 1 and Rutherford's explanation of compatibilist Lutheran passivity. I do not think it unlikely that Milton's scorn for Rutherford is also behind this speech.

trap then; it would only have been unfair had he perceived it as unfair. He is free to accept, though not free to reject, and the odd status of this ambiguous freedom is a perfect emblem of how the capacity for self-origination can originate outside of the self.

Mauss's systematic anthropological study of the system of gift exchange confirms the ubiquity and strictness of Hobbes's fourth law in human societies. As for Shakespeare in Sonnet 94, for Mauss, too, power can take the form of expenditure imitative of the divine generosity of being, the form of what might be called imitative expenditure. His great essay on the gift arises from observations about the nature of contract and obligation in prejuridical society:

> In the economies and legal systems which precede our own, there is no real evidence for the simple exchange of goods, of wealth, and of products through a market occuring between individuals. . . . These prestations and counter-prestations take place rather in a voluntary form, through presents, through gifts, although they are at bottom rigorously obligatory, on pain of war, public or private. (*Sociologie*, pp. 150–51)[24]

To give a gift, in the societies Mauss is studying, is to oblige the recipient to give a gift in return. The structure of this relationship (by no means a necessarily binary one: gifts can circulate through extraordinarily intricate networks) is self-amplifying. To give someone a gift is to utter a challenge, and the recipient can meet that challenge only through something more than simple reciprocation. He or she must outgo the original gift. So Timon is described by two of his parasites:

> *1 Lord*:   [Come], shall we in
>   And taste Lord Timon's bounty? he outgoes
>   The very heart of kindness.
> *2 Lord*:   He pours it out: Plutus, the god of gold,
>   Is but his steward. No meed but he repays
>   Sevenfold above itself; no gift to him
>   But breeds the giver a return exceeding
>   All use of quittance.
>
>   (1.i.272–80)

In 1897 Franz Boas understood Kwakiutl gifts and the return of greater gifts as a version of an ecomonic structure based on lending out at interest. But, as Pierre Bourdieu tirelessly reiterates, the psy-

---

24. Fumerton implies too strongly that gifts remove the threat of war. That threat always haunts gift exchange.

chological manifestation of this functional system does not reduce to
the practice of lending at interest: the value of the gift depends on its
not being given with any hint of ulterior motives.[25] (Thus Mauss
quotes countless beautiful formulae in which the gift giver deprecates
the value of the gift, lest it should appear that he or she is angling
after credit for it, in all senses of the term.)

People compete to outdo each other in the gifts they make each
other; this generosity is agonistic because it is also a struggle to get the
upper hand in the balance of obligation. The practice of gift giving
undergirds a power structure in which the powerful lay the less powerful under an obligation they cannot fully repay.[26] Social dominance
consists in a general power to place others under obligation. Timon's
desire for such dominance is inextricable from his generosity, because
generosity and dominance name the same thing. A nearly sticho-
mythic interchange makes this clear. Ventidius's messenger reports his
master's imprisonment for debt:

> *Timon*:   . . . I'll pay the debt and free him.
> *Messenger*:   Your lordship ever binds him.
>   (1.i.103–4)

It is clear that some unproductive generosity is at work in these acts
of obligation (of rendering the beneficiary obliged); the powerful do
not get back all that they give. Thus Timon proclaims to the freed
Ventidius: "I gave it freely ever, and there's none / Can truly say he
gives if he receives" (I.ii.10–11); this anticipates Mauss's insight about
the more radical case of the spectacular destruction of gifts called the
potlatch: "In a certain number of cases, destruction replaces the process of giving and receiving, in order that the benefactor might not
appear to desire a return" (*Sociologie*, p. 201). Indeed this non-
reciprocity is the foundation of the benefactors' power. At the same
time, it would appear that they do get a fair, or even generous, return
in the form not of goods but of prerogative.

Gift giving, of course, is only the form taken by something we
recognize as exchange, and in all eras the powerful sometimes buy
people's obligation rather than their goods. But this trade in obliga-

25. The necessity of a theory of practice, and not simply a functional theory of laws
describing practice, is the polemical thrust of *Outline of a Theory of Practice*. Descriptive
laws are fine, Bourdieu argues, but they are not the immediate causes of practice.
Bourdieu derives his critique of a certain tendency in structuralism from Wittgenstein's
meditations on rule following, in *Philosophical Investigations*.

26. For an example of the ideal of an unreturnable gift important to my argument
below, see Mauss, *Sociologie*, p. 212 n.2.

tion can become interestingly phantom when gifts take on pure gift-exchange value without any use value at all. The Kwakiutl traded copper coins that had no use except as gifts—conferrals, that is, of (tokens of) obligation, which were eventually returned; obligation then develops and circulates with no precipitate in use value. Just as the promise made by generality promises only itself, the token of obligation stands for the obligation to return that token; in such a situation, seemingly clear-cut distinctions between giving and taking come undone. This situation is, in fact, ubiquitous. What counts is not the objects or commodities that are traded, but the display of generosity. For this display, the objects are only props, but they only work as props if they are costly and represent a great deal of exchange value despite the fact that they have no use value (except, of course, their usefulness in having exchange value).[27]

Expenditure squanders wealth in conspicuous consumption functionally indistinguishable from conspicuous generosity. What most fascinated Bataille in Mauss's essay was the guise that the attempt to oblige took on among the tribes of the Northwest territories of North America, the radical institution of the potlatch. In this spectacular destruction of wealth, expenditure takes on its most unproductive form and seems least like a disguised form of simple exchange. Mauss's description of the potlatch adumbrates Bloom's theory of the ambivalence of influence, where poems also engage in an agonistic struggle over which poem is source and which beneficiary—a priority whose only reward is the sense of public strength it consists in. Mauss's description enables a correlation between Bloom's theory of poetic struggles for power and the new historicism's insights into the place that carnival and spectacle have in the production of the illusion of power (of power as illusion):[28]

> "Potlatch" basically means "nourishment" or "consumption." Those very rich tribes that live in the Islands or between the Rockies and the coast pass their winter in perpetual feasting: banquets, fora and markets,

27. Marx rejected the notion that the use value of a commodity, e.g., gold, could fundamentally inhere in its exchange value; he argued that the choice of medium of exchange is limited to commodities already being exchanged. This may be true at the moment that the choice is being made; but after that the commodity serving as money will have a special status, and its exchange value will be the primary component of its use value.

28. See, for example, Mikhail Bakhtin, *The Dialogic Imagination: Four Essays*, trans. Michael Holquist (Austin: University of Texas Press, 1981); Orgel, *Illusion of Power*; Greenblatt, *Renaissance Self-Fashioning* and *Shakespearean Negotiations*; Pye, *Regal Phantasm*; and Leonard Tennenhouse, *Power on Display: The Politics of Shakespeare's Genres* (New York: Methuen, 1986).

which are at the same time the solomn assembly of the tribe. The tribe is ranged according to its hierarchical fellowships, its secret societies, often indistinguishable from the first and from the clans; and everything, clans, marriages, initiations, shamanistic and cultic sessions dedicated to the gods, the totems, or the collective or individual ancestors of the clan, everything mingles into an inextricable network of rites, of juridical and economic prestations, of fixations of political ranks in the society of men, in the tribe, and in the confederations of tribes, and even internationally. But what is remarkable in these tribes is the principle of rivalry and of antagonism which dominates all these practices. They go so far as battle, as the killing of the chiefs and nobles who thus come to grips with each other. And on the other hand they go so far as the purely sumptuary destruction of the riches accumulated to eclipse the rival but associated chief (commonly the grand-father, father-in-law or son-in-law). . . . [There is] on the part of the chief a highly marked agonistic attitude. It is essentially usurious and sumptuary. (*Sociologie*, pp. 152–53)

Here expenditure really is unproductive, since the obligations it creates do not stem from anything that could be called an exchange. Although from a long perspective the clan "profits" from this agonistic mechanism in that it settles the hierarchy (p. 153), the mechanism itself seems a deeply unproductive way to secure that profit, and the system as a whole is clearly wasting goods. As for Bloom, the agon in the family romance (against "grandfather, father-in-law, or son-in-law") takes the form of a contest in generosity. This is generosity that no one wants to benefit from, an influx (or influence) that causes anxiety. That generosity should take the form of the destruction of goods indicates how utterly involuntary, unbargained for, is the status of the person on whom it imposes obligation. That person gets no material benefit in return for being obliged. It is the spectacle of generosity, the limiting case of benefaction—benefaction without an object—that creates power, the spectacle and not the generosity itself, which is useless and empty. But this spectacle gains power only to the extent that it is precisely not the purchase of power. This is why, Mauss and Bataille argue, the potlatch in the Pacific Northwest often took the form of throwing money into the ocean.[29] The intent was

29. It's just conceivable that a knowledge of this sort of practice among North American Indians can solve the Iudean/Indian crux in *Othello*, where Othello says of himself that he "Like the base [Indian]) threw a pearl away / Richer than all his tribe" (V.ii.347–48). Forms of ostensive gift giving were widespread among the North American Indians (the expectation of return is probably what leads to the later term "Indian giver"), and it is possible that Shakespeare had heard or read a potlatch narrative. As James Boswell *fils* points out (*Boswell's Malone* [New York: AMS, 1966], 9:495), a slightly later work is relevant here: William Habington's sonnet "To Castara Weeping" (1634). Bos-

not, as in the similar Venetian ritual, to oblige the grace of the sea but to imitate the spectacular generosity that gives utterly without return.[30] Timon is described in almost these marine terms when one character asks whether he is "Still in motion / Of raging waste?" Foucault will develop Bataille's account of power as spectacle and will focus on the carnivalesque as one of its modes. But it is useful, especially with regard to Shakespeare, to look specifically at the origin of spectacle in mimetic generosity—in spending, as nature or being spends, without return.

This mimesis of natural generosity is a mode of power (of the display of power) in Shakespeare. True, the young man addressed in "They that have power" is praised (with some bitterness) for the fact that he can "husband nature's riches from expense," not for any sumptuary destruction or expense of spirit. But that poem, I have argued, means to paralyze its addressee, not valorize him. He is not to

---

well quotes only part of the following passage; what he doesn't quote helps suggest the possibility that something close to the potlatch was known to Europeans by then:

> *Castara!* O you are too prodigall
> Oth'treasure of your teares; which thus let fall
> Make no returne. . .
> So the unskilfull Indian those bright jems,
> Which might adde majestie to Diadems,
> 'Mong the waves scatters, as if he would store
> The thanklesse Sea, to make our Empire poore.
> (*Castara* (*1634–40*), ed. Edward Archer
> [London: English Reprints, 1870], p. 67)

Castara as a whole alludes to Shakespeare with some frequency, so Habington at least may think that Shakespeare is thinking of something with some currency: the Indian who demonstrates his own powers to impoverish his rivals by destroying the wealth that they covet, despite the fact that this destructive potlatch is a gift that makes no return. This would explain why the Indian is base in *Othello*. He throws the pearl away out of self-destructive defiance, which is what Othello has done. The notoriously unreliable Steevens claims to recall dimly an Elizabethan story of a Venetian Jew casting a pearl into the sea to defy those who could not or would not buy it from him (*Othello: A New Variorum Edition*, ed. H. H. Furness [New York: Dover, 1963], pp. 328–29), but this sounds untrue to the English sense of Jewish avarice (as Furness points out), and I speculate that it is a misremembering of a story about a potlatch. Stanley Cavell's reading of *Othello* as about Othello's skeptical refusal to acknowledge Desdemona's existence as an other ("Othello and the Stake of the Other," in his *Disowning Knowledge in Six Plays of Shakespeare* [New York: Cambridge University Press, 1987], pp. 125–42) could lend support here: by destroying Desdemona Othello asserts his power over her as power over an object (and not a human being), but this is what makes him base and what leads him to the ultimate act of self-objectifying self-destruction that he is about to perform.

30. See Bataille, *Oeuvres*, 1:310. This is contrary to Sahlins's view; for him gifts to nature expect a return from nature. On a deeper level, as Bourdieu suggests, Sahlins is probably right, but the manifest practice of destructive expenditure cannot maintain its good faith if it expects reciprocity from elsewhere, including the gods.

use the power that he has. Power in that poem means a kind of ownership of its potential victims. This ownership requires preservation and not only a spendthrift charisma. This is the ambiguity between power as possession and power as essence. An equivocation such as the sonnet implies enables the scheme whereby for the young man to use his power would be for him to use it up, to lose ownership by displaying power. For this reason the poem is intent on imagining the young man's power not as generosity but as thrift, and for this reason it is intent on recommending thrift to him. His power is self-discrepant, since either he doesn't use it or he uses and loses it. Display of self-sufficiency becomes imagined in the poem as display of self-containment, a containment in turn made to appear as paralysis.

The larger issue here is the relationship between having and being, between having riches (and so being the beneficiary of their source) and being wealth—being their source. The line "They rightly do inherit heaven's graces" mediates this relationship. To inherit means to be the beneficiary. But it also means to replace the benefactor (who, once dead, can no longer represent self-coincident generosity), to become, like him, source and not only beneficiary. And to inherit *rightly* means to *be* oneself in an ontologically privileged relation to the riches that one comes to possess, not to be alienated from them.[31]

This doubleness of relation to the generosity of being, used in the sonnet against the young man, haunts Shakespeare's work. In the plays it tends to appear under the form of the "political theology," as Ernst Kantorowicz calls it, of the king's two bodies.[32] Kantorowicz's

31. Compare France's line in *King Lear* about Cordelia: "She is herself a dowry." Still, France is the beneficiary here, and Cordelia is only secondarily the beneficiary of her own status as wealth, through France's acceptance of her. Lynda E. Boose cites this line in her analysis of the relation between the father and the bride in Shakespeare's plays, an analysis she couches in the terms Levi-Strauss derives from Mauss's account of gift exchange. Boose suggests that it is Cordelia's gain to be regarded as wealth ("Father and Bride," p. 333). In this Boose differs from the slightly later work of critics such as Eve Sedgwick and Lars Engel (who applies Sedgwick's ideas to *The Merchant of Venice*), as when Boose writes of the father giving away the bride: "While at first glance the church ceremony might seem only to dramatize the transfer of a passive female object from one male to another, in reality it ritualizes the community's coercion, not of the bride, but of her father. Ultimately, it is he who must pay the true 'bride price' at the altar and, by doing so, become the displaced and dispossessed actor" (p. 341). I think the difference is one of emphasis. The question is what the father is getting out of the ritual; Boose agrees that he gets a displaced sexual thrill (read by Boose as incest, where Sedgwick sees it as homoeroticism between father and son-in-law; see Boose, p. 327). Boose reads Sonnet 129 ("Th'expense of spirit") as expressing precisely the equivalence between expenditure of a Maussian sort and sexuality (p. 344 n. 11).

32. See his *The King's Two Bodies: A Study in Medieval Political Theology* (Princeton, N.J.: Princeton University Press, 1957).

reading of *Richard II* in these terms is exemplary and convincing: as a man, with a human body, Richard turns out to be vulnerable to every need, and to be utterly mortal; and his tragedy consists in his own (mistaken) belief that his superbody, the mystical body politic of the king as a corporation sole, would be inseparable from his body natural. But just as Bullingbrook takes possession of Richard's body natural, he also takes possession of that superbody, and he takes possession of it precisely by becoming it.

What interests me in the sonnet, however, is the way this doubleness instantiates an ambiguity that Kantorowicz also expounds, in the terms of power and kingship, in his analysis of the much earlier but still theologically relevant work of the Norman Anonymous. Shakespeare (along with Sidney and Spenser) may be thought of as importing certain theological paradoxes to the erotic sphere. The Anonymous's description of the "twin person" that a king constitutes fits also with the status of the young man imagined in Sonnet 94:

> We thus have to recognize [in the king] a *twin person,* one descending from nature, the other from grace[,] . . . one through which, by the condition of nature, he conformed with other men: another through which, by the eminence of [his] deification and by the power of the sacrament [of consecration], he excelled all others. Concerning one personality, he was, by nature, an individual man: concerning his other personality, he was, by grace, a *Christus,* that is a God-man.[33]

This is nearly a description of the young man, who is genuinely charismatic but whose charisma comes from the grace of heaven. As for Shakespeare, for the Anonymous this by no means implies that such grace is merely adventitious. On the one hand, although kings were consecrated and so deified "shadows" and "imitators" of Christ, they differed from him as to the source of their divinity: "Christ was King and *Christus* by his very nature, whereas his deputy on earth was king and *christus* by grace only" (Kantorowicz, *Two Bodies,* p. 47). But this opposition between nature and grace could also be undone. Kantorowicz continues:

> The antithesis served the Anonymous, it is true, to observe very strictly the inherent difference between the God and the king; but it served him also to blur that line of distinction, and to show where the difference between "God by nature" and "god by grace" ended; that is in the case of

33. Quoted in ibid., p. 46.

potestas, of power. Essence and substance of power are claimed to be equal in both God and king, no matter whether that power be owned by nature or only acquired by grace. (P. 48)[34]

Power, then, becomes a mediating or transferential term. To exercise power would mean to be more than a recipient, because in the case of power, essence and substance are the same. Because power is finally purely functional and because its sphere is purely instrumental, the question of its original provenance loses its meaning. Rather, that question becomes a question of legitimacy, not a question of status. Nature (or God) is nothing but power (the power to originate). To have power is to be like nature, or like God: "He is a god and knows / What is most right," says Cleopatra of the conquering Caesar (*Antony and Cleopatra*, III.xiii.60–61). Whoever *has* power *is* powerful.

This quality of power can undo the difference between king and Christ, and it can undo that difference through its very invocation. Kantorowicz continues his exposition of the Norman Anonymous by describing just this undoing of difference: "The king, otherwise an individual man, is *in officio* the type and image of the Anointed in heaven and therewith of God" (*Two Bodies*, p. 48). And thus it turns out that he is like Christ, because like Christ he is a twin being. That the king should be not like Christ is the way that he is like Christ, at least under the sign of power. He is like the twinned Christ in that he is both like Christ and unlike him. Thus the king, "the anointed by grace, parallels as a *gemina persona* the two-natured Christ" (ibid., p. 49).

The language that the Anonymous uses in his analyses is typological. The king is typologically related to Christ. At once type and antitype, he "in spiritu et Christus et deus est, et in officio figura et imago Christi et Dei est."[35] It is interesting that this typological analysis should lead to ontological consequences. Typology shades into ontology when the type represents (by foreshadowing) an antitype who is similarly an essentially representational being, and not only a representational being but a typological one. Although it is *in officio* that the king is the image of Christ, this makes him like Christ. The distinction between office and nature in the person of the king mir-

---

34. In my analyses I prefer to render the meaning of Kantorowicz's distinction between "owning by nature" and "acquiring by grace" in terms that oppose being to possessing rather than describe two kinds of ownership.

35. Quoted in ibid., p. 56n. (The king is "in spirit *Christus et Deus*; and in his office he acts as antitype and image of Christ and God" [modification of Kantorowicz's translation].)

rors the two natures of Christ. This confers upon the office an on-tological status. Indeed, according to the Anonymous, the king im-ages the divine office of Christ (while the priest images his human office) so that the king's office has the status of a being. Kantorowicz's summary makes the shading of typology into ontology clear. He writes that the Anonymous's focus

> on the idea *Rex imago Christi* . . . makes it evident that the analogy pre-vailing between the God-man and his image should not be sought in a functional distinction between "office" and "man." For it would be diffi-cult, nay, impossible, to interpret the divine nature of Christ as an "of-fice," since the divine nature is his "Being." And the Anonymous likewise visualizes in his king two different forms of "being": one natural or individual, and the other consecrated or (as the author calls it) deified and apotheosized. In short, the Norman author's vision of the king as a *persona geminata* is ontological and, as an effluence of a sacramental and liturgical action performed at the altar, it is liturgical as well. His vision is, on the whole, more closely related to the liturgy, to the holy action which is image and reality at the same time, than to the distinction of functional capacities and constitutional competencies, or to the concepts of office and dignity as opposed to man. (P. 59)

To put it schematically: analysis of a representational relationship to an ontological object whose very essence is representational will either undo all ontological security (the program of deconstruction, when it elaborates a "mise-en-abîme") or will confer that security and priority even upon representations of the primordial, divine representation.[36] Ontology might turn out to be simply typological; alternately, typol-ogy may lead to an unassailable ontological position. As I argued about Herbert, the latter route is the avenue explored by many of the Reformers, for whom the granting of grace will have ontological con-sequences. Herbert's "Aaron" could be taken as the liturgical version of the undoing of the difference between being and seeing, an undo-ing that subsumes them both under the rubric of being and not the deconstructive rubric of seeming. "Thus are true Aarons drest," he writes, and the pluralizing of the proper name indicates how it refers both to the individual "Poore priest" and to Aaron himself (both particular and general), both of whom merge in the last line "Come people; Aaron's drest."

36. In fractal geometry this is known as self-similarity, and its stability has been proved. This proof may pose a challenge to deconstruction, on its own uneven terrain.

Eternity More Short Than Waste or Ruining

> . . . time was money in those days. . . .
>   He was "in his prime"
> At three score ten. But money was not time.
>   —James Merrill, "The Broken Home"

On this theory of typology's approach to ontology, the beneficiary's grace and the benefactor's being could become synonymous through their telescoped and congruent structure. But Shakespeare does not share this theory. In Shakespeare, power is indeed equivalent to being. By definition, power is the source of its own capacity to manifest itself. It has the inalienable self-coincidence of being, unlike humans, whose every possession is alienable. Power's generosity comes from itself. And yet, as Sonnet 94 makes clear, limitless power is not so limitless after all. Seasonal lilies, not eternal stones, come to emblematize natural self-coincidence. Power is lost in its own exercise and can only be maintained at the cost of paralysis, so that what is maintained is not really power. In Shakespeare, the exercise of power consists in often ritualized, often quasi-liturgical displays of generosity, but these displays use up the substance that makes power possible. Power in Shakespeare's plays tends always to its own undoing. This is one of Timon's bitterest discoveries, issuing in his misanthropic recommendation to the gods: "For your own gifts, make yourselves prais'd; but reserve still to give, lest your deities be despis'd" (iii.vi.71–73).

It seems inevitable to think that the specter of expenditure and dissipation broods over Shakespeare's plays as the dangerous heart of power. I call this manifestation of power dangerous particularly because so many of the plays stage the clash between an older generation still given to the ideology of the gift and a newer generation intent on accumulation and not generosity. If Sonnet 94 is written from the point of view of one of the ambivalent beneficiaries of the idle generosity of narcissistic self-sufficiency, part of that ambivalence consists precisely in the young man's being a typically Shakespearean young man, or new man, and so husbanding his riches from expense.[37] But many of Shakespeare's greatest plays are written from

37. Something like this refusal of the ambiguities of the gift underlies the precisarian language of Claudio's cadishness in *Much Ado About Nothing* when he spurns Hero:

> *Claudio:*   Father, by your leave,
> Will you with free and unconstrained soul
> Give me this maid, your daughter?

the opposite perspective of Sonnet 94 and describe the experience of the end of generosity from the viewpoint of the putative source of being, not only from that of its beneficiary. One of Shakespeare's greatest achievements—one that corresponds to the dethronement of "his majesty the baby," the narcissist in every person—is the depiction of the adventures of power and the loss of power from the perspective of the source of that power. The difficulty of this achievement consists partly in the sense that there should be no such perspective because, to put it schematically, the narcissist is more an object of the gaze of other people than himself or herself a gazer. Narcissus gives up what Freud calls primary narcissism the moment he begins gazing, even at his own reflection.

Richard, in *Richard II*, governs spectacularly—governs, that is, through the spectacle he both embodies and controls. That spectacle is the almost ritualistic theater of wastefulness. The trajectory of the play is one in which wastefulness returns to destroy its own, as in Richard's astonishing lapidary formula: "I wasted time, and now doth time waste me" (v.v.49). While Richard's profligacy has long been deplored, it is simply the obverse of his power.[38] Under the aegis of the gift, wasting time is one of the marks of power, and not of feckless-ness.[39] Richard can temporize by wasting Gaunt's and Bullingbrook's

---

> *Leonato:* As freely, son, as God did give her me.
> *Claudio:* And what have I to give you back whose worth
>   May counterpoise this rich and precious gift?
> *Don Pedro:* Nothing, unless you render her again.
> *Claudio:* Sweet Prince, you learn me noble thankfulness.
>   There, Leonato, take her back again. (IV.i.23–31)

Macbeth is also about the opposition between two different ideologies of value. Malcolm's famous description of the rebel Cawdor's execution praises Cawdor for returning to the ideology of the gift: "He died / As one that had been studied in his death, / To throw away the dearest thing he ow'd, / As 'twere a careless trifle" (I.iv.8–11). Macbeth himself is interested in accumulation, and violates the laws of hospitality so clearly linked in the play to the gift economy. That link is made in the compliments of greeting that Duncan and Lady Macbeth make when Duncan graciously apologizes for the obligation that his love confers on those he loves, and Lady Macbeth replies that nothing she can return will make up for the honor of Duncan's presence (I.vi.10–18). Shakespeare intensifies our shock at the violation of the laws of hospitality when the doomed Banquo (also fated to be killed by the host who has invited him to a feast) brings Duncan's last gift to Macbeth: "the King's a-bed. / He hath been in unusual pleasure, and / Sent forth great largess to your offices. / This diamond he greets your wife withal, / By the name of most kind hostess, and shut up / In measureless content" (II.i.12–17).

38. In *Henry V* the Chorus will praise Hal for the way "A largess universal, like the sun, / His liberal eye doth give to every one" (IV.prologue.43–44); unlike Richard's, though, Hal's largess does indeed seem inexhaustible.

39. This is one of the major sociological insights of Thorstein Veblen's *Theory of the Leisure Class*, an insight central as well to the work of Bourdieu and Baudrillard. It

time because he can also afford (he thinks) to waste his own time, and prodigal as he is, Richard takes no thought of the inevitability of Bullingbrook's return from banishment, coupled with his inevitably intensified resentment. Under the new dispensation that Bullingbrook represents, however, time is money, or at least a measure and a goad to efficiency.

Nevertheless, Richard's own ability to wield power is not inconsiderable. He stages his spectacles with nearly as much canniness as Bullingbrook does his own public appearances (or as Richard III does).[40] The opening scenes can be read as a contest, a kind of chess game, between Richard and Bullingbrook for the central position on the stage of power. Richard is intent on playing Mowbray and Henry against each other in order to maintain a triangulated preeminence:

> call them to our presence; face to face,
> And frowning brow to brow, ourselves will hear
> The accuser and the accused freely speak.
>
> (I.i.15–17)

The enjambment here is significant. We expect Richard to frown at these two troublemakers, but it turns out that he will watch them frown at each other,[41] at the apex of the triangle of which they form the stable base. Each confronts the other, and so neither can confront Richard. This is a scenario he encourages, and the emblem for this insistent triangulation could be his interruption of the combat that would destroy the triangle. Through that combat the shrewd Henry seeks (or so it seems to Richard) to collapse the triangle whose apex is the king, in order to be left with a binary opposition: first between himself and Mowbray, then (after Mowbray's presumed defeat) be-

---

might be added in illustration that one impressive way that Achilles manifests his power in *The Iliad* is by willingly wasting prodigious amounts of time in inglorious fashion, despite the fact that he knows that his own life will be short.

40. John D. Cox compares and contrasts Richard III with Hal; he sees both of them as theatrical but describes Hal as managing an opacity that Richard III does not. That opacity, I think, is also something Bullingbrook manages. See *Shakespeare and the Dramaturgy of Power* (Princeton, N.J.: Princeton University Press, 1989) p. 109. My reading here takes issue in many ways with David Kastan's important article "Proud Majesty." Although I basically agree with Kastan's analysis of Bullingbrook I disagree that Richard is unable to manage the theatrical devices of power.

41. Harry Berger, Jr., makes a similar point in his article "Psychoanalyzing the Shakespearean Text: The First Three Scenes of the *Henriad*" in *Shakespeare and the Question of Theory*, p. 226. I agree also with his sense in *Imaginary Audition: Shakespeare on Stage and Page* (Berkeley: University of California Press, 1989) of Richard's slyly extravagant self-destructive theatricality, though I don't share his feeling that Richard outplays Henry.

tween himself and Richard. (And Bullingbrook knows that even a victory unlikely as it would be for Mowbray would put the king in an awkward situation, since Mowbray would call him to account for the mortal danger he has incurred on Richard's behalf and without Richard's protection, in a battle where the odds are against him.) Bullingbrook knows (and knows that Richard knows) that Richard cannot win if the combat goes on.

By stopping the combat Richard attempts to skirt these potential binary oppositions. He stages the triangular pomp of ritual preparation to which he is central (another spectacle of kingship), but he avoids the spectacle of combat from which he would be absent and in which Bullingbrook would become the cynosure. The marshal directs everyone's attention: "Sound, trumpets, and set forward, combatants. / Stay, the King hath thrown his warder down" (1.iii.117–18). At the very moment when he would become backgrounded,[42] Richard establishes himself once more as the spectacular center of attention.[43] Far from showing Richard's vacillation and uncertainty, this scene exemplifies his exercise of power. The way Richard continues to command attention is not only spectacular, it is also shrewd. Richard's is not a thoughtlessly self-destructive charisma. Like Bullingbrook he belongs to a new generation that has contempt for the sacralizing beliefs of the generation of their uncles, even as they make use of its rhetoric whenever convenient. But Richard's contempt is hidden, and he mimes (and exaggerates) the sacred but wasteful prodigality people accuse him of as a way of maintaining power through the spectacle of expenditure. But, as Mauss shows, the imitation of expenditure (in the return of the gift or in the competition associated with potlatch) necessarily manifests itself only as expenditure. Richard may not entirely believe in the divinity of expenditure, but his expenditure must be no less real for that. Here, in effect, Richard displays, cannily but prodigally, his ability to exercise a canny prodigality even with the

42. See Graham Holderness, *Shakespeare: The Play of History* (Iowa City: University of Iowa Press, 1988): "Technically the king's authority over the legal procedure is absolute: it is his prerogative to grant or deny combat, and his right to terminate the combat at his own inclination. But the very nature of the feudal institution of judicial combat, if permitted to run its course, deprives the king of any real authority or control. . . . The true conflict fought out at Coventry on St. Lambert's Day is not, then, a trial of arms between Bolingbroke and Mowbray, but a trial of strength between two agonistic ideologies, absolutist and feudal" (pp. 28–32).

43. See Scott McMillin, "Shakespeare's *Richard II*: Eyes of Sorrow, Eyes of Desire," *Shakespeare Quarterly* 35 (1984), 43. This would also occur in most stagings of the play. The marshal's speech must redirect the attention of the theater audience, as well as the attention of the audience at the combat, to Richard.

prodigal theatricality he lives by (such as the trial by combat), a generosity bordering on wastefulness of the power of theatrical ritual.

This effect is plotted, not spontaneous, and the plot turns on another game of generosity. It soon emerges that, tricked in his expectations, Gaunt has recommended the sentence of banishment against
both Mowbray and his son Bullingbrook. His analysis of his motivations indicates that he expected his own generosity to be met with an
answering generosity on Richard's part: "Alas, I look'd when some of
you should say / I was too strict to make mine own away" (I.iii.243–
44). What he calls strictness is also a kind of expenditure, a calculated
willingness to engage in sacrifice: he's thinking of Abraham and Isaac.
He miscalculates, however, in thinking that Richard will provide the
ram to save him from the sacrifice of his son. He expects Richard also
to be generous. That Richard is not comes as a shock. (Indeed,
Richard's laconic "Thy son is banish'd upon good advice, / Whereto
thy tongue a party-verdict gave" [I.iii.233–34] anticipates Bullingbrook's much pithier mode of power, as when he remarks to Richard
"I thought you had been willing to resign" [IV.i.190].) Richard, however, is even here unwilling completely to give up the power associable
with generosity.

Having extracted from Gaunt what he needs, Richard attempts to
efface his refusal of an answering generosity, and displays a counterfeit of the generosity that Gaunt had expected from him before. He
takes great care to tell Mowbray that he cannot possibly go back upon
a sentence once pronounced: "After our sentence plaining comes too
late" (I.iii.175); but then he shrewdly squanders that authority to temper Bullingbrook's sentence. Indeed, this display is particularly important because it occasions a colloquy thematizing the correlation
between authority and expenditure:

> *Richard:*   Uncle, even in the glasses of thine eyes
>   I see thy grieved heart. Thy sad aspect
>   Hath from the number of his banish'd years
>   Pluck'd four away. Six frozen winters spent,
>   Return with welcome home from banishment.
> *Bullingbrook:*   How long a time lies in one little word!
>   Four lagging winters and four wanton springs
>   End in a word: such is the breath of kings.
> *Gaunt:*   I thank my liege that in regard of me
>   He shortens four years of my son's exile,
>   But little vantage shall I reap thereby;
>   For ere the six years that he hath to spend
>   Can change their moons and bring their times about,

> My oil-dried lamp and time-bewasted light
> Shall be extinct with age and endless [night];
> My inch of taper will be burnt and done,
> And blindfold Death not let me see my son.
> *Richard:*   Why, uncle, thou hast many years to live.
> *Gaunt:*   But not a minute, King, that thou canst give.
> Shorten my days thou canst with sullen sorrow,
> And pluck nights from me, but not lend a morrow;
> Thou canst help time to furrow me with age,
> But stop no wrinkle in his pilgrimage;
> Thy word is current with him for my death,
> But dead, thy kingdom cannot buy my breath.
>   (I.iii.208–32)

Richard manifests his power through his pronouncements of exile in two ways. On the one hand, he displays an imperial efficiency—the efficiency of the fiat that can waste the irrecuperable time of other people simply by pronouncing the command (and Lear too will banish Kent with just this magisterial offhandedness); on the other hand, it is just this apparent irrecuperability that is supposed to throw a magical light on the partial reversal of the sentence he pronounced, a reversal that is meant to appear to be an act of stunning and almost insouciant generosity. At least Richard wishes it to be understood as insouciant when, having wasted time, he unwastes it again just as easily. In fact, both these displays of power represent the same thing. Richard shows himself spectacularly liberal with everything, and by doing so he asserts his ownership of everything. What one can waste, one has power over. He wastes his subjects' time, and so he has power over their most intimate possessions. But, as is evident in Bullingbrook's and Gaunt's chafing at his magnaminity and not at the original sentence, he wastes his own authority as well—the authority of his fiat. The question at this point of the play is whether Richard's squandering of authority, through his display of all the power he has, increases that authority or decreases it, uses it up (as the young man is liable to use it up in Sonnet 94).

Of course Henry is shrewder still than Richard, and he takes care to display his own gracious stoicism even as he denies that Richard is the source of the sunlike generosity he will several times be associated with:

> This must my comfort be,
> That sun that warms you here shall shine on me,

And those his golden beams to you here lent
Shall point on me and gild my banishment.
(I.iii.144–47)

He takes care too to display the oppression that his magnanimity
labors under: six winters will pass quickly "to men in joy, but grief
makes one hour ten" (I.iii.261). Bullingbrook's rhetoric lengthens
time, stretches it out, as Richard cannot. His own and his father's
language re-image shortening not as the generosity Richard would
see it as ("Thy sad aspect / Hath from the number of his banish'd
years / Pluck'd four away") but as laying hold of what is not his—
Gaunt's life ("Shorten my days thou canst"). Bullingbrook's banishment and the graciousness with which he accepts it lay the king under
an obligation to him, at least in the public eye, and reverse Richard's
attempt to make Henry appear the obligated one. The stable triangular structure has now been undone.

This exchange shows another characteristic of Richard's exercise of
power through expenditure. It only goes one way. His power takes the
form of an ability to dissipate itself, more or less theatrically, but not
an ability to consolidate itself. Power as consolidation will belong to
Henry as it does not belong to Richard.

Richard's theatricality has often been noted, usually under one or
another species of failure to rule adequately. On the other hand, some
recent critics aligned with the new historicism, like Leonard Tennenhouse and David Kastan, argue that it is Bullingbrook who successfully utilizes the theatrical machinery of power in order to stage
his own inheritance. There is much to be said for this view. But I do
not agree with Tennenhouse that Richard eschews theatricality: "In
assuming the authority of blood is absolute, Richard neglects those
displays of political authority which establish the absolute power of the
monarch over the material body of the subject. . . . With a consistency
that suggests he could not do otherwise, Richard avoids those occasions where scenes of violence ordinarily would be staged" (*Power on
Display*, pp. 77–78). Yet Richard is the most theatrically self-expressive
of kings, as Scott McMillin argues very persuasively in terms that
sometimes anticipate mine.[44]

44. Ibid., esp. p. 43. McMillin contrasts theatricality in the play with self-expression.
He sees the tight-lipped Bullingbrook as mastering the effects of theater, and Richard
as losing his command of them. This is true, but I would insist that theatricality and its
dissolution or waste are not opposed; the latter is simply the most extreme form of the
former. I do not think that I am really contradicting him, however.

I agree with Pye that theatricality—Richard's constant self-display—means to and does contribute to the exercise of power. It does so through the mode of expenditure. That Henry, too, exercises power through the theater of expenditure cannot be doubted, but Henry represents the burgeoning capitalist ethic.[45] For him such a

45. Walter Cohen's *Drama of a Nation* is the best account of Shakespeare as deeply concerned with the transition to modern capitalism. (See also Raymond Southall's essay on *Troilus and Cressida* in his *Literature and the Rise of Capitalism* [Norwood, Pa.: Norwood Editions, 1975], pp. 70–85.) Cohen's careful analyses of *The Merchant of Venice* and *King Lear* are of particular importance. In the former he reads Shakespeare as trying to harmonize aristocratic and capitalist ideology; in the latter he reads *King Lear* as a despairing critique of the rising bourgeois ethos and as expressing a forlorn hope that feudalism might be ameliorated (through an informed and enlightened absolutism) where the (neofeudal) capitalism of Goneril, Regan, Cornwall, and Edmund is not. It is of course a commonplace to stress generational distinctions in Shakespeare; I have learned most from the way Cohen and others align these distinctions with economic transitions.

Lawrence Stone's historical account *The Crisis of the Aristocracy: 1558–1641* describes the transition as one in which conspicious consumption played a great part. (Conspicuous consumption is the term Veblen uses to describe the potlatch and its later cousins in Western civilization; see *The Theory of the Leisure Class* [Boston: Houghton Mifflin, 1973], p. 65.) The aristocracy effectively ruined itself by continuing a practice of rivalry based on conspicuous consumption, at the cost of selling its holdings, and giving up its feudal prerogatives. As with Richard, the imperative to wastefulness generally led to a runaway spiral; where generosity had once consolidated power, it now squandered it in rivalries that came to have less and less to do with the real economic life of the kingdom. The aristocracy depended on this economic life to provide the cash that could purchase its unproductive ostentation. Thus the language of Gaunt's complaint about Richard contrasts two modes of economic life in which England's magic abundance is seen as devastated by its being marketed or leased out (II.i.40–60). See Stone, pp. 50, 162–64, 505–86.

One might argue that the sixteenth century saw an almost literalized economic example of generosity or expenditure imitative of its divine source, or at least an example of power turning imitation of the source of benificence into an actual source, since (as Stone argues, pp. 409–16) the Tudors' gifts of land tended to be out of the monastic estates seized by Henry VIII. Of course, Elizabeth became more and more parsimonious, having nothing to spare from the Anglo-Spanish War. But the relevance of this for Shakespeare's career (though not, obviously, for *Richard II*) stems from the contrast between Elizabethan parsimony and Jacobean extravagance that Stone analyzes. Stone writes that Elizabeth's policies effectively led to a change in the economic culture of the court; in an economy of scarcity thrift and corruption took hold, and James's atavistic extravagance no longer made up part of a generalized atmosphere of largess but simply enriched corrupt functionaries who hoarded what they received from both James and the bribes of the burgeoning class of merchants. See Stone, pp. 470–75. Compare this with *King Lear*.

Other critics (such as Novy, Fumerton, Kastan, Engel, Kahn, and Montrose) use Stone in their description of the place of gifts in a culture of patronage, but my interests are different and are closer to Rosalie Colie's focus: "Mr Stone's crisis was a prolonged affair, during which the aristocracy, although it never lost its favorable position in English society, lost its relative importance and was forced to alter its own self-image from that of an entrenched chivalrous and 'feudal' group, with particular military obligations of service and general obligations of largesse, to that of a group involved in private lives and obligations precariously facing the problems of an expanding econ-

display must take place according to an economy of scarcity and not abundance. His virtue is shrewdness and not sumptuousness: he proceeds, as Richard says punningly, by opposing "shrewd steel against our golden crown" (III.ii.59). Nevertheless, it is clear from his rebuke to Hal in *1 Henry IV* that he regards theatricality as necessary even to his power, as an unavoidable expenditure of royalty and the royal presence. There he reminds Hal of Richard's unwillingness or inability to dispense himself in narrow measure, expanding on the earlier play's characterization of him as "the wasteful King" (*Richard II*, III.iv.55). Nevertheless, he acknowledges that the exercise of royal power consists in some form of expenditure, even if he thinks that Hal is being spendthrift:[46]

> Had I so lavish of my presence been,
> So common-hackney'd in the eyes of men,
> So stale and cheap to vulgar company,
> Opinion, that did help me to the crown,
> Had still kept loyal to possession,
> And left me in reputeless banishment,
> A fellow of no mark nor likelihood.
> By being seldom seen, I could not stir
> But like a comet I was wond'red at,
> That men would tell their children, "This is he";
> Others would say, "Where, which is Bullingbrook?"
> And then I stole all courtesy from heaven,
> And dress'd myself in such humility
> That I did pluck allegiance from men's hearts,
> Loud shouts and salutations from their mouths,
> Even in the presence of the crowned King.
> Thus did I keep my person fresh and new,
> My presence, like a robe pontifical,
> Ne'er seen but wond'red at, and so my state,

---

omy and a society increasingly articulate" ("Reason and Need," p. 186). Colie finds a critique of conspicious consumption in the existence of counterfeit characters like Osric, Oswald, and Parolles. She summarizes: "The lavish expenditure characteristic of the medieval noble way of life was simple . . . compared to the new ways a nobleman might spend his money—the new commerce, the New World, and the aristocratic need for show accounted for remarkable outlays of income" (pp. 188–89).

46. Stephen Orgel, in "The Spectacle of State," in *Persons in Groups: Social Behavior as Identity Formation in Medieval and Renaissance Europe*, ed. Richard Trexler (Binghamton, N.Y.: Medieval and Renaissance Texts and Studies, 1985), pp. 101–21, and Kastan argue that the theatricality of kingship is at best double-edged, since the same theatricality that makes greatness imposing also risks making it familiar. As against Greenblatt, Kastan thus sees subversive possibilities available in theater.

> Seldom but sumptuous, show'd like a feast,
> And wan by rareness such solemnity.
>
> (*1 Henry IV*, iii.ii.39–59)

"Seldom but sumptuous": what terser phrase for the counterfeit of generosity or abundance? Henry's generosity is contrived. It appears indeed only within an economy of scarcity or "rareness." That scarcity may perhaps mark one difference between Henry's theory of power and that of Sonnet 94: where the young man *inherits* heaven's graces, Henry *steals* all courtesy from heaven. He wins loyalty by establishing the expectation of scarcity in order to outgo that diminished expectation with a factitious abundance, that of apparently "sunlike majesty / When it shines seldom in admiring eyes" (iii.ii.79–80). But, paradoxically, the bourgeois theory of value that Henry represents and articulates makes real abundance the depreciation of all value. To be lavish is to lose what Henry sees as the struggle for possession rather than for being. Henry does win the struggle, co-opting Richard's mode of power but also spelling the defeat of that mode in its pure form. For Richard does rule simply through unthriftiness (as Henry calls this trait in Hal), through lavishness, of his presence as well as of his goods, as Henry goes on to indicate in scornful terms:

> The skipping King, he ambled up and down,
> With shallow jesters, and rash bavin wits,
> Soon kindled and soon burnt, carded his state,
> Mingled his royalty with cap'ring fools,
> Had his great name profaned with their scorns,
> And gave his countenance, against his name,
> To laugh at gibing boys, and stand the push
> Of every beardless vain comparative,
> Grew a companion to the common streets,
> Enfeoff'd himself to popularity,
> That, being daily swallow'd by men's eyes,
> They surfeited with honey and began
> To loathe the taste of sweetness, whereof a little
> More than a little is by much too much.
>
> (iii.ii.60–73)

Lavishness of presence leads to excess in the Falstaffian mode, when the eyes that should admire become bored, "being with his presence glutted, [gorg'd], and full" (iii.ii.84).

Hal, of course, is even more canny than his father. Yet he actually embodies an alloyed strength made up of elements of both the old economy of lavishness and the new economy of scarcity. Hal represents, I think, a figure able to subsume and hold together the apparently irreconcilable opposition between absolutism and bourgeois capitalism. (One can similarly argue of the young Bullingbrook that he reconciles feudalism and absolutism.) Hal is an absolutist utterly at home in both worlds. His own improvisatory abundance is so full and so varied that he can be free with his presence and yet nevertheless come to give his ultimate self-revelation the impressiveness of the seldom—that seldomness being only one more role that the ubiquitous Hal can lavishly play.[47] The theory of majestic visibility that Hal puts forward in his first soliloquy is no different from Henry's. It does not, however, require genuine scarcity, since Hal is supremely confident that the copiousness of his own mana—his own Bataillean solar glory—will allow him to outgo not merely a carefully diminished expectation but any sense of his presence that anyone has of him, no matter how lavish that sense is:

> I know you all, and will a while uphold
> The unyok'd humor of your idleness,
> Yet herein will I imitate the sun,
> Who doth permit the base contagious clouds
> To smother up his beauty from the world,
> That when he please again to be himself,
> Being wanted, he may be more wond'red at
> By breaking through the foul and ugly mists
> Of vapors that did seem to strangle him.
> If all the year were playing holidays,
> To sport would be as tedious as to work;
> But when they seldom come, they wish'd for come,
> And nothing pleaseth but rare accidents.
> So when this loose behavior I throw off
> And pay the debt I never promised,
> By how much better than my word I am,
> By so much shall I falsify men's hopes,
> And like the bright metal on a sullen ground,
> My reformation, glitt'ring o'er my fault,
> Shall show more goodly and attract more eyes
> Than that which hath no foil to set it off.
> I'll so offend, to make offense a skill,
> Redeeming time when men least think I will.
>
> (I.ii.195–217)

47. See Greenblatt, "Invisible Bullets," in *Shakespearean Negotiations*, pp. 21–65.

It is true that the language here, in its meditation on the relation between the seldom, the rare, and the "wish'd for," is in many respects no different from that of Henry IV. "When they seldom come, they wish'd for come / And nothing pleaseth but rare accidents" is Hal's less solemn anticipation of Henry's otherwise very similar "and so my state, / Seldom but sumptuous, show'd like a feast, / And wan by rareness such solemnity." Hal's strategy, like Henry's before him, is to boost people's sense of his own worth through an impression of scarcity or rarity. Like his father, he is aware that scarcity breeds value, and like his father, he intends to imitate that "sunlike majesty" that is majestic because it "shines seldom in admiring eyes."

However, Hal conceives of his own essential worth with considerably more self-confidence than his father. Henry has always been the Machiavellian politician, whose theatricality is a way of managing and manipulating scarcity rather than a mode of abundance. But Hal is certain that he contains within himself a natural abundance of charisma, an abundance so great as to make the apparently lavish squandering of presence he has heretofore engaged in turn out to be scarcity by comparison with the way he will appear.

Unlike his usurping father, Hal will be a complete king. He will combine Henry's canniness in manipulating the display of power with Richard's more grandly theatrical dissipation of his own theatrical substance.[48] Hal's formulations hold these two apparently incompatible modes of kingship together. Like his father in *Richard II*, he is the figure of knowledge in the play and so, as Foucault would insist, the figure of power. Like his father, he is himself essentially unknown and unknowable to those around him. That is why he will "falsify men's hopes." He will do this when he comes to "pay the debt I never promised," as though people are hoping, not that Hal will pay what he gave them reason to hope he would pay, but that he won't pay what he never promised to pay to begin with. It is of course his parasitical friends whose hopes Hal will falsify. Nevertheless, the rhetoric of the speech manifests its fusion of apparent irreconcilables. From Henry's bourgeois perspective (and Falstaff's), a debt means a promise to pay,[49] but Hal's handsome intention to pay something he does not owe comes from the kind of lavish extravagance more associable with Richard's or Falstaff's world than with Henry's.

48. Cf. McMillin, "Shakespeare's *Richard II*," p. 46, on the paradox by which "the experience of self-loss tries to take shape" (p. 44), although McMillin argues that only its absence can appear.

49. Obviously the language of debt precedes capitalism, and its sanctions go back to the twelve tables; but as a legal status its scrupulous specificity contrasts with the implicit, unpromised "debt" of gift exchange.

Hal's intention comes from a gift economy. Mauss argues (against Marx) that the institution of credit precedes the institution of equivalent exchange.[50] The sense of obligation to pay a debt that is not promised is characteristic of a gift economy, where any promise or any formalization of the debt would vitiate the original obligation. A loan is not a gift, and only a gift truly obliges. To pay such an unpromised debt is to oblige in return: to oblige through the magnanimity of the gift that such a payment constitutes.

I do not mean to assert that Hal already lives explicitly within such an economy. Rather, his magnanimity consists in his freely establishing such an economy by freely beginning the cycle of gift exchange. This is true magnanimity (and hence true power), since whoever begins such a cycle cannot come out ahead (except of course in power, the shadow of the gift). Under the sign of magnanimity or abundance

50. Marxist critics of *The Merchant of Venice* have nevertheless noticed that Shylock is represented as the archaic figure, which seems a Maussian sequence. See Terry Eagleton, *William Shakespeare* (New York: Blackwell, 1987), and this very important passage from Cohen's *Drama of a Nation*: "From [the Italian] point of view, the hostility between Antonio, the openhanded Christian merchant, and Shylock, the tightfisted Jewish usurer, represents not the conflict between declining feudalism and rising capitalism, but its opposite. It is a special instance of the struggle, widespread in Europe, between Jewish quasi-feudal fiscalism and native bourgeois mercantilism, in which the indigenous forces usually prevailed. Both the characterization and the outcome of *The Merchant of Venice* mark Antonio as the harbinger of modern capitalism. By guaranteeing an honorable reputation as well as a secure and absolute title to private property, the exemption of the Italian merchant-financier from the stigma of usury provided a necessary spur to the expansion of the new system. Shylock, by contrast, is a figure from the past, marginal, diabolical, irrational, archaic, medieval. Shakespeare's Jacobean tragic villains—Iago, Edmund, Macbeth, and Augustus—are all younger men bent on destroying their elders. Shylock is almost the reverse, an old man with obsolete values trying to arrest the course of history" (p. 202). Shylock has the uncanny ability to efface the difference between the animate and the inanimate. I think the archaic always has the feel of such an undoing of distinction: when the dead speak, it is not clear whether there is a difference any more between life and death. This comes out even in Portia's pun "Thus is the will of a living daughter ruled by the will of a dead father." The death's head in the gold casket may feel quite different from Portia's portrait in the lead casket, but that difference is not so obvious as may at first appear. At any rate, much of the play is about the animation of specie and the inanimation of human beings, and although Marx speaks of commodity fetishism in the same way, his commodities are jejune and childish, cartoon characters, and not uncanny. From this perspective, Shylock's great speech "Hath not a Jew eyes . . . ?" makes him out to be a machine, like all other humans. This speech is entirely consistent with the bond to repay a pound of flesh, which also confuses animate and inanimate matter. From another point of view, of course, Shylock (who can't know that Antonio won't be able to pay his debt on time) is in fact making a gift of his loan—lending his money gratis—and "the merry bond" really is only a joke. Only after Jessica's elopement does he treats the bond seriously. I certainly do not mean simply to align Shylock with a gift economy and those in Belmont with an exchange economy; rather, Shylock stands for everything disturbing about both capitalism and the archaic barbarity of the endless demands of a gift economy, whereas those of Belmont stand for a free and easy generosity and a capitalism that harmonizes (as Cohen argues) with aristocracy. But Shylock certainly does foreground the less idealized aspects of the gift, and among those is the inevitable fact of interest.

Hal integrates the two modes of kingship—Richard's and Henry's—
in his own person, a person at once secret and invisible (as Greenblatt
essentially reads him), as well as highly visible, like the sun (as Pye
might read him).[51]

The comparison with Christ that the speech invites is apposite.
What makes Hal complete is this integration of the dualities represented by abundance and scarcity. Since such an integration is itself
abundant, Hal achieves what Richard cannot, "Redeeming time when
men least think I will." Richard's power consists in his power to waste
or dissipate time. The reverse he cannot do, but Hal intends to redeem the time he has so insouciantly wasted. This is the insouciance
of generosity, that generosity which also renders him a redeemer, like
Christ paying the debts that he hasn't promised. As the succesfully
integrated representative of insouciant generosity, magnificently
combining the attributes of seeing all and dazzling all,[52] Hal can serve
as a standard to which to compare those Shakespearean figures whose
generosity comes at some cost, whose expenditure depletes a substance or charisma that is not inexhaustible.

Hal is the exception among Shakespeare's kings. His magic is inexhaustible; it consists partly in his insouciant shrewdness and partly in
his shrewd sense that he really is charmed or really is a charm.
Richard too attempts to rule by dazzling, but the sources of his power,
or his powers as source, are not inexhaustible. Although he grandly
manages the ritual that appears to defuse the danger both Bullingbrook and Mowbray pose for him, he ends up playing into Bulling-

---

51. On this combination of the visible and the invisible in Henry, cf. Goldberg, *James
I*: "The sovereign displays in public . . . his own unobservability" (p. 150).

52. Following Lacan, Pye argues for the priority of seeing over either the seeing
subject or the object seen in *Richard II* (*Regal Phantasm*, pp. 82–105). Less radical is
Goldberg's formulation that the "moment of self-consciousness remains a theatrical
scene, for the king sees himself being seen—by the audience without, and by one
within, the eye of God observing him as he is observed. Conscience/consciousness,
which treads the boundary between interiority and exteriority, and which makes interiority exteriorized and imposes an outward gaze upon the inner self, leads to an all-
pervasive theatricality and the effacement of other normative distinctions. The theatre
of conscience . . . makes the boundary between the spectator and the spectacle elusive"
(*James I*, p. 148). For both Pye and Goldberg any relation to sight comes after sight
itself, as though (in my terms) sight were the source or the unmoved mover, the
authority that cannot itself be a consciousness. I am interested in Hal's self-
representation as the sun (a common enough topos in the Henriad) and in the way he
manages to combine both the apparently secondary capacity to see (which is the mark
of consciousness) and the primary status of being that which is seen—being the source
of other people's sight, the Bataillean source "sans contre-partie." On this aspect of sun
mythology Joel Fineman has a beautiful couple of pages in his *Shakespeare's Perjur'd Eye:
The Invention of Poetic Subjectivity in the Sonnets* (Berkeley: University of California Press,
1986), pp. 12–13.

brook's hands. On his departure Henry evidences the shrewder theatricality he will later boast of to Hal through his "courtship to the
common people," through the false anti-economy of the "reverence
he did throw away on slaves, / Wooing poor craftsmen with the craft of
smiles" which is "observ'd" and described by Richard (1.iv.23–36).
Subsequent events will intensify the impression of injured merit that
Henry encourages, when Richard through his military activity gives
himself a further pretext for the squandering of England's substance
that Gaunt warns him against. The accusations traded by Mowbray
and Bullingbrook make clear that decking the military provides
Richard with an excuse to waste money and to waste his country's
prosperity by wasting that money:

> *Bullingbrook:*   Look what I speak, my life shall prove it true:
>   That Mowbray hath receiv'd eight thousand nobles
>   In name of lendings for your Highness' soldiers,
>   The which he hath detain'd for lewd employments,
>   Like a false traitor and injurious villain. . . .
>
> *Mowbray:*   Three parts of that receipt I had for Callice
>   Disburs'd I duly to his Highness' soldiers;
>   The other part reserv'd I by consent,
>   For that my sovereign liege was in my debt,
>   Upon remainder of a dear account,
>   Since last I went to France to fetch his queen.
>   (1.i.87–91; 126–31)

The garrison at Callais may be a legitimate expense, but military
funds are being used for what can only be a quasi-public debt;
Richard is certainly getting a kickback. Northumberland later expresses the general sentiment as to the falsity of Richard's military
expenses when he says of the money that Richard has raised, "Wars
hath not wasted it, for warr'd he hath not, / But basely yielded upon
compromise / That which his noble ancestors achiev'd with blows. /
More hath he spent in peace than they in wars" (II.i.252–55). The
unimportant Irish rebellion appears a golden opportunity for
Richard: he will be able to destroy the house of Lancaster and leave
Henry powerless, display his own heroism by fighting in person, and
leave the kingdom in the less resented control of York, whom he is
shrewd enough to trust. Once more however, he has played into Bullingbrook's hands, since Bullingbrook now has a legal justification for
the return he has already intended. (He is already waiting off the
coast when Richard makes off with his inheritance [II.i.289–90], per-

haps anticipating the mistake that will enable him to return as a victim.)

That these egregious examples of Richard's wastefulness tend toward the justification of Gaunt's accusations do not diminish a certain efficacy in Richard's rule by expenditure. Of course, almost by definition this rule is finally not susceptible of being called technically efficient. Like Stone, Norbert Elias, in his book on court society in France, argues that the archetypal story of the ruin of an aristocratic family is the structural result of an exercise of social power that displays itself as prestige. The prestige that enables power also prevents those frugalities that would guard and maintain it.[53] In *The Merchant of Venice* Bassanio gets into the trouble from which merchant capital has to save him, at least for a while, because of the display that he has to keep up.[54] For the king, as Elias points out, the absolutist power he displays requires his own submission to the ritual, and the costs of the ritual, in which he displays that power. What better description of Richard's procedure?

But it is nevertheless power that Richard does wield, even when he is himself girt round with weakness. Bullingbrook acknowledges Richard's power and his mastery in the mode of display, and he acknowledges that power in word and action through the consistency with which he refuses to attempt to outshine or outdisplay Richard. He analyzes his own maneuvers tellingly, displaying his power in a mode as understated as Richard's is dazzling, for example, when he asks Northumberland to convey his message to Richard:

> thus deliver:
> Henry Bullingbrook
> On both his knees doth kiss King Richard's hands,
> And sends allegiance and true faith of heart
> To his most royal person; hither come
> Even at his feet to lay my arms and power. . . .
> Let's march without the noise of threat'ning drum,
> That from this castle's tottered battlements

53. Norbert Elias, *Power and Civility*, trans. Edmond Jephcott (New York: Pantheon, 1982).

54. Because *The Merchant of Venice* is about the possibility of annealing the difference between bourgeois and aristocratic wealth, Bassanio can borrow money from Antonio that will thriftily win him self-originating aristocratic substance in the form of the very valuable Portia, who is treated like a commodity whose value is precisely that she is no mere commodity (i.i.161–76).

Portia later describes herself as a commodity to Bassanio (iii.ii.149–67), and of course Antonio is a commodity, not only to Shylock, but to Bassanio and Portia, who attempt to "purchase" him in order to save him.

Our fair appointments may be well perus'd.
Methinks King Richard and myself should meet
With no less terror than the elements
Of fire and water, when their thund'ring shock
At meeting tears the cloudy cheeks of heaven.
Be he the fire, I'll be the yielding water;
The rage be his, whilst on the earth I rain
My waters—on the earth and not on him.
March on, and mark King Richard how he looks.
                    (III.iii.34–39; 51–61)

   The last line characterizes in a nutshell Richard's and Henry's differing modes of power. Henry's efficiency mirrors his own efficient
order to "march on." The langorous repetition of the same sounds—
as "march" extends into *"mark* King Ri*ch*ard"—captures Richard's
unthrifty indolence. Although Henry here makes a show of his own
power—silent king that he is, he marches silently so that "our fair
appointments may be well perus'd"—he continues to treat Richard,
not himself, as the center of vision: "mark King Richard how he
looks." Indeed the entire speech witholds the display of catastrophic
power—of power as catastrophe—that it appears to promise. Not
only is Henry not hasty as fire, as Richard had described him, but his
watery qualities mean not the deafness of the sea, but silence. For even
the meteoric clash of elements that would produce the most violent
and violently destructive of spectacles gives way immediately to Henry's shrewder refusal to grapple with Richard in the mode of the
spectacular. Henry's refusal to clash with Richard directly recapitulates Richard's halting of the duel between Henry and Mowbray. But
this recapitulation repudiates the spectacle central to Richard's action.
Instead of making himself the center of attention, Henry repeatedly
gives way, and does not insist on spectacle.
   Or rather, the spectacle he insists on is Richard's, not his own.
Visibility will center on Richard as fire, and what will be visible will be
Richard's spectacularly burning out. Even if Henry did not anticipate
the specific ways in which Richard would spectacularly squander his
power of spectacle, it is clear that by now he knows the uses to which
Richard's grandeur may be put. Richard's grandeur is real power, as
Henry and York confirm when Richard appears:

Bullingbrook: See, see, King Richard doth himself appear,
   As doth the blushing discontented sun
   From out the fiery portal of the east,
   When he perceives the envious clouds are bent

To dim his glory and to stain the track
Of his bright passage to the occident.
York: Yet looks he like a king! Behold, his eye,
As bright as is the eagle's, lightens forth
Controlling majesty. Alack, alack for woe,
That any harm should stain so fair a show!

(III.iii.62–71)

That Hal's mode of rule is at least partly Ricardian may be gleaned from the echoes between the description of Richard here and Hal's prospect for himself in the "I know you all" soliloquy, where he intends to

imitate the sun,
Who doth permit the base contagious clouds
To smother up his beauty from the world,
That when he please again to be himself,
Being wanted, he may be more wond'red at
By breaking through the foul and ugly mists
Of vapors that did seem to strangle him.
(*1 Henry IV* II.ii.197–203)

This display *is* power, and indeed the display of power is not—as he will indicate in *1 Henry IV*—something that even Henry can do without, even if his prestige is a function of the scarcity of his display. In *Richard II* Henry's displays of power tend to be reported rather than staged. Though this has much to do with the limitations of staging the kind of progresses he leads, it serves as well to preserve the audience's sense of him as powerful through the mode of surveillance rather than display. He *is* powerful as a surveyor, as one who will always "mark King Richard, how he looks," as one told by Richard to "mark, silent king, the moral of this sport" in the mirror scene. When he does stage-manage displays for himself, Henry calculates carefully, in contrast to Richard who depends on more instinctive judgments. Henry's departure for banishment, his parade outside Flint Castle, his return to London in which he may almost be said to be leading Richard in a Roman triumph,[55] and his wish to see Richard murdered—all exemplify his care. His expression of this wish could easily have been shown on stage, but instead we get it in Exton's report, where it is King Henry, not King Richard, who has been marked, but marked in secret: "Didst thou not mark the King, what words he spake? / 'Have I

55. The explicitly theatrical language of York's description of this has often been noted.

no friend will rid me of this living fear?'/. . ./And speaking it, he wishtly look'd on me / As who should say, 'I would thou wert the man / That would divorce this terror from my heart'" (v.iv.1–2; 7–9).

Henry is the shrewdest, least spectacular of kings. He amasses power silently. In this he would seem to represent the opposite of Richard's lavishings of himself. Yet Henry's nascently bourgeois mode does not exclude the expenditure it subsumes. The play itself bears witness to the spectacle of Henry's rise, a spectacle that takes the form of Richard's extravagant fall. Westminster describes the abdication scene as well as the play quite tellingly: "A woeful pageant have we here beheld" (iv.i.321). This pageant Henry has produced, much as Essex will try to produce it in 1601, and Elizabeth will resist its production, preventing the abdication scene from being played.

In his extreme care to accommodate Richard's theatricality, Henry aims also at consolidating his own power. Now, if that power, like Elizabeth's, consists in the very shrewd managing of spectacle, and if, on the other hand, spectacle necessitates the expenditure of prestige, power would seem to be caught in its own toils. Richard has demonstrated all too well that power exercises itself by undoing itself. Henry will confirm that he can conserve and amass power only by making himself scarce—in both the colloquial and the noncolloquial sense— scarce, but not absent. Since power is theatrical, it must display the scarcity of its own display, and this display, even of scarcity, can occur only in the mode of the expenditure of power.

How can Henry avoid this paradox? How can he maintain a power whose very maintenance requires its expenditure? He solves this problem in characteristic fashion, by staging a spectacle in which theatrical expenditure and power are split from each other, are doubled. An example of a parallel practice might make this clear. Bataille describes Aztec human sacrifice as a particularly thoroughgoing mode of expenditure. He is intrigued by the confluence of two facts. On the one hand, the humans who are sacrificed are captives of a war fought for the purposes of obtaining such captives, so that the society that sacrifices them is not quite engaging in the self-sacrifice that total expenditure would seem to require (although the war itself leads to expenditure productive only of victims to be sacrificed unproductively). The Aztecs find scapegoats for that sacrifice. On the other hand, those scapegoats are taken very seriously indeed. The chief victim is treated like a king for an entire year preceding his sacrifice. In the last days before the ritual, the real king withdraws, and the imminent victim is treated with the most elaborate courtly deference by the entourage that has left the king to follow the victim. The symbolism of the sacrifice is obvious: the victim represents the supreme power; the spectacular destruction of so supreme a power represents the spectacular magnitude of the sacrifice. But the king sacrifices only the symbolic king, only his symbolic double.

This can describe the relationship between Henry and Richard. The course of the play transforms Richard, transforms him from a real into a symbolic king: he becomes a king of griefs (IV.i.193), "a mockery king of snow" (IV.i.260), even (as the noble lion by comparison to which the queen tries to rally him) "A king of beasts indeed—if aught but beasts, / I had been still a happy king of men" (V.i.35–36). Henry's elaborate displays of courtesy and respect toward Richard render *symbolic* the theatricality that had been Richard's real power. From the start Henry overdoes his deference to Richard. He accuses Mowbray of plotting against Richard for the crime that Richard himself has plotted. He publicly gives thanks that in his exile the same sun that shines on Richard will shine on him (I.iii.144–47). Later, when he has the upper hand, he intensifies Richard's now symbolic kingship with all sorts of theatricalizing gestures: "See, see, King Richard doth himself appear, / As doth the blushing discontented sun," (III.iii.62–63), he urges, and shortly thereafter he commands his followers to "stand all apart, / And show fair duty to his Majesty" (III.iii.187–88). One speech of Richard's in the abdication scene summarizes the differing modes of exhibition that Henry has marshaled, with Richard "looked upon," gazed at as the center of a display that he predicts will be "mark'd with a blot" and that consists not only in the display of himself but in an ostentations "show" by those now Henry's allies:

> Nay, all of you that stand and look upon me
> Whilst that my wretchedness doth bait myself,
> Though some of you, with Pilate, wash your hands,
> Showing an outward pity, yet you Pilates
> Have here deliver'd me to my sour cross,
> And water cannot wash away your sin.
>
> (IV.i.237–242)

Henry takes power by sacrificing a king become symbolic, much as Hotspur in turn will attempt to render Henry symbolic in *1 Henry IV*. Informed of the magnificence of Henry's force coming against him Hotspur cries:

> Let them come!
> They come like sacrifices in their trim,

And to the fire-ey'd maid of smoky war
All hot and bleeding will we offer them.
The mailed Mars shall on his [altar] sit
Up to the ears in blood. I am on fire
To hear this rich reprisal is so nigh,
And yet not ours.

                              (IV.i.112–19)

The important question in Hotspur's speech is, Who is to be the sacrifice? Who is "hot and bleeding"? The fire-eyed maid of war hardly cares who comes out ahead, so long as the losses are spectacular. Either side can be the offering: either can take the place of the other. "Reprisal" must mean something like substitute—the prize that, like the Aztec victim, is a rich object substituting for the extravagant expenditure that Hotspur longs for. Here the fact that the symbolic and sacrificial king is the real King Henry intensifies a sacrifice no longer purely ritual. It is real. Hotspur too may be (will be) the victim. He is already on fire with his own spectacular glory, and to sacrifice Henry and Hal would only mean to displace the object of spectacular expenditure.

In the same way, Richard becomes the sacrificial king. His destruction symbolizes the expenditure of power in the spectacle that Henry stages (though Henry himself, unlike Hotspur, is cool to the extravagant glory of the situation and merely plays to and uses other people's passionate interest in the spectacular dissipation of power). Power does dissipate itself in the spectacle Henry stages—all the power of an absolutist monarch. The control of its expenditure is Henry's—that is the point—but the power expended is not his, but Richard's. "Fetch hither Richard, that in common view / He may surrender" (IV.i.155–56), he commands, and Richard's surrender is indeed a display of expenditure. Power consists in its expenditure, but now the power is only Henry's, the expenditure only Richard's.

From its start on the coast in Wales Richard's long abdication does not oppose but rather continues the dissipative extravagance that marks his rule. Commentators jeer at the extraordinary rapidity with which he shuttles between hope and despair, but rapidity and instability are simply facets of his extravagance. What but emotional extravagance is it for him to give everything up when he hears that Bushy, Green, and Wiltshire are dead? He responds by declaring that he has nothing and by giving up all title to the appurtenances of kingship: "Let's choose executors and talk of wills; / And yet not so, for what can we bequeath / Save our deposed bodies to the ground?" (III.ii.148–50). After briefly taking comfort from Aumerle he despairs

again, this time in terms recalling the death of Gaunt: "Go to Flint
castle, there I'll pine away—/ A king, woe's slave, shall kingly woe
obey. / That power I have, discharge, and let them go" (III.iii.209–11).
If the idea of pining away recalls Gaunt's composition, Gaunt's death
is also described as the spending of everything, "Words, life, and all,
old Lancaster hath spent"; death leaves him "bankrout," like Richard
having nothing left to bequeath but his body to the ground (II.i.150–
51). And Richard continues to image his ruin as a *giving away* of his
own substance:

> I'll give my jewels for a set of beads,
> My gorgeous palace for a hermitage,
> My gay apparel for an almsman's gown,
> My figur'd goblets for a dish of wood,
> My sceptre for a palmer's walking-staff,
> My subjects for a pair of carved saints,
> And my large kingdom for a little grave,
> A little little grave, an obscure grave—
> Or I'll be buried in the king's high way.
>
> (III.iii.147–55)

Hal will echo these lines, but in the mode of his magical prodigality,
when he squanders the dignity of his own inheritance for the purposes of farce. But Hal has the self-sufficient resources to be able to
absorb Falstaff's debasement of the currency of kingship in the play-
acting scene. To Falstaff's ostensive "This chair shall be my state, this
dagger my sceptre, and this cushion my crown," Hal replies, as
though daring the comparison with Richard that he means to outgo,
"Thy state is taken for a join'd stool, thy golden sceptre for a leaden
dagger, and thy precious rich crown for a pitiful bald crown" (*1 Henry
IV*, II.iv.378–82). For Hal to make this exchange manifests yet again
his invulnerability to his own extravagance; but for Richard, to give
everything away is to lose contact with the general, here present in the
eerie and haunting use of the word *king* as a possessive adjective: "the
king's high way." Richard will no longer participate in the generality
that he once embodied. The adjectival form of *king* marks how far
from that pastoral state of belonging to the world, to the world as
geography, Richard has gone now that he (or his language) imagines
being buried in the king's high way as a kind of pastoral, as a final
participation, even in the most debased way, in the daily life of the
kingdom.

The abdication scene literalizes the language of giving away. Henry
stages, or shrewdly allows Richard to stage, an exhibition of expendi-

ture where the display of Richard's dissipation of his power redounds to an increase in Henry's and not Richard's. Once again all eyes mark Richard even as he forswears all pomp and majesty:

> Now mark me how I will undo myself:
> I give this heavy weight from off my head,
> And this unwieldy spectre from my hand,
> The pride of kingly sway from out my heart;
> With mine own tears I wash away my balm,
> With mine own hands I give away my crown,
> With mine own tongue deny my sacred state,
> With mine own breath release all duteous oaths;
> All pomp and majesty I do foreswear;
> My manors, rents, revenues I forgo;
> My acts, decrees, and statutes I deny;
> God pardon all oaths that are broke to me!
> God keep all vows unbroke are made to thee!
> Make me, that nothing have, with nothing griev'd,
> And thou with all pleas'd, that hast all achiev'd!
> Long mayst thou live in Richard's seat to sit,
> And soon lie Richard in an earthy pit!
>
> (IV.i.203–19)

Even this is not the end. Richard must genuinely become grieved with the nothing that is there, and he has more to play in this sad pageant. Henry continues to be accommodating. He dispatches his servants to bring a mirror after Richard asks for one so that he may be *shown* his own emptiness, "That it may show me what a face I have / Since it is bankrout of his majesty" (IV.i.266–67). Indeed in what might be called a transumptive moment from Henry's point of view, Richard does more than merely continue making of himself the symbolic sacrifice that ends his power and confirms Henry's. As though to make stronger his status as (only a) symbolic representation of Henry (something he will also do, with more ambiguous overtones, when he becomes a prophet without honor and predicts that Northumberland will come to regard Henry as he now regards Richard [V.i.55–68]), he actually plays Henry's part as well as his own in the sacrificial ritual under way. In general, the victim differs from the king in that the king has a symbolic scapegoat where the victim does not. The victim thus fails to be a complete symbol for the king; he has everything the king has *except* the king's power to be symbolized by the victim—which is the king's power *tout court*. In a reversal of the hierarchical value of possessing and being explored above, the king generally *has* a symbol and the victim *is* one (although this merely schematizes in reverse the fact that the king is a source of the symbolic, the victim a recipient of the conferred symbolism). But Richard, both true and symbolic king, becomes an even truer symbol. He manifests himself as the most representational symbol possible, for he actually enacts both sides of the symbolic sacrifice, sacrificing his own power but also mirroring the king who makes his mirror-image victim undergo that sacrifice. Both king and victim, he attempts to maintain some glory by sacrificing his own glory. But to his woe he maintains glory only symbolically, and the real glory all still goes to Henry's political power:[56]

> Give me that glass, and therein will I read.
> No deeper wrinkles yet? Hath sorrow struck
> So many blows upon this face of mine,
> And made no deeper wounds? O, flatt'ring glass,
> Like to my followers in prosperity,
> Thou dost beguile me! Was this face the face
> That every day under his household roof
> Did keep ten thousand men? Was this the face
> That, like the sun, did make beholders wink?
> Is this the face which fac'd so many follies,
> That was at last out-fac'd by Bullingbrook?
> A brittle glory shineth in this face,
> As brittle as the glory is the face,
> For there it is, crack'd in an hundred shivers.
> Mark, silent king, the moral of this sport,
> How soon my sorrow hath destroy'd my face.
>
> (IV.i.276–91)

Henry's terse reply—"The shadow of your sorrow hath destroy'd / The shadow of your face" (292–93)—exemplifies the tendency of his power to work laconically and silently (as Richard has just insisted). To sustain itself, that power must prevent Richard's abdication from ever appearing other than more theater of the kind he squandered his authority on to begin with. Henry's authority derives from the theatrical rejection of the theatrical, from the sacrifice of the king of theater. As though to perfect this sacrifice by perfecting the adequacy of Richard's symbolic theater—seen in his representation of the king—Henry returns Richard's eerie characterization of him as the "silent king" by effectively calling Richard a "king of shadows," of theatrical

56. Pye makes a similar point in his deconstructive elaboration and critique of Greenblatt's insights into the inextricability of theatrical power and its erosion (*Regal Phantasm*, pp. 82–105).

actors, so that the end of Richard would mean only the end of a play-acted kingship.[57]

Again, Henry may have two reasons for his response. He may be effacing or disguising the theatrical nature of his own surveying power by having Richard symbolize even the tendency to theatricalize through someone else while remaining silent and in the background. And he may be responding to the slight but ominous threat that identifies him with the mirror image of the king—shadowy, perhaps, and silent, and liable to destruction. In *1 Henry IV* Douglas, having killed three people disguised as Henry, comes upon him and asks, "What art thou / That counterfeit'st the person of a king?" (v.iv.27–28)—a question that looks forward to Falstaff's meditation on counterfeiting death as counterfeiting a counterfeit (v.iv.111–24).[58] Henry seems to acknowledge the justice of Douglas's formulation, and ultimately of Richard's, in his reply:

> The King himself, who, Douglas, grieves at heart
> So many of his shadows thou hast met
> And not the very King.
>
> (v.iv.29–31)

The strangeness of this formulation is worth considering. Who counterfeits the person of a king? The king himself counterfeits the person of a king.[59] The king himself mourns that Douglas has not met the very king. Perhaps one can read this too as an allusion to the doctrine of the king's two bodies. "A king" connotes a concrete general term, and it is *the* particular king who counterfeits this general status. Douglas meets a particular theatrical manifestation of the general, nonphysical king several times, and the particular manifestation he now meets is different in degree, not in kind, from the other shadows. This is overly literal, I know, but I think it describes the precariousness of Henry's sense of himself as king: the very king feels grief as we all do, and the word *very* seems susceptible of disappearing.

Henry's response to Richard in the earlier play, on the other hand, denies the efficacy of the attempt to read Henry as himself a shadow.

57. McMillin reads shadows as actors also; see "Shakespeare's *Richard II*," p. 46.
58. Compare Sigurd Burckhardt, *Shakespearean Meanings* (Princeton, N.J.: Princeton University Press, 1968), pp. 147–49.
59. James Winny, in *The Player King: A Theme of Shakespeare's Histories* (London: Chatto and Windus, 1968), sees in this scene a dramatization of the "doubtfulness of [Henry's] identity" as king (p. 100), although he does not understand Henry's answer to confirm that doubtfulness.

He closes Richard off. Richard may try to turn the tables on Henry and make him only symbolic or at least representational—the silent reflection. But Henry insists that it is Richard who is pure representation, that Richard contains the circuit of representation within himself. A shadow on both sides of the mirror, Richard's shadowiness represents the theatricality and vulnerability of Richard alone, though Richard himself may theatrically represent Henry.

And yet that Henry should now be speaking in the vocabulary of shadows and that he should participate with Richard in the eeriness of the language at this moment in the play shows that something besides last-ditch sparring is going on here. Henry, at least briefly, is pulled into the spooky atmosphere of insubstantiality that the play associates with Richard, as though the shadow complement of his substantiality and plenitude had now become prominent. Richard's reply to Henry is not the origin of the shadow logic of the play's imagery, but it does explain that logic:

> Say that again.
> The shadow of my sorrow! Ha, let's see.
> 'Tis very true, my grief lies all within,
> And these external [manners] of laments
> Are merely shadows to the unseen grief
> That swells with silence in the tortur'd soul.
> There lies the substance; and I thank thee, King,
> For thy great bounty, that not only giv'st
> Me cause to wail, but teachest me the way
> How to lament the cause.
>
> (IV.i.293–302)

Of course Richard descends in this speech to the bitterest and most impotent sarcasm. Yet the bounty Henry is supposed to manifest here does not go utterly without genuine acknowledgment on Richard's part. I think he acknowledges the fact that Henry permits him to play this last scene, acknowledges Henry's attention to him. Though that attention may have its origin in Henry's sacrifice of Richard, its content is not without a strange intimacy.

Such an intimacy is present elsewhere in the play as well. It is present in Henry's final regretful speech, "I hate the murtherer, love him murthered" (v.vi.40), where it is not only the fact that Richard is murdered but Richard himself that the already aging Henry loves. Intimacy is present also in the strange interchange outside Flint Castle when Richard gives up entirely:

Richard: Cousin, I am too young to be your father,
Though you are old enough to be my heir.
What you will have, I'll give, and willing too,
For do we must what force would have us do.
Set on towards London, cousin, is it so?
Bullingbrook: Yea, my good lord.
Richard: Then I must not say no.
(III.iii.204–9)

I hear the same tone here as in Cordelia's "We are not the first /
Who with best meaning have incurr'd the worst. / . . . / Shall we not see
these daughters and these sisters?" (*King Lear*, v.iii.3–4, 7), the same
recognition of the intimacy of a familial relation, an intimacy without
hope or comfort. Richard's willingness here deserves notice. "What
you will have, I'll give, and willing too": the word "too" means not only
that he is emphatic about his being willing to give his substance to
Henry's possession, but also that he is just as willing as Henry, who
"will have" what he wants, even though *taking* has now come to stand
for power, and *giving* has come to stand for its loss. This is why Henry
can later say, "I thought you had been willing to resign" (IV.i.190):
there is in Richard some muted version of *amor fati* that takes the form
of an intimacy with fate or necessity. "How brooks your Grace the air /
After your late tossing on the breaking seas?" asks Aumerle on
Richard's return from Ireland; and Richard's joyful response, couched
as it is in the language of necessity, is already not without a sense of his
sorrowful intimacy with his own mortality: "Needs must I like it well; I
weep for joy / To stand upon my kingdom once again" (III.ii.2–5).
Later his neediness will become more pressing when he feels the
proximity of necessity. He tells his queen, in lines with an odd buoyan-
cy at the word "sweet", "I am sworn brother, sweet, / To grim Necessity, and he and I / Will keep a league till death" (v.i.20–22).[60] Richard
has descended to this strange willingness from the heights of a Ma-

---

60. Milton, as I'll suggest, remembers this in *Paradise Lost*, when Satan apostrophizes
Adam and Eve:
League with you I seek,
And mutual amity so strait, so close,
That I with you must dwell, or you with me
Henceforth.   (4.375–78)
Empson reads this scene as truthfully testifying to Satan's desire for intimacy with
Adam and Eve, not simply bitter sarcasm, and I think he is right to say that here Satan
makes "the eerie offer to them of all he has" (*Milton's God* [New York: Cambridge
University Press, 1981], p. 67). Satan's sense of intimacy for them echoes the odd
intimacy between Henry and Richard.

chiavellian power that claims to take place in the feigned unwillingness of its exercise. His protégé Mowbray's fate he declares "I with some unwillingness pronounce" (1.iii.149); this is not true, but it counterfeits the real unwillingness of Gaunt's sentence against his real son, pronounced because "you gave leave to my unwilling tongue / Against my will to do myself this wrong" (1.iii.245–46). Gaunt's tone here can serve as a standard to measure how different is Richard's tone outside of Flint Castle, how much closer to Cordelia's. Henry, the David to Richard's Saul in this modern book of Kings, seems to share David's regret at the scene of humiliation that he stages and from which he benefits. The double spondee of "Yea, my good lord" participates in Richard's tone, and Richard picks up this participation again when he finishes the line by not saying no to Henry's "Yea."

This intimacy also haunts the abdication scene, where Henry almost continuously accommodates Richard's desires. True, he has his own reasons for this, some of which are explored above, but even Richard cannot deny the reality of Henry's accommodation and the sympathy it requires, no matter what their origin and no matter how bitter Richard is about that origin. Even the bitterness of Richard's thanks in that scene acknowledges Henry's charismatic power over him, a power whose marvelous extent is figured in the fact that even this scantiness should be construable as bounty, however sarcastically. Richard is so little compared with Henry's greatness now that any kindness on Henry's part, even the most cursory, is to be wondered at.

In a sense Richard and Henry have changed positions, not only politically but also thematically. Now Henry appears bountiful. Henry's charisma is now such as to imbue the smallest and least sympathizing of his gestures with the affect of great generosity. This is an odd generosity, generous in the way it transmogrifies its own paucity: Henry's economy of scarcity works that way. Still, Henry has indeed become generous, in the imaginings of this speech, and if this makes him more like Richard, Richard, for his part, has become the king associated with silence. It is not Henry but Richard himself and his grief "that swells with *silence* in the tortur'd soul." It is not about Henry but about himself that Richard now uses the language of substance after all the talk (his own and others') about his emptiness or vanity. The language of substance here has become eerie, however. What is substantial turns out to be what cannot make its way into the world. But this is because the world is only a world of shadows. Shadow and substance have changed positions as well.

Richard now belongs to what I call a shadow economy, a preterite space where all things are reversed. Richard's substance—secret, silent, and grievous—is a shadow of Henry's, next to whom he too is merely a shadow. But the play insists that Richard's shadowy substance still is a kind of substance, one less vulnerable than wealth to evaporation through expenditure. Henry stages Richard's abdication, which means that he stages Richard's own staging of the abdication. Richard does his own share of directing the events, especially at the emblematic moment when he gives the crown to the man who has just seized it:

> Give me the crown. Here, cousin, seize the crown;
> Here, cousin,
> On this side my hand, [and] on that side thine.
> Now is this golden crown like a deep well
> That owes two buckets, filling one another,
> The emptier ever dancing in the air,
> The other down, unseen, and full of water.
> (iv.i.181–87)

All the imagery of the *Henriad* pressures the interpretation of this metaphor in one direction. The emptier bucket, ever dancing in the air, would have to represent Richard, the skipping, ambling king. And the other bucket, unseen and full of water, would have to stand for Henry, the silent king who represents himself as yielding like water. But the next two lines undo this interpretation:

> That bucket down and full of tears am I,
> Drinking my griefs, whilst you mount up on high.
> (iv.i.188–89)

Those tears are the return on Richard's expenditure. In this shadow gift economy he succeeds where he fails in the real economy. He increases substance as he gives everything away. The shadow economy is not itself symbolic but results from the experience of being rendered purely and completely symbolic. A king of griefs, Richard has become utterly separated from his power, and the kingship left to him now symbolizes that separation. But his perspective, the preterite perspective of the symbol rather than the 'real' perspective of its user, contains its own laws of expenditure. In this negative space, substance (in the form of grief, for example) does not conserve itself (as in the world of physics), nor does it evaporate (as in the experience of the world) but only increases. It increases because its expenditure *is* its increase. This negative space is akin to the terrifying Freudian space of insomnia, where the ego becomes too weakened to sleep, too weakened, that is, even to collapse into unconsciousness. Consciousness for

Freud is a negative, not a positive, and past a certain zero point, the removal from consciousness of libido—its life force—results not in consciousness's depletion but in its intensification.[61] Richard tells Bullingbrook that he is indeed willing to resign his crown, "but still my griefs are mine. / You may my glories and my state depose, / But not my griefs; still am I king of those" (IV.i.191–93). Like Christ's in Herbert's "The Sacrifice," Richard's symbolic kingship intensifies as the intensity of his griefs increases, and their intensity increases as he gives away his real kingship. So does the intensity of his cares, given away but increasing nonetheless:

> *Bullingbrook:* Part of your cares you give me with your crown.
> *Richard:* Your cares set up do not pluck my cares down:
>   My care is loss of care, by old care done,
>   Your care is gain of care, by new care won;
>   The cares I give I have, though given away,
>   They tend the crown, yet still with me they stay.
>
>   (IV.i.194–99)

Care here names one of the modalities of vanity or nothingness to which the play confers the most spectral but exigent of substances. A shadow economy parallels the real economy of the play. In that economy, as in the real, nothing increases perpetually; but in that economy the increase of nothing takes on its own blankly positive meaning, as in Richard's famous chiasmus: "What e'er I be, / Nor I, nor any man that but man is, / With nothing shall be pleas'd, till he be eas'd / With being nothing" (v.v.38–41). The bucket that is Richard fills with tears because he is filled with nothing. He fills with nothing as he is emptied out. In Richard substance and the lack of substance that is its shadow converge, as in the gardener's odd metaphor to the Queen about Richard's insufficiency compared to Henry's capability: "Their fortunes both are weigh'd. / In your lord's scale is nothing but himself, / And some few vanities that make him light" (III.iv.84–86). Richard's vanities (both the emptiness of his purposes and the useless parasites that attend him), far from adding even a trivial amount to the weight on his side of the balance, make him even lighter than if they were nothing. Theirs is a strange negative mass, befitting Richard's increasing spectrality.

Richard's spectrality is the spectrality of grief, which renders Richard a king of grief. Grief is the first of many entities in the play to

---

61. See addendum C to Freud's *Inhibitions, Symptoms, and Anxiety*, in *Standard Edition*, 20:169–72, and J.-B. Pontalis, *Entre le rêve et la douleur psychic* (Paris: Gallimard, 1977).

become oddly reified, to take on its own shadowy being. Gaunt tells Henry that grief is merely the name for absence: "Thy grief is but thy absence for a time." "Joy absent, grief is present for that time," Henry replies (I.iii.258–59), echoing his aunt's simultaneous anthropomorphizing and deanthropomorphizing of grief:

> *Duchess of Gloucester:*   Farewell, old Gaunt! thy sometimes brother's wife
>   With her companion, grief, must end her life.
> *Gaunt:*   Sister, farewell, I must to Coventry.
>   As much good stay with thee as go with me!
> *Duchess:*   Yet one word more! Grief boundeth where [it] falls,
>   Not with empty hollowness, but weight.
>
> (I.ii.54–59)

This might be called an impersonal anthropomorphizing. It anticipates Richard's similarly impersonal intimacy with necessity. Here, no sooner does the Duchess personify grief than she treats it as massiveness again. It weighs with the heaviness of what should be hollow or empty like the inside of a ball. Richard later will "give this heavy weight from off my head" (IV.i.204) but, having done so, will lament "the heavy day" (IV.i.257) whose weight comes from the removal of the heavy crown. For Richard too grief will become a kind of companion, replacing his spouse. When the Queen asks him, "Why should hard-favor'd grief be lodg'd in thee?" he responds, "Join not with grief, fair woman, do not so, / To make my end too sudden" (V.i.14; 15–16). The substance of nothingness haunts Richard's hope for himself. "Make me, that nothing have, with nothing griev'd" (IV.i.216) he wishes; and that wish becomes too literally true, as it has previously for the Queen, who like Richard speaks the simple but spectral language of impotence. Her answer to Bushy's reminder that she has promised to be cheerful anticipates Richard's "I have been studying how I may compare / This prison where I live unto the world; / And for because the world is populous, / And here is not a creature but myself, / I cannot do it" (V.v.1–5). This last phrase echoes the Queen's reply to Bushy's entreaty to show cheer:

> I cannot do it; yet I know no cause
> Why I should welcome such a guest as grief,
> Save bidding farewell to so sweet a guest
> As my sweet Richard. Yet again methinks
> Some unborn sorrow, ripe in fortune's womb
> Is coming towards me, and my inward soul

> With nothing trembles; at some thing it grieves,
> More than with parting from my lord the King.
>   (II.ii.6–13)

In the space of grief, hollowness and substance join. In Gaunt, "Grief hath kept a tedious fast" (II.i.75) and so emptied him out and made him gaunt, "gaunt as a grave, / Whose hollow womb inherits nought but bones" (II.i.82–83). Grief with its oddly hollow weightiness resembles in its logic the vanity whose etymological meaning of emptiness or hollowness is constantly present, the vanity that makes Richard lighter than nothing: "Light vanity, insatiate cormorant / Consuming means, soon preys upon itself" (II.i.38–39). For the Queen, grief and nothingness come into apposition through the apparent contradictoriness of her claim that her soul "with nothing trembles; at some thing it grieves" (II.ii.12). This is nothing as positive negation again, and here the word works as a transition, since she does tremble, even if with nothing. The play of language whereby "nothing" attains to its negative heaviness verges on the baroque in this scene:

> *Queen:*   How'er it be,
>   I cannot but be sad; so heavy sad,
>   As, [though] on thinking on no thought I think,
>   Makes me with heavy nothing faint and shrink.
> *Bushy:* 'Tis nothing but conceit, my gracious lady.
> *Queen:* 'Tis nothing less: conceit is still deriv'd
>   From some forefather grief; mine is not so,
>   For nothing hath begot my something grief,
>   Or something hath the nothing that I grieve—
>   'Tis in reversion that I do possess
>   But what it is that is not yet known what,
>   I cannot name; 'tis nameless woe, I wot.
>   (II.ii.29–40)

This speech may feel a little labored, but it is important. What she possesses "in reversion" is some nameless woe, whereas Henry leaves the kingdom acting "as were our England in reversion his" (I.iv.35). It is his in reversion because Richard and Isabel have no heir of their own. The absence of an heir presents itself for the Queen as the negative presence of grief. This is the "unborn sorrow, ripe in fortune's womb" (II.ii.10) which images her grief that it should be grief and not a child that she harbors as her guest, that her womb should be as hollow as the grave. Heavy nothing has begot grief; Richard has failed to beget a child. And Green's report of Bullingbrook's rebellion causes grief's birth:

> So, Green, thou art the midwife to my woe,
> And Bullingbrook my sorrow's dismal heir.
> Now hath my soul brought forth her prodigy,
> And I, a gasping new-delivr'd mother,
> Have woe to woe, sorrow to sorrow join'd.
> (II.ii.62–66)

She has already joined with grief, and Richard's later imperative, "Join not with grief," (v.i.16) comes too late. Bullingbrook is old enough to be her heir as well. The language of this scene, through its dense intrication with the motifs of Richard's degradation, assimilates the Queen to Richard as an already preterite figure. Bushy's strange attempt to talk her out of her grief—strange because no one would argue that the representations hidden in an anamorphosis were insignificant because hidden—shows her even now a denizen of the shadow world that Richard will come to inhabit. The language of Bushy's arguments anticipates the mirror scene, as does the Queen's reponse, with its introspective attention to the inward or tortured soul:

> *Bushy:* Each substance of a grief hath twenty shadows,
>   Which shows like grief itself, but is not so;
>   For sorrow's eyes, glazed with blinding tears,
>   Divides one thing entire to many objects,
>   Like perspectives, which rightly gaz'd upon
>   Show nothing but confusion; ey'd awry
>   Distinguish form; so your sweet Majesty,
>   Looking awry upon your lord's departure,
>   Find shapes of grief, more than himself, to wail,
>   Which, look'd on as it is, is nought but shadows
>   Of what is not; then, thrice-gracious Queen,
>   More than your lord's departure weep not—more is not seen,
>   Or if it be, 'tis with false sorrow's eye,
>   Which for things true weeps things imaginary.
> *Queen:* It may be so; but yet my inward soul
>   Persuades me it is otherwise.
>
> (II.ii.14–29)

Expenditure is a mode of power in the world that tends to its own undoing, and there seems to be a limit to that undoing, a zero point where nothing remains to be expended. But beyond the zero is a shadow world where expenditure is infinite and endless, where grief's multiplications of its shadows increase the darkness of the world of shadows, endlessly. This preterite, and in *Richard II* clearly poetic or literary, space is not only the obverse of power. It draws even power into its strange negativity. The regret that seems to haunt Henry and that will haunt him more and more in the two parts of *Henry IV* until he too "is gone wild into his grave" (2 *Henry IV*, v.ii.123) has its origin in the sacrifice he makes of Richard. It is as a symbol that Henry can love Richard: "I . . . love him murthered" (v.vi.40). As a symbol Richard, alienated from himself, stands in strange proximity to Henry. This is proximity without presence, the hallmark of the literary, whence the peculiar and preterite power of Richard's language.

By becoming symbolic, Richard has as it were become grief, or has attained to the peculiarly impersonal status that the personification of grief has imaged. Herbert, I think, remembers *Richard II* in "Confession" ("O what a cunning guest / Is this same grief!"); at any rate, his use of the third person, as I argued above, tends toward a similar impersonality, the impersonality of what is excluded from intercourse with the quotidian (as Blanchot would say) or the ordinary (in Cavell's language). The space of the preterite has a peculiar impersonal intimacy, an intimacy without affection, which I will explore more fully in *King Lear*, in the next section of this chapter.

For Henry to sacrifice this preterite power as he does is to sacrifice the possibility of a relationship with the alterity that Richard has come to represent, a sacrifice that by a strange and natural antithesis eventuates in Henry's being marked by this alterity or wildness as well. In the shadow world of expenditure, the world of Shakespearean language, nothing remains to be spent except language, which spends itself and spends itself without recompense and without any depletion of the grief that is its substance. This hyperexpenditure, expenditure below zero, need not necessarily originate in grief; rather, grief is one of its forms. Shakespeare remained fascinated with the kind of extravagance that means a wandering beyond the limit, a wandering into literary space—an extravagance not only with possession but with being itself. When Shakespearean characters have less than nothing but continue to give what they have away, the evaporation of their own being seems to transform itself into language. To give everything away is to attain to the shadow possibility of literary utterance, as Richard does, and as Lear and Antony will do.

To Boot and Boot

Surely oppression maketh a wise man mad; and a gift destroyeth the heart.

—Ecclesiastes 7:7

Was Du für ein Geschenk hältst, ist ein Problem, das Du lösen sollst.

—Wittgenstein

Beyond beyond . . .

—*Cymbeline*

Vastly different as their characters are, Lear and Richard resemble each other in the way they seek to confer the onus of obligation along with their gifts. *King Lear* may also be considered a play which marks the transition from a gift economy (an economy of reciprocation, of mutual obligation, like feudalism) to the nascent bourgeois exchange economy of the early seventeenth century. The *Henriad* makes Richard the last and most manipulative representative of the old order, shrewdly managing for a time his youthful extravagance so as to keep such old-style elders as Gaunt and even York loyal (at least until the pressure of the new order that Bullingbrook represents becomes too much for him) and shrewdly making his wildness stand for what is sacred about him—as though his erratic behavior signifies the magical inconsistency of the divine. Richard's not inconsiderable mode of power may come down to the way he represents himself as divinely able to afford his spendthrift eccentricity, and as divinely proof against anything in the world, his own behavior included, that would "wash the balm off from an anointed king" (III.ii.55). Henry, however, belongs to a new and secular order for which the category of the sacred has lost its meaning, and Henry is its shrewdest representative before Hal. Hal is shrewdest of all, particularly in the way he reconciles gift and exchange economies. But this reconciliation no longer holds in *King Lear*.

Lear imagines obligation on the part of Regan and Goneril, obligation that they do not feel. But in this play—and, as I shall argue, in Shakespeare's late plays in general—there is no chance of the reconciliation between old and new order, gift and capitalist economy, that Hal embodies. Cordelia, as the good daughter and a gentler and less ambivalent version of the uncanny Hal, might be expected to provide the solution that would combine both orders. But, surprisingly, it is Regan and Goneril who are willing to straddle epochs (of course only for the self-interested ends of the new epoch), whereas Lear's rage against Cordelia has its roots in her refusal to compromise with the old ways, her refusal to give more than "nothing."

Unlike Richard, Lear recognizes something like contract. The pure gift economy in which Richard operates tends to be an economy in which exchange takes place in some deep sense without even an implicit contract. Bataille stresses that any notion of gift exchange that simply posits a different manifestation of the structure schematized in a capitalist marketplace will lead to a genuine and deep inconsistency. For, given the equation of generosity with power in the gift economy, to give someone a gift with the conscious or explicit expectation of return means to be aware of conferring on her or him not only obligation but also power—the power to outdo and so shame the giver: "The original giver *suffers* the apparent gain resulting from the difference between his gifts and those which are returned to him. Only the person who returns has the sense of acquisition—the acquisition of power—and of victory. The truth is . . . that the ideal potlatch would be one that could not be returned. The gift in no way corresponds to the desire for gain" (*La part maudite*, in *Oeuvres*, 7:73). Bourdieu makes a similar point in the last chapter of *Outline of a Theory of Practice*. He does not argue that there is no quid pro quo, but that it cannot be acknowledged. The repression of an open expectation of reciprocity makes for a temporal element in exchange: the gift cannot be returned immediately, since that would be to acknowledge that indeed only bartering is going on. The deferral that makes the gift seem a genuine gift also lays the recipient under an obligation for that time, and there is no way to get out of that obligation gracefully (least of all by repaying the debt quickly, which would be a sign of ingratitude). Culture (as the unequal distribution of symbolic capital) is formed by the repression of the fact of equivalent exchange.[62]

62. Bourdieu is perhaps more hardheaded than Bataille, although Bataille may have more to say to the manifest content of literature, which is my concern; and the meaning of this manifest content may not yield to the reductionism that Georges Lukács (*History and Class Consciousness: Studies in Marxist Dialectics* [Cambridge, Mass.: MIT Press, 1971]) argues is typical of capitalism. Reductionism is only a part of Bourdieu's program, however, and the part he warns most stringently against taking as final. What finally counts for the Wittgensteinian Bourdieu, as opposed to the Freudian structuralists, is practice and not the latent mental contents that issue in practice.

The Merchant of Venice can be taken as just as hardheaded (and as softhearted) as Bourdieu. In *Sociologies*, Mauss describes "certains potlatch [où] on doit dépenser tout ce que l'on a et ne rien garder" (p. 200) ("where you are to expend all that you have and keep nothing"). He may have been thinking of the lead casket and its requirement—

There is indeed a sense in which Lear begins the play desiring to make something close to Bataille's ideally unrepayable gift. But he nevertheless makes this desire explicit in a contract. True, this contract's spectacular imbalance is meant to attest to Lear's generosity. Nevertheless, the play begins in a mode that attempts to reconcile gift and contractual exchange, attempts to regulate free gifts by contract, and yet preserve their essence as gifts. In his opening challenge Lear negotiates the two modes, but far more ineptly than Hal:

> Tell me, my daughters,
> (Since now we will divest us both of rule,
> Interest of territory, cares of state),
> Which of you shall we say doth love us most?
> That we our largest bounty may extend
> Where nature doth with merit challenge?
> (I.i.48–53)[63]

Nature and merit, gifts and deserts, challenge each other here, and their part in each daughter challenges the nature and merit of the others. But the language of competition also speaks to a kind of rivalry with the benefactor characteristic of gift economies. Lear's daughters are to attempt the challenge of matching his goodness with their flattery. He speaks the language of generosity—"our largest bounty"—but the generosity (churlishly) contracts for and announces its expectation of a quid pro quo in gratitude from his daughters. Lear's odd formulation "Which of you *shall we say* doth love us most" indicates that he knows he wants flattery. Flattery means the acknowl-

---

"Who chooseth me must give and hazard all he hath" (II..ix.21)—in contrast with the ideologies of primitive accumulation ("Who chooseth me shall gain what many men desire" [l. 24]) and equivalent exchange ("Who chooseth me shall get as much as he deserves" [l. 35]) of the gold and silver caskets. At any rate, under the sign of harmonious marriage, giving and hazarding all leads Bassanio to the possession of the rich lady as both person and commodity. (The pun that ends the play makes the connection vivid, although explicit only for the servant or sidekick class and not for the aristocracy.) But this demonstration of the harmonizing of bourgeois exchange with an ethos of generosity does not withstand the insights of the later plays, for example, *Hamlet*. Hamlet's rebuke to Ophelia "I never gave you aught" (III.i.95) marks his utter rejection of any of the conventions of the gift economy, as does his parody gift to Polonius upon the old man's taking leave: "You cannot take from me any thing that I will more willingly part withal—except my life, except my life, except my life" (II.ii.215–17). *King Lear* also articulates the impossibility of harmonizing gift and equivalence, successfully repressing the self-interest of equivalence.

63. I use the conflated text because, among other reasons, I am treating Shakespeare's work as a whole and in general, and I am not paying a great deal of attention to the boundaries between particular plays.

edgment of obligation. Lear desires such acknowledgment: he desires
to reduce his daughters to an acknowledgment of the kindness that
obliges them to something so easy as flattery.

In this way *King Lear* begins with a happy coincidence of gift and
contract. Lear makes explicit the finality of the generosity he offers
here. The exchange is to be made once and for all, as an explicit
trade: territory and sovereignty (with Lear's small reserve) for the
language of love and loyalty. As a contract this fixes the terms of the
exchange. The contract is final. Lear is not to get back anything beyond this at some future date, since the future for him holds, he
imagines, nothing: "'Tis our fast intent / To shake all cares and business from our age, / Conferring them on younger strengths, while
we / Unburthen'd crawl towards death" (i.i.38–41). Of course this
contract is, in its very imbalance, a gift. It is for the magnanimity of
this contract that Lear admires himself. Empson points out the reiterated occurrences of the sentence "I gave you all."[64] Indeed he does
give them all, and in such a manner as to prevent them from making a
return—not that they would have done so. But his misreading of their
characters, especially of their economic characters, might make him
believe that he would otherwise find himself, as Bataille says, vulnerable to their countergifts. Lear has left himself terribly vulnerable to
Regan and Goneril, as he is soon to discover, but he has foreclosed one
possibility: that they will shame him through their own lavish return
of his generosity.

This behavior is very much in keeping with Lear's paternal imperiousness. His gifts to his daughters are meant to secure him an in-
superable paternal power. In a gift economy, power finally belongs to
those whose gifts their beneficiaries cannot repay. Henceforth those
beneficiaries remain obliged to their benefactors. Lear goes farther;
he attempts to *contract* such an impossibility of repayment.[65] But to
make obligation explicit, as every child knows, is to undo the internal-
ization that makes obligation an effective power, the beneficiary's in-
ternalization of debt or guilt. Thus, at the end of the first scene
Goneril and Regan begin to talk themselves out of any guilt or obliga-

64. William Empson, *The Structure of Complex Words* (Norfolk, Conn.: New Directions,
n.d.), p. 137. Empson regards his own reading of the play as indebted to Orwell's
summary of its moral, that renunciation ought to be serious. My own reading hardly
differs from this: the question here is whether renunciation need also renounce its
public merit, and the moral answer, for Empson and Orwell, would probably be yes.
65. See Boose on fathers giving away daughters in "Father and Bride." She very
beautifully reads the scene between Lear, Cordelia, and France as densely allusive to the
marriage ceremony.

tion to Lear.[66] His generosity manifests itself in the fact that the contract he offers—kingdoms for the mere declaration of love—is so one-sided. He wants only the indebted acknowledgment of a kindness that obliges his daughters to something so easy as flattery and hardly indebts them further. But finally, just because he makes the debt explicit in a contract, he gives away even the sense of indebtedness he meant to impose.

It is partly France's role to show the magnanimous power of the countergift Lear has sought, at too great a cost, to escape. His beneficence to Cordelia necessarily underscores Lear's rash and unpremeditated niggardliness toward her. Shakespeare makes an audience feel the difference between the two men at that moment by contrasting their capacities for generosity, for generosity in their valuations of Cordelia. France declares of Cordelia, "She is herself a dowry" (i.i.241), and so he himself effectually bestows upon her the wealth her father has withheld when he addresses her as "Fairest Cordelia, that art most rich being poor, / Most choice, forsaken, and most lov'd, despis'd" (i.i.249–50). The same gift that France munificently (though of course accurately) values so highly, Lear regards as worthless, "cast away" (i.i.253). With respect to Cordelia, he utterly refuses to conform to the laws of generosity. He gives vent to his hatred by stressing their abrogation:

> Thou hast her, France, let her be thine, for we
> Have no such daughter, nor shall ever see
> That face of hers again. Therefore be gone,
> Without our grace, our love, our benison.—
> Come, noble Burgundy.
>
> (i.i.261–65)

And yet Lear's abrogation of these laws is not the first in the play. For Cordelia has already violated the vestigial norms of the gift economy that Lear is attempting to assimilate into the newer bourgeois order. Regan and Goneril are willing to accept the obligation to please that they incur with the gift, or at least they appear to accept it. But in contrast to her sisters, who offer the sacrifice of everything—"eyesight, space, and liberty" (i.i.56)—Cordelia insists on the primacy of equivalent exchange and refuses to acknowledge boundless obliga-

66. On Goneril's possible near-reasonableness, see Gary Taylor, *To Analyze Delight: A Hedonist Criticism of Shakespeare* (Newark: University of Delaware Press, 1985), pp. 171–77.

tion. Like Shylock, she talks the language of economics even within familial relations:

> *Cordelia:*   I love your Majesty
>   According to my bond, no more nor less.
> *Lear:* How, how, Cordelia? Mend your speech a little,
>   Lest you may mar your fortunes.
> *Cordelia:*   Good my lord,
>   You have begot me, bred me, lov'd me: I
>   Return those duties back as are right fit,
>   Obey you, love you, and most honour you.
>   (1.i.92–98)

Cordelia's unnecessary inflexibility here has often been called her one flaw. Her language conceives exchange not under the rubric of generosity and countergenerosity but under that of equivalences.[67] Cordelia accepts from Lear not gifts but "duties," and she returns precisely what she has received and "no more." "No more" is a crucial phrase in the play, and this interchange illustrates its function. Cordelia's precision contrasts with Lear's deliberate understatement, an understatement consonant with what he offers: fortunes for speech. Cordelia need only mend her speech "a little," (another crucial phrase) to avoid the major catastrophe of ruining her future. So little, obligation or language, will yield so much in return, in the gift economy that Lear defends. For Lear, equivalent exchange reduces only to the spare and equal nihilism that has often been seen as the final truth of the play. "Nothing will come of nothing" (1.i.90) describes equivalent exchange, and Lear opposes this to the gift economy, where much comes from "a little." The language of equivalence can become nihilistic indeed:

> The barbarous Scythian,
> Or he that makes his generation messes
> To gorge his appetite, shall to my bosom
> Be *as well* neighbour'd, pitied, and reliev'd,
> As thou my sometime daughter.
>   (1.i.116–20)

67. Franco Moretti reads this in the opposite way; he sees Cordelia as asserting an "untainted feudal spirit" and maintains that she "still inhabits a world of reciprocal obligation, of feudal rights and duties, whereas Lear aspires to absolute omnipotence" ("'A Huge Eclipse': Tragic Form and the Deconsecration of Sovereignty" in *The Power of Forms in the English Renaissance*, ed. Stephen Greenblatt [Norman, Okla.: Pilgrim Books, 1982], p. 15).

The gift economy is an economy of inequalities. A gift obliges its recipient to return a gift of greater value than the gift he or she has received. It is not Cordelia, at the start of the play, who speaks the language of inequality. This language would insist on moving "beyond all manner of so much" (I.i.61). At the end of the play, however, Cordelia does speak this language. She effectually undoes the impulses behind her opening speech when she thanks Kent for his aid: "O thou good Kent, how shall I live and work / To match thy goodness? My life will be too short, / And every measure fail me" (IV.vii.1–3). Her words are not utterly different from her language in act 1 only because they momentarily preserve a remnant of the notion of an obligation to equivalent exchange, but this is an obligation she knows she cannot meet. The word *match* suggests a quid pro quo, but it also picks up the sense appropriate to a gift economy that beneficence is a challenge which must be met, and not merely a good available for sale. Kent's reply—"To be acknowledg'd, madam, is o'er-paid" (IV.vii.4)—completes the transformation of language to that appropriate for the gift economy.

Lear shares a deluded version of this language with his elder daughters. Goneril's first speech, from its opening line, insists on comparative adjectives and adverbs, and strange quasi-rhymes of the comparative play like what John Hollander calls virtual morphemes in, all the other words ending in an *er* sound—*Sir, matter, rare, honor, e'er, father,* and *manner,* as well as in *word* and *liberty*:

> Sir, I love you more than [words] can wield the matter,
> Dearer than eyesight, space, and liberty,
> Beyond what can be valued, rich or rare,
> No less than life, with grace, health, beauty, honor;
> As much as child e'er lov'd, or father found;
> A love that makes breath poor, and speech unable:
> Beyond all manner of so much I love you.
>
> (I.i.55–61)

Against this assertion, Regan claims that Goneril "comes too short" (I.i.71), using rhetoric that Cordelia will echo only when she thanks Kent ("My life will be too short"). Cordelia wins over at least the audience when she too speaks a version of this language: "I am sure my love's / More ponderous than my tongue" (I.i.77–78). The truth about Cordelia, of course, is that she is the only one of Lear's daughters entitled to this language since she alone acts with real generosity toward him. Regan and Goneril show all too well the perilous success of Lear's placing them under an unfulfillable obligation. Their refusal to house Lear's knights or, at last, Lear himself testifies to a depth of resentment whose familial countours make it necessarily familiar to an audience. It is the child's resentment—to be echoed by Satan—of the unpayable obligation, the debt immense of endless gratitude, owed the parent. Lear's demands are inconsequential. As such they at once create and symbolize an obligation that cannot fully be met: endless "dues of gratitude" (II.iv.179). The very insubstantiality of what Lear requires means that Regan and Goneril can make no substantial return to him. This imposed sense of obligation toward an object of contempt, I think, causes their otherwise unmotivated malignity.

The family romance so recognizable in *King Lear* always has just this dynamic. Sexist critics have tended to take Lear too much at his word in imagining Regan and Goneril as entirely "unnatural monsters." Act 2, scene 4, however, shows them in one of several familial situations in which they put on a sort of oedipal bravery, identifying with the authorities they now seek to supplant. Premeditated evil could not issue in the need for sisterly ratification, in the tentatively self-excusing and confirmation-seeking language of an exchange like this one, after Lear has gone out into the storm:

> *Regan:*   This house is little, the old man and 's people
>   Cannot be well bestow'd.
> *Goneril:* 'Tis his own blame hath put himself from rest
>   And must needs taste his folly.
> *Regan:*   For his particular, I'll receive him gladly,
>   But not one follower.
> *Goneril:*   So am I purpos'd.
>   (II.iv.288–93)

Cordelia's belated but genuine generosity to Lear contrasts with the specious generosity that Lear attempts to codify in a contract (a contract that we all feel Cordelia is right to refuse, even though her refusal does display a seemingly mean-spirited obstinacy on her part). Lear attempts the language of comparatives, but of course his language is resolutely imperious. In the course of the play Lear will discover the endlessness of the comparative—the interminability of alienation and loss—that is *King Lear*'s deeper moral. The play opens, however, with Lear resisting this interminabilty and seeking to put an end to the space opened by the comparative. Although the comparative is the mode of the gift, Lear aspires to the equalizing language of

absolutism and finality. This aspiration is clear in the very first interchange of the play, where Lear's greater affection for Albany gives
way to a scrupulous regard for equivalence in their portions:

> *Kent:*   I thought the King had more affected the Duke of Albany than
> Cornwall.
> *Gloucester:*   It did always seem so to us; but now in the division of the
> kingdom, it appears not which of the Dukes he values most, for [equal-
> ities] are so weigh'd, that curiosity in neither can make choice of either's
> moi'ty.
>
> (i.i.1–7)

What here comes out as a zealous evenhandedness will soon take on
the relentless tones of Lear's bitter "Nothing is got for nothing." His
chiasmatic curse on Cordelia undoes the comparatives that frame it,
since what is "better" has not happened: "Better thou / Hadst not
been born than not t' have pleas'd me better" (i.i.233–34). His imperiousness comes out in his consistent use of the superlative form.
"Which of you shall we say doth love us most, / That we our largest
bounty may extend" (i.i.51–52), he asks, and later he mourns Cordelia's faithlessness (as he thinks it) by a kind of negative gift, in the
weird formulation "I give / Her father's heart from her":

> I lov'd her most, and thought to set my rest
> On her kind nursery. Hence, and avoid my sight!—
> So be my grave my peace, as here I give
> Her father's heart from her. Call France. Who stirs?
> Call Burgundy. Cornwall and Albany,
> With my two daughters' dow'rs digest the third;
> Let pride, which she calls plainness, marry her.
> I do invest you jointly with my power,
> Pre-eminence, and all the large effects
> That troop with majesty. Ourself, by monthly course,
> With reservation of an hundred knights
> By you to be sustain'd, shall our abode
> Make with you by due turn. Only we shall retain
> The name, and all th' addition to a king;
> The sway, revenue, execution of the rest,
> Beloved sons, be yours.
>
> (i.i.123–138)

Unlike Goneril's this speech abounds with anagrams of the superla-
tive: *most, rest* (twice), *sight* perhaps, and *stirs, digest, invest, effects*, possibly, *majesty* (of course), perhaps *knights*, and *sustain'd*. Those com-

parative rhymes that are there tend to assimilate themselves to super-latives. *Power* is surrounded by *invest* and *effects* and by itself seems curiously weak, stuttering its way into *pre-eminence*. A counter-parsing of word endings haunts phrases like "father's heart," which threatens to collapse into an *est* ending, as well as phrases like "daught*ers'-dowers* *d*igest," so that a competition between comparative and superlative can be heard in the twice repeated *ersd* (very close to *erst*), with the gift-marking comparative pun in *dower* finally resolved into the *est* of *digest*.[68]

Lear continues the language of absolutism through the rest of the scene. To Kent's intercession ("Revoke thy gift," Kent pleads a few lines later [1.i.164]) he echoes Cordelia when he threatens, "Kent, on thy life, no more" (1.i.154). He asks Burgundy the ungenerous question, "What, in the least, / Will you require in present dower with her?" (1.i.191–92). Burgundy replies that he wants "no more than hath your Highness offer'd, / Nor will you tender less" (1.i.194–95), but Lear refuses even this compromise formulation in which he will have to deliver "no more" than he's contracted to give:

> Right noble Burgundy,
> When she was dear to us, we did hold her so,
> But now her price is fallen. Sir, there she stands:
> If aught within that little seeming substance,
> Or all of it, with our displeasure piec'd,
> And nothing more, may fitly like your Grace,
> She's there, and she is yours.
>
> (1.i.195–201)

This speech plays on the difference between an economy based on gifts and one based on equivalent exchange. When she was dear, her father would have paid dearly whoever took her hand in marriage, not sold her dearly. That "her price is fallen" means that Lear is not willing to *give* Burgundy as much; it does not mean (as it might appear out of context) that he can purchase her at a cheaper rate. Price here means a valuation measured in the generosity of the giver; he

68. The names Edgar and Edmund might reflect a similar divergence; Edmund would be the worldly version, that which belongs to the *mundus*, but Edgar would be more than this. In this connection Edmund's line "The better best" (11.i.14; it appears thus in both quarto and folio) would ambiguously combine comparative and superlative. Certainly Edgar's later meditation on the relation of the worst to the worse resonates with this interjection. I thank Joseph Kramer for discussing some of these ideas with me; it was he who suggested the epigraph "Beyond beyond" and who cited "The better best."

will pay a high price along with his gift to mark its worth and a lower price (or none at all) once he denies that worth. In the gift economy, the value of the gift is pieced out with a further inequality—the beneficiary receives the gift and more: he also receives a dowry, which makes for a difference between the animate bride and the commodities she brings with her. Now, however, she is cheapened in all ways: divested of a dowry and treated as a mere commodity, and a not very valuable one at that. In refusing her a dowry Lear refuses Cordelia the generous gesture of indefinite increase; he rejects the undefined language of inequality and instead invokes the all-or-nothing terminology of absolutism. Burgundy can have "all of it . . . and nothing more." It is only to avoid breaking decorum with France and to prevent offense that Lear returns to the diplomatic language of comparatives when he beseeches him "T' avert your liking a more worthier way" (1.i.211).

Lear reduces Cordelia's dowry to his curse (1.i.204) and her truth (1.i.108). Thus he intends to equalize all inequality in the nothing that he gives her. France, however, values her because "she is herself a dowry," and this line suggests a kind of spectral and residual gift economy that continues or subsists even when Lear's generosity ends. Cordelia underscores the strangeness of this spectral residue of the comparative when she expresses her eerie gratefulness that she should display a "want of that for which I am richer" (1.i.230).

This want that makes her rich is her truthfulness. Truth in the play appears to speak a language of flat, nihilistic equality. There is a sense in which things are worse, however, and in which truth participates in the inequality of the gift economy without that inequality signaling increase. Gifts are designed to express affection, but the world of *King Lear* is a world of intimacy without affection. It is an alien world or a world in which the alien and the intimate become synonymous. All affection in the play does indeed reduce to nothing (in Cordelia's case, through the arbitrary violence Johnson lamented). But a spectral intimacy continues. The play evokes the intimacy of the gift without its substance.

Lear imagines *nothing* as an absolute, a superlative, the bottommost. In his absolutist scheme, giving can come to an end: "Nothing. I have sworn, I am firm" (1.i.245). His lament at his own powerlessness comes out when he tells his daughters, "I gave you all," all that they have, but also all that he once had (except the title of fool: "All thy other titles thou hast given away," says the Fool [1.iv.149]). But the play describes something beyond that limit, beyond the zero. It is there that truth resides. Edgar formulates this lesson most starkly at the start of act 4, when the bottom falls out for him:

> Yet better thus, and known to be contemn'd,
> Than still contemn'd and flatter'd. To be worst,
> The lowest and most dejected thing of fortune,
> Stands still in esperance, lives not in fear.
> The lamentable change is from the best,
> The worst returns to laughter. Welcome then,
> Thou unsubstantial air that I embrace:
> The wretch that thou hast blown unto the worst
> Owes nothing to thy blasts.
>
> (IV.i.1–9)

Here Edgar imagines something like Lear's initial absolutism, or superlativism, as it might be called. Lear begins the play thinking he is at the very end of his life—speaking the fifth act's language of ultimates. Stephen Booth, in his remarkable analysis of *King Lear* in his *King Lear, Macbeth, Indefinition, and Tragedy*, notes all of the play's false endings and the way it seems to go on interminably. Much of his argument is congruent with my own.[69] In fact, things have hardly begun for Lear. Edgar's metaphor is derived, rather, from the wheel of fortune, but like Lear's it imagines a limit to descent. This is a strange limit, since somehow the superlatives nevertheless slip into comparatives: to be worst is better than not to be worst. The laughter to which the worst returns once more rhymes with the comparative. Here, of course, the comparatives mean to mitigate the disaster signified by the limits they qualify; they return from rather than exceed the superlative. This theory of the worst, as Empson calls it, is not to last, however. The appearance of Gloucester undoes it:

> But who comes here?
> My father, poorly led? World, world, O world!
> But that thy strange mutations make us hate thee,
> Life would not yield to age.
>
> (IV.i.9–12)[70]

Strange here is the nonsymmetrical contrast between life and age, where we expect life and death. Age comes out here as opposed to the

---

69. Stephen Booth, *King Lear, Macbeth, Indefinition, and Tragedy* (New Haven, Conn.: Yale University Press, 1983). Rereading Booth and Empson repeatedly spurs me to acknowledge how many of my points their obiter dicta anticipate.
70. I follow the Folio here, preserving "poorly led."

life it is nevertheless part of. To yield to age must mean something like this: to attempt to end mutation by conceding everything to the finality of death, but to fail even at that attempt at finality. Lear, who begins the play ready to die, only to discover that his true aging has hardly begun, experiences that failure. These haunting words undo the experience of limits. Life enters the interminable region of the comparative. Edgar laments this a short while further on: "O gods! Who is't can say, 'I am at the worst'? / I am worse than e'er I was. . . . / And worse I may be yet; the worst is not / So long as we can say, 'This is the worst'" (IV.i.25–28). By saying *this* is the worst, we try to use language referentially to put an end to the comparative; but the nonreferential comparative haunts endlessly and undoes the attempt at the referential stability of the here and now as the bottommost. The comparative form has no fixed limit:[71] this is the shadow cast by the gift in this world without generosity. Life yields to the interminable comparative form of age, and age is indeed interminable in *King Lear*. The last lines of the play provide a resolution, as Edgar finally moves the language into the realm of finality and of the superlative; but the strangeness of the lines nevertheless subsists, and the superlative is more a blank description than a judgment as to absolutes:

> The oldest hath borne most: we that are young
> Shall never see so much, nor live so long.
> (v.iii.326–7)

How, one might ask, does Edgar know this? How does he know that he won't outlive Lear? This is partly an echo of Cordelia's thanks to Kent: "How shall I live and work / To match thy goodness? My life will be too short, / And every measure fail me" (IV.vii.1–3), and so suggests an odd reprisal of the language of the gift. Edgar's attempt to achieve a superlative fails again when confronted with age: as life yields to age, the superlative here yields to a description of something

71. Reuben Brower (*Hero and Saint: Shakespeare and the Graeco-Roman Heroic Tradition* [New York: Oxford University Press, 1971]) gives a sensitive account of the adventures of the word *worst* in the play, seeing it as responding to the question (which I think erroneous) "What happens to heroic man when faced with the absolute 'worst'?" (p. 384). He finds hope in the way the play finally acknowledges a Christianizing possibility of retreat from the worst, and he is quite eloquent on these lines. He argues that for Edgar to discover that "life holds the possibility of a horror beyond the present one . . . is a source of strength: 'so long as we can *say*', can articulate, we stand, though perilously, above the horror that opens before us" (p. 400). But Edgar is in error to say "this is the worst," because things risk getting even worse, not because he feels this as a way out or a retreat. The interminability and endless comparativity of language is exactly what these lines bring out.

beyond an absolute limit. Others, besides the oldest (Lear and Gloucester),[72] will not have been and will not be exposed to this mode of pure comparativity. Thus Gloucester, as Regan and Cornwall are about to blind him, implores aid in language whose inefficacy becomes immediately apparent. "He that will think to live till he be old, / Give me some help!" (ii.vii.69–70) he cries, but the return on the gift of help is the instantaneous death Gloucester will helplessly crave and not a ripe old age: "O! I am slain" (iii.vii.80) says Gloucester's would-be savior.[73] Only the oldest in the play exceed the natural limit of life. "Age is unnecessary" (ii.iv.155) to the new capitalist economy; it has no use value; but in the play this also means that age has exceeded the limits in which necessity works its grim but finite finalities; age has surpassed the limits of the absolute. Lear has inhabited a strange temporal zone of aging that extends beyond death. Edgar knows, with the full knowledge of the play, that Lear has gone beyond the boundary which is the natural limit of life. "The wonder is he hath endur'd so long, / He but usurp'd his life" (v.iii.317–18) is how Kent puts it. This too is the lesson of the Fool's uncanny wit: "If thou wert my Fool, nuncle, I'ld have thee beaten for being old before thy time" (i.v.41– 42). Age here no longer refers to temporal measure. To be old as the Fool says Lear is old means to have lived a prodigal and contingent relationship to time. Age does not belong to a temporal continuum any more.

Lear begins at the limit of continuous temporality. He has given away "all." He has reserved next to nothing and is ready to die. But he has yet to learn the secret art of necessity, which works on him and takes him beyond the zero. The negative moment of generosity, or of Bataillean expenditure, is yet to come. It will manifest itself as an undoing of superlatives when Lear realizes that there is no limit to the possibility of expenditure, that no poverty will relieve the inexorable necessity of a further dissipation of substance. To his daughters' de-

72. The first folio makes *oldest* singular: "The oldest hath born most." The first quarto makes it plural but gives the speech to Albany. I think the plural in the quarto and the singular in the folio finally are similarly indeterminate but that the singular is slightly preferable since it underlines the contrast between the undoing of distinction in old age versus the easily discriminable plurality of youth. This is a plurality different from the plurality I examine below. I think this is a prime instance of a Shakespearean revision (if it is one) working as a palimpsest; I think that the singularization of "the oldest" has to be understood as though the plural is still there, only with reference to plural objects (discriminable persons) effaced. The analogy here would be to the "un-numbered . . . pebble" of iv.vi.21, which I discuss below.

73. This is in the folio but not in the quarto; if it is a genuine addition, it again can be taken to show Shakespeare returning to what he would have considered the important relation between generosity and age.

mands why he needs any followers at all, he cries, "O, reason not the need! our basest beggars / Are in the poorest thing superfluous" (ii.iv.264–65; note again the interplay of the virtual morphemes *est* and *er*, the latter echoing through *our, beggars, are, poorest,* and *superfluous*), so that the extreme limit of baseness turns out still to be a superfluity. Gloucester will echo this in act 4 when he begins his extravagant treatment of the madman who he thinks is guiding him:

> Here, take this purse, thou whom the heav'ns' plagues
> Have humbled to all strokes. That I am wretched
> Makes thee the happier; heavens, deal so still!
> Let the superfluous and lust-dieted man,
> That slaves your ordinance, that will not see
> Because he does not feel, feel your pow'r quickly;
> So distribution should undo excess,
> And each man have enough.
>
> (iv.i.64–71)

The self-laceration here does not fully explain the speech. Gloucester pities Edgar, not himself; the moral for this Ancient Mariner is to accept one's own punishment and to pity others, and his acceptance of this moral should bring him "enough" if it brings him peace. The prayer that affirms this moral, however, would not resolve the disasters of the world through an equable distribution. Gloucester prays instead for an endless inequality: the heavens are to continue to make the wretchedness of one person the source for another person's being happier: "happier," not "happy," introduced to the minimal beneficence of the comparative. This is hardly a case of each man having enough, the zero grade of the adjective. But even here Gloucester becomes aware of an endless superfluity in his situation which he cannot shuck off. The fact that he has more than one purse indicates this, as though he can never give away all his wealth and as if, no matter how degraded he gets, he will remain a kind of minimal Adonis, always able to "repair the misery thou dost bear / With something rich about me" (iv.i.76–77) and thus to make Edgar marginally, asymptotically "happier."

For his part, Lear is horrified when he first becomes aware of the negative limitlessness of superfluity. But later he will participate in it more fully. Edgar, in taking on the disguise of Tom, says that Bedlam beggars, even when they meet the poor—"low farms, / Poor pelting villages, sheep-cotes, and mills"—will "enforce their charity" (ii.iii.17–18), as though they too are simultaneously impoverished and susceptible to the demands of an endless largess. So it will be when he meets Lear, reduced already to utter poverty. Lear responds to Edgar's request, "Do poor Tom some charity" (III.iv.60), by shucking off those sophistications he still recognizes in himself: "Off, off, you lendings!" (III.iv.108). Though this still aims at approaching a limit— the limit represented by Edgar as unaccommodated man—it also goes beyond the previous limit Lear had postulated, in which warm clothing, at least, is conceived as a necessity: "If only to go warm were gorgeous / Why, nature needs not what thou gorgeous wear'st, / Which scarcely keeps thee warm" (II.iv.268–70). Nature here would still need some warmth (though even here need's near superfluity is marked by the fact that Regan seems scarcely to need warm clothes). Lear thinks Tom is beyond even the most minimal need for warmth and so is beyond all obligation for the "necessary" as well as the more obviously superfluous: "Thou ow'st the worm no silk, the beast no hide, the sheep no wool, the cat no perfume" (III.iv.103–5). But of course Edgar is soon to discover that he is, as yet, hardly at the worst.

The comparative mode of expenditure is eeriest and grimmest in the play when applied to aging. For life to yield means for life to expend itself and approach a zero point represented by death. If life yields to age, and not to death, then the expenditure of life becomes endless. All life is superfluous, but its dissipation leaves simply a more tenuous superfluity, the superfluity of age.

Old age in the play means being unable to die and so being unable to put an end to dying. Regan and Lear are equally deceived about the possibility of achieving some limit:

> O Sir! you are old,
> Nature in you stands on the very verge
> Of his confine!
>
> (II.iv.146–48)

This is Regan well before the halfway point of the play. Meant to warn Lear of the precariousness of his command on his own life, it also emphasizes the wishful assumption that to go a little—perhaps a foot—farther will mean Lear's death. Lear passes that "confine" and transgresses the limits of life to find not death but an interminable quasi-life, a strange parody of the normal life he has led. The nature of this transgression, of this going beyond the final term or terminus into the interminable, will be underscored in an uncannily literal way when Gloucester believes that he has come to the "cliff, whose high and bending head / Looks fearfully in the *confined* deep" (IV.i.73–74). The sea is confined here, not the land, so that life on land, for

Gloucester and Lear at any rate, is already uncanny because already beyond the verge of the deep's confine. Edgar, disguised as a madman in act 4, has led Gloucester, as the latter thinks, to the cliffs of Dover. There a strange farewell ritual of gift exchange takes place:

> *Edgar:* Give me your hand. You are now within a foot
> Of th' extreme verge. For all beneath the moon
> Would I not leap upright.
> *Gloucester:*   Let go my hand.
> Here, friend, 's another purse; in it a jewel
> Well worth a poor man's taking. Fairies and gods
> Prosper it with thee! Go thou further off:
> Bid me farewell, and let me hear thee going.
> *Edgar:* Now fare ye well, good sir. . . .
> *Gloucester:*   O you mighty gods!
> This world I do renounce, and in your sights
> Shake patiently my great affliction off.
> If I could bear it longer, and not fall
> To quarrel with your great opposeless wills,
> My snuff and loathed part of nature should
> Burn itself out. If Edgar live, O bless him!
> (IV.vi.25–32; 34–40)

"Give me your hand. . . . Let go my hand." A strange, purged humanity comes out here, readable in the way that it is Edgar now, and not the cliff, who "looks fearfully into the confined deep." He attempts a gift of kindness to Gloucester, makes him an offering of some companionship in the lonely and impersonal world his previous speech has just evoked: "The murmuring surge, / That on th' unnumb'red idle pebble chafes, / Cannot be heard so high. I'll look no more." (IV.vi.20–22). This speech is in the play's language of denatured generosity, of comparatives without substance. The pebble is unnumbered, idly indeterminate (even between singular and plural). The surge murmurs endlessly, but its murmuring affects not the ear (which cannot hear it) but the eye, which requires an act of will to draw it from the hypnotizing seductions of the comparative: "I'll look no more." In this minimal and denatured world Edgar directs toward Gloucester a countergenerosity: he leaves looking to the high and bending head of the cliff. He does not blind himself in any way, but he does offer Gloucester a spare minimalization of the difference between blindness and sight. Neither sees anything of note—this is also the *literal* truth for Edgar, since he is not at the cliff's edge—and in this world not given to sight, he offers Gloucester poetic language instead—the language of an empty description that describes nothing—and offers him too the minimal gift of his hand. He holds Gloucester's hand until Gloucester asks him to let go. In return, Gloucester makes him the second gift of his purse, continuing to distribute his endless superfluity. That a sort of kindness has taken place between them in this minimal and radically contingent world may be inferred from the odd and indirect exchange of blessing here performed, a blessing, I think, like the one the blind Isaac confers on Jacob. Gloucester asks Edgar to bid him farewell, partly in order to assure himself that Tom has left him alone, but also to leave on a note of blessing. Tom's "Now fare ye well, good sir" is not Edgar's but an austere, impersonal blessing belonging only to language, and this blessing Gloucester returns with a directness that is not his own but language's as well when he blesses Edgar. For it is Gloucester's language, not Gloucester, that returns Tom's blessing in blessing Edgar. Gloucester does not know that Edgar is there in person, and Edgar's presence, as evoked in Gloucester's language, is as spectral as Gloucester's generosity. (This too represents a strange inversion of the Isaac and Jacob story.)[74]

Gloucester imagines that he is about to put an end to the comparative mode which he can bear no "longer" and that he is now finally going to give away everything as he "renounces" the world and "shakes patiently his great affliction off" (IV.vi.36). The adverb *patiently*, however, already suggests that the comparative will not come to an end so quickly. And the grim eeriness of this scene inheres in the fact that the limit, the extreme verge, is no limit at all. Gloucester plunges beyond the extreme verge of his confine to find that nothing has changed, that he has not shaken his great affliction off but must continue to be "patient," as both Edgar (IV.vi.80) and Lear (IV.vi.178) tell him. Patience in *King Lear* means finally something different from its usual worldly meaning: (suppressed) *impatience*. Lear says "I can be patient" but means merely "I can wait *until* you come round." But the true patience of the play is patience that does not await anything, patience that is endless and that meets the interminable on its own terms.[75]

---

74. Brower remarks that act 4 "is a kind of subconscious 'recognition' scene, father and son meeting in sympathy before there is any actual recognition" (ibid., p. 399).

75. This is to be sharply differentiated from the two modes of patience—Stoic and Christian—that John F. Danby focuses on in "King Lear and Christian Patience" (*Cambridge Journal* 1 [1948], 305–20). Patience in *King Lear* ultimately means neither resignation nor hope but a relationship to a purely phantom temporality, that of time perpetually giving itself without any teleology.

That the cliff scene spatializes the temporal scheme of aging in the play is indicated not only by the echoes from Regan's speech but also by Edgar's momentarily deceived apprehension that Gloucester has, in fact, died:

> And yet I know not how conceit may rob
> The treasury of life, when life itself
> Yields to the theft. Had he been where he thought,
> By this had thought been past. Alive or dead?—
> Ho, you, sir! friend! Hear you, sir! speak!—
> Thus might he pass indeed; yet he revives.
> (IV.vi.42–47)

Thought is never past in *King Lear*, at least for the "oldest." (It is past for the servant who "thinks to live till he be old" and attacks Albany.) It continues relentlessly. Edgar's speech conceives Gloucester's temporal survival as well as his possible death in spatial terms analogous to the topographical fiction Edgar has foisted upon Gloucester. He might pass indeed and leave thought behind, leave it "past" or in the past. Edgar's fear that Gloucester has thought himself to death imagines one last time that what life yields to can indeed be death, not age. Should life yield its treasures to conceit, in a despairing access of generosity, it may be able to conceive its own death and so ultimately surpass itself. Gloucester's survival, however, shows life yielding to age, not to death. (For the youngest it will lead to death, in the inverse scene between Lear and Cordelia). Gloucester himself laments the interminable negative superfluity of his situation: "Is wretchedness depriv'd that benefit, / To end itself by death?" (IV.vi.61–62). For wretchedness to be deprived of this means for it to be deprived even of the finality of the nothingness that has too often seemed the play's ultimate moral. Wretchedness here must continue to live, that is, it must continue to be submitted to the excessive demands of a life that ceaselessly impoverishes. Edgar's theory of the worst invoked a benefit belonging to absolute poverty: there would be nothing more to lose. But Gloucester here confirms on his own pulse the axiom that he has lately taught Edgar: there is no absolute poverty, because even the basest beggars are in all things superfluous. Lear and Gloucester experience the comparative mode in its most austere form: the inability to die.[76] This comparativity governs the very odd precision of Lear's declaration to Cordelia: "I am a very foolish fond old man, / Fourscore and upward, not an hour more nor less"

---

76. See Maurice Blanchot, *L'espace littéraire* (Paris: Gallimard, 1955), pp. 104–34.

(IV.vii.59–60). The Fool had recommended a niggardly and accumulative version of comparative arithmetic in one of his first songs, where he encourages the Henrican virtues at the expense of Ricardian visibility:

> Have more than thou showest,
> Speak less than thou knowest,
> Lend less than thou owest,
> Ride more than thou goest,
> Learn less than thou trowest,
> Set less than thou throwest;
> Leave thy drink and thy whore,
> And keep in a' door,
> And thou shalt have more
> Than two tens to a score.
>   (I.iv.118–127)

The tone in Lear's speech to Cordelia, by contrast, may be perhaps described as a minimal comparative. Lear demands *next to* nothing. The infiniteness of the comparative borders on the nothing it comes infinitely close to. Lear describes his age to the hour, and yet what he describes is a comparative time: upward of four score. This translates into time the Fool's lesson about money—how to increase a score beyond its arithmetical limits.[77] But the pure temporality that the comparative mode evokes more and more starkly in the play has nothing to do with material increase. It is, rather, generosity without substance, or intimacy without affection.

It is the smallest of generosities that Lear requires of his last intimacy with Cordelia at the end of the play. There he echoes or shadows forth his initial imperiousness toward her. "Cordelia, stay a little" (V.iii.272), he addresses her dead body in the most minimal of recollections of his earlier demand: "Mend your speech a little" (I.i.94). But

---

77. W. R. Elton discusses arithmetical imagery in the play very interestingly, in *King Lear and the Gods* (San Marino, Calif.: Huntington Library, 1968), pp. 121–25. He sees the cries of "more, more" in the play as coming only from the mistaken capitalist souls in Edmund's camp. Obviously I disagree. Robert Heilman, in *This Great Stage: Image and Structure in King Lear* (Baton Rouge: Louisiana State University Press, 1948), p. 161, and Colie, who reads the play as staging a contest between aristocratic magnanimity and bourgeois calculation ("Reason and Need," pp. 212–16), both see Lear himself as exemplifying the new ethos of purchase in the love contest. They see him as trying to buy love, where I see that contest as a fundamental attempt to bring the gift relationship into a new context. Leir in the source is much shrewder, in this regard, than Lear, since he wants to use Cordelia's claim to obey him as an opportunity to marry her where he pleases.

even this hope that at last the inability to die should come to benefit Lear gets blasted here. Cordelia's death empties out the little, the short time, that Lear himself must still stay, empties it of any substance of kindness or hope.

This last inability on Cordelia's part to grant Lear the gift he wants reverses and so confirms the endlessness of life. Lear's desperate request confers upon her at that moment, in his mind at least, a quasi-life. But it is not only in his mind, I think: this last moment of parental gentleness on Lear's part, after all his cruelty, must feel to an audience as though it is not entirely lost. Although Lear and Cordelia have already expressed profound emotion at their reconciliation, only at her death does he resume the role of loving parent, protecting her and addressing her as a child. As in Gertrude's room in *Hamlet*, the eeriness of this moment comes from the strangeness of the reconstitution of family relationship. The play's last, impotent generosity is to make possible the parent-child relationship that had been lacking until this moment—to make it possible even as it becomes impossible. The Cordelia thus addressed must in some way be regarded as still there, even though she has already died. The difference between life and death is here eroded yet again. Yet it is not that Cordelia in some sense haunts her own absence (as Edgar may be said to have haunted his own presence as Tom when he exchanges blessings with Gloucester); rather, her absence haunts the Cordelia that Lear so desperately wills to be present. The strange and empty generosity of her death returns to Lear a capacity not only for love (since he has already discovered how to love her again) but for parental love, even as it deprives him of its object.

Cordelia's death participates at once in the absolute and in the comparative, and it is finally under the rubric of the comparative that any overlap—any *comparison* between them—must belong. There is a final echo of the comparative in the chill, absolute statements that Lear makes about her death—statements he makes even as he continues to hope for and believe in her continuance:

> Howl, howl, howl! O, [you] are men of stones!
> Had I your tongues and eyes, I'ld use them so
> That heaven's vault should crack. She's gone for ever!
> I know when one is dead, and when one lives;
> She's dead as earth. Lend me a looking-glass,
> If that her breath will mist or stain the stone,
> Why then she lives.
>
> (v.iii.258–64)

Cordelia may be dead, and Lear alive, but their relation is symmetrical, and there is a great deal of Richard in Lear's request for a mirror. In Cordelia dead he may see himself alive: to so little does the difference between them come, and to so little does the difference between all life and death come. She is dead as earth; but the living are men of stones, and Lear's own living sounds of anguish, those of a reversed Orpheus or Antony, as opposed to the other witnesses' imperturbability, would crack the stone vault of heaven.[78] Lear's hope in the possibility of her life takes the form of wishing her to affect the stone that represents the inanimateness to which she now belongs. She's gone for ever, Lear says, even as he attempts to undo the difference between life and death, between absolute and comparative, and he repeats this formulation ten lines later: "Now she's gone for ever! / Cordelia, Cordelia, stay a little" (v.iii.271–72). Once again what is now the endlessness of the absolute Lear tries to wrest back into the minimal comparative mode of the living, even as he acknowledges her death. The demand to "stay a little" opposes the frailest of differences to "nothing" by the interminable comparative marked by the *er* in "ever." What is being emphasized is not the finality of her death but its endlessness. Thus, the ultimate version of this lament in this play without ultimates formulates a negative version of the endless comparative of death and sees death as both the end of the comparative and as its inescapable and final establishment:

> No, no, no life!
> Why should a dog, a horse, a rat, have life,
> And thou no breath at all? Thou'lt come no more,
> Never, never, never, never, never.
>   (v.iii.306–309)

The moment that the absoluteness of Cordelia's death comes home to Lear manifests itself also as the moment when he recognizes an interminable and eternally insubstantial mode of loss. "No more" and "no breath at all" slide into the repetitive iterations of "never"—as though the word itself were never to cease.

78. Cf. Booth, *King Lear*, pp. 23–24.

On the Plurality of Gods

Was es, scheinbar, geben *muß*, gehört zur Sprache.

—Wittgenstein

He saw himself then, so little, so poor. And now, littler, poorer. Was that
not something?
So sick, so alone.
And now.
Sicker, aloner.
Was not that something?
As the comparative is something. Whether more than its positive or less.
Whether less than its superlative or more.

—Beckett, *Watt*

Intimacy without affection, the space of the comparative, generosity without substance: I have tried with these phrases to evoke the
strange and empty kindness of King Lear. It is an indeterminate
kindness, a negative version of Protestant grace, since what is promised here is something other than fulfillment. Its own indeterminate
gods preside over this kindness. The gods in King Lear are not anthropomorphized, and yet they are in some relation to the humans in
the play: they draw those humans into their own residual and anonymous region. I hoped to show this in the way comparatives, or quasi-
comparatives, without substance make up Lear's final vocabulary.

Those emptying forms, it is true, would seem to go beyond the
relics of hope for divine chastisement that Lear has engaged in on the
heath:

Let the great gods,
That keep this dreadful pudder o'er our heads,
Find out their enemies now. Tremble, thou wretch
That hast within thee undivulged crimes
Unwhipt of justice. Hide thee, thou bloody hand;
Thou perjur'd, and thou simular of virtue
That art incestuous! Caitiff, to pieces shake,
That under covert and convenient seeming
Has practis'd on man's life! Close pent-up guilts,
Rive your concealing continents, and cry
These dreadful summoners grace. I am a man
More sinn'd against than sinning.

(iii.ii.49–60)

By act 4 Lear will, of course, out of a strange, forgiving nihilism, grant grace to the hypocritical universe of sinners that he sees all around him. That he progresses, as Elton argues, to disbelief even in these gods "deanthropomorphized during the violent storm into their elements" (*King Lear and the Gods*, p. 180), indicates the extent of Lear's despair by act 4, scene 6. Nevertheless, by act 5 he has achieved, at least for a while, a renewed faith in the gods' generosity, specifically their generosity toward precapitalist expenditure or sacrifice: "Upon such sacrifices, my Cordelia, / The gods themselves throw incense" (v.iii.20–21). Bataille distinguishes between sacrifice (which aims at a reward from the gods) and potlatch, but for the gods partly to contribute to the sacrifice—to reward it only by making it more beautiful—blurs the distinction. There is a continuity between the great curse on the heath and the Lear of acts 4 and 5, for even that curse, ending with the negative obligation marked by the comparative "I am a man / More sinn'd against than sinning" conceives the elements— "these dreadful summoners"—as potentially the agents of a minimal generosity or "grace." The generosity of the heavens or of the gods will become more and more an issue as the play progresses, precisely as the possible particular *content* of their general generosity becomes more and more spectral.

Paralleling this trajectory toward spectrality, the object of imperious language changes. In act 3 Lear can still direct his absolutizing imperatives toward those whom he conceives as sinners. But characters learn humility as they come into greater and greater proximity to the minimality of all value in the play. This kind of humility even Goneril learns, as the oddly scrupulous minimality of her homecoming boast shows (although still in the mode of equivalent exchange):

> *Goneril:* I have been worth the whistle.
> *Albany:*   O Goneril,
>   You are not worth the dust which the rude wind
>   Blows in your face.
>
>   (IV.ii.29–31)

Whether Goneril marvels (sarcastically, but not entirely sarcastically) that Albany has indeed come to meet her even now or whether this marks the difference between his past, perfect-tense love for her and his indifference to her now,[79] she displays the near but not entire

---

79. Edmund's sense of this past-perfect generosity—the empty generosity of a past whose wealth has become phantom—comes out in his great line "Yet Edmund was belov'd."

emptiness of the world they live in. There is a residual generosity in this play; it is stripped-down and barren but still able to confer a minimal value on Goneril. I think that Shakespeare's alteration of the proverb ("It is a poor dog that is not worth the whistling") tends to show this.[80] Her language does not say, "It is worth whistling for me." Goneril is worth a whistle as a physical object, a kind of prize for the achievement of some utterly minimal decency or love, but that would mean that she is still worth something. Albany's reply, although it denies her even this, repeats her sense of the stark and bare generosity that still continues to confer the most minimal value on this utterly exterior world. Even the dust is worth something, and Albany's residual love for Goneril—the impotent charity of his past love for her—still haunts his characterization of the wind that blows the dust into her face as rude.

Albany here refuses the absolutist language that even Edgar had continued to employ in his proud address to the rude wind: "Thou unsubstantial air that I embrace: / The wretch that thou hast blown unto the worst / Owes *nothing* to thy blasts" (iv.i.7–9). The word *nothing* is wrong here, because it still accepts the illusion of equivalent exchange—experiencing the worst means having nothing and owing nothing. But Edgar is soon to revise this language implicitly in the lessons he gives to his father: "Hadst thou been aught but goss'mer, feathers, air / (So many fathom down precipitating), / Thou'dst shiver'd like an egg: but thou dost breathe, / Hast heavy substance" (iv.vi.49–52). Edgar tells Gloucester that he is not "aught but" unsubstantial "air" but also that he has "heavy substance." This recognizes something like the continued generosity of the air (to which Edgar would now acknowledge he does not owe nothing), even at the moment of its extreme insubstantiality. Like Albany's bare and muted lament about the wind's rudeness, this utterly minimal anthropomorphism revises in an ascetic mode Lear's earlier address to the elements. That address still displays imperiousness, but even there imperiousness is shifting into an uncanny register:

> Blow, winds, and crack your cheeks! rage, blow!
> You cataracts and hurricanoes, spout.
> . . . .
> Rumble thy bellyful! Spit, fire! spout, rain!
> Nor rain, wind, thunder, fire are my daughters.
> I tax not you, you elements, with unkindness;

80. Even if we assume that Shakespeare did revise, he lets quarto *a*'s "whistle" stand in the folio, over quarto *b*'s "whistling."

> I never gave you kingdom, call'd you children;
> You owe me no subscription. Then let fall
> Your horrible pleasure. Here I stand your slave,
> A poor, infirm, weak, and despis'd old man;
> But yet I call you servile ministers,
> That will with two pernicious daughters join
> Your high-engender'd battles 'gainst a head
> So old and white as this. O, ho! 'tis foul.
>
> (III.ii.1–2, 14–24)

The elements owe him no obligation because they have never been the objects of his generosity. They are now, however: he has in fact given the elements everything in the exterior space, beyond the limit of the social and of reciprocity, to which he has crossed over—hence the Gentleman's description of Lear as "Contending with the fretful elements; / Bids the wind blow the earth into the sea. / . . . / And bids what will take all" (III.i.4–5, 15). At first Lear's speech suggests an end to anthropomorphism. The elements are not unkind, since Lear was never "so kind a father" to them. He does not *tax* them with unkindness—does not require of them something like an acknowledgment of their own despicability. Yet an impersonal anthropomorphism returns, here where he calls them "servile ministers" and, a few lines later, when he calls them "dreadful summoners" (III.ii.59).

The difference between these two formulations also matters—as servile ministers the elements would seem to be ministering to Regan and Goneril. Still, their battles are "high-engender'd," which must mean above lowly human concerns. When Lear calls them "dreadful summoners," *anthropomorphism* seems the wrong word. There is no court that these summoners summon to: they themselves are both messengers and authorities from whom some minimal grace might be sought. That grace would not be Lutheran grace. It would be the generosity that their *indifference* would manifest. "The great gods" (III.ii.49) and the dreadful summoners are indistinguishable; the gods manifest their "justice" (III.ii.53) not at the trial to which humans are summoned, but in the very act of summoning. This is both an anthropomorphism and something more—as though in anthropomorphism it was the human that was being changed and rendered suitable to an alien but condign exteriority. Humans are not summoned to a trial, like those with which the play begins and ends or the quarto's mock trial: they are summoned to *know* that the deanthropomorphized elements are at once nonhuman and summoners. Their grace would be in this knowledge of a nonhuman generosity that confers only such knowledge, summoning humans to know the summoners' indifference to whether they answer the summons or not.

Already intimated in this scene is an aura of the play that may be called an exterior comparativity. It is exterior because it is beyond all human exchange—all exchange based on the hope of a gain in substance. The oedipal paradigm of the superhuman father with which the play begins, and which Goneril, Regan, and Edmund remain prey to, dissolves in this nonhuman universe. This is a universe in which justice and generosity merge in their being equally austere, equally exigent, equally without substance, and indeed without human or humanlike intention of any sort. Edgar articulates a still shockingly oedipalized version of the gods' justice when he speaks to the dying Edmund:

> *Edmund:* What you have charg'd me with, that have I done,
>   And more, much more, the time will bring it out.
>   'Tis past, and so am I. But what art thou
>   That hast this fortune on me? If thou'rt noble,
>   I do forgive thee.
> *Edgar:*   Let's exchange charity.
>   I am no less in blood than thou art, Edmund;
>   If more, the more th'hast wrong'd me.
>   My name is Edgar, and thy father's son.
>   The gods are just, and of our pleasant vices
>   Make instruments to plague us:
>   The dark and vicious place where thee he got
>   Cost him his eyes.
>   (v.iii.163–74)

This errs as much as Gloucester's anguished claim that "As flies to wanton boys are we to th' gods, / They kill us for their sport" (iv.i.36–37); Gloucester is shortly to change his mind about his Hobbesian theology. However, I think that Edgar is paradoxically instancing the play's austere generosity, not by saying what he believes, but by expressing himself, for Edmund's benefit, in the oedipalized language of equivalent exchange and accumulation that he takes Edmund to understand. Hence Edgar says he will "*exchange* charity," acknowledging Edmund's genuine, if useless, gesture toward a useless generosity in his offer to "forgive" Edgar and generously meeting that generosity halfway by speaking his brother's customary language: the language of calibrated exchange. (I think the type for this scene is the meeting of Jacob and Esau after Jacob crosses the Jordan, which results in their unexpected mutual generosity. Here that eerie scene Shakespeare nearly matches in eeriness.) In his charity, Edgar forgives Edmund his calculation; Edgar's charity consists in his allowing Edmund to believe that the wrong he has done to his father participates in a humanized (and so oedipalized) divine scheme of justice, as though divine justice obeyed the exact and exacting calculations of the *lex talionis*. And Edgar also does Edmund the charity of pretending to his own parallel oedipal desire to see Gloucester symbolically castrated (hence his parallel self-identification as "thy father's son"); and so avoids seeming to lord it over Edmund.

But Edmund too has changed. His speech marks his dying return to the aristocratic mode of gift exchange. Where else is the charity Edgar sees in him? That charity, of course, is marked by ambivalence, perhaps like the charity enforced from pelting farms and poor villages. It is both anonymous and fastidious. It is fastidious in the way it requires the nobility of its object, as though so interested in its own aristocratic status that it requires an aristocratic setting. But it is anonymous because it forgives Edgar without knowing who he is, just as he has generously fought the anonymous challenger against Goneril's advice. He is concerned only with the spare generality of the situation. His charity is useless, substanceless, and of no possible concern, at last, to his anonymous vanquisher; yet its residual generosity finds residual reciprocation in Edgar's acknowledgment that, empty as it is, it remains charity.

Edgar's charity further manifests itself in the way Edgar recognizes, or his language recognizes, the development of Edmund's profound ambivalence. Edmund's final nobility consists in a return to the aristocratic mode he associates with Edgar and Gloucester. He simultaneously wants to engage Edgar in this mode—hence his hope that Edgar was not motivated by a calculated desire for gain—and he wants to believe himself more noble, finally, than they are, debased though he may be. This negotiation, I think, gives rise to the tonal complexity of the scene. It is as though both Edmund and Edgar acknowledge the sharp external law of human psychological and economic self-interest in a world too impoverished and demanding to permit its relaxation, and yet communicate a kind of generosity in that law's interstices.

Still that law is not wholly blind. The language of Edgar's speech aligns the gods with the ananke or necessity it evokes, the necessity of the poetic and so inhuman justice by which Gloucester loses his eyes. The *lex talionis* here goes beyond simple equivalence, which is always contingent and humanly weighed, not necessary. Equivalence takes the form of the exchange of two otherwise unrelated commodities. Their values are determined beforehand and not in some necessary and a priori relation to each other. (Their relation is always mediated by their human producers through labor.) The justice based on equivalent exchange also exacts a punishment that retrospectively fits the crime rather than being inherently connected to it. The poetic justice of ananke, however, makes crime and punishment necessarily related. There need be no human or humanizing intervention to establish the comparison it makes palpable.

Behind much of the Gloucester subplot, I think, is the Jacob and Esau story, and the subplot ends with the same surprising and eerie, dehumanized, and almost anonymous exchange of generosity that marks Jacob's and Esau's reunion in Genesis. "I have seen thy face as though I had seen the face of God," Jacob tells Esau, when we would expect the reverse, since he has just wrestled with God and "seen God face to face" (Gen. 33:10, 32:30).[81] So too has Edmund fought with a kind of divine summoner, whose face he now sees. And like the gifts Jacob and Esau give to each other, Edmund and Edgar exchange the litany of the comparative: "And more, much more"; "If more, the more." Edmund admits "more, much more" than he has been charged with, and Edgar suggests, but only suggests, the possibility that he is "more" wronged because he is more than Edmund's equal, and so increases the minimal charity of his forgiveness.

A verbally similar interchange shortly follows this scene of Edgar's reluctance to persevere in the comparison of wrongs. Here Edmund displays a kind of charity or unselfishness in encouraging the detail of the woes for which he now intends to take responsibility. This interchange again underscores the excessive and interminable quality of the comparative—its transit beyond all limits and above all strangeness:

> *Edmund:*   But speak you on,
>   You look as you had something more to say.
> *Albany:*   If there be more, more woeful, hold it in,
>   For I am almost ready to dissolve,
>   Hearing of this.
> *Edgar:*   This would have seem'd a period
>   To such as love not sorrow, but another,
>   To amplify too much, would make much more,
>   And top extremity.
>   (v.iii.201–8)

---

81. In Genesis it is not an angel that Jacob wrestles with. Genesis says "a man"; Jacob says, "I have seen God face to face, and my life is preserved" (32:30). Not until much later does Hosea call the nocturnal visitor an angel (12:4). On the face of Esau, see Blanchot, *L'entretien infini*, p. 188.

Edgar's overtone of a declaration of love for sorrow points again to the region of phantom gifts. But even the slightly earlier interchange with Edmund, the play's most austere and nihilistic evocation of the apparently equivalent exchange of the *lex talionis*, contrasts, in this last scene, with the nihilistic motto of equivalent exchange at the beginning: "Nothing will come of nothing." Nor ought the kindness to Edmund of Edgar's account of justice to distract from some other, even more uncanny, characterizations of justice, which participate more fully and more eerily in the rarefied or rarefying atmosphere of the gift. Thus Lear, in sight of beggars whose baseness seems unending, develops a more just idea of superfluity than that which saw even beggars as being in all things superfluous:

> This tempest will not give me leave to ponder
> On things would hurt me more. But I'll go in.
> In, boy, go first.—You houseless poverty—
> Nay, get thee in; I'll pray, and then I'll sleep.
> Poor naked wretches, whereso'er you are,
> That bide the pelting of this pitiless storm,
> How shall your houseless heads and unfed sides,
> Your [loop'd] and window'd raggedness, defend you
> From seasons such as these? O! I have ta'en
> Too little care of this! Take physic, pomp,
> Expose thyself to feel what wretches feel,
> That thou mayst shake the superflux to them,
> And show the heavens more just.
>
> (III.iv.24–36)

The storm might seem here to be the worst, but the speech describes its terror as less than the "things would hurt me more." Nevertheless, the confrontation between the king whose life has been extravagance and the specter of interminable poverty addresses the question of the justice of the gods.[82] The oddness here consists in the

82. The elements here still mean the gods to Lear—the gods keeping this dreadful pudder over their heads. If not, there would be nothing to credit to divinity about pomp's exposing itself to what the wretches feel. The dreadful summoners chastise pomp here, and they do so pitilessly, without grace. Yet the storm is pitiless to the poor as well. This speech makes the strange claim that the justice of the heavens will be evident in pomp's expenditure of superfluity on behalf of the poor. This is distributive justice, since it matters to Lear that the superflux should be shaken to them. And yet the logic seems to be the logic of retribution. Pomp will be punished for its superfluity, but the speech does not even say that. Rather than calling upon the gods to punish pomp (as he had earlier), Lear calls upon pomp to transform itself, to expose itself to what wretches feel. And this will show the heavens "more just." The heavens do not show themselves just (as opposed to unjust). They show themselves more just. Their

fact that the distribution of excess comes out also as a comparative kindness *to* the heavens, not just by them. Their justice may seem *corrective*, consisting in the vengeance they take on Pomp, but it is pomp's distribution of the superflux that does the heavens the charity of showing their distributive justice.[83] That minimal comparative appearance of justice (show the heavens more just) is a gift that even the basest beggars can make with the superfluity of even the poorest things. This distributive generosity of the heavens is spectral indeed if it depends on human gestures of kindness—and kindness for the sake of these nearly empty heavens. Theirs is a justice without any intention to be just—that is, any intention to redistribute substance in either a more equitable or a more generous fashion. The generosity of this justice is generosity without substance. The heavens *do* appear more just here, and they do so only because the pompous Lear is now willing to shake his superflux to the poor. But he has no superflux left (at least using that term the way he would have in act 1, scene 1), and so justice here is purely comparative, since utterly without substance other than what Laura Quinney calls in *Antony and Cleopatra* "the impotent generosity of language."[84]

The play confirms this by making Gloucester echo these lines when he attempts to "shake patiently my great affliction off" (IV.vi.36): there what's shaken off is at once superflux and affliction, and Gloucester declares something far beyond the naively normalizing intention expressed in Lear's opening speeches when Lear declares "our fast intent / To shake all cares and business from our age" (I.i.38–39).

Albany too evokes a strange phantom justice in his response to Gloucester's blinding and to Cornwall's consequent death. Upon this news he echoes Lear when he marvels, "This shows you are above, / You [justicers], that these our nether crimes / So speedily can venge!"

---

justice is a pure comparative endowed upon them by the spectral extravagance of a king or dignitary become a pauper. The expenditure of superflux redounds not to his own prestige but to that of the gods.

83. See J. C. Maxwell's elegant, Christianizing reading: "This is a curiously elusive phrase, which is possible only in the religiously undefined world of the characters in the play. A paraphrase would presumably be 'make the heavens appear more just than they do in the light of your present behavior'" ("The Technique of Invocation in 'King Lear,'" *Modern Language Review* 45 [1950], 145). He reads this as Lear's cautious agnosticism, which recommends acting "*as if*" it were a Christian world, a step to seeing it as being one indeed (as in Gloucester's "Heavens, deal so still" [IV.i.64]).

84. Laura Quinney, "Enter a Messenger," in *William Shakespeare's Antony and Cleopatra: Modern Critical Interpretations*, ed. Harold Bloom (New York: Chelsea House, 1988), p. 167.

(iv.ii.78–80). The emphasis here is partly on the word "above"—the rapidity of justice confirms its place in a supernatural realm balancing the natural "nether" realm. Edgar is shortly to undo this pious invocation of the word "above." He renders it only a marker of the comparative when he tells Gloucester that what he has witnessed in the latter's "so many fathom *down* precipitating" (iv.vi.50) is "*above* all strangeness" (iv.vi.66). Albany's speech primarily makes the claim, however, that the gods exist. Yet the terms of that claim are strange. It is not the gods who show themselves to be above: rather, something that happens here in this nether world shows them above.

The apostrophes to the gods recur throughout the play, and not only to the gods, but also to "all you unpublish'd virtues of the earth" (iv.iv.16) or, as in Lear's great speech, to the eerie abstraction "You houseless poverty."[85] The address to the inhuman here is not, I think, an instance of de Manian prosopopoeia (of which Shakespeare may never be said to be guilty). It is a direct address to the inhuman, an acknowledgment of the direct generosity of the impersonal or the general. One might have expected Albany to say, "You show yourselves in this, you justicers." Instead his language evokes the impersonal agency or stratum to which the event also belongs, and he sees this impersonal agency as conferring upon the justicers an existence as impersonal as its endower. That this is true needs confirmation only from what follows immediately: the report that Gloucester lost his other eye as well.

Like the immediate death of the servant who responds to Gloucester's appeal to him "that will think to live till he be old" (iii.vii.69), this is an instance of what Empson has stressed: the chilling regularity in which all invocations of the gods become ironized. Kent thanks Gloucester on the heath: "The gods reward your kindness" (iii.vi.5). In the next scene Gloucester loses his eyes. In turn Gloucester blesses the disguised Edgar in response to his hope "that the right may thrive" and his promise that "If ever I return to you again, / I'll bring you comfort." "Grace go with you, sir!" Gloucester replies; Edgar exits, there is an alarum and a retreat, and Edgar reenters with the words, "Away, old man, give me thy hand, away! / King Lear hath lost, he and his daughter ta'en" (v.ii.2–6). In the comfort to which Edgar

---

85. Brower, whose readings are always sensitive, prefers the opposite valuation: he sees an advance in the less eerie "thou" of the address to pomp which comes a few lines later: "Take physic, pomp, / Expose thyself to feel what wretches feel, / That thou mayst shake the superflux to them" (iii.iv.33–5). This he regards as a "change to the intimate second person, 'thou', in contrast with 'You houseless poverty—'" (*Hero and Saint*, 397n).

has referred, he meant also to include the revelation of his own identity. This revelation kills his father. It is again Albany, as Empson writes,[86] whose language falls prey to the 'starkest moment of this irony:

Albany: The gods defend her! Bear him hence awhile.

Enter LEAR, *with* CORDELIA *in his arms.*

(v.iii.257)

After Gloucester's death, Albany replaces him as a second and uncanny double to the now uncanny Lear. He rejects Regan's desire to marry Edmund with a remark far more chilling than Lear's attempt at ironically giving Cordelia away as a bride "dower'd with our curse": "For your claim, fair [sister], / I bar it in the interest of my wife; / 'Tis she is sub-contracted to this lord" (v.iii.84–86). He echoes Lear's opening challenge when he demands Lear and Cordelia from Edmund, "so to use them / As we shall find their merits and our safety / May equally determine" (v.iii.43–45). This recalls Lear's intent to reward his largest bounty "where nature doth with merit challenge" (I.i.53), as does Albany's more comparative and giftlike assignment of Edgar and Kent "to your rights, / With boot, and such addition as your honors / Have more than merited" (v.iii.301–3). Having behaved like Lear, the now widowed Albany is about to experience a telescoped version of Lear's generosity's coming to grief in the death of its beneficiaries, as he, like Lear, sees cursed the person he had intended to bless. "Know our intent; / . . . / we will resign, / During the life of this old majesty, / To him our absolute power" (v.iii.297–301), he says, reversing the opening of the play, in which Lear declares his "fast intent" (I.i.38) to resign his majesty. Albany's unwitting jinx in fact initiates a spectral generosity opposite from what it intends; his implicit desire to see Lear live is answered almost at the end of Lear's next speech by the now unexpected death of someone who long ago topped extremity. Yet even Lear's death, though utterly arbitrary in de Man's sense, may not be final. Kent still speaks the language of comparatives, although he rejects them, and his description of the dead Lear is hard to distinguish from a description of a living person. Both ghost and human, he may be where Kent thinks he is, but Kent does not think that by this has thought been past:

---

86. *Structure of Complex Words*, p. 150.

> Vex not his ghost. O, let him pass, he hates him
> That would upon the rack of this tough world
> Stretch him out longer.
>
> (v.iii.314–16)

It is not only Albany and Gloucester whose blessings can so speedily be venged. Even Edmund falls prey to the same temporal irony: a blessing or prophecy that promises time and increase results in the hard charity of the gods, here as genuine vengeance (come a moment too late to prevent what it avenges). "If thou dost / As this instructs thee, thou dost make thy way / To noble fortunes" (v.iii.28–30), he tells his captain, giving him Cordelia's death warrant but also the captain's.

The justice of the gods is of an extreme minimality in the play. It displays itself, if it displays itself, in the perverse severity of its near emptiness and insubstantiality. Elton concluded that the play is a document of skepticism. Yet the trajectory he locates in the play's major character—a trajectory from pagan belief to pagan disbelief—seems as untrue to the play as complacently Christianizing readings do. It seems untrue because the invocations of the gods in the play become more and more pressing, more and more part of the deep current of the language, as the universe of the play becomes less and less substantial. The play begins, as has always been noticed and often lamented, with Lear and Kent (as Kent and as Caius) exchanging interjected vows: "By Jupiter," "By Juno," and "By Apollo"; "by the sacred radiance of the sun, / The [mysteries] of Hecat and the night; / By all the operation of the orbs / From whom we do exist and cease to be." (i.i.109–112). But the language in the play moves toward more anonymous gods. They become pluralized. In being pluralized they become indeterminate, and what they offer becomes indeterminate.

At the same time, the language of their invocations undergoes a transformation. Lear begins with the imperious invocation of the gods as underwriters of his oaths. "Thou hast sought to make us break our [vow]— / Which we durst never yet," (i.i.168–69) Lear tells Kent, but it is not fear of Hecate or Apollo that prevents Lear from daring to break his vows; it is the fact that his vows objectify his own absolute performative power.[87] Lear does not dare to go against his

87. Cf. Burckhardt, *Shakespearean Meanings*, pp. 239–43. Burckhardt, whose reading is consonant with mine, argues that the play describes the difference between an old, quasi-magical, self-guaranteeing realm of self-enacting performative truths and a new realm of fact, in which language asserts correspondence with the external world and includes the possibility of lying, as meaning and reference cease to be necessarily identical.

own pronouncements. But the language of the play shifts from the mode of invocation as interjection to that of direct address. Lear curses Goneril in language at once more intimate and less anthropomorphized than he has used to curse Cordelia:

> All the stor'd vengeances of heaven fall
> On her ingrateful top! Strike her young bones,
> You taking airs, with lameness. . . .
> You nimble lightnings, dart your blinding flames
> Into her scornful eyes! Infect her beauty,
> You fen-suck'd fogs, drawn by the pow'rful sun,
> To fall and blister her.
>
> (II.iv.162–168)[88]

Like Cordelia's address to the unpublished virtues of the earth, the invocation here is not a moment of prosopopoeia or anthropomorphizing apostrophe. This speech may indeed still distinguish the natural or even preternatural summoners and vengeances from the gods they serve, but the imperious tone with which the play begins here gives way to imploration:

> O, reason not the need! our basest beggars
> Are in the poorest things superfluous.
> . . . .
> But for true need—
> You heavens, give me that patience, patience I need!
> You see me here, you gods, a poor old man,
> As full of grief as age, wretched in both.
> If it be you that stirs these daughters' hearts
> Against their father, fool me not so much
> To bear it tamely.
>
> (II.iv.264–65, 270–76)

Here more than ever, patience means patience without an object or reward, except for its own empty generosity. The gods, or their absence, preside over the negative and insubstantial fullness now Lear's. Like Isabel in *Richard II*, he is "as full of grief as age"; this fullness overflows into the second-person address. This address, it is true, still participates in a kind of wordly rhetorical structure through the same

---

88. Compare this particularly Shakepearean use of the verb *fall*—meaning *make fallen*—to Antony's "Fall not a tear, I say," considered below. (Here I am following Kenneth Muir's emendation in the Arden edition of *King Lear* [London: Methuen, 1972].)

transferred epithet by which Lear will soon call the gods servile ministers: the emphasis is on the way the gods too may be called cruel if
they encourage the manifest cruelty of these children (Gloucester's
children too: "As flies to wanton boys are we to th' gods, / They kill us
for their sport" [iv.i.36–37]). The scale of Goneril and Regan's cruelty
is divine. Gloucester comes close to a similar (but more pious) accusation against the gods at the moment of his blinding: "He that will
think to live till he be old, / Give me some help! O cruel! O you gods!"
(iii.vii.69–70).[89] Though this implores aid from the gods, it also despairs over the cruelty that they allow to happen.

Yet, as though Gloucester too were beginning to witness the gods'
insubstantial generosity, his tone begins to change after he loses his
other eye and discovers Edmund's treachery: "O my follies! Then
Edgar was abus'd. / Kind gods, forgive me that, and prosper him!"
(iii.vii.91–92). For, Cordelia to call the gods kind—"O you kind
gods!" (iv.vii.13) she cries in prayer for her father's cure—witnesses
to her continued hopefulness that all may yet be well. But Gloucester's
language, even if ascribable to a sudden acceptance of the gods' justice
according to the *lex talionis*, is nevertheless shocking. What sort of
kindness is this? In what does the gods' generosity consist? Gloucester
represents here a new mode of relationship with the gods. The second person of these invocations made in times of the sorest need is
not a second person of presence, of the mutual presence of human
and God. The very indeterminacy and anonymity of the gods show
this. No one invokes any god by name after act 2; there Lear last
names a god negatively, in a new and less imperious strain: "I do not
bid the thunder-bearer shoot, / Nor tell tales of thee to high-judging
Jove" (ii.iv.227–28),[90] and the gods are entirely pluralized for the rest
of the play.[91] The inadequacy of the Christianizing interpretations of
King Lear is manifest in the terrible difference in tone that would
occur if these eerily general gods were singularized or particularized
in any way. Such a particularization would imply the possibility of
material kindness, of material benefit from some god's generosity.
The kindness of the gods in *King Lear* benefits no one, yet it becomes
more and more the rhythm of the play.

89. I follow the folio; the quarto has "*ye* gods."

90. Cf. Maxwell, "Technique of Invocation," p. 143: "We hear nothing hereafter of
classical paganism. It is too exclusively a civil cult to satisfy Lear now, or to stand up
against the tumult of the storm."

91. With the possible exception of "Gods spies" (v.iii.17). In fact I agree with those
who modernize this as "God's," as against Muir who has "Gods'"; but the point (as
Burckhardt notes most eloquently) is that this idyll is fantasy. The contrast between
Lear's brief wishfulness here and the actual tutelary deities in the play underscores my
point.

The kindness of the gods seems to me the empty return of the empty gift that Lear makes to the gods and to their unwitting representative Cordelia. Cordelia is dowered with truth (with the curse of the truth); Lear gives all to his daughters, but when he has nothing left to give, except his own superfluous poverty, he addresses the insubstantial and deanthropomorphized elements ("you taking airs") and gives to them the shadow of what he has already given to his daughters: "unbonneted he runs, / And bids what will take all" (III.i.14–15).[92] But the gods give as well as take, and this is what makes for their eerie kindness: "I tax not you, you elements, with unkindness" (III.ii.16) is Lear's early and negative version of this recognition (couched as it is in litotes). Though for a moment he does tax them with servility, only for a moment is this the play's language. After this the gods are invoked more and more—by Albany, by Cordelia, by Kent, by Gloucester, as, earlier, even by Regan—in language that acknowledges their uncanny kindness, and often in the strange mode of plural and indeterminate intimacy borne by the second-person plural.[93] This is the play's language, not merely the language of the characters. While many of them indeed speak from hopes soon to be proved vain, Gloucester, at least, has a deeper knowledge of what their kindness consists in.

> O you mighty gods!
> This world I do renounce, and in your sights
> Shake patiently my great affliction off.
> If I could bear it longer, and not fall

92. Emile Benveniste remarks that the English word *take* preserves some of the original indistinction between giving and receiving characteristic of the vocabulary of the gift in Indo-European languages, as in the phrase *to take to*. See *Problèmes de linguistique générale* (Paris: Gallimard, 1966), 1:310. Thus the "taking airs" are active, Goneril passive, in Lear's curse. The word *tax*, as used in English, seems to have some of the same antithetical sense, as when Lear considers taxing the elements with unkindness. *Tax* derives from a proto-Indo-European root meaning *touch*, which can obviously be both active and passive.

93. I think the strange intimacy of tone in the address to the gods in *King Lear* has not been sufficiently noticed (although J. C. Maxwell's article provides a sensitive Christianizing interpretation). E. A. Abbott remarks of Shakespeare's usual practice in his plays, "*ye* seems to be generally used in questions, entreaties, and rhetorical appeals" (*A Shakespearean Grammar*, new ed. [London: Macmillan, 1875], §236) (he's talking about the second person generally, not the specific case of addresses to the gods): hence Gloucester's cry (in the quarto), "O cruel! O ye gods!" But generally in *King Lear* people use the far eerier *you* (as in the folio version of Gloucester's line), eerier because it doesn't assume the informality of the vocative—the implied claim to attention of normal interpellation.

Both "you gods" and "ye gods" are rare formulations in Shakespeare; "ye gods" appears frequently only in *Julius Caesar*, and "you gods" is frequent only in *King Lear* and the two plays that share its eerie, impoverished intimacy, *Pericles* and *Timon*.

> To quarrel with your great opposeless wills,
> My snuff and loathed part of nature should
> Burn itself out. If Edgar live, O bless him!
>   (IV.vi.34–40)

This echoes his earlier blessing, after he has discovered that his blinding is due to Edmund's treachery: "Then Edgar was abus'd. / Kind gods forgive me that, and prosper him." The gods' "great opposeless wills" are a far cry from Lear's bidding "*what* will take all." Defiance has given way to intimacy. True, even here Gloucester's invocation to the gods will be disappointed, since he is about to fail in his impatient attempt to commit suicide, but his failure gives rise only to a further acknowledgment of the gods' kindness. For Edgar's explanation of Gloucester's survival ought not wholly to be contextualized as a white lie "done to cure" him (IV.vi.34). Even if the gods' kindness is confined only to the language that people use to describe them (since they are beings spectral as language), the play nevertheless evokes the kindness of language, insubstantial as the kindness of the gods but no less kind for that. There is kindness indeed in Edgar's recommendation to Gloucester: "Think that the clearest gods, who make them honors / Of men's impossibilities, have preserved thee" (IV.vi.73–74). The superlative here has the same puzzling opacity as the superlative in his concluding lines: "The oldest hath borne most." "Clearest" is not a clear but an opaque word, suggesting so little against the finality of the word "impossibilities." "The clearest gods" almost means the most transparent gods—the gods so far other to this muddied world as to have almost no relationship to it at all. "The clearest gods"—does this mean a certain subset of the gods: the clearest as opposed to the less clear? No, it means something like a determinacy that is indeterminate to us.[94] The gods are most clear, but their clarity is anonymous, not because of the epistemological commitments of language, but because their clarity is so other to the substance of our world. Yet substanceless as this clarity is and confined as it may be to the language it nevertheless escapes, Gloucester still has access to an intimacy

94. Again Brower gives the opposing side: Gloucester "has been saved, appropriately, by 'the clearest gods', *dei clarissimi*, deities of brightness and purity, very unlike the dark gods he had served while living in Edmund's world. . . . The introduction of '*clearest*' in Edgar's speech expresses precisely Gloucester's change in mood and moral attitude, with a nice adjustment to his easier optimism and to this moment of peace after the storm" (*Hero and Saint*, p. 402). The clearest gods have not saved Gloucester, but Edgar has; and whatever brightness belongs to them comes only from the language that invents them. The association with an "easier optimism" seems to undervalue the strangeness of the phrase and its context.

with this substanceless generosity that enables him to pray for death rather than take action to procure it: "You ever-gentle gods, take my breath from me" (IV.vi.217).

This, it seems to me, is the dominant tone of the play—the tone that evokes the substanceless generosity of the comparative. This generosity restores Lear and Cordelia to each other only to extend the anguish of their estrangement, the estrangement that granted restoration to begin with. Lear's vain willingness to acknowledge a wishful parity in exchange fails, but just fails, to give up the notion of material presence as coordinate with the gods' generosity: "This feather stirs, she lives! If it be so, / It is a chance which does *redeem* all sorrows / That ever I have felt" (v.iii.266–68).[95] The play's generosity, however, can only allow Cordelia to "stay a little," not to be present as an exchange for the losses Lear has experienced. And she does stay a little for Lear even after her death, since Lear can no longer tell the difference between life and death, as though the difference has come to mean only "a little."

This minimizing of the difference between life and death also occurs in Edgar's characterization of life as an hourly death (a characterization like that which contrasts life to the interminable dying of old age). This description, while unhappy, is accurate to the moral of the play. Edgar, in telling Edmund and Albany what has happened to him, also experiences a version of the inability to die, of being consigned endlessly to language:

> List a brief tale,
> And when 'tis told, O that my heart would burst!
> The bloody proclamation to escape,
> That follow'd me so near (O our lives' sweetness!
> That we the pain of death would hourly die
> Rather than die at once!), taught me to shift
> Into a madman's rags, t' assume a semblance
> That very dogs disdain'd; and in this habit
> Met I my father with his bleeding rings,
> Their precious stones new lost; became his guide,
> Led him, begg'd for him, sav'd him from despair;
> Never (O fault) reveal'd myself unto him,
> Until some half hour past, when I was arm'd.

95. Compare the exchanges that Gloucester is willing to make after his blinding: "Might I but live to see thee in my touch, / I'd say I had eyes again" (IV.i.23–24) and Antony's "Fall not a tear, I say. One of them rates / All that is won and lost" (considered below).

> Not sure, though hoping, of this good success,
> I ask'd his blessing, and from first to last
> Told him my pilgrimage. But his flaw'd heart
> (Alack, too weak the conflict to support!)
> 'Twixt two extremes of passion, joy and grief,
> Burst smilingly.
>
> (v.iii.182–200)

What Edgar has cured in Gloucester he has taken upon himself. Not only does he lead him, he also begs in his stead. The suicidal despair that he talks Gloucester out of has now apparently become his: "O! that my heart would burst," he cries in despairing contrast to the fact that Gloucester's has "burst smilingly." Edgar here also lives the same relation to time, and in similar language, as Lear. "Never" did he reveal himself to Gloucester: this seems to have been his crime, but the finality of that "never" becomes oddly less final by the unassuming qualification, "until some half-hour past," which recalls Lear's "Fourscore and upwards, not an hour more nor less" (iv.vii.60). Of course, since telling Gloucester kills him, it becomes less clear that he should consider his keeping the truth from Gloucester a fault that shows ugly in him.[96] Yet even, or precisely, in this most despairing of speeches, Edgar still recognizes an entirely gratuitous—or gracious— sweetness to life. This must be an insubstantial sweetness indeed, if it belongs even to a life whose every hour is like a death, but these are hours like the comparative hours and half-hours that change the meaning of words like "never" from something having the character of the absolute to the interminable empty charity of time.

In a sense, I am arguing that the play constitutes an endlessly elaborating expansion of Lear's first great imploration of the gods. Lear thinks he has left Goneril behind forever, but in Gloucester's castle, upon seeing her enter as Regan's ally, he cries:

> O heavens!
> If you do love old men, if your sweet sway
> Allow obedience, if you yourselves are old,
> Make it your cause; send down, and take my part.
>
> (ii.iv.189–92)

96. This speech too, with the good son asking a blessing from the blind father, recalls Isaac and Jacob, although Edgar takes off his disguise before he asks for the blessing.
 Stanley Cavell, in his great essay "The Avoidance of Love: A Reading of *King Lear*" in *Disowning Knowledge*, pp. 39–123, asks very probingly *why* Edgar waits so long; his whole essay, about the avoidance of love and the avoidance of the other's knowledge of who you are, may be taken as an answer to this question.

This is the first of the direct, second-person addresses to the gods. Yet it is to the heavens that it is addressed, so that apostrophe does not blend into prosopopoeia. The gods are rendered indeterminate here. The heavens are pluralized in a way that undoes any certain reference to anthropomorphic divinities. The play begins to conceive of the gods—always under the irresolvable uncertainty of the "if"—as old, a word whose uncanny resonances the play will work henceforth to develop. What does this language expect from the heavens? What are they supposed to do? It is not merely an accelerating alternation in his impetuous impulses that causes Lear to say a few lines later,

> But I'll not chide thee,
> Let shame come when it will, I do not call it.
> I do not bid the thunder-bearer shoot,
> Nor tell tales of thee to high-judging Jove.
> Mend when thou canst, be better at thy leisure,
> I can be patient.
>
> (II.iv.225–30)

Something other than an imperious demand that Jove shoot his thunder is at work in Lear's plea that the heavens send down and take his part. What are they supposed to send? I think that Lear's language here aleady recognizes the insubstantiality of the generosity manifested by the gods of the play or (what is the same thing) the absence of the gods.

It recognizes this, for example, in the strange use of the word *allow*. In 1748 Upton had to gloss this word as meaning "to be well pleased with, approve of," but Tate had already felt the necessity of revising the word to *hallow* as early as 1681.[97] This means, I think, that *allow* cannot be kept free of the resonances of the words that surround it— *sway* and *obedience*. It must have a strong connotation of permission as well as of approval. (Indeed, in our bureaucratic use of the word *approve*, the same senses merge as those the *OED* says are both originally present in *allow*, as when the question arises whether Reagan or Bush approved of North's activities. The two meanings are not to be separated.) This connotation of permission is strange in the speech. The generosity of the heavens consists less in their rewarding than in their "allowing" obedience—allowing a relationship to them empty but for the fact that the relationship is allowed. Their sway is as sweet as "our lives' sweetness"—a sweetness without substance or reward.

---

97. *A New Variorum Edition of Shakespeare*, vol. 5, *King Lear*, 2d ed., ed. H. H. Furness (Philadephia: Lippincott, 1880), note on II.iv.188.

I think Lear's prayer here is granted. The heavens do send down and take his part, but only because the difference between helping Lear and not helping him, between helping Gloucester and not helping him, is undone. The generosity of the gods, the generosity of the language of the play, consists in their allowing a conception of an interminable generosity that has nothing to do with substance and that can coexist and render itself indistinguishable from an extreme poverty. Kent laments for Lear that he "must approve the common saw, / Thou out of heaven's benediction com'st / To the warm sun!" (II.ii.60–62).

But the play makes warmth something desirable: poverty in the play results in coldness, for Edgar ("Poor Tom's a cold"), for the Fool ("Art cold boy?"), and for Lear himself ("I am cold myself"; "If only to go warm were gorgeous, / Why, nature needs not what thou gorgeous wearest, / Which scarcely keeps thee warm" [II.iv.268–70]). The warmth of the sun is not, in this play, the proverbial excess of heat that it means in the common saw. It is "a little" kindness, something without the substance of heaven's benediction but nevertheless, as in the Sermon on the Mount, not entirely without a random and impersonal benificence.

The substanceless generosity of the gods is recognized more by the language of the play than by any specific character (with the possible exception of Gloucester). It is a generosity recognized by language that occurs in and through language—in and through what language allows in an address to the plural, anonymous, indeterminate, and absent gods. The language in *King Lear* becomes oddly more imperious and oddly more exacting as the play progresses and as its characters call upon the gods, in both second- and third-person imperatives, to do things that they simply never do. Yet language itself, if it cannot invoke the gods, nevertheless evokes them. The gods in *King Lear* are general and anonymous, not specific. They have no specific existence, and their generosity is the generosity of the general without any specifying and localizing substance.

Their evocation makes for the presence in *King Lear* of what might be a called a purely literary language—a language whose need and neediness is met only by the charity of its own insubstantial evocations. The characters in *King Lear* come into this insubstantial relation to the generosity of their own language, come to live it. This is the extreme minimalization of the gift economy, lived as a patient relation to language, to a language whose imperiousness is indistingishable from its neediness.[98]

98. Richard Halpern, in his *The Poetics of Primitive Accumulation: English Renaissance Culture and the Genealogy of Capital* (Ithaca, N.Y.: Cornell University Press, 1991), reads

Bounty Overplus

In the Dark

Come, try this exercise:
Focus a beam
Emptied of thinking, outward through shut eyes
On X, your "god" of long ago.

Wherever he is now the photons race,
A phantom, unresisting stream,

For nothing lights up. No
Sudden amused face,
No mote, no far-out figment, to obstruct
The energy—

        It just spends
And spends itself, and who will ever know

Unless he felt you aim at him   and ducked

Or you before the session ends
Begin to glow

                          —James Merrill

And looked and looked our infant sight away

                          —Elizabeth Bishop

King Lear describes a trajectory from the happy mode of generous expenditure of wealth to an unhappy world of generosity without substance, of a pure formal intimacy without mutual presence. In one way it parallels *Richard II*; in another, it does not. *Lear* follows *Richard II* in the way it shows expenditure conceived as a mode of power give way to the negative expenditure of the powerless. It goes beyond *Richard II* by evoking spectral generosity, the phantom generosity of the phantom divinities that preside over the powerless realm the play draws its audience into. *King Lear* represents the intimacy of the hu-

King Lear from the same Maussian and Bataillean perspective that I do, although he maximizes the expenditure that I have been seeking to minimize or residualize. He describes "the play's attempt to create or manifest value through its destruction" (p. 268), and this orientation toward the superlative is connected for him with the zero sum game that I think the play's comparatives undo: "Tragedy assumes the absence of any miraculous supplement to overcome loss. It is predicated on the zero sum" (p. 253).

man with the gods as an impotent imperiousness whose demands stand for the endlessness of its needs and not for any kind of power. No generosity can satisfy the demands of an endless need, and so the generosity that the language of such an imperiousness evokes is as needy, as indeterminate and endless, as the imperatives that address it.

Nevertheless, the minimalization of the gift economy in *King Lear* does not represent that economy's final manifestation in Shakespeare. For in *Antony and Cleoptara* Antony's absolute generosity or bounty manifests itself in an absolute imperiousness of language that never fails, even when confronted with its own absolute poverty. *King Lear* may be said to represent a negative generosity or, better, an imaginary generosity. I use the word *imaginary* to sum up my argument that *Lear*'s generosity is not simply the negation or reversal of what we ordinarily call generosity but occurs in a space oblique to the space, positive or negative, of the quotidian world, just as imaginary numbers do not fall on the number line that intersects every number from the infinitely negative to the infinitely positive; they fall outside of the real. *King Lear* represents an imaginary generosity. And *Antony and Cleopatra* outgoes even *King Lear* in its dissipation of divinity: "'Tis the god Hercules, whom Antony lov'd, / Now leaves him" (iv.iii.16–17), the soldiers say to account for the music that they hear. One expects "who lov'd Antony," but Hercules never loved Antony. And yet, despite the withdrawal of this god, who is so careless of the intimacy that Antony bestows upon him, so divinely and nonchalantly above it, Antony's impetuous and imperial generosity remains utterly positive.

If the linguistic mood of *King Lear* is defined by the opaque intimacy of the second-person plural imperative, *Antony and Cleopatra*'s mood is defined by the third-person imperative. From the start, Antony manifests his power in gestures of prodigality whose grandeur outdoes anything Timon will be able to display, gestures whose insouciance rivals that of the departing Hercules.[99] Indeed, Hercules sym-

---

99. See Eugene Waith, *The Herculean Hero in Marlowe, Chapman, Shakespeare and Dryden* (New York: Columbia University Press, 1962); Maurice Charney, *Shakespeare's Roman Plays: The Function of Imagery in the Drama* (Cambridge, Mass.: Harvard University Press, 1961); Janet Adelman, *The Common Liar: An Essay on Antony and Cleopatra* (New Haven, Conn.: Yale University Press, 1973), Peter Erickson, *Patriarchal Structures in Shakespeare's Drama* (Berkeley: University of California Press, 1985); and esp. Howard Jacobson's *"Antony and Cleopatra:* 'Gentle Madam, No'" in Jacobson and Wilbur Saunders's *Shakespeare's Magnanimity: Four Tragic Heroes, Their Friends and Families* (New York: Oxford University Press, 1978), pp. 95–135. Jacobson would disagree fundamentally about the nobility of Antony's generosity. He thinks that readers who admire Antony's prodigality in fact are mimicking the Roman views that they mean to distance themselves from, since they participate in Roman voyeurism. In most ways Jacobson's view is

bolizes one attribute of Antony in the inexhaustible delight his music signifies. However, unlike Hercules' nonchalance, Antony's comes at his own expense. It is true that Antony's gestures of prodigality alternate with impulses to the prudence and carefulness that make for Roman virtue. Much of the drama, not of the play but of the first half of the play (until act 3, scene 6), centers on the competition of these alternating features of his character. Nevertheless, Antony's impulses to prudence function ultimately as a foil to set off his dazzling prodigality. They show his prodigality dazzling because it is the prodigality not of a Herculean god but of a human who cannot imaginably afford it and for whom prudence would be life-saving. And Cleopatra's similar moments of imperious prodigality take the form of an expenditure of her own claims to divinity, on behalf of Antony.

Both Antony and Cleopatra underscore their power in their willingness to dissipate all that makes for that power. Bataille follows Mauss in describing where expenditure must end when it insists on not seeming to be a purchase of obligation: with the potlatch that consists in the destruction rather than the conferral of gifts (compare Veblen's "conspicuous consumption"). Such dramatic destructiveness nevertheless still purchases prestige and so remains open to the charge of calculation and the accumulation of power. But there is a sense in which Antony and Cleopatra even go beyond that, since they are willing to destroy not only the appurtenances of their power but that power itself. The play ends with their suicides, but for neither of them is suicide a final act of self-affirmation. Antony's suicide turns out to be based on a misapprehension, and, besides, he botches it. Both Brutus and Eros are more impressive. Cleopatra is anticipated by Iras, who does not need an asp to die, and she cannot escape Caesar's mocking (and no doubt true) accusation that "She hath pursu'd conclusions infinite / Of easy ways to die" (v.ii.355–56). But these are only the final manifestations of features central to their characters. From the start there is a sense in which Antony and Cleopatra's power results from their genuine and prodigal carelessness about that power.

This power arises from the fact that their very nonchalance is impe-

---

interestingly the reverse of my own: his is an exciting and stimulating article, and he pays a fundamental attention to the oppressive aspects of Antony's generosity.

Jacobson's view is similar to that of L. C. Knights (*Some Shakespearean Themes* [London: Chatto and Windus, 1959]), who complains of Antony's generosity that it violates the "exclusive trust" which goes with his wealth and that finally it is a "vain and arrogant pomp" (pp. 181–82 n. 3).

rious. It is couched in the third-person imperatives of those born not
to sue but to command. Yet their carelessness dispenses with the very
subjects of their command, makes away with them. Antony first displays his grandeur in the great speech refusing to hear the messenger
from Rome:

> Let Rome in Tiber melt, and the wide arch
> Of the rang'd empire fall! Here is my space,
> Kingdoms are clay; our dungy earth alike
> Feeds beast as man; the nobleness of life
> Is to do thus—when such a mutual pair
> And such a twain can do't, in which I bind,
> [On] pain of punishment, the world to weet
> We stand up peerless.
>
> (i.i.33–40)

Antony's first imperative, and the play's first of many third-person
imperatives, extravagantly demands the destruction of the object of
his power. The language here recalls Lear's developing skeptical prodigality with the difference between man and beast, but where Lear
speaks out of a deep and misanthropic despair, Antony here merely
demonstrates his extravagance and the extravagant difference he locates between human eroticism and any other desire, human or otherwise. If this recalls Lear, it looks forward to Cleopatra's twin demands:
"Melt Egypt into Nile! and kindly creatures / Turn all to serpents!"
(ii.v.78–79) and "Sink Rome, and their tongues rot / That speak
against us!" (iii.vii.15–16). The latter of these commands, it is true,
expresses aggression against an enemy. Even so, it shares the former's
violent self-destructiveness, since Cleopatra here disregards the Roman advice Enobarbus gives her not to participate in the battle lest
she distract Antony.

Antony and Cleopatra begin in a mode of expenditure that Lear
does not reach until act 3, when he bids what will take all. This, I
think, is indicated by the very first speech of the play: "Nay, but this
dotage of our general's / O'erflows the measure" (i.i.1–2). *Lear* is an
endless demonstration of what it means to move beyond the last
boundary, but Antony may be said to begin already beyond that
boundary. Yet what in *King Lear* produces the experience of an endless poverty (the endless generosity that such poverty witnesses) comes
out in *Antony and Cleopatra* as perpetual wealth and eternal delight. I
do not think that this is because *Antony and Cleopatra* represents a
retreat from the boundless extremity of *King Lear*. Rather, it refuses

the reduction to *Lear*'s "a little"; it refuses the temptation of intimacy without affection in the predicate that there is nothing else, and it insists instead on an extravagance continued through every loss. "O'erflowing the measure" means extravagant prodigality in the play—means the kind of wealth that has nothing to do with husbanding nature's riches from expense. Iras tells the soothsayer, "There's a palm presages chastity, if nothing else," and Charmian replies, "E'en as the o'erflowing Nilus presageth famine" (i.ii.47–50). In a Roman mood Antony explains to Caesar how the harvest is predicted:

> Thus do they, sir: they take the flow o' th' Nile
> By certain scales i' th' pyramid; they know,
> By th' height, the lowness, or the mean, if dearth
> Or foison follow. The higher Nilus swells,
> The more it promises; as it ebbs, the seedsman
> Upon the slime and ooze scatters his grain,
> And shortly comes to harvest.
>
> (ii.vii.17–23)

This is partly couched in terms meant to show Caesar the reasonableness of Egyptian practice. The overflowing Nile may represent a most un-Roman beneficence of nature, but the Egyptians reassuringly follow the rest of the civilized world by numbering, weighing, and measuring. Nevertheless, even here Antony describes the uncommodifiable nature of the source of Egyptian wealth. In contrast to what happens in the utilitarian Roman economy, labor, though stressed in his speech, does not give rise to value. It is secondary to the whims of the Nile and only manifests itself as another kind of dissipation: the scattering of grain over slime and ooze.

To o'erflow the measure, for Antony, is to go beyond any limit through the prodigality of his generosity.[100] *Lear*'s interminability minimizes. It is always a little more than a little. By contrast, *Antony*'s is always by much too much. The contrast is, I think, intentional. Antony's principles directly reverse Lear's ungenerous impetuosity at the start of *King Lear*. Lear wants flattery and likens truth to nothing: "Thy truth then be thy dower!" But Antony's response is the reverse:

Antony: Well, what worst?
Messenger: The nature of bad news infects the teller.

100. Derek Traversi writes, "The 'dotage' which Philo ascribes to him, is expressed by his very critic through an image of abounding generosity, 'o'erflows the measure'" (*Shakespeare: The Roman Plays* [Stanford, Calif.: Stanford University Press, 1963], p. 81).

Antony: When it concerns the fool or coward. On:
   Things that are past are done with me. 'Tis thus:
   Who tells me true, though in his tale lie death,
   I hear him as he flatter'd.

(1.ii.94–99)

Cleopatra's reaction to the bearer of the bad news of Antony's marriage to Octavia will of course be different. To that messenger's question, "Shall I lie, madam?" she responds, "O, I would thou didst; / So
half my Egypt were submerg'd and made / A cestern of scal'd snakes!"
(11.v.93–95). Yet in Alexandria contradictions complicate into a larger
amassing harmony: even here she continues a prodigal destructiveness on Antony's behalf. Her alternations demonstrate this. She
wishes the destruction of all she owns, but this manifests the violence
of her love for Antony, and does it in language in which she seeks by
echoing his earlier imperative to identify herself with him: "Melt
Egypt into Nile!" Like Lear, she promises the messenger Croesus's
wealth in exchange for the simplest words. He need only make his
language at once pleasant and truthful. This may be an impossible
request, but it is merely a concatenation of two purely linguistic
choices, each easy in itself. (It is as though language is the final object
of the demands made by her imperatives.)

Cleopatra's imperiousness is nearly as unlike Lear's as Antony's, but
Antony voices what seems a more direct rebuke to Lear. Lear hears
flattery as though it were truth and truth as the quintessence of the
untender. Antony hears truth as though it were flattery. Other echoes
also underscore the contrast. Antony's question "What worst?" recognizes implicitly that the worst is not yet. His impatience is manifest in
the odd superlative of the question (which Hanmer and Rann
changed to "worse").[101] Yet this does not indicate merely a desire to
know the bottom line or "the sum" at once. After all, he demands a
narrative and has just been asking details: "*Messenger*: Fulvia thy wife
first came into the field. / *Antony*: Against my brother Lucius?"
(1.ii.88–89). Rather, it marks his typical extravagance, which meets the
comparative head on, superlatively. Antony never shares Edgar's expectation that thought might be past. Only things can be past and
done, and Antony is utterly undisturbed by letting them go, even if
only death remains.

It is this robust contrast with the characters of *Lear* that the opening
of the play emphasizes. The whole of *King Lear*, as Stephen Booth

101. See *New Variorum Edition*, vol. 15, *Antony and Cleopatra* (1907), note on 1.ii.91.

argues, demonstrates the excruciating anguish of passing beyond boundaries. But *Antony and Cleopatra* moves into that mode from the start. I want to quote much of the beginning of the play in order to show the velocity and directness with which it represents the efface-ment of all boundaries by uncontrollable prodigality:

> *Philo:*   Nay, but this dotage of our general's
>   O'erflows the measure. Those his goodly eyes,
>   That o'er the files and musters of the war
>   Have glow'd like plated Mars, now bend, now turn
>   The office and devotion of their view
>   Upon a tawny front; his captain's heart,
>   Which in the scuffles of great fights hath burst
>   The buckles on his breast, reneges all temper,
>   And is become the bellows and the fan
>   To cool a gipsy's lust.
> *Flourish. Enter* ANTONY, CLEOPATRA, *her* LADIES, *the* TRAIN, *with eunuchs fanning her.*
>   Look where they come!
>   Take but good note, and you shall see in him
>   The triple pillar of the world transform'd
>   Into a strumpet's fool. Behold and see.
>
>   (i.i.1–13)

Antony's heart has lost temper and has become a billows and fan in conformity with Alexandria's character. It is a world of insubstantial air mocking eyes with substance, from the fans "whose wind did seem / To [glow] the delicate cheeks which they did cool, / And what they undid did" (ii.ii.203–5) and the air which Antony is left alone to whistle to (ii.ii.215–16), to the air and fire to which Cleopatra sub-limes herself at her death (v.ii.289). For Philo this airy nothingness contrasts with the solid substance of Roman virtue. In overflowing the measure, Antony has given up substance and has become a windy dotard. A not quite parallel formulation points this up. Philo says that Antony has shifted his attention from war to Cleopatra. He now gazes on her as once he had gazed on war. When he gazed on war, however, his own act of seeing had been the cynosure of other people's view. His eyes glowed like Mars's. He had the theatrical power consisting in privileged visibility. Caesar implicitly recognizes this power in scene 4 when he describes the reports of Antony's valor: "and all this / . . . / Was borne so like a soldier, that thy cheek / So much as lank'd not" (i.iv.68–71). Now Antony has apparently given up that visible power and has become a servile viewer. He devotes his vision to Cleopatra, where before his vision had itself been visible in the way it glowed with the radiance of his own warlike power. The glowing of his eyes is replaced by the glow that Cleopatra's fans seem to produce but that, in fact, they cool, just as his heart cools her lust. Her artificial visibility contrasts with the more honest and workmanlike glow of Antony as soldier.

Yet Philo's account does not quite make sense. He still asks Demetrius to "behold and see." And it's not quite clear whether his imagery is coherent. If Antony's dotage now o'erflows the measure, this does no more than parallel the image of Antony's heart bursting (unlike Gloucester's or Edgar's) the buckles on his breast. Philo contrasts this with reneging all temper, but the metaphor is somewhat mixed, since a well-tempered heart would not be bursting out. The confusion subsists at the end of the scene when Philo answers Demetrius's question "Is Caesar with Antonius priz'd so light?" His response reverses the original image, in a figure of speech raising odd questions about the nature of Antony's personal identity: "Sir, sometimes when he is not Antony, / He comes *too short* of that great property / Which still should go with being Antony" (1.i.57–59). I will return to the nature of this evocation of Antony's personal identity. Here, I note only that even Philo treats the proper name of his general like a general term, as though "being Antony" described a state of being rather than designated a person. Demetrius's question suggests Antony's nonchalance even about the value he should more prudently set on Caesar. In describing Antony as short of the property that should go with him, Demetrius may be trying to reimagine careless aristocratic grandeur as a bad husbandary of nature's riches.

Against Philo's paralleling of Antony to Caesar and Lepidus as the triple pillars of the world, Antony will claim, "We stand up peerless." Philo's pillars would stand near each other and support the world or the roof of the world, but Antony and Cleopatra rise like monoliths or towers, not pillars, o'ertopping them all. Philo's opening speech shows that Antony is not entirely wrong. Antony, in his excess, is, for Philo and Demetrius, remarkable in a way he would not be otherwise. He and Cleopatra go on to demonstrate the ways in which they do o'erflow every measure:

Cleopatra: If it be love indeed, tell me how much.
Antony: There's beggary in the love that can be reckon'd.
Cleopatra: I'll set a bourn how far to be belov'd.
Antony: Then must thou needs find out new heaven, new earth.

Enter a MESSENGER

Messenger: News, my good lord, from Rome.
Antony: Grates me, the sum.
Cleopatra: Nay, hear them, Antony.
   Fulvia perchance is angry; or who knows
   If the scarce-bearded Caesar have not sent
   His pow'rful mandate to you: "Do this, or this;
   Take in that kingdom, and enfranchise that;
   Perform't, or else we damn thee."

                                         (I.i.14–24)

Commentators have noted the echo of the beginning of *King Lear* in Cleopatra's opening question. Antony's answer asserts a love that goes beyond every bourn or boundary. His claim is not like Cordelia's but like a more truthful version of Goneril's flattering assertion, "Beyond all manner of so much I love you." In contrast to the always minimal extravagance of *King Lear*, Antony's extravagance maximizes. Synecdochical of the difference between the two plays is their differing conceptions of beggary. For Lear, our basest beggars are in all things superfluous. For Antony, even the most ardent superfluity of love may still be accused of beggary, of not being superfluous enough, if it does not find out new heaven, new earth. This grand notion of beggary remains constant in the play. Of Cleopatra, Enobarbus tells Agrippa, "For her own person, / It beggar'd all description" (II.ii.197–98), a much truer claim than Goneril's that her love "makes breath poor, and speech unable" (I.i.60). What there is beggary in is the news from Rome. Love ought not to be able to be reckoned, but as for the news from Rome, Antony only wants it reckoned—summed up—without delay. It is Cleopatra who wishes to dilate, as though langorously, the telling of the news, or rather, she delights in the grand and easy prodigality she imagines for Antony: "Take in that kingdom or enfranchise that." But Antony prefers a purer prodigality and so dispenses with even the apparent purpose of prodigality, which is to be the privileged focus of all attention:

Antony: Now for the love of Love, and her soft hours,
   Let's not confound the time with conference harsh;
   There's not a minute of our lives should stretch
   Without some pleasure now. What sport to-night?
Cleopatra: Hear the ambassadors.
Antony: Fie, wrangling queen!

Whom every thing becomes—to chide, to laugh,
To weep; [whose] every passion fully strives
To make itself (in thee) fair and admir'd!
No messenger but thine, and all alone,
To-night we'll wander through the streets and note
The qualities of people. Come, my queen,
Last night you did desire it.

(I.i.44–55)

Visible prodigality here dissipates its own visibility. North's Plutarch describes what Antony here proposes: "And sometime also, when he would goe up and downe the citie disguised like a slave in the night, and would peere into poore mens windowes and their shops, and scold and brawle with them within the house: Cleopatra would be also in a chamber maides array, and amble up and downe the streets with him, so that oftentimes Antonius bare away both mockes and blowes."[102] Antony and Cleopatra cease, at least for a time, putting forth their glory. In wasting visibility, they waste not only their actual substance—they waste the potential glory that their wastefulness might procure.

I think Antony's wonderful and strange urging that "There's not a minute of our lives should stretch / Without some pleasure now" captures the peculiarity of their dissipations. This line must mean something like, "Time is short [hence the word *now*]; and so we cannot afford to waste any time doing anything else but—wasting time in frivolous pleasure." They will make time run (as Marvell will say), shorten what would otherwise stretch its briefness tediously out, by wasting time in pleasure.

Alexandria distinguishes itself from Richard II's England, then, by the genuine frivolity of Antony's and Cleopatra's pleasures. Richard, to be sure, indulges his every whim; but his whims are for power, and his indulgences aim at maintaining his power. Antony and Cleopatra take pleasure in disguise, cross-dressing, fishing, and sex. This may sound like one version of Hal, but no one could be less like Hal than Antony and Cleopatra are. They may be more like Falstaff, but their plangent commitment to frivolity at all costs assures that they are not self-serving. Falstaff only does what he thinks will bring gain, but Antony and Cleopatra do not seek gain. Octavius Caesar, an avatar of

102. *Antony and Cleopatra*, ed. M. R. Ridley (London: Arden, 1954), p. 249. There may be an echo of this in *1 Henry IV*: "The skipping king, he ambled up and down" (III.ii.60).

Bullingbrook, evinces disgust with Antony for the vulgar display with
which he reasserts his place in Alexandria:

> *Caesar:*   Contemning Rome he has done all this, and more
>   In Alexandria. Here's the manner of't:
>   I' th' market-place, on a tribunal silver'd,
>   Cleopatra and himself in chairs of gold
>   Were publicly enthron'd. At the feet sat
>   Caesarion, whom they call my father's son,
>   And all the unlawful issue that their lust
>   Since then hath made between them. Unto her
>   He gave the stablishment of Egypt, made her
>   Of lower Syria, Cyprus, Lydia,
>   Absolute queen.
> *Maecenas:*   This in the public eye?
> *Caesar:*   I' th' common show-place, where they exercise.
>   His sons [he there] proclaim'd the [kings] of kings:
>   Great Media, Parthia, and Armenia
>   He gave to Alexander; to Ptolemy he assign'd
>   Syria, Cilicia, and Phoenicia. She
>   In th' abiliments of the goddess Isis
>   That day appear'd, and oft before gave audience,
>   As 'tis reported, so.
>   (III.vi.1–19)

This frivolous ceremony would hardly have been Richard's procedure. It can hardly be considered a coup de theatre. Caesar's description, unlike Enobarbus's earlier evocation of Cleopatra, heaps
ridicule on its object. For Enobarbus and Agrippa, Cleopatra had
"appear'd indeed"; here appearing as a goddess, she is made to look
silly. It is not only Antony and Cleopatra, however, who waste the
opportunity for a genuine theatrical effect. Shakespeare himself, as
though in procedural sympathy with them, gives up the effect an
audience waits for most expectantly: the reunion of Antony and
Cleopatra. We last saw Antony in scene 4, bidding Octavia farewell as
she goes to attempt a mediation between her husband and her brother. His conversation with her there seems not notably more cold, holy,
and still than usual:

> *Antony:*   Gentle Octavia,
>   Let your best love draw to that point which seeks
>   Best to preserve it. If I lose mine honour,
>   I lose myself; better I were not yours

> Than [yours] so branchless. But as you requested,
> Yourself shall go between's. The mean time, lady,
> I'll raise the preparation of a war
> Shall stain your brother: make your soonest haste;
> So your desires are yours.
> *Octavia:*   Thanks to my lord.
> The Jove of power make me most weak, most weak,
> [Your] reconciler! Wars 'twixt you twain would be
> As if the world should cleave, and that slain men
> Should solder up the rift.
> *Antony:*   When it appears to you where this begins,
> Turn your displeasure that way, for our faults
> Can never be so equal that your love
> Can equally move with them. Provide your going,
> Choose your own company, and command what cost
> Your heart [has] mind to.
>
> (III.iv.20–38)

Although Antony has reported his intention to return to Egypt, this interchange with Octavia seems designed to set up a dramatic contrast between the sober faithfulness of a relationship with her—including the last speech's sober generosities—and the wild instabilities of his relationship with Cleopatra. It must surprise an audience that what seemed to set the tone for one option should actually represent his manipulating her into departing so that he can return to Alexandria. More surpising is the fact that Shakespeare denies himself the opportunity to show Antony and Cleopatra's reunion. This is the least likely event one would expect to take from report, and yet, on the metatheatrical level, where Antony and Cleopatra may be said to live, this wasted opportunity for theatrical extravagance seems most extravagantly appropriate.

Alexandria, like the world of *King Lear* but unlike Richard's court, represents a place where generosity is, in the last analysis, divorced from the desire for power. In *King Lear* generosity is minimal and empty. In *Antony and Cleopatra* its extravagance extends to the dissipation of its own being or activity. The second scene of the play portrays the thriftless economics that characterize Alexandria concisely. The soothsayer in *Antony and Cleopatra* attempts to set the tone of that seriousness associated with ananke. He appears grimly out of place, and the way the seriousness of his language contrasts with the frivolity of Cleopatra's retinue identifies him as one of those monitory characters who can read the writing on the wall. The generic situation of act 1, scene 2, seems resolvable in one of two ways: either people will believe the soothsayer and take seriously his prognostications, or they will ominously ridicule him to their own later comeuppance. Ridicule the soothsayer they do, at least to an extent, and yet the soothsayer's presence turns out not to control the tonality of the scene:

> *Charmian:*   Is this the man? Is't you, sir, that know things?
> *Soothsayer:*   In nature's infinite book of secrecy
> A little I can read.
>
> (1.ii.9–11)

His language is grandiloquent and serious and attempts to put hers to shame, but she continues, oblivious to any insult, even in her response to the oracular litany of hinted disaster that the soothsayer utters:

> *Charmian:*   Good, sir, give me good fortune.
> *Soothsayer:*   I make not, but foresee.
> *Charmian:*   Pray then, foresee me one.
>
> (1.ii.14–16)

What he foresees is chilling: although Charmian shall be far fairer than she is now (presumably at her death), she will be more beloving than beloved, will outlive Cleopatra (by moments), and will only see her fortunes decline. That these predictions are not arbitrary his terse summary of Iras's future confirms: "Your fortunes are alike" (1.ii.55). When she asks for details, he draws himself up with the assured brevity of truth: "I have said" (1.ii.57). His grim finality echoes Lear's refusal to show any flexibility to Cordelia: "Nothing. I have sworn, I am firm" (1.i.245). And yet it is impressive to see so firm and uncanny a figure reduced, as he is in this scene, to exasperation. To Charmian's question, "Prithee, how many boys and wenches must I have?" he responds with some peevishness, "If every of your wishes had a womb, / And [fertile] every wish, a million" (1.ii.36–39). Strange in *Antony and Cleopatra* is the way the soothsayer's otherworldly power falters when confronted with the careless riot and frivolity of Antony and his retinue. In the same way, when he articulates and confirms Antony's most secret fears in act 2, he does so with a kind of cranky grumpiness, divested of the authority that his Delphic office would be expected to confer upon him:

> *Antony:*   Now, sirrah; you do wish yourself in Egypt?
> *Soothsayer:*   Would I had never come from thence, nor you thither!
> *Antony:*   If you can, your reason?

Soothsayer: I see it in my motion, have it not in my tongue;
   But yet hie you to Egypt again.
Antony: Say to me whose fortune shall rise higher,
   Caesar's, or mine?
Soothsayer: Caesar's.
   Therefore, O Antony, stay not by his side.
   Thy daemon, that thy spirit which keeps thee, is
   Noble, courageous, high unmatchable,
   Where Caesar's is not; but near him thy angel
   Becomes a fear, as being o'erpow'r'd: therefore
   Make space enough between you.
Antony: Speak this no more.
Soothsayer: To none but thee; no more but when to thee.
   If thou dost play with him at any game,
   Thou art sure to lose; and of that naturai luck
   He beats thee 'gainst the odds.

                                                        (II.iii.11–28)

In *Antony and Cleopatra* it is Caesar who has the mana.[103] Like Hal,
he combines a secret prudence with an inexhaustible and magical
resourcefulness, emblematized in his youth. His prudence, like Hal's,
can afford to be secret. A supremely self-confident resourcefulness
makes possible an imprudent version of prudence, and he's willing to
gamble with Antony against all the odds. (Only, of course, in unimportant matters; later he won't gamble the outcome of the war on
single fight: his impersonal power there measures both his prudence
and his uncanny otherworldliness.) This magical resourcefulness
frightens Antony's angel.

It does not frighten Antony, however. Antony's intention to go to
Egypt should be read neither as non sequitur nor as manifestation of
his fearfulness before Caesar. The soothsayer, in desiring him to return to Egypt, wants simply to fly. Indeed he wishes that Antony had
never been there. The advice to return cannot come to good, however, and indeed it does not. Antony knows that his better cunning
consisted in marrying Octavia. This should procure him peace. Yet his
recognition of Caesar's "natural luck" spurs him to defiance in the
realm in which Caesar's privileged relation to being should weigh
most heavily against Antony. Antony risks all for the frivolous pursuit
of pleasure after he has managed to dampen the danger Caesar rep-

103. I think Antony's description of how, at Phillipi, Caesar held his sword like a
dancer is not pure scorn: he's also describing Caesar's grace, his ease with the world he
now owns. Cf. J. Leeds Barroll, *Shakespearean Tragedy: Genre, Tradition, and Change in
Antony and Cleopatra* (Washington, D.C.: Folger Books, 1984), p. 102.

resents. He does not so much hie himself to Egypt as recklessly give himself over to a nonchalant defiance.

This kind of frivolity, both in Antony and in Cleopatra's retinue, vexes the soothsayer's prescience. To put it bluntly, he imagines himself a character like the soothsayer in *Julius Caesar* or perhaps like the fool in *Lear*, but the play treats him more like Malvolio than like Feste. His own sense of privileged communication with the truth is ridiculed, not only by the other characters, but in a sense by the play itself. Not that in any particular he resembles Malvolio. He does have access to the hidden authority of truth. His claim to be an uncanny character is legitimate, but it is surprising that this legitimate claim wanes when confronted with the more frivolous characters in Alexandria. The soothsayer makes an odd double for Caesar. Though they differ in their ability to improve the occasion afforded by their magical gifts, both are closer to the sources of truth than are the surface-loving Egyptians. The Alexandrian defiance of the soothsayer's prognostications corresponds to a defiance of Caesar. The soothsayer's plaintive wish "Would I had never come from thence, nor you / Thither," echo of his vexed exasperation against Charmian, signifies not only that he is a prophet without honor but that his questioners in some way outgo him despite their slenderer (because less supernatural) resources; they manage to oppress him because his seriousness bears no great weight in their lightness. They *have* less, but they *live* more grandly. Theirs is the extravagance of the request Charmian makes anent Alexas:

> Alexas,—come, his fortune, his fortune! O, let him marry a woman that cannot go, sweet Isis, I beseech thee! and let her die too, and give him a worse! and let worse follow worse, till the worst of all follow him laughing to his grave, fifty-fold a cuckold! Good Isis, hear me this prayer, though thou deny me a matter of more weight; good Isis, I beseech thee!
>
> (1.ii.62–69)

The bargain offered here belongs to a gift economy, not to an economy of equivalent exchange. Charmian is spendthrift with her prayers, willing to throw away whatever claim she might have to Isis's intercession in a matter of importance in return for the granting of a frivolous wish. This trade fits with an evaluative system that can make an informative—that is, potentially surprising or noteworthy—statement of what to the bourgeois Romans, as to Shakespeare's audience, would seem too obvious for comment, in the wonderful line "I love long life better than figs" (1.ii.32). This line parodies equivalent exchange in the way it treats long life and figs as in some sense commensurable and in the way it pretends that there is some choice to made there. And of course, as has often been noted, the play returns to this formulation when Cleopatra ends her life by means of what is supposed to be a basket of figs. Thematically, the play agrees with the hilarious valuation that Charmian puts on things.

The unequal bargains Charmian makes can introduce the whole series of extravagant and self-dissipating gestures in the play. Cleopatra puts a high price on her letters to Antony: "Who's born that day, / When I forget to send to Antony, / Shall die a beggar" (i.v.63–65). Her extravagant formulations would use up her own subjects in the delivery of those letters: "He shall have every day a several greeting, / Or I'll unpeople Egypt" (i.v.77–78). This may sound typically hyperbolic, but Cleopatra's hyperboles are themselves hyperbolically reckless. Indeed, it is a kind of hyperbolic recklessness of language that induces Antony to commit suicide. Cleopatra's own suicide seeks to come up to the hyperbolic, but fundamentally true, vision of Antony that she invokes for Dolabella:

> His legs bestrid the ocean, his rear'd arm
> Crested the world, his voice was propertied
> As all the tuned spheres, and that to friends;
> But when he meant to quail and shake the orb,
> He was as rattling thunder. For his bounty,
> There was no winter in't: an Antony 'twas
> That grew the more by reaping. His delights
> Were dolphin-like, they show'd his back above
> The element they liv'd in. In his livery
> Walk'd crowns and crownets; realms and islands were
> As plates dropp'd from his pocket.
>
> (v.ii.82–92)

In contrast to Philo's vision, here Antony's voice has all the properties of the spheres. The possible echo of that earlier speech, in which Philo complains that Antony comes short of that great property which still should go with being Antony, helps justify the mounting resistance to Theobald's emendation of *Antony* to *autumn* in line 87. Antony here does not fall short of himself but is in some sense capacious enough, o'erflows his own measure enough, to contain the bounty he is synonymous with. (This is Shakespeare's anticipation of Milton's treatment of Adam and Eve as their own ancestors, considered in my introduction.) Antony's generosity exceeds fancy's and rivals nature's: "It's past the size of dreaming. Nature wants stuff / To vie strange forms with fancy; yet t' imagine / An Antony were nature's piece 'gainst fancy, / Condemning shadows quite" (v.ii.97–100). Nature produces "an Antony" in the same way that Antony's bounty is "an Antony" and, as Cleopatra had described earlier in one of the most mysterious passages in the play, the cause of her being tongue-tied:

> Courteous lord, one word:
> Sir, you and I must part, but that's not it;
> Sir, you and I have lov'd, but there's not it;
> That you know well. Something it is I would—
> O, my oblivion is a very Antony,
> And I am all forgotten.
>
> (i.iii.86–91)

Cleopatra is forgotten by oblivion as she would (playfully) accuse Antony of forgetting her. This is a very odd description of her own forgetfulness, but it registers, I think, a sense of Antony's capaciousness here. The difference between oblivion and presence is somehow effaced, as it is in Antony's parting lines: "Our separation so abides and flies, / That thou residing here, goes yet with me; / And I hence fleeting, here remain with thee" (i.iii.102–4). Taken in conjunction with Antony's joking rebuke of Cleopatra—"But that your royalty / Holds idleness your subject, I should take you / For idleness itself" (i.iii.91–93)—these lines suggest that, for Antony and Cleopatra at least, their lives together are one continued allegory.

To be forgotten by oblivion is for Cleopatra the same as to be forgotten by Antony, and yet it also means something like being in the presence of Antony, since the allegorical presence of oblivion would signify the forgetfulness she is experiencing. She forgets herself when she is with Antony, or when she is with the forgetfulness and absence that Antony signifies, and in forgetting herself she becomes in some way part of the vast and bounteous and carelessly inexact order that Antony exemplifies. It is part of that bounty that even Antony's forgetfulness nevertheless leaves room for a forgotten Cleopatra, just as their separation nevertheless can signify a kind of presence to each other—the allegorical presence represented by the figure of separation.

Nevertheless, this allegorical way of instancing plenitude comes at a cost—the cost of Antony's actual presence. In Antony generality and extremity come together in a generosity so hyperbolic that it dislimns the specificity of his relation to the world. Thus it makes sense for

Philo to complain that "he comes short of that great property / Which still should go with Antony" (1.i.58–59), a complaint that registers (though wrongly) the difference between the individual Antony and the property of being "Antony." (Wrongly, because Antony's great property is indeed his light valuation of Caesar.) Antony's loss, as Canidius grieves, was his own fault: "Had our general / Been what he knew himself, it had gone well" (iii.x.26–27). Antony's use of nearly the same language in his dolorous lament that Caesar is "harping on what I am, / Not what he knew I was" (iii.xiii.142–43) will make sensible a deeper self-discrepancy. However, this self-discrepancy does not yet vitiate the claim he makes fifty lines earlier, "I am Antony yet" (iii.xiii.92), since Cleopatra ends the scene with her great affirmation:

> It is my birthday,
> I had thought t'have held it poor; but since my lord
> Is Antony again, I will be Cleopatra.
> (iii.xiii.184–87)

Evocations of Antony's generality can take on many tones. Cleopatra opens the play by teasing that she will "seem the fool I am not. Antony / Will be himself" (1.i.42–43), that is, the fool that emblematizes the great property named Antony. Antony himself is frequently made to seem merely one of many Antonys, so that he both does and does not coincide with the general term that he has become. Cleopatra thinks langorously of "betraying" (crucial word) the fishes she angles for, and she muses, "as I draw them up, / I'll think them every one an Antony, / And say, 'Ah, ha! y' are caught'" (ii.v.13–15); here Antony stands for a mode of being that even the fishes may instantiate (as objects of desire and seduction). Conversely Cleopatra's grievance that "my oblivion is a very Antony" sounds as though Antony and oblivion are on the same level, the word *Antony* naming an absolute form of oblivion rather than the person Mark Antony. The person would merely stand for Antonian carelessness: and yet, contrariwise, that carelessness is human, not allegorical or divine; it's careless as only a human as insouciant as Antony could be. Antony himself will think of an Antony as a person, but a person different from himself, another example of the person that is Antony:

> I wish I could be made so many men,
> And all of you clapp'd up together in
> An Antony, that I might do you service
> So good as you have done.
> (iv.ii.16–19)

The language of the last act tends to merge completely these two connotations of the phrase "an Antony." In act 5 Antony turns out to be the unique instance of the class or property named Antony. Caesar's comment on the dead Cleopatra's beauty—"she looks like sleep, / As she would catch another Antony / In her strong toil of grace" (v.ii.346–7)—takes the subjunctive. There is no other Antony, and she is dead. But her beauty and its intimate *directedness* toward Antony seem able, momentarily at least, to replenish the world with Antonys (as though Antony might simply be the goodliest man of men since born his sons, and the fairest of her daughters Cleopatra). Yet for Cleopatra too, Antony is unique. His bounty was as himself, "an Antony . . . / That grew the more by reaping." Antony here is an instance of bounty, but bounty is the same as Antony ("thou mine of bounty" [iv.vi.31]), not something he merely instances. Cleopatra tells Dolabella that "t' imagine / An Antony were nature's piece 'gainst fancy" (v.ii.98–99), so that the hypothetical being "an Antony" whom nature might imagine becomes the single Antony whom she *has* imagined. And nature here is hardly different from Cleopatra:

> I dreamt there was an Emperor Antony.
> O, such another sleep, that I might see
> But such another man!
>
> (v.ii.76–78)

This means both "I dreamt that Antony was Emperor" and "I dreamt that the Emperor was Antony." Office and person are made equivalent here; this king has only one body, simultaneously corporeal and mystical. Meaning and instance, intension and extension, of the concept Antony coincide. Like Caesar, Cleopatra imagines the possibility of "another Antony," but only as a possibility of the replenishment of uniqueness. Dreams are not accretive experiences, continued night to night. Another sleep would mean another world, another life, new heaven, new earth. For Caesar to say that she looks like sleep hints at a poetic truth to the lovers' ideas that they will marry in the dreams that come after they shuffle off this mortal coil. Such another man would be another instance of the unique, the absolutely singular. Specific and general merge in these evocations of an Antony who was Antony himself.

And yet replenishment does not occur in the play. His inexhaustible bounty finally empties him. The motto for this might be the inverse of his claim that "I am Antony yet," the sorrowful proverb he proffers to his followers after the battle of Actium: "Let that be left / Which leaves itself" (iii.xi.19–20). Enobarbus marvels at Antony's own dream: "that he should dream, / Knowing all measures, the full Caesar will / Answer his emptiness!" (III.xiii.34–36). Indeed, as for the characters in *King Lear*, Antony is more than emptied. He passes beyond the zero. His dazzling and amazing grandeur consists in the way he sustains his generosity when he is less than empty. This sustained generosity seems to indicate infinite resource; but beyond the zero it means, instead, a negative infinity, the endlessness of loss, as his generosity preys on itself and eats away at its own substance.

But Antony, in contrast to the minimalism of the characters in *Lear*, never fails at continuing his endless casting away of substance; he keeps up and intensifies his voluntary extravagance. This mirrors his interminable loss through an absolute fullness: "For his bounty, / There was no winter in't" (v.ii.86–87). Giving all to Caesar by insisting on fighting him at sea, "throwing away" his advantage on land just as Pompey has "laughed away his fortunes" and as his side will have "kiss'd away kingdoms and provinces," Antony declares, "Our overplus of shipping will we burn" (III.vii.50), as though the unfair advantage lay on his side. After losing that battle he manifests his despair finally through the intensified generosity with which he addresses his followers:

> Hark, the land bids me tread no more upon't,
> It is asham'd to bear me. Friends, come hither:
> I am so lated in the world, that I
> Have lost my way for ever. I have a ship
> Laden with gold, take that, divide it; fly,
> And make your peace with Caesar.
>
> (III.xi.1–6)

The third line is an example of the astonishing prosody in this play, with its enjambment between subject and auxiliary verb.[104] The word "I" frames the line, but its appearance at the end of the line exemplifies the lateness described. After the heavy, quasi-final stress on "world" at the end of the fourth foot, it maintains itself in the line in so precarious a fashion as to seem ready to fall or dissolve over the line break. The prosodic undoing of the first person here corresponds to the meaning of the passage. To be lated and lost means not to be

---

104. Cf. also the lines lately quoted:
> the full Caesar will
> Answer his emptiness.

Enjambments around auxiliary words make for a perilous prosody just right for this play.

where you wish to be; but where you would wish to be is a place somewhere in the world, and to be lated in the world means there is no place at all that you could be. Antony here describes himself not as an allegorical figure of ubiquity and plenitude but as so reduced to singularity as to be reduced further to nothing and less than nothing. He has left himself behind.

I think these lines are an answer to the question asked several times about Antony: "Where is he now?" This question signals Antony's potential for plenitude and ubiquity but also for the ways in which it is possible for him to be absent, to be lost. Caesar preys on the possibility of Antony's self-discrepancy through a counterubiquity when he gives his chilling order about Antony's abandoners: "Plant those that have revolted in the vant, / That Antony may seem to spend his fury / Upon himself" (IV.vi.8–10). Caesar intends Antony's expenditure of power to be useless and insubstantial, like a disengaged gear. Caesar throughout proceeds so as to disengage real generosity from power. His own instances of generosity are couched in the shrewd terms of equivalent exchange: "feast the army; we have store to do't / And they have *earn'd* the waste" (IV.i.15–16). The new heaven and new earth of bourgeois imperialism that Shakespeare imagines Caesar as establishing renders the Antonine mode of generosity empty, a mangled shadow. Caesar's motto might come from the first words of his careful command to Taurus: "*Do not exceed* / The prescript of this scroll" (III.viii.4–5).[105]

Antony's ubiquity in the play, his generality, is too often proportioned to his inefficacy. His is the ubiquity of absence.[106] The play counterpoints the generalizing phrase "an Antony" with another re-

---

105. At Antony's death, though, he too recognizes a version of Antony's generality: "The death of Antony / Is not a single doom, in the name lay / A moi'ty of the world" (V.i.17–19).

106. Jonathan Dollimore comments nicely: "Caesar . . . is reminiscent of Machiavelli's Prince; he is inscrutable and possessed of an identity which becomes less fixed, less identifiable as his power increases. Antony by contrast is defined in terms of omnipotence (the more so, paradoxically, as his power diminishes): the 'man of men' (I.iv.72), the 'lord of lords' (IV.viii.16)" (*Radical Tragedy: Religion, Ideology, and Power in the Drama of Shakespeare and his Contemporaries* [Chicago: University of Chicago Press, 1984], p. 208). But Dollimore sees only overcompensation in Antony. Frank Kermode calls Caesar "*fortunatus*, the man of destiny" (introduction to *Antony and Cleopatra* in *The Riverside Shakespeare*, ed. G. Blakemore Evans [Boston: Houghton Mifflin, 1974], p. 1345), which anticipates Dollimore and also Jacobson's beautiful sentence "If it is austerity that is before us [in Caesar] then it is austerity wrought to splendour" ("*Antony and Cleopatra*," p. 103). John Danby's earlier remark that Caesar is "a kind of impersonal embodiment" of Rome, "a cold and universal force . . . invulnerable as no human being should be" (*Poets on Fortune's Hill: Studies in Sidney, Shakespeare, Beaumont and Fletcher* [London: Faber and Faber, 1952], p. 144) also strikes me as correct.

iteration, the apostrophe "O Antony." These words are addressed to
Antony absent more than to Antony present. They make his absence
felt. Antony becomes in these vocatives something other than another
person; he becomes a spirit with all the power but also all the impotence of language. Of course, as with "an Antony," their invocation
can correspond to all the tones in the play, from Caesar's rebuke
"Antony, / Leave thy lascivious [wassails]" (i.iv.55–56) to Cleopatra's
extravagantly mediated "O happy horse, to bear the weight of Antony!" (i.v.21). But on the whole, apostrophe to Antony tends to be an
indication of need. Pompey makes his peace with the triumvirate and
fights back his misgivings: "O Antony, / You have my [father's]
house—But what, we are friends" (ii.vii.127–28). Enobarbus sorrows
over Cleopatra's mollifications of Thidias: "Sir, sir, thou art so leaky /
That we must leave thee to thy sinking, for / Thy dearest quit thee"
(iii.xiii.63–65; this is another instance of the most audacious prosody). Having left him, Enobarbus apostrophizes him incessantly. "O
Antony, / Thou mine of bounty, how wouldst thou have paid / My
better service, when my turpitude / Thou dost so crown with gold!"
(iv.vi.30–33), he responds to Antony's sending his treasure after him
"with / His bounty overplus" (iv.vi.20–21), and he dies invoking
Antony:

> O Antony,
> Nobler than my revolt is infamous,
> Forgive me in thine own particular,
> But let the world rank me in register
> A master-leaver and a fugitive.
> O Antony! O Antony!
>
> (iv.ix.18–23)

We would expect Enobarbus's infamy to be directly related to Antony's nobility: the nobler Antony is, the more infamous the betrayal.
Antony's bounty exceeds the proportional logic of equivalence, however, and can be apprehended only in doleful or in gay comparatives:
"Nobler than my revolt is infamous." Even Caesar feels Antony's loss,
and if his first apostrophe rebukes, his last laments: "O Antony, / I
have follow'd thee to this" (v.i.35–36). And Cleoptra dies (or tries to)
also invoking Antony (v.ii.312).

These invocations of the absent are the apostrophes of generosity.
Voice and presence are given away to the absent. Enobarbus and
Cleopatra give more than that—they give their lives, dying as a way of
joining Antony in absence. But there is nothing pious in this. As

Cleopatra wishes, Mardian falsely reports "that the last word [she] spoke was 'Antony'" (IV.xiii.8):

> the last she spake
> Was "Antony, most noble Antony!"
> Then in the midst a tearing groan did break
> The name of Antony; it was divided
> Between her heart and lips. She render'd life,
> Thy name so buried in her.
>
>   (IV.xiv.29–34)

Apostrophe articulates need, and yet that need can speak only of the absence and loss out of which it arises.[107] Whatever Cleopatra may think about the possibility of attaining, in one world or the other, to the presence of Antony (and I do not think that she, any more than Antony, believes literally in this possibility of mutual presence), the play works hard to disabuse its audience of that idea. Mardian's setup marks the fact that Cleopatra's timing is slightly off when she actually dies: "O Antony!—Nay, I will take thee too: / What should I stay—" (V.ii.312–13).

The play can be still more direct: Antony gives up his life to run toward a posthumous Cleopatra whose phantasmal nature actually consists not in the fact that she is dead *but in the fact that she is not dead.* Antony apostrophizes Cleopatra by name only twice (as opposed to using the more generalizing terms "my queen," or "Egypt"): when he seeks to tell her of Fulvia's death (I.iii.26) and when he thinks that she herself has died: "I will o'ertake thee, Cleopatra, and / Weep for my pardon" (IV.xiv.44–45).[108] Life in *Antony and Cleopatra* itself becomes

---

107. Quinney puts this quite well: "For a long stretch of *Antony and Cleopatra*—until the battle at Actium, late in act 3—Antony's presence in the play is curiously pervasive but abbreviated. He appears in only half the scenes, and, while Cleopatra appears in even fewer, he seems particularly elusive, since so many of the scenes from which he is absent concern his absence itself. . . . The host of [the] apostrophes to Antony both make his presence pervasive, and, with their epitaphic drive, imperil it ("Enter a Messenger," p. 151).

108. This is another astonishing example of the play's prosody, especially with the lines that follow it:
> I will o'ertake thee, Cleopatra, and
> Weep for my pardon. So it must be, for now
> All length is torture: since the torch is out.   (IV.xiv.44–46)
Close to breathtaking are the caesura after the ninth syllable in line 44, followed by an "and" which barely resists elision with the last syllable of Cleopatra, and the difficult enjambment with which the word conjoins two verbs (as opposed to two clauses), followed again by trochaic inversion in the first foot of the next line. The line may instance some of the torturous drawing out that I have argued is the theme of *King Lear*, a

insubstantial, as insubstantial as the nonexistent posthumous relationship between Dido and Aeneas (since she spurned him and kept silent)[109] to which Antony compares his relationship with Cleopatra
(IV.xiv.50–54). The insubstantiality of life is the lesson of the apostrophes, verbal gestures that undo the difference between absence
and presence. If absence appears to be a kind of presence in apostrophe, the converse is still truer: presence is a kind of absence, and
generality is a kind of dissipation and attenuation of substance: "O my
oblivion is a very Antony, / And I am all forgotten" (I.iii.90–91). The
emptiness of the gestures of apostrophe shows that in some sense they
are pure generosity's pageants—offerings of passion and life to phan-
tasms unable to be repositories for them.

Of course Antony is not the only absent subject of apostrophe.
Enobarbus laments, "Caesar, thou hast subdued his judgment too";
Cleopatra addresses the dead "Broad-fronted Caesar"; and she her-
self is the subject of much apostrophe. Even when Cleopatra is absent,
Pompey can address her in his hope that Antony will not join Caesar
and Lepidus in their war against him:

> all the charms of love,
> Salt Cleopatra, soften thy wan'd lip!
> Let witchcraft join with beauty, lust with both,
> Tie up the libertine in a field of feasts,
> Keep his brain fuming; Epicurean cooks
> Sharpen with cloyless sauce his appetite,
> That sleep and feeding may prorogue his honor,
> Even till a Lethe'd dullness—
>
> (II.i.20–27)

Yet this apostrophe concerns Antony more than it does Cleopatra,
and structurally it is hardly apostrophe at all. Though Pompey addresses Cleopatra, the imperatives are *third-person*, not second. The
subjects of these sentences—"all the charms of love," "witchcraft,"
"lust," "Epicurean cooks," "sleep and feeding," "Lethe'd dullness"—
are distinct from the vocative Cleopatra. Cleopatra focuses an imperative that aims at other grammatical subjects. There is some argument
within linguistics as to how anomalous it is to have an imperative

---

torturous lengthening compounded by the strange and difficult pun: torture/torch is
out.

109. Despite much scholarship, the main allusion must be to the story as told in the
Aeneid, as though Shakespeare's play were the Antonian counter to Vergil's Octavian
epic.

whose subject is different from the addressee, but everyone agrees that it is fairly anomalous, especially in English.

The third-person imperative construction is relatively rare. That this should be especially true of English is due, I think, to the tendency to introduce it with *let* or *may*, where the French, for example, would have *que*. Thus, in English, third-person imperatives tend to be assimilated to those of the second person, to whom *let* or *may* would be addressed. Often the second person is only putative—God, for example—and optative or contrary-to-fact third-person imperatives look a lot like prayers—"let the test results be negative," for example.[110] We tend to register the third-person imperative only in particularly transitive or efficacious or violent verbs, strong cases of what linguists call agentive verbs: "Let her be hanged by the neck until dead" doesn't really mean "permit her to be hanged"; "let him go to hell" isn't a prayer but a refusal to pray. Third-person imperatives, impatient of mediation through a second-person agent, demand or require immediate and complete change, at any cost.

Striking in *Antony and Cleopatra* are the large number of third-person imperatives, as Pompey's speech helps to underscore in distinguishing vocative from subject. Occasionally these imperatives do seem to make use of verbs with a requisite vividness or violence: "their tongues rot / That speak against us!" (III.vii.15–16). In general, however, the verbs that Antony and Cleopatra use for their third-person imperatives are remarkable for their non-agentive or (figuratively speaking) *intransitive* properties. When they demand alteration at all, the changes they demand are less than immediate and, indeed, sometimes imperceptible. Their formulations preserve the sense that what they require, they require at any cost; but the gradualness and insubstantiality of what they desire underscore how incommensurably great is the price that Antony and Cleopatra are willing to pay. Even the imperative just quoted shares this feature:

110. Maynard Mack writes eloquently of the radically optative mode of the play in "*Antony and Cleopatra*: The Stillness and the Dance" in *Shakespeare's Art*, ed. Milton Crane (Chicago: University of Chicago Press, 1973), pp. 91–92. I am trying to distinguish a more specific feature. I think that the third-person imperatives in the play are too common to make it helpful to read some of them as optatives and others as true imperatives. Abbott comments in the article "Subjunctive used optatively or imperatively": "Often it is impossible to tell whether we have an imperative with a vocative, or a subjunctive used optatively or conditionally" (*Shakespearean Grammar*, §364). Two of his four examples are from *Antony and Cleopatra*: "*Melt* Egypt into Nile! and kindly creatures / *Turn* all to serpents!" (II.v.78) and "Now to that name my courage *prove* my title!" (v.ii.288).

> Sink Rome, and their tongues rot
> That speak against us! A charge we bear i' th' war,
> And as the president of my kingdom will
> Appear there for a man.
>
> (III.vii.15–18)

The enjambment at the end of line 17 at an auxiliary verb anticipates Antony's "I / have lost my way for ever." The verb that follows—
"appear"—is curiously weak or phantasmal—close to non-agentive—
but it recalls the other moments Cleopatra "appears": "There she
appear'd indeed"; "she / in th' abiliments of the goddess Isis / That
day appear'd" (III.vi.16–18). Here the verb's spectrality (and yet this is
not a particularly spectral passage) comes out in the lack of a proper
subject. There is a grammatical solecism in the sentence. Its subject is
the first-person plural, "we," but what will appear "as the president of
my kingdom . . . for *a* man" is singular. The spectrality of the verb
appear shares the spectrality of the third-person imperatives *sink* and
rot. Violent though these demands are, they do not have the putative
efficacy of a curse of different aspect, a curse that would demand that
Rome be sunk, that *their tongues be rotted*. The present tense or aspect of
the imperative precludes the efficacious immediacy of result because
sinking and rotting, no matter how swift, are gradual processes. The
verbs belong to the class linguists call stative rather than agentive.

Consistent throughout the play is this anomaly of the vocabulary of
third-person imperatives, in which non-agentive verbs appear in the
imperative mood. A list of quasi-intransitive verbs appearing in the
imperative (usually in the third person) would include, in addition to
Pompey's *soften, join, keep, sharpen,* (I agree that *tie up* is fully transitive),
Cleopatra's *sink* and *rot* and words like *melt, fall, weet, know, foresee, find,
mend, marry, lose, sit, be strew'd, look, turn, be kind, comfort, be inform'd,
o'ertake, be left, repent, fever, dissolve, yield, grow, disponge, discandy, be
gentle grave,* and many others. I do not claim that there are more
imperatives in *Antony and Cleopatra* than in Shakespeare's other plays
but that they are more anomalous in this play.[111] The very first scene

---

111. There may be more of them as well. In *Shakespeare's Grammatical Style: A
Computer-Assisted Analysis of Richard II and Antony and Cleopatra* (Austin: University of
Texas Press, 1973), Dolores M. Burton tabulates the number and kinds of imperatives
in *Richard II* and *Antony and Cleopatra*. She counts 460 imperatives in *Richard II*, compared with 780 in *Antony and Cleopatra* (p. 37), and notes, "When the subjects of all
optative imperatives were divided into those that refer to deities or supernatural
powers . . . and those that refer to human beings, there were twenty-nine of the former
in *Richard II* as opposed to seventy-one of the latter; the proportion in *Antony* was twelve
to ninety-two" (p. 41n), which confirms a sense of the peculiarity of the imperatives in
Antony and Cleopatra.

of the play (I.i.33–40) uses imperatives to signal Antony's imperiousness, an imperiousness that makes demands that o'erflow the measure of transitivity.

Antony's extravagance manifests itself not only in what he shows himself willing to cast away for the company of Cleopatra but in the imperious way he casts it. His language commands that Rome melt and that the arch of empire fall, rather than merely permitting destruction through neglect. Such a command is anomalous, as is the command that ends this speech: "I bind / On pain of punishment, the world to weet / We stand up peerless." One would expect him to require the world to acknowledge their peerlessness but a command to know something, when not purely performative (as in a be-*hereby*-informed construction: "Know but that I loved the gentle Desdemona"), is close to what Wittgenstein would call a grammatical solecism. Either you know something or you don't. Force will not cause knowledge, even if it may compel an assertion or concession of knowledge. But Antony imagines his own extravagant power as overcoming the spectrality of his verbs and as giving efficacious substance to inefficacious quasi-intransitives and non-agentives: *melt, fall,* and *weet.* Indeed, *melt* and *fall* are canonical examples in linguistics of a class of intransitive verbs defined by the fact that they cannot be modified by the adverb "purposely,"[112] but Antony consistently uses these verbs as though they were susceptible of the voluntarist jussivity that is his mode. His power rejoices in what it takes to be its capacity to overcome these verbs' phantasmal relation to agency, or their resistance to the language of agency, and its capacity to assimilate them to the intentional and to endow them with graspable, workable substance from its own efficacious plenitude of will. Or rather, their substance comes from the plentiful substantiality of the objects on which Antony's imperious will legitimately can exercize itself and which thus symbolize it. The subjects of Antony's opening imperatives—Rome and the wide arch of the ranged empire—are so large and so weighty that they come close to making the weight necessary to endow mass to the spectral verbs *melt* and *fall.*

And yet this imperious will to substance eventually comes, in *Antony and Cleopatra*, to mean that even for his *ordinary* Antony pays his heart, for what his eyes eat only—the ordinary can appear indeed but cannot be engaged.[113] By this I mean that Antony himself falls into the

112. They are called unaccusatives. The other class is called unergative. *Know* or *weet* could be added to the list of things you can't do on purpose. *Run* would be an example of an unergative, something you can do intentionally.

113. By the ordinary I mean something close to what Stanley Cavell means: the world we live in, the world that language games apply to, the opposite of the extrava-

phantasmic verbal space that he has spent everything in trying to draw into the efficacious ambit of his power. His generosity goes beyond a reasonable boundary, o'erflows a calculated measure, and ends up spending the capital that has made it possible. He does not, unlike Octavius, venture his capital simply in order to amass more, to extend

---

gant. And yet Cavell is interested in how the extravagant can coincide with the ordinary—the extravagance of skepticism, for example, and also the extravagance of the rescue from skepticism. His profound reading of *Antony and Cleopatra*, in many ways complementary to mine, sees Cleopatra in her great speech to Dolabella as "making a present of the world" to Antony: "My guiding (in)tuition is that the invention of marriage *is* the (is Cleopatra's, whoever that is) response to Antony's abandonment; it is a return of the world through the gift of herself, by becoming, presenting herself as, whatever constitutes the world" (*Disowning Knowledge*, p. 28). This seems to me ultimately in accord with Bloom's apparently contradictory sense that Antony and Cleopatra are catastrophes for each other (introduction to *William Shakespeare's Antony and Cleopatra*, p. 3). In this play the difference between gift and catastrophe comes undone; Cleopatra, as a pure giver and a pure gift, is necessarily also a catastrophe, but this in no way implies that there is anything ambivalent about her gifts or about receiving them. The gift of catastrophe is a very rare and very desirable thing; this seems to me one place where you can imagine Cavell and Bataille agreeing.

   Rosalie Colie also argues eloquently for Cleopatra's generosity, and of the speech to Dolabella she writes, "Cleopatra's imagination is as bountiful as Antony's generosity" (*Shakespeare's Living Art* [Princeton, N.J.: Princeton University Press, 1974], p. 193). That speech itself is significant for the way it conceives bounty, her own and nature's, as competitive—in contrast to Antony's—as though nature's condemning bounty consisted in creating a generosity (contra Jacobson) that unimaginably did not condemn. This speech can be taken to reply to Jacobson's article "Gentle Madam, No":

   You lie up to the hearing of the gods!
   But if there be, or ever were one such,
   It's past the size of dreaming. Nature wants stuff
   To vie strange forms with fancy; yet t' imagine
   An Antony were nature's piece 'gainst fancy,
   Condemning shadows quite.   (v.ii.95–100)

This contrasts with Caesar's far more standard attempt to manipulate the economies of capital and obligation in the message he sends to Cleopatra that "he partly begs / To be desir'd to give" (iii.xiii.66–67), which courteously displays Caesar's willingness to act as though the obligation would be all his if he were permitted to be beneficent to Cleopatra. Cleopatra's description to Dollabella means to oppose Antony to Proculeius's description of Caesar:

   Y'are fallen into a princely hand, fear nothing.
   Make your full reference freely to my lord,
   Who is so full of grace that it flows over
   On all that need. Let me report to him
   Your sweet dependency, and you shall find
   A conqueror that will pray in aid for kindness
   Where he for grace is kneel'd to.   (v.ii.22–28)

"Pray in aid," as the Arden note effectually points out, means that he will beg to be desired to give all that she needs. This is a strange parody of Lear's idea that he and Cordelia will kneel to each other in prison. Talk is cheap, as Caesar knows when he claims "Caesar's no merchant, to make prize with you / Of things that merchants sold" (v.ii.183–84). All this boasting contrasts with Antony's real generosity, which does not aim at power, and this is Cleopatra's point.

his holdings.[114] Generosity's imperious and amassing investment of substance in the phantasmic reverses into its own spectral dissipation.[115] Enobarbus describes this with his usual bluntness. "A diminution in our captain's brain / Restores his heart. When valour [preys on] reason / It eats the sword it fights with" (III.xiii.197–9), he says, and this characterization extends to a self-sustaining process of ruin his earlier description of Antony: "And for his ordinary pays his heart / For what his eyes eat only" (II.ii.225–26).

In his great speeches to Eros, Antony's spectrality manifests itself most strikingly. It manifests itself in the way his relation to the most ordinary of verbs has now become spectral. Here it is no longer Antony's substance that fails to engage phantom, non-agentive verbs; Antony's own spectrality cannot engage even the most agentive of verbs:

Antony: Eros, thou yet behold'st me?
Eros: Ay, noble lord.

My own reading is more about Antony than about Cleopatra because the stuff of Antony's bounty is not inexhaustible, whereas the stuff of Cleopatra's is. No one objects to Enobarbus's description of Cleopatra's infinite variety, but people do object to her corresponding description of Antony's bounty because Cleopatra really does seem self-originating in a way that Antony ultimately cannot sustain. Why this should be so is, I think, the argument of Cavell's work on the difference between male and female characters in Shakespeare, the former open to a skepticism that can harm the latter but that the latter will not share.

114. That Antony should squander his capital so easily is the surest sign of his antibourgeois sensibility. Caesar's wealth is centripetal, Antony's centrifugal; Caesar's mass, like a neutron star's, draws everything to him and spirals inward, whereas Antony's spirals outward, exploding like a supernova.

For good Marxist readings of the different economic orders in Rome and Egypt, see Eagleton, *William Shakespeare*, pp. 86–89, and Dipak Nardy, "The Realism of *Antony and Cleopatra*," in *Shakespeare in a Changing World*, ed. Arnold Kettle (Norwood, Pa.: Norwood Editions, 1964), pp. 172–94.

115. Freud's account of mourning presents a similar economy. Mourning is painful because libido drains only into a sievelike phantom or memory and not into a presence that can contain and sustain it. Libidinal investment is like filling a form with content; loving that form gives it life. But if the object of investment is gone, present only as an image, the form becomes a sieve, and its apparent life comes at the cost of a continuous drain of the psychic energy of the self. Antony's self-description, which I am about to consider, works the same way, when he says that he "cannot hold this visible shape," as though his form, like the images of the dead in the mourner's mind, were stationary and stable only through continual and exhausting replenishment of a substance endlessly "leaky" (to use Enobarbus's word). In her *Suffocating Mothers: Fantasies of Maternal Origin in Shakespeare's Plays, Hamlet to The Tempest* (New York: Routledge, 1992), pp. 174–92, Janet Adelman gives a psychoanalytic account of the similarities and differences between Antony and Cleopatra. Her emphasis on Cleopatra's "imaginative fecundity" (p. 192) as the model and matrix for Antony's male bounty is a useful complement to my reading of Antony.

Antony: Sometime we see a cloud that's dragonish,
A vapour sometime like a bear or lion,
A [tower'd] citadel, a pendent rock,
A forked mountain, or blue promontory
With trees upon't that nod unto the world,
And mock our eyes with air. Thou hast seen these signs,
They are black vesper's pageants.
Eros: Ay, my lord.
Antony: That which is now a horse, even with a thought
The rack dislimns, and makes it indistinct
As water is in water.
Eros: It does, my lord.
Antony: My good knave Eros, now thy captain is
Even such a body. Here I am Antony,
Yet cannot hold this visible shape, my knave.

(IV.xiv.1–14)

He is Antony yet, but more than authority melts from him here.
Not to be able to hold one's own shape, as though even so agentive a
verb as *hold* had become no longer in the control of his agency: this is
to have as spectral a relationship to the most ordinary verbs as the
phantom relationship that the third-person imperatives witness
throughout. It is the culmination of the Alexandrian use of verbs,
from their most jocular to their most solemn appearances. These
verbs stand for or instance expenditure. Charmian asks the soothsayer to give her good fortune and replies hilariously to his stern
admonition that "I make not, but foresee,"—that is, that the business
of fortune telling is not entirely agentive—by demanding, "Pray then,
foresee me one" (I.ii.15–16). This easiness with verbs is the same
easiness that makes it possible to weigh long life against figs and to ask
Isis to cuckold Alexas even if she denies prayers of greater weight. In
Alexandria weighty considerations are insouciantly laughed away for
the purpose of lending piquancy to trivial verbs.

Charmian's joke is to use *foresee* as an agentive verb, as though one
could forsee good fortune intentionally; *hold* reverses this, when Antony uses it as though he is powerless even to will the coherence of his
own soul. Perhaps the most eerily anomalous reversal of category is
Cleopatra's response to the news of Fulvia's death: "Can Fulvia die?"
The retort might be, Who can *fail* to die? Cleopatra's question may
look back to the failure to die in *King Lear* and the endless spectrality
that failure leaves behind. It is difficult to decide whether *die* is agentive or not, whether it is something that happens to the subject of the
verb or something which that subject does. Dying is the transition

from intention to its utter absence (from the agentive to its opposite), and the question *Can she die?* registers her entry into a space where she is no longer the agent of the verb, a space where the verb is no longer agentive. Cleopatra's sympathy for Fulvia comes out in the way she marvels that so great a figure could fall, could, *in dying*, be rendered so powerless as to be perhaps powerless *to die*.

What happens to the verb *die* in this question represents what happens to the verbs throughout the play. Even Octavia can have this impoverishing, dissipatory relationship to the imperative: "The Jove of power make me most weak, most weak, / [Your] reconciler!" (III.iv.29–30), she says as she leaves to mediate between Antony and Caesar. The pathos of these lines inheres in the way her self-acknowledged frailty nevertheless expends what power or imperious efficacity of will it has on willing or wishing the most powerful of gods to act as she desires and supply her own lack of power. Antony's and Cleopatra's imperatives differ from Charmian's and Octavia's, however, in that they do not solicit the aid of any of the gods: they are not optatives. Octavia's appeal can be thought of as a quasi-vocative address to Jove, but when Antony and Cleopatra speak, their commands make no appeal at all.

But the tonalities of their imperatives change. These changes, especially in Antony's, describe the trajectory of his life from a dissipatory plenty to an even more dissipatory poverty, from the imperious "Let Rome in Tiber melt" to the astonishing moment when he casts away even the anger that seems to be the only possession he has left, after the loss of the battle of Actium. Cleopatra enters, and Antony begins twenty lines of anguished beratement by asking,

> O, wither hast thou led me, Egypt? See
> How I convey my shame out of thine eyes
> By looking back what I have left behind
> 'Stroy'd in dishonour.
>
> (III.xi.51–54)

Even these lines speak to an extravagant economy of dissipation. Antony foregrounds the dishonor of the destruction of his own life in order to escape the much more minor shame or dishonor of having Cleopatra look directly upon his grief. He absorbs the expense of the terrible and shameful vision of disaster rather than the much smaller expense of the shame of having her see him weep. His shame is a simple emotion, but it means several things: shame at losing, shame at losing because of her, shame at her seeing him lose (partly because he still idolizes her and he is ashamed before her authority), and shame because he scorns her and is ashamed to feel reduced to an object of derision for what he now derides, reduced thus both because he has lost and because he now weeps. His vision still pays all it has, still pays his heart, by looking on the wreckage of its world to avoid her vision's observation of his shame: her vision here is being rated as worth all the expense his undergoes, even as he thinks he thinks her worthless. These remarkable lines convey the character of their intimacy as well as any lines in the play. Antony feels himself the focus of Cleopatra's most intimately comprehending look: he knows she will understand how ashamed he feels *before her*, over what (he says) she has led him to. Yet what she will see is how he obscures himself from her; his opacity will become for her another purchase for the intimacy between them. She will understand what his turning his visage away from her, out of her eyes, means: Antony will rather face the dishonor of his utter loss than dishonor himself before her. Such a thing is a courtesy on his part. It occurs where courtesy and intimacy overlap, where the smallest points of courtesy—not to confront someone else with your own problems, no matter how terrible—become the occasion for the deepest intimacy. Only for someone like Cleopatra will Antony continue his courtesy even in this extreme situation.

I agree that he is, of course, having it both ways, since he does complain; but it is a sign of their intimacy that she accepts this and is, indeed, expected to accept it. Still, he does excoriate her for another fifteen lines. The crucial point, however, is the way he changes his tone with no warning at all:

> *Antony:*   Now I must
>   To the young man send humble treaties, dodge
>   And palter in the shifts of lowness, who
>   With half the bulk o' th' world play'd as I pleas'd,
>   Making and marring fortunes. You did know
>   How much you were my conqueror, and that
>   My sword, made weak by my affection, would
>   Obey it on all cause.
> *Cleopatra:*   Pardon, pardon!
> *Antony:* Fall not a tear, I say, one of them rates
>   All that is won and lost. Give me a kiss.
>   Even this repays me.
>
>   (III.xi.61–71)

"Fall not a tear": is this second- or third-person imperative? It does not seem adequate to me to say that *fall* is simply transitive or that it may be sometimes used transitively (as possibly in Lear's "Fall and blister her"). Clearly it means "let not a tear fall" and means it more than it means "drop not a tear." Both are second-person imperatives, but "let not a tear fall" preserves the non-agentive quality of *fall*. In "Fall not a tear," *tear* is the subject of the sentence: something other than an agent is the subject of an imperative with a non-agentive verb. I think that the line hovers between second- and third-person imperative and that Antony is putting everything into an imperious desire that not so much as a tear (to speak nothing of a sparrow) shall fall if he wills it otherwise. To Cleopatra he says that she should not permit a tear to fall, but the extravagance and extremity of his own will goes to using all the authority that is left to him to prevent the tear from falling. His authority goes to making the verb agentive, as though to make that authority possible: authority can only affect the actions of agents (who submit to that authority). He once again commands the verb to be susceptible to the authority of command, as though his substance will cancel out the insubstantiality of the verb's capability of agency. This squandering of will upon a verbal phantom is what the next words describe: "one of them rates / All that is won or lost: give me a kiss, / Even this repays me."

Antony's linguistic practice gives everything, huge tracts of willing, in order to attempt to confer the slightest residuum of resistance upon purely phantom verbs. I have argued that the rebound of this is the way substantial verbs lose their resistance or substance, so that even a verb like *hold* becomes non-agentive and phantom. Now, Antony's astonishing generosity consists in its extravagance even when its resources are utterly depleted, when the verb *to give* maintains its agency despite the fact that Antony's life has rendered it, for him, non-agentive. Enobarbus is made to feel this when the soldier comes in with the treasure that Antony, despite his extremely precarious situation, has sent after him:

> *Soldier:*   Enobarbus, Antony
>   Hath after thee sent all thy treasure, with
>   His bounty overplus. The messenger
>   Came on my guard, and at thy tent is now
>   Unloading of his mules.
> *Enobarbus:*   I give it you.
> *Soldier:*   Mock not, Enobarbus,
>   I tell you true. Best you saf'd the bringer
>   Out of the host; I must attend mine office,
>   Or would have done't myself. Your emperor
>   Continues still a Jove.
>
>   (IV.vi.19–28)

Continue may be the verb most precariously poised between agentive and non-agentive. Antony continues to be himself—continues still a Jove. He continues still a Jove despite the fact that Hercules—cause, sign, and manifestation of his power—has left him at the same time as Enobarbus. He wins the day's battle, despite the fact that all he has to match against the full Caesar is his own emptiness. To continue to be something seems non-agentive: continue here seems entirely stative. As with *hold*, however, it is no such thing. To continue his preternatural generosity requires for Antony the most intense intention imaginable. His generosity is preternatural precisely in its having no supernatural sponsorship. The genuineness of his generosity, like Christ's or God's in Herbert, consists in its coming at more cost than he can possibly bear, since there is nothing—no divinity—still conferring upon him substance to supply the emptiness he has already been reduced to, an emptiness that nevertheless does not hobble his generosity. His generosity is entirely his own, not itself the endowment of a richness in being to which he would stand in a privileged relation and not the gift of an ontological plenitude whose organ he would be. Antony continues generous despite his extreme poverty: his generosity is real in direct proportion to that poverty. It is the converse of the way the young man in the sonnets can combine being and having: Antony continues his generosity even when both his being and his having have come to an end. His generosity and his poverty are indistinguishable: his poverty is felt as a lack so extreme that it has become an alterity. Enobarbus recognizes this, and he recognizes it in the stunning immediacy with which he accepts the truth of the soldier's report (an immediacy the soldier misreads as immediate skepticism). Antony's impotent generosity draws Enobarbus into its atmosphere. "O, my fortunes have / Corrupted honest men" (III.v.17), he says, but in fact his generosity does more and draws them, as it draws Eros, with him into the sphere of alterity.

This is the alterity of literary language, language that speaks despite its utter insubstantiality and its utter inefficacy, speaks for something different from the linguistic play of power, and glows not with superabundance but with solitude. *Paradise Lost*, to which I turn in my last chapter, thematizes directly the question of the relation of language to power, to the power of the determination of being. It thematizes directly the relation that is a nonrelation between being and the language of poetry.

CHAPTER THREE

The Majesty of Darkness:
Idol and Image in Milton

Thou art immortal and this tongue is known
But to the uncommunicating dead.

—P. B. Shelley

Abyss is its own apology.

—Dickinson

I began this book with Herbert in order to make an argument about the relation of Protestantism to generality and the relation of the latter to generosity. In both the Herbert and the Shakespeare chapters I tried to characterize a certain literary mode—the mode of the experience of the exhaustion of generosity. Herbert describes this experience from the point of view of the dependent beneficiary; Shakespeare describes it from the point of view of the benefactor. In this last chapter, I try to return to the Protestant experience of what I called a community of preterition.

Paradise Lost is one of the severest exponents of a Puritan movement opposed to idolatry in all its forms, and so opposed to the theatrical mode of power which it has been the strength of recent criticism to see as one of Shakespeare's main concerns. Werner Gundersheimer has argued that radical Reformation iconoclasm must be seen as having had an economic as well as religious impetus. It sought to overturn the hierarchy based on a patronage system that took the form of ostentatious display and exchange.[1] If Protestantism and the spirit of capitalism are internally related, part of that relation would consist in

1. See "Patronage in the Renaissance: An Exploratory Approach," in *Patronage in the Renaissance*, ed. Guy Fitch Lytle and Stephen Orgel (Princeton, N.J.: Princeton University Press, 1981), pp. 3–23. Gundersheimer specifically compares the patronage system to the "Big Man system" in which power is a function of gift exchange.

their rejecting the specificity of the icon for the generality of a system in which there are no local distinctions between sacred and profane, in which all values are commensurable, and where the only real distinction is between the specificity of this world and the ineffability of God. I have argued that generality and generosity went together, that those sympathetic to an archaic gift economy saw it as one in which all individual personalities may be viewed as functions of a general deployment of generosity. But, unlike Herbert and the Luther and Calvin he followed, the Puritans did not see things this way, and their radicalism consisted in undoing the hierarchy (and the consequent focus on particularity) natural to any system of gift exchange.

And yet the gift can be conceived as opposed to idolatry, and not only as an idol. The gift can be thought of as opposed to idolatry if its ultimate value does not reside in itself but in the relations it makes possible and that it stands for. On this conception, the least idolatrous of gifts would be the gift without substance, the invisible gift (say of grace) that opposes all materiality and stands for generosity without substance. Such a notion of the gift might be seen as the sacralized version of the substanceless generosity present in *King Lear*. Such a notion of the gift, the gift of poetry or of a mortal voice—opposed to idolatry in all its forms—*Paradise Lost* articulates.

Like the Shakespearean plays I have considered, *Paradise Lost* can be thought of as describing a transition from a gift economy to an exchange economy, from an economy that promotes an ideology of abundance to an economy that promotes an ideology of scarcity. In discussing Herbert I tried to describe this transition in theological terms. Salvation, for Herbert, would mean the discovery that we have not really fallen utterly and that what looks like scarcity is a disguised abundance. The real fall into foresakeness comes with the discovery that there are, in fact, limits even to divine abundance and that God, too, lives, or suffers, the experience of scarcity and loss.

In my discussion of *King Lear* I described an empty or substanceless generosity conferred by gods become anonymous. I argue similarly about Milton's God, that at his best he too is nearly anonymous and that he too offers a substanceless generosity.

Paradise Lost also conceives the transition from abundance to scarcity as a fall—indeed as The Fall. The Fall results in the destruction of paradisal abundance and in its replacement by the labor economy of the postlapsarian world. Prelapsarian abundance itself, however, is a highly ambivalent blessing, at least for Satan. I argued above that Satan's ambivalence about God's generosity is a classic instance of the ambiguity of the gift. That the gift cannot be repaid constitutes its burden as a gift—an instance of generosity that places its recipient under an impossible obligation. The obligation is impossible to fulfill because it demands so little: only the gratitude on which such stress is laid throughout *Paradise Lost*. What return can Satan make to demands so great, because so little, except revolt? But how can such a revolt ever provide satisfaction?

> Ah wherefore! he deserv'd no such return
> From me, whom he created what I was
> In that bright eminence, and with his good
> Upbraided none; nor was his service hard.
> What could be less than to afford him praise,
> The easiest recompense, and pay him thanks,
> How due!
>
> (4.42–48)

The ease of this recompense is also its impossibility, however, and so Satan turns this acknowledgment into its opposite:

> I 'sdein'd subjection, and thought one step higher
> Would set me highest, and in a moment quit
> The debt immense of endless gratitude,
> So burdensome, still paying, still to owe;
> Forgetful what from him I still receiv'd,
> And understood not that a grateful mind
> By owing owes not, but still pays, at once
> Indebted and discharg'd, what burden then?
>
> (4.50–57)

By owing, the grateful mind owes not. By feeling its obligation, it is discharged of obligation. This movement of thought is similar to Herbert's, but its opposite is necessarily just as present to Satan. By not owing, he is made continually to owe; he is indebted *because* he is discharged. The simultaneity and mutual amplification of debt and its forgiveness is familiar from Seneca's *De Benificiis*:

Yet thou demaundest what I think of the matter: and thou wilt have mee too saye thee a full answere. I say, let the one think his good turne requyted: and let the other assure himself he hath not requyted. Let the giver hold the receyver discharged, and let the receyver acknowledge himselfe bound still. Let the one say, I have it: and let the other say I owe it. . . . I have doone all that might bee. Yea and doo so still. . . . Thou hast doone what thou couldst too requyte. Let him accept it as sufficient, but think thou it too little. For like as if hee can fynd in his hart too passe

over thyne earnest and vigilent indever unregarded, he is unworthie too
be requyted with kindnesse: Even so also art thou a verie Churle, if thou
on the othersyde, in respect that he acceptheth thy good will for payment, bee not so muche more willingly beholden too him because thou
art released.[2]

I do not deny that Milton thought this a piece of accurate moraliz-
ing and that the unfallen Adam and Eve are perfect examples of
beings who feel the debt of gratitude as utterly lightsome and delightful. Adam's first speech acknowledges his delight in God's liberality,
manifest in the "ample world" he has created. God is "infinitely good,
and of his good / As liberal and free as infinite, / That rais'd us from
the dust and plac't us here / In all this happiness" (4.414–17). ("All
this happiness" is the prelapsarian phrase corresponding to "all our
woe," brought into the world with the Fall, and to "all that pain" that
Ceres felt in searching for Proserpin.) The only return required, he
continues, is not to eat of the fruit of the tree of knowledge, and
Adam regards the apparent ease of this obligation as being *in fact* easy
and not a burden:

> Then let us not think hard
> One easy prohibition, who enjoy
> Free leave so large to all things else, and choice
> Unlimited of manifold delights:
> But let us ever praise him and extol
> His bounty, following our delightful task.
>
> (4.432–37)

Adam and Eve continue extolling God's bounty in their evening
hymn. Anticipating their own fruitfulness they see their children as
sharing this plenty: "thy abundance wants / Partakers," and they
thank God for his "gift of sleep" (4.730–31, 35). For them the miracle
of life consists precisely in their awareness of a divine liberality that
does not seem extravagant only because it comes from infinite resources. It is the fullness with which they partake of or share in this
liberality that enables them to return praise, gratitude, and even gifts
without any sign of anxiety or oppression. The contrast with Satan is
clear when Adam asks Eve to prepare entertainment for Raphael:

> But go with speed,
> And what thy stores contain, bring forth and pour
> Abundance, fit to honor and receive

2. Seneca, . . . *Concerning Benefyting* . . . , trans. Arthur Golding (London: 1578),
pt. 7, chap. 16, pp. 113–14.

Our Heav'nly stranger; well we may afford
Our givers thir own gifts, and large bestow
From large bestow'd, where Nature multiplies
Her fertile growth, and by disburd'ning grows
More fruitful, which instructs us not to spare.
                                        (5.313–320)

Eve agrees that she will "entertain our Angel guest, as hee / Behold-
ing shall confess that here on Earth / God hath dispenst his bounties
as in Heav'n" (5.328–330). The point obviously does not need to be
labored. Perhaps the most beautiful examples of "the Maker's high
magnificence" (8.101) are the descriptions in books 8 and 9 of the
abundance and speed of the tributes of light that the earth, or the
inhabitants of earth, receive.

   Nevertheless, Adam and Raphael, as John Guillory has pointed out,
speak in the vocabulary of a possible scarcity.[3] Adam marvels at "How
Nature wise and frugal could commit / Such disproportions, with
superfluous hand" (8.26–27) as to have so many heavenly bodies
shine on and circle earth with numberless swiftness. Raphael, while
famously hedging his answer, continues this language of frugality, so
opposed to the language of creation in book 7, by suggesting that
even if all of these celestial splendors really are solely for the benefit
of the inhabitants of earth, their value might be relatively trivial
despite the fact that Adam supposes

That bodies bright and greater should not serve
The less not bright, nor Heav'n such journeys run,
Earth sitting still, when she alone receives
The benefit: consider first, that Great
Or Bright infers not Excellence: the Earth
Though, in comparison of Heav'n, so small,
Nor glistering, may of solid good contain
More plenty than the Sun that barren shines.
                                        (8.87–94)

---

3. "Superfluity has two different Paradisal economies, meaning abundance . . . or
[else] waste" (lecture at Brandeis University, May 14, 1987). In "The Father's House:
Samson Agonistes in Its Historical Moment," in *Re-membering Milton: Essays on the Texts and
Traditions*, ed. Mary Nyquist and Margaret W. Ferguson (New York: Methuen, 1987),
pp. 148–76, Guillory argues that Samson is caught between two conflicting paternal
authorities: that of Manoa, who wants him to follow his (protestant) vocation, and that
of Yahweh (the superego), who demands some great work. Destruction on the order of
the potlatch—destruction of the temple of Dagon—is for Samson the only way to fulfill
both demands. I am interested in Milton's sense of what is left after the expenditure or
destruction of infinite bounty and of general belongingness to a prelapsarian generality. Following Regina Schwartz (see below), one could say that what is left are shadowy
types no longer representing more general truths.

This is a warning against idolatry, against the premium placed on looking, and against the voyeuristic "gazing" that progressively rots Satan's character and brings the humans to their downfall. But it is a rather prosaic response after all the extraordinary imagery of the tireless expenditure of light beginning in book 3. In general for both Adam and Raphael, though, an impulse toward generosity and distribution, not prosaic devaluation, almost inevitably coexists with their aesthetic sense of the superiority of frugality. Thus Adam cannot conceive all these goods as his or theirs alone, and in his colloquy with his creator, he asks,

> how may I
> Adore thee, Author of this Universe,
> And all this good to man, for whose well being
> Thou hast provided all things; but with mee
> I see not who partakes.
> ....
> Among unequals what society
> Can sort, what harmony or true delight?
> Which must be mutual, in proportion due
> Giv'n and receiv'd; but in disparity
> The one intense, the other still remiss,
> Cannot well suit with either, but soon prove
> Tedious alike.
>   (8.360–64, 383–89)

As in his conversation with Raphael, and as in his talk with Eve about the children who will soon share in all this plenty, Adam expresses a sense of proportion that is finally utilitarian. All this wealth must have some use. There must be a reason for all this abundance. This utilitarian concept of the gift risks denying of at least one aspect of divinity: the ease and freedom of its generosity. (As we shall see, it also leaves Eve vulnerable to one of Satan's arguments.) Satan in his worst moments also speaks such a language of frugality or scarcity and of calculation, as when he speculates, in book 9, on God's reasons for creating humans:

> To mee shall be the glory sole among
> Th'infernal Powers, in one day to have marr'd
> What he Almighty styl'd, six Nights and Days
> Continu'd making, and who knows how long
> Before had been contriving, though perhaps

> Not longer than since I in one Night freed
> From servitude inglorious well nigh half
> Th'Angelic Name, and thinner left the throng
> Of his adorers: hee to be aveng'd,
> And to repair his numbers thus impair'd,
> Whether such virtue spent of old now fail'd
> More Angels to Create, if they at least
> Are his Created, or to spite us more,
> Determin'd to advance into our room
> A Creature form'd of Earth.
>
> (9.135–49)

This is typical of Satan's wishful sense that all beings in the universe are as subject to their own finitude as he is. Even conceding what he sometimes will not concede, that God is the creator, Satan imagines this creation coming at some expense. It costs labor. The creative virtue may be spent, or partly spent. The number of God's host is impaired, and it will take some doing to repair that lack. (God, of course, has already said that he can "repair / That detriment," if it is a detriment, "in a moment" [7.153–54]; but this means that Satan's perspective is not entirely unshared.)

Yet in this same speech Satan continues to display some of his own magnificence, inextricable though it may be from what by book 9 is utterly base in his character. His courage continues, and in his own desire to make a potlatch of paradise ("For only in destroying I find ease" [9.129]), he is willing to absorb all the expense of punishment that his destructive actions will entail: "maugre what might hap / Of heavier on himself" (9.56–57). This idea is repeated several times, and even in its most debased form it shows a grandeur in Satan. Satan is willing to absorb a cost far greater than any benefit he can possibly obtain and far greater than any injury he can inflict. Debased as he is by book 9, he is still in some ways an avatar of Antony. This can be seen, I think, in his language of expenditure, far more magnificent and far more Miltonic than Raphael's or Adam's, in his invocation to the Earth:

> Terrestrial Heav'n, danc't round by other Heav'ns,
> That shine, yet bear thir bright officious Lamps,
> Light above Light, for thee alone, as seems,
> In thee concentring all thir precious beams
> Of sacred influence.
>
> (9.103–7)

Unlike Raphael, Satan echoes God's blessing on the elect that "Light after light well used they shall attain" (3.196). Obviously God means a more figurative and inward irradiation than what Satan refers to, but the echo and the hedging formula "as seems" indicate that Satan's words of helpless praise represent Milton speaking in full voice. This claim can also be supported by the linguistic transaction that follows God's line in book 3. There God speaks the language of justice and scarcity and says that after the Fall a rigid requirement of exchange will prevail. Grace, and the sense of abundance that the promise of "light after light" manifests, can only come after the payment of "the rigid satisfaction, death for death" (3.212). The demand for this payment is a demand for a gift of mercy that will satisfy justice's requirement of equivalent exchange. But the Son's language of mercy when he volunteers to become human translates this strict quid pro quo into its opposite and recalls the abundance of these lights: "Behold mee, then, mee for him, life for life / I offer" (3.236–37).

In this chapter I will partly follow the Romantic reading of *Paradise Lost*, at least so far as to insist on the tragic cast of Satan's experience. That tragic affect may be described as a loss of abundance or of access to abundance. This experience of depletion and exhaustion, which is a loss of substance, carries a ghostly gain: the gain of one sort of literary experience, or the experience of a certain type of extremity, impoverishment, or solitude. Satan's power as a tragic figure—a power whose limits will nevertheless be one of my main claims in this chapter—is manifest in his opposing an adverse finitude and the most limited of resources in his rivalry with God. He is willing to absorb from his own finite resources the tremendous loss entailed by the punishment he will receive for the trivial challenges he mounts to God. The gifts, the generosity that he is himself able to confer, are empty and nearly meaningless. Nevertheless, in their emptiness they share something of the intimacy of the nearly empty generosity that is evoked by *King Lear*.

I think that Satan's attempt to rival God's fullness with his own emptiness can be seen in the way he tempts Eve. His first speech to her praises her in subtly idolatrous terms, but as though the praise is also a praise of God:

> Wonder not, sovran Mistress, if perhaps
> Thou canst, who are sole Wonder, much less arm
> Thy looks, the heav'n of mildness, with disdain,
> Displeas'd that I approach thee thus, and gaze
> Insatiate, I thus single, nor have feared

Thy awful brow, more awful thus retir'd.
Fairest resemblance of thy Maker fair,
Thee all things living gaze on, all things thine
By gift, and thy Celestial Beauty adore
With ravishment beheld, there best beheld
Where universally admir'd: But here
In this enclosure wild, these Beasts among,
Beholders rude, and shallow to discern
Half what in thee is fair, one man except,
Who sees thee? (and what is one?) who shouldst be seen
A Goddess among Gods, ador'd and serv'd
By Angels numberless, thy daily Train?

(9.532–48)

The modulations of this speech depend on a subtle interplay of the notions of abundance and waste. Eve is open to such arguments because she herself is ambivalent about paradisal luxuriance (9.205–12). All things belong to Eve by gift. So far this is true, but, according to Satan, this comes to mean that she is owed these gifts because she herself is the sole wonder of the earth, the sole object magnificent enough in its visibility to be worthy of insatiate gazing. The generosity of her own being—so Satan argues—requires a greater return than can possibly be hers in Eden. Her fairness is wasted in this narrow boundary; she should have the abundant service of angels numberless.

Satan now transfers the language of privileged visibility, the idolizing language of gazing applied throughout to his admiration for the humans, to the fruit of the tree of knowledge. He tells her that he saw the fruit and "nearer drew to gaze" (9.578) and, because he has eaten the fruit, he is now compelled "to come / And gaze, and worship" Eve (9.610–11). Eve's reply celebrates the abundance of the garden:

But say, where grows the Tree, from hence how far?
For many are the trees of God that grow
In Paradise, and various, yet unknown
To us, in such abundance lies our choice,
As leaves a greater store of Fruit untoucht,
Still hanging incorruptible, till men
Grow up to thir provision, and more hands
Help to disburden Nature of her Birth.

(9.617–24)

Here too Eve tends to return to the utilitarian language of frugality, even as she praises the abundance of the garden. These fruits are partly burdens for nature, but they will eventually be put to use when her children consume them. Nevertheless, both Satan and Eve have stressed the plenitude of the garden, and this bounty is the context for Eve's regret when Satan brings her to the tree of knowledge:

> Serpent, we might have spared our coming hither,
> Fruitless to mee, though Fruit be here to excess.
>   (9.647–48)

Her vocabulary still maintains its ambivalent sense of frugality. "We might have spared" the wasted journey; the fruit of the tree is "here to excess." Yet this is her first confrontation with scarcity, a scarcity that looks to her indistinguishable from waste. This idea that waste and scarcity should go together can be said to prepare her for the counter-vailing sense of the genuine abundance of the world, an abundance with which the limitations implied by envy cannot be thought to co-exist. She gazes fixedly on the fruit (9.735) and reasons that it cannot be denied to humans and reserved for beasts (9.767–68). Finally she accepts Satan's reasoning that an economy of abundance cannot be an economy marked by envy (9.729–30), and she completely mistakes *his* envy for generosity: "yet that one Beast which first / Hath tasted, envies not, but brings with joy / The good befall'n him" (9.769–71). Such a sense of unenvied abundance still implies her innocence. Only after the Fall does she contrast the liberality of the tree to divine envy:

> O Sovran, virtuous, precious of all Trees
> In Paradise, of operation blest
> To Sapience, hitherto obscur'd, infam'd,
> And thy fair Fruit let hang, as to no end
> Created; but henceforth my early care,
> Not without Song, each Morning, and due praise,
> Shall tend thee, and the fertile burden ease
> Of thy full branches offer'd free to all;
> Till dieted by thee I grow mature
> In knowledge, as the Gods who all things know;
> Though others envy what they cannot give;
> For had the gift been theirs, it had not here
> Thus grown.
>   (9.795–807)

This speech returns to the vocabulary of a subtle frugality. The fruit should be eaten; otherwise it would be a burden hanging to no end. Its abundance cannot be the gift of the gods; otherwise it would not have grown here. The idea of useless abundance which the potlatch celebrates is alien to Eve, and her impulse toward a sense of frugality is one of the determinants of her fall, even as it witnesses her capacity for gratitude. Her frugality appears early on, when she asks Adam of the stars, "But wherefore all night long shine these, for whom / This glorious sight, when sleep hath shut all eyes?" (4.657–58). This frugality is what Satan had first worked on in her dream, when he ventriloquizes Adam: "now reigns / Full Orb'd the Moon, and with more pleasing light / Shadowy sets off the face of things; in vain, / If none regard" (5.41–44).

An intolerance of waste leads to utter loss of Eden, and yet this can also mean that loss, as in *King Lear*, still maintains the aura of generosity. The parodic version of this linkage, as I suggested above, is Satan's making a potlatch of his destruction of humanity. He demonstrates his power through his power to destroy and to absorb the pain and loss that such destruction will entail. I think, however, that there is real generosity, real intimacy—utterly empty though it is—in the earlier Satan of book 4 and in the regret that suffuses his words. What he has to offer Adam and Eve is nothing compared with the "grace" that

> The hand that form'd them on thir shape hath pour'd.
> Ah gentle pair, yee little think how nigh
> Your change approaches, when all these delights
> Will vanish, and deliver ye to woe,
> More woe, the more your taste is now of joy:
> Happy, but for so happy ill secur'd
> Long to continue, and this high seat your Heav'n,
> Ill fenc't for Heav'n to keep out such a foe
> As now is enter'd; yet no purpos'd foe
> To you whom I could pity thus forlorn
> Though I unpitied: League with you I seek,
> And mutual amity so strait, so close,
> That I with you must dwell, or you with me
> Henceforth; my dwelling haply may not please,
> Like this fair Paradise, your sense, yet such
> Accept your Maker's work; he gave it me,
> Which I as freely give; Hell shall unfold,
> To entertain you two, her widest Gates,
> And send forth all her kings; there will be room,
> Not like these narrow limits, to receive
> Your numerous offspring; if no better place,
> Thank him who puts me loath to this revenge
> On you who wrong me not for him who wrong'd.
>
> (4.365–87)

I agree with Empson that this ought not to be taken as sneering irony.[4] Satan does pity Adam and Eve, and he offers only what he can: the space of his own version of freedom in return for the loss of abundance and grace. I do not deny that his plea of necessity here is tyrannical, but I think nevertheless that necessity has some of the resonances it has in *Richard II* and that Satan is thinking of Richard's speech to Isabel: "I am sworn brother, sweet, / To grim necessity, and he and I / Will keep a league till death" (v.i.20–22). It seems to me that Satan's offer, an offer whose emptiness is ultimately manifest in the fact that his character does rot over the course of the poem, is an offer of the empty generosity of language for the generosity of paradisal abundance. The one thing that the fallen Adam and Eve receive from this offer is, I think, a sense of the generosity of language, in opposition to the ostentatious generosity of the visible or iconic.

According to this argument, Satan is something of a Protestant; yet I will attempt to justify Milton's God. I will urge what I only half-jokingly call the novel view that Milton is of God's party in *Paradise Lost*. Not that theodicies of *Paradise Lost* are wanting, but I think they defend the wrong God and the wrong kind of God. Perhaps the extremity I described in Herbert and Shakespeare is not likely to touch so robust a God as Milton's. Nevertheless, I want to argue against that robust conception. I describe my view as novel because, as Keats says, axioms of philosophy are not axioms until they are proved upon the pulse, and most readers, on both sides of this vexed issue, have had to go elsewhere even for the terms of an argument about God's justifiability (for example, to theology.)[5] But on my reading, *Paradise Lost* dramatizes a series of more or less mistaken interpretations of God in order to claim a terrific prerogative for poetry as the only human endeavor pitched high enough to be adequate to the God

4. William Empson, *Milton's God* (New York: Cambridge University Press, 1981), p. 67.

5. I know of no convincing reading of *Paradise Lost* that justifies God without bringing in doctrinal contexts whose apparent necessity would seem to vitiate Milton's avowed purpose. The argument about whether Milton succeeds in this purpose turns into an argument about what sufficient justification would mean; the angelic side seems to think that *Paradise Lost* need only rehearse old arguments, that the justification is clear from the outset, and that if you look to *Paradise Lost* for the justification you have not found elsewhere, there is no hope for you anyway. I also depend on some doctrinal context but only to try to make explicit what I think is a successful justification within the terms of the poem alone. A formula for this—which I hope will seem less gnomic later—might contend that Shelley (who died just before the doctrinal contextualizing provided by the "Christian Doctrine" appeared) was of God's party without knowing it. This means, at the least, that Milton would have been glad to have been the major influence on *Prometheus Unbound*.

the poem imagines. The poem may load the deck in poetry's favor, then, but it still must convince you to play with that deck: that, I argue, is what Milton conceived of as his task. Justifying the ways of God to men becomes equivalent to proving poetry upon the pulse: making the reader go the same steps as the author until the reader reaches the point where God is his own apology. It will become clear, I hope, that this is not a claim for the vatic fullness of poetry, a fullness that would attest to the presence of God.[6] Rather Milton's God is justified through poetry; he derives his own authority from poetry. For poetry is the only thing that Milton conceived of as being inherently antipathetic to idolatry as worship. Perhaps such a claim to the novelty of the identification of creator and poet needs justification. Its novelty consists in a reversal of what I take to be the usual (Platonic) relationship of tenor to vehicle in such a metaphorical identification. Most assertions of the vatic fullness of poetry ultimately reduce to the Ionic view that poetry is a metaphor for creation. But for Milton, creation is a metaphor for poetry.[7]

I want to define idolatry in a broad sense as understanding God to be a *particular* object or entity, marked by some particular ostentation, rather than sharing the generality that omnipresence would imply. Such a Spinozean account of Milton's God is shared by critics as radically divergent as William Empson (in *Milton's God*) and Dennis Danielson (in *Milton's Good God*). I want to understand God's generality more radically than they do, however, and to relate it to the shadow generality that I have been claiming for poetry. Milton's God seems to me ultimately to preside, much like Herbert's God, over Bataille's "negative community: the community of those who have no community."

Most readers agree on Milton's hatred of idolatry. Christopher Hill

---

6. Compare Maureen Quilligan, *Milton's Spenser: The Politics of Reading* (Ithaca, N.Y.: Cornell University Press, 1983). Her Milton, like Fish's Herbert, finds his own writing completely taken over by the absolute presence of God, so that Milton "did not need a language in which the divine presence was other, or *allos*" (p. 152).

7. This may sound idolatrous in its own way, but the point is how terrifically difficult Milton makes poetry. Thus I cannot agree with Florence Sandler's emphasis when she writes of *Eikonoklastes* that "it is as if Milton's career as iconoclast and enemy of sacramentalism had brought him to the point of rejecting not only *Eikon Basilike* but the Gospel of John" ("Icon and Iconoclast" in *Achievements of the Left Hand: Essays on the Prose of John Milton*, ed. Michael Leib and John T. Shawcross [Amherst: University of Massachusetts Press, 1974], p. 183). She implies that in *Paradise Lost* Milton produces whatever theology is necessary to justify his ways to Charles; my claim is that Milton rejected Charles for the same fundamental reasons that he wrote *Paradise Lost*. Poetic affect is not for Milton a substitute idol but the uncanny residue—so I argue—left when all idolatry is gone.

is most succinct on political implications: "Idolatry is a short summary of all he detested: regarding places as holier than people; interfering with the strongly-held convictions of Christians about how they should and should not worship God; use of financial and corporal punishments in spiritual matters; all the sordidness of church courts progging and pandering for fees."[8] The concept of idolatry does much— even all—of the work of coordinating the poetical, political, and religious dimensions of Milton's thought: readers of all camps find Eve's worshiping of the tree the clearest sign of her degradation, a degradation to find its latest avatar in what Milton calls in "Of Reformation" "the new-vomited Paganisme of sensuall Idolatry" that was the target of the Puritan revolution. Idolatry makes the soul forget "her heavenly flight."[9] For Milton, idolatry was the exact antithesis of freedom, the alienation of one's own free will. Even Calvinism becomes a mode of idolatry, enslaved by the particular and unable to rise to an apprehension of the general. The Arminian rejection of Calvinist predestination in the "Christian Doctrine" is couched in the terms of an iconoclasm that would refuse the gratuitous magnification of some individuals over others:[10] "It seems, then, that predestination and election are not particular but only general: that is, they belong to all who believe in their hearts and persist in their belief. Peter is not predestined or elected as Peter, or John as John, but each only insofar as he believes and persists in his belief" (*Complete Prose*, 6:176).

Determining which party Milton was of, then, depends on deciding which is the party of the iconoclasts. Percy Shelley—who can represent the radical tradition from Blake to Empson—sees Satan as a forerunner of his own explicitly revolutionary hero Prometheus, and it is hard to quarrel with him that even for Milton Satan was on the side which saw itself as resisting oppression. I agree that there are problems with Satan—I insist on it—but certainly he spends a lot of time defending his attempted regicide in terms like those of Milton's defenses of the English people.[11] If we are to admire Milton's refusal

8. Christopher Hill, *Milton and the English Revolution* (New York: Viking, 1978), p. 64.

9. *The Complete Prose Works of John Milton*, ed. Don Wolfe (New Haven, Conn.: Yale University Press, 1953–82), 1:520, 522.

10. The best theological account, I think, of Milton's doctrines of free will, fixed fate, and foreknowledge absolute is Dennis Danielson's in *Milton's Good God* (New York: Cambridge University Press, 1982). I disagree with him on most matters of interpretation, but his book convincingly shows Milton rejecting the human compatibilism between free will and fixed fate that I argued is closest to Herbert's doctrine.

11. It is of course generally agreed that Satan's position at least partly bases itself on the Puritans'; even C. S. Lewis can write that "he begins by fighting for 'liberty,' however misconceived." And, as will be seen, I agree with the rest of the sentence: he "almost at

to idolize the name of king—"a name then which there needs no more among the blockish vulgar, to make it wise, and excellent, and admir'd, nay to set it next the Bible, though otherwise containing little els but the common grounds of tyranny and popery, drest up, the better to deceiv" (*Complete Prose*, 3:339)—it is difficult not to admire much of what Satan says to the same purpose. Throughout the first two books of *Paradise Lost* Satan denounces what he sees as "the Tyranny of Heav'n" (1.124) or what Mammon calls a "state / Of splendid vassalage" (2.251–52). His incitement of the rebel angels can couch itself as a plea for liberty from servile pomp, whose ceremonies seem to be important in heaven. Satan's objection to God's command about the Son that "to him shall bow / All knees in Heav'n, and shall confess him Lord" (5.607–8),[12] seems justified since the Son has not yet demonstrated his worth. While Milton wants us to admire the Son because he volunteers to redeem humanity through his sacrifice, this reason for exaltation comes after Satan's rebellion (although earlier in the

---

once sinks to fighting for 'Honour, Dominion, glorie, and renoune' (VI, 422)," (*A Preface to Paradise Lost* [New York: Oxford, 1942], p. 99). I insist on the connection between the nature of Satan's rebellion and that of idolatry. Kenneth Gross has a fine piece, "Satan and the Romantic Satan: A Notebook," in *Re-membering Milton*, pp. 318–41.

12. Satan is not wrong to understand the letter and not the spirit of this command (unless all the angels are deceived, which I think they are) since bending knees to one's superiors is a general rule among the angels (see, e.g., 3.736–38). Adam in Eden also conforms to the custom of "bowing low" (5.360; this phrase first appears in 1.434 when Israel turns from God "bowing lowly down / To bestial Gods"). Adam has apparently not read the "Christian Doctrine," where Milton writes apropos of idolatry, "We are forbidden to pray to angels and saints" and glosses "Rev. xix. 9 [*sic*]: I fell on my face to worship him. . . . See that you do not do it. I am your fellow-servant, similarly xxii. 8.9. The reason given is that God is nearer and kinder to us than any of the saints and angels either are or can be" (6:694). Raphael, who likes showing off in front of Adam and who likes having Adam think of him as one of God's privileged, does not respond to Adam's bowing the way Christ does in Revelation, probably because he's a follower (as he shows a hundred lines later) of Cornelius Agrippa: see Robert H. West, *Milton and the Angels* (Athens: University of Georgia Press, 1955), p. 12.

Irene Samuel points out that, for Milton, "through the pagan Neoplatonists the Ideas became Intelligences as well as intelligibles, and thence by easy steps the angels of Neoplatonic Christians" (*Plato and Milton* [Ithaca, N.Y.: Cornell University Press, 1947], pp. 145–46). Samuel quotes a passage from the *Convivio* which there is some evidence that Milton knew—a passage that makes Dante sound like Raphael. While Dante does say that ideas became intelligences, he goes on to say, as she does not point out, that the intelligences they became were the pagan gods (*Convivio*, 255); if Milton believed this, then he would have to be seen as anti-Platonist, since in *Paradise Lost* the Platonic ideas would be associated with the fallen angels worshiped as the pagan gods. I want to minimize the difference between fallen and unfallen angels, however, in order to demonstrate that both belong to a kind of Platonism that can accommodate idolatry (and hence was to be rejected).

poem).[13] Satan's objection to the Son stems, at least in part, from the
same impulse that caused Milton to inveigh against arbitrariness in
law giving. It would not be out of character for Satan to urge, with
Milton, that "in the publishing of humane lawes, which for the most
part aime not beyond the good of civill society, to set them barely
forth to the people without reason or Preface, like a physicall prescript, or only with threatnings, as it were a lordly command, in the
judgment of *Plato* was thought to be done neither generously nor
wisely." The judgment Milton is approving is about human and civil
laws, it is true, but Milton's heaven (and at this point, Milton's God)
does not seem fundamentally different in quality from civil society. If
God's purpose is to evoke love in the angels, one would think he'd do
better to use persuasion which is "a more winning and more manlike
way to keepe men in obedience than feare," since it "would so incite,
and in a manner, charme the multitude into the love of that which is
really good, as to imbrace it ever after, not of custome and awe, which
most men do, but of choice and purpose, with true and constant
delight" (*Complete Prose*, 1:746). But God does not give Satan any
persuasive reason for the law proclaiming the Son's glorification; to
Satan it does indeed seem an arbitrary and lordly command:

> by Decree
> Another now hath to himself ingross't
> All Power, and us eclipst under the name
> Of King anointed.
>
> (5.774–77)

There is no reason to doubt that Satan's expectations were encouraged by a genuine belief that God ruled only through what Milton
scornfully calls "custome and awe" and Satan calls "Consent or cus-

---

13. W. B. Hunter tries to naturalize the strangeness of chronology in "The War in
Heaven: The Exaltation of the Son" in *Bright Essence: Studies in Milton's Theology*, ed.
Hunter et al. (Salt Lake City: University of Utah Press, 1971). In order to do so, he has
to minimize the importance of narration so completely that Satan's sin seems to be that
he does not see how wonderful the Son's redemption of not-yet-created fallen humanity
is. I agree that we already know we are fallen and so could be predisposed in the Son's
favor as early as 1.4, but Milton never has Satan sneer at this line of reasoning, as he
does at all the arguments that can be thought of as orthodox: this reasoning is simply
not available to him. This unavailability would mean, on my argument, that the poetic
force driving *Paradise Lost* is also not available to him, and this will be his greatest lack. If
this still seems a sacrifice of a figure who could not possibly have known better for the
sake of aesthetic response, at least my point is that Milton does not, in the end believe in
the existence of any of these supernatural figures; their problem is that they do believe
in their own existence (that is, their problem is the opposite of Calliope's).

tom" (1.640). Satan's grandeur, even if it is the grandeur of archangel ruined, comes from his iconoclasm, from his desire for liberty.

Obviously there is an important difference between Milton and Satan. Satan is both admirable and deluded in this speech: admirable in his rejection of royalty ratified only by tradition; deluded in thinking that the only other ratification of God's regal power is force. Unlike Satan, Milton can ground his iconoclasm on the worship of the true God. Killing kings is permissible because, as he says in the *First Defense* (relying on the doctrine of the king's two bodies), God has not approved of the person who acts as magistrate but of his office (*Complete Prose*, 4:386). It would be idolatry to confuse the two, to equate the office with the person when speaking of the temporal order and so to mistake the particular for the general; but it is different on high. God, Milton very much wants to argue, combines both functions. If there is no power but of God, then a rebellion against God is not a rebellion against a temporary vessel of power but against the source of power itself. Satan's error is, first, in not understanding the difference between a normative iconoclasm, which has the worship of God as its end, and one without teleology, but it must be urged in his defense that he never had an opportunity to learn this difference because heaven is run so much like an earthly state.

Nevertheless, there are other problems with Satan. His superiority to his conception of God may consist in his perseverance "in some purpose which he has conceived to be excellent, in spite of adversity and torture," as Shelley put it in his "Defence of Poetry," but it is not at all clear how excellent his purpose is. Empson and Bloom see *Paradise Lost* as chronicling Milton's struggle with the nobility of his own conception of Satan, a struggle that forced him into debasing or "rotting" his own noble conception as Satan's grandeur threatened to get out of hand.[14] But Shelley's analysis of Satan in the preface to *Prometheus Unbound*, that he is not "exempt from the taints of ambition, envy, revenge, and a desire for personal aggrandisement," seems as true of Satan early (both in the poem and in the time frame) as later. Satan desires to conquer God so that he can reign in God's place: the liberty

14. See Empson, *Milton's God*, pp. 66–69, and Harold Bloom, *The Anxiety of Influence* (New York: Oxford University Press, 1973), p. 22. A.J.A. Waldock, in *Paradise Lost and the Critics* (New York: Cambridge University Press, 1947), of course takes this as a sign of Milton's own incoherent conception of the character: "I do not think, in other words, that the term 'degeneration,' when applied to the downward course of Satan, has any real validity. . . . Satan does not degenerate: *he is degraded*" (p. 83). As far as I know, Sir Walter Raleigh was the first to argue Milton's own struggle with Satan, although he rejects the "progressive degradation and shrinkage" view, in *Milton* (London: Edward Arnold, 1900), pp. 139–41.

he would achieve would be for himself alone. His rejection of Christ's authority comes ultimately from his sense that his own power is being diminished. He refuses to worship the name of king in God: yet for himself and his crew he claims that their "Imperial Titles . . . assert / Our being ordain'd to govern, not to serve" (5.801–2). He will not acknowledge as true of himself what he argues against God, that titles of nobility are "merely titular" (5.774). Satan's revolt is not against tyranny. It is against a tyrant whose place he wishes to usurp.

We should admire, then, the iconoclastic traits that urge Satan to revolt against a figure who looks and acts very much like a tyrant, but we should not overlook his own similar tendencies. Satan never sustains the iconoclasm that makes him admirable because it exists side by side with a desire to be the worshiped icon. I think this accounts for our ambivalent feeling about Satan: heroic in his rebellion against idolatry, he never gets beyond it himself.

Even Satan's analysis of his fall reifies the dubious battle. The rebels (with the partial and hypocritical exception of Mammon) all follow Satan in ascribing God's victory only to the superior *degree* of his power, a degree they might hope to match. Beelzebub articulates their idolatrous conception of the true God (and yet it is this idolatrous conception that allows them to imagine themselves iconoclasts) when he anticipates Satan's claim that God has overcome them by force. His name for God is "our Conqueror (whom I now / Of force believe Almighty, since no less / Than such could have o'erpow'rd such force as ours)" (1.143–45). As in Satan's speech about testing God's traditional kingship, the idolatrous strain subverts the speaker's admirable iconoclasm. Beelzebub's pun echoes Milton's objections to imposing laws by force instead of reason, but at the same time it takes the term *almighty* to refer only to superior force. For the rebel angels, the war in heaven was a war to determine who was first in strength. Their rejection of traditional power offers nothing but a new power in its place: they do not rise above the particularities of power. They conceive of God as great because of his power; he is the victor "whom Thunder hath made greater" (1.258).

To be fair to Satan, he is different from the other rebels by being the only one who seems really (if inconsistently) outraged by the equation of greatness with power. He is most noble when most stoical, when least impressed by the force that has vanquished him. His claim that thunder made God greater misconceives God, but it also rejects such a conception of greatness. Although he ends up by repeating it, Satan deplores what he takes to be God's idolatry of force:

> Hail, horrors, hail
> Infernal world, and thou profoundest Hell
> Receive thy new Possessor: One who brings
> A mind not to be chang'd by Place or Time.
> The mind is its own place, and in itself
> Can make a Heav'n of Hell, a Hell of Heav'n.
> What matter where, if I be still the same,
> And what I should be, all but less than hee,
> Whom Thunder hath made greater? Here at least
> We shall be free.
>
> (1.250–59)

Satan is the only rebel whose character is complex, and that complexity manifests itself in almost all his speeches. His irreconcilable impulses toward self-sufficient iconoclasm and toward his own iconic glory besiege him with contraries. We feel the authentic power of his affirmation of self-reliant freedom, independent of place: he anticipates Michael's doctrine that "God áttributes to place / No sanctity" (11.836–37). But that freedom too often resolves into nothing more than freedom to attempt to regain only the lost place, "once more / With rallied Arms to try what may be yet / Regain'd in Heav'n" (1.268–70).

We do get a sense of the nobility of Satan's rebellion when we hear that his name was blotted out of the book of life. There is unintended pathos in Raphael's sneer, "Nameless in dark oblivion let them dwell" (7.380). Satan's willingness to give up his name stems from that part of him which scorns terms of honor, scorns what Milton, writing as Charles's iconoclast, calls "the gaudy name of majesty." All the angelic names double as titles, deriving their glory from God, (who appears in all of them, via the el suffix, except Zephon's.) In the "Christian Doctrine," Milton says that angels take on God's name to image him:

> The name of God seems to have been attributed to the angels because they were sent from heaven bearing the likeness of the divine glory and person and, indeed, the very word of God. . . . Angels or messengers, even though they may seem to take upon themselves, when they speak, the name and character of God, do not speak their own words but those specified by God, who sent them. . . . Exod. xxxiii. 20: *no one can see me and live.* Also John 1.19: *no one has ever seen God,* and v. 37: *you have never heard his voice nor seen his shape;* I Tim. vi. 16: *dwelling in unapproachable light, whom no man has seen or can see.* It follows, then, that whoever was heard or seen was not God. (*Complete Prose*, 6:236–37)

Although this passage is primarily about the identity of the messengers who speak to humans, I think that for Milton the names of all the angels implied their conditions as images of God, just as Adam is created in God's image. (I insist, however, on the importance for Milton of the interpretation that Adam's name alludes to the ground he comes from.) Satan's rebellion entails the loss of his Godlike name, and this loss would mean two things to him. It would first of all signify his own kenosis, his refusal to bear the name and be the image of God, in favor of a radically unidolatrous freedom. But for Satan this freedom would also come to mean supplanting God.

By giving up a title that invests him with God's image, Satan seems to attempt to rival God's invisibility and inaccessibility. This attempt is double-edged. It proceeds from a less iconic and more admirable understanding of God than the other angels (both fallen and unfallen) possess (even the unfallen angels think they can see God); but it erroneously and idolatrously considers a visible, accessible, irremediably particularized and subjective being like Satan capable of rivaling God. Pride engenders Satan's fall, but I think that that pride is not accurately described as pride of place alone. Satan's nobility does, for many acute and powerful readers, rival and even exceed God's. As a projection of Milton's repressed pride in his own insightfulness that tempts him (if Sandler is right) to reject the authority of the Bible, Satan can be understood to be imagining himself to know more about Godlike inaccessibility than any of the other angels, and perhaps even than God himself. But Satan (or Milton in Satan) thinks, and not without some very good evidence, that his conception of godliness is poetically superior to God's. He certainly speaks better poetry than God is allowed to. I am going to argue that not only is Satan's conception of God inadequate, but also his conception of godliness; nevertheless, Satan comes closer than any other angel to the understanding of godliness that was Milton's.

The loss of his name indicates Satan's nobility, and his reaction to that loss distinguishes him, for a time at least, from the rest of the fallen angels. Milton's scorn for the other rebels is boundless. They are not complex like Satan, and their only desires are gluttonous: to be feasted and adored as idols. Satan sustains for a time (and only partially) his noble and impossible condition of namelessness, a truer image of God's invisible glory than are the idols. The other rebels, however, seem avid to get new names, avid to be particularized and idolized in their own names:

>   of thir Names in heav'nly Records now
> Be no memorial, blotted out and ras'd
> By thir Rebellion, from the Books of Life.
> Nor had they yet among the Sons of *Eve*
> Got them new Names, till wand'ring o'er the Earth,
> Through God's high sufferance for the trial of man,
> By falsities and lies the greatest part
> Of Mankind they corrupted to forsake
> God thir creator, and th' invisible
> Glory of him that made them, to transform
> Oft to the Image of a Brute, adorn'd
> With gay Religions full of Pomp and Gold,
> And Devils to adore for Deities:
> Then were they known to men by various Names,
> And various Idols through the Heathen World.
>   (1.361–75)

This passage catches one of the most profound contrasts in the poem—that between the puerile, cartoonish infestation of these ridiculous deities and "God's high sufferance" which inflects "all our woe" with the sense that it is God's as well (otherwise why *high* sufferance?). To the extent that the rebels find their greatest delight in "gay Religions full of Pomp and Gold" they are ridiculous. Yet Satan does differ from them. Milton arouses our disgust at these lesser rebels, but in large part we are disgusted because they contrast with Satan. They are parasites, ready to swarm in, for the rewards only, when he has done his job. No reader can see this passage as referring to Satan, however, and Milton explicitly aligns himself with Satan's distrust of names when, at the beginning of book 7, his invocation of the Muse is to "the meaning, not the Name" (7.5).

Satan is not able to maintain his impossible namelessness. To be like God he would really have to be unchanged by place and time, but his response to his fall is too often close to the obsessive concern with outward show that characterizes the pervasive idolatry of the fallen angels. For the most part, Satan's actions are ultimately reactions and so are based, however indirectly, on the exterior constraints that Satan as iconoclast wants to think himself entirely independent of. Even in book 1 he spends a lot of time playing the adolescent inverter that Harold Bloom finds he has become by book 9. His first speech to Beelzebub asserts his desire for revenge, a reactive passion (1.107), and fifty lines later he takes up his adversarial role decisively: "To do aught good never will be our task, / But ever to do ill our sole delight, / As being the contrary to his high will / Whom we resist" (1.159–62). This resolution finally leads to his ultimate degradation, in which he wholly accepts the adversarial name that heaven had given him and revels in its meaning: "*Satan* (for I glory in the name, / Antagonist of Heav'n's Almighty King)" (10.386–87). The Son ultimately manifests himself as Satan's better when he refuses this reactive, adversarial role in book 10; his willingness "to clothe his Enemies" (10.219) enriches the possibilities of human life instead of turning the world into the theater of antagonism that Satan wants it to be.

At the end of book 2 Milton provides an objective correlative to the fallen angels' idolatrous overestimation of names. Many readers echo Johnson's discomfort with the allegorization of Sin and Death, as being unworthy of the grandeur that has come before. But this unworthiness allegorizes the idolatry of the rebels. They never learn what it will be Adam's and Eve's burden to discover, that sin and death are something more than the names of horrid personages. For Satan, the words *sin* and *death* become the names of exterior beings instead of signifiers of interior states. The externalization of sin and death allegorizes Satan's refusal to understand the pertinency of a figurative understanding of allegory. He takes the image as the essence, and he worships the image. According to Sin's account—the force of which neither of them understands—Satan "full oft / Thyself in me thy perfect image viewing / Becam'st enamor'd" (2.763–65). He falls in love with sin as a narcissistic self-image and so evinces his sinful idolatry of himself. That he could find a sufficient, indeed a perfect, idol for himself within so decayed an allegory shows how debased his self-idolatry has become.

Idolatrous narcissism is on one level the cause of all the falls in the poem. Abdiel interprets narcissism as the opposite of real liberty when he upbraids Satan, echoing Sin, as being "Thyself not free, but to thyself enthrall'd" (6.181). Satan tempts Eve, who had already manifested her narcissistic tendencies in her attraction to her reflection at the pool (4.460–66), with the promise of what she might become; Adam's reproach to her, that she insisted on going off alone because she was "longing to be seen" (10.877), does not seem unfair. But Adam consents to eat when he finds that Eve has fallen because he feels "The Link of Nature draw me: Flesh of Flesh, / Bone of my Bone thou art" (9.914–15) and that "to lose thee were to lose myself" (9.959).

Commentators often try to distinguish Satan's narcissistic attraction to Sin from what looks like a similar trait in God by calling it a parodic version of the Father's glorification of his Son. The invocation of parody, however, means that the distinction is not internal to the comparison. The Son is called worthy of God's surpassing love because he is "the radiant image of his Glory" (3.63); God praises him as "thou, in whom my glory I behold / In full resplendence" (5.719–20), and when he addresses him, "O Son, in whom my Soul hath chief delight, / Son of my bosom, Son who art alone / My word, my wisdom, and effectual might" (3.168–70), the Son seems to have sprung from God's bosom as Sin will spring from Satan's head and Eve from Adam's side. Obviously Milton did feel a difference between God's love for his Son and Satan's desire for Sin, but the difference does not seem available for the heavenly audience, except by decree.[15]

In fact, it is impossible, from a heavenly perspective, to distinguish between Satan and God except as different in degree. I have been arguing that one of the signs of the rebel angels' idolatry is their belief that might makes right, that only force ratifies the pretension to sovereignty, and thus that the only difference between Satan and God—both particular beings—is one of degree (except that Satan sometimes imagines himself as deploring this state of things). A less vicious version of the rebels' doctrine manifests itself in the idea of the great chain of being, in which every link has its place in a hierarchy. A defense of hierarchy can of course be mounted: "Orders and Degrees / Jar not with liberty, but well consist" (5.792–93)—but this is Satan speaking. His initial objection is not to the chain but to having his position as its second link (after God) usurped by the Son. Abdiel is exceptional among the angels in perceiving a radical discontinuity between the highest of the angels and the Son (5.841–45), who is himself, according to the Arian "Christian Doctrine," only the first of all *created* beings (*Complete Prose*, pt. 1, chap. 5). But Abdiel's interpretation is not the one encouraged in heaven, since the Father's predic-

---

15. On narcissism in *Paradise Lost*, see William Kerrigan's interesting discussion of Eve's narcissism in *The Sacred Complex: On the Psychogenesis of Paradise Lost* (Cambridge, Mass.: Harvard University Press, 1983), pp. 70–74, and Regina Schwartz's *Remembering and Repeating: Biblical Creation in Paradise Lost* (Cambridge: Cambridge University Press, 1988), pp. 99–103. Schwartz argues, as I do, that narcissism must be contrasted to the alterity of the other; but it is interesting to consider Kerrigan's fine discussion—which would implicitly analyze the relationship with the Father in narcissistic terms—of how the alterity of the superego preserves the narcissism no longer directly available to the ego (pp. 169–70). But the apparent narcissism of the Father in *Paradise Lost* does not seem to be otherwise discussed at any length.

tion that "God shall be All in All" (3.341) seems an easy induction from the continuous version of the chain that Raphael explains to Adam. Thus his repetition of "all" enforces a continuity in being—a continuity that does seem to attribute sanctity to place:

> O *Adam*, one Almighty is, from whom
> All things proceed, and up to him return,
> If not deprav'd from good, created all
> Such to perfection, one first matter all,
> Indu'd with various forms, various degrees
> Of substance, and in things that live, of life;
> But more refin'd, more spiritous, and pure,
> As nearer to him plac't or nearer tending
> Each in thir several active Spheres assign'd,
> Till body up to spirit work, in bounds
> Proportion'd to each kind.
> . . . .
> . . . time may come when men
> With Angels may participate. . . .
> . . . .
> And from these corporal nutriments perhaps
> Your bodies may at last turn all to spirit,
> Improv'd by tract of time, and wing'd ascend
> Ethereal, as wee.
>   (5.469–79, 493–94, 496–99)

Empson notices some of Raphael's unwitting echoes of Satan's dream temptation in this passage (*Milton's God,* esp. p. 147). I think that Raphael sounds so much like Satan because they have very similar ideas about God and heaven. Raphael and Beelzebub both seem to have the same conception of what it means to be almighty. For Beelzebub, in his claim that God demonstrated himself to be almighty by defeating a force next to almightiness in power (1.144–45), almightiness implies a position at the top of the scale of power, commensurable with lesser might. Raphael takes a similar view when he describes Michael and Satan battling with "next to Almighty Arm" (6.316). For both Raphael and Beelzebub, God is a Platonic form: if he is the origin of ontology, he is likewise approachable through ontology, with being becoming purer (or mightier) as you are placed or tend nearer to him.[16]

16. Waldock (*Paradise Lost,* pp. 67–68) notices this and again ascribes to Milton a weakness that belongs perhaps to the angelic view of the world: "Actually, if the text is watched closely it will be seen, I think, that there is a certain equivocation in the use of

Again, Raphael does not seem far from the lesser rebels in his conception of God's invisibility. Milton subscribes to the Arian tenet that the Father is absolutely unknowable. He is radically different from all created beings, even the Son, who is the voice we hear and the sight we see when we imagine that we are seeing God: "*The Word* must be audible, but God is inaudible just as he is invisible, John c. 37; therefore the Word is not of the same essence as God" (*Complete Prose*, 6:239). The rebels, with the intermittent exception of Satan, possess a debased notion of this doctrine. God's inaudibility and invisibility are parodied when the rebels corrupt human beings "th'invisible / Glory of him that made them, to transform / Oft to the Image of a Brute" (1.369–71), which is to have the unknown degenerate into the monstrous. Mammon's attempt to persuade the fallen angels that they can make a material heaven of hell also presents God's invisibility in material terms:

> This deep world
> Of darkness do we dread? How oft amidst
> Thick clouds and dark doth Heav'n's all-ruling Sire
> Choose to reside, his Glory unobscur'd,
> And with the Majesty of darkness round
> Covers his Throne; from whence deep thunders roar
> Must'ring thir rage, and Heav'n resembles Hell?
> (2.262–68)

This somewhat literal-minded conception of God's hiddenness is not restricted to hell, however. Raphael always presents God as either within a covering cloud (6.28 and 56–57) or hidden by a dazzling brightness. It is worth comparing Milton's conception of God's dazzling invisibility with Raphael's. Raphael seems to believe that his inability to tolerate the direct sight of God comes merely from his being too far down on the chain of being. God is dazzling, yes, but his inaccessibility is finally relative. Raphael and the other angels cannot see God, but they take this invisibility as proceeding from the weakness of their sight (a weakness Satan refuses to acknowledge), not as one of God's fundamental attributes. Adam echoes Raphael when he laments the weakness that the Fall has produced in him:

---

the word 'omnipotent'. When it is convenient to do so Milton uses it with full literal force; but on occasion it can seem not much more than a grandiloquent synonym for 'supreme'. There is a certain latitude to 'play' in the use of the word; and this is for the benefit of the narrative."

> How shall I behold the face
> Henceforth of God or Angel, erst with joy
> And rapture so oft beheld? those heav'nly shapes
> Will dazzle now this earthly, with thir blaze
> Insufferably bright.
>
> (9.1080–84)

For Raphael, God speaks "as from a flaming Mount, whose top /
Brightness had made invisible" (5.598–99), which, at first, sounds like
Milton's hymn in book 3 to:

> thee Author of all being,
> Fountain of Light, thyself invisible
> Amidst the glorious brightness where thou sit'st
> Thron'd inaccessible, but when thou shad'st
> The full blaze of thy beams, and through a cloud
> Drawn round about thee like a radiant Shrine,
> Dark with excessive bright thy skirts appear,
> Yet dazzle Heav'n, that brightest Seraphim
> Approach not, but with both wings veil thir eyes.
> Thee next they sang of all Creation first,
> Begotten Son, Divine Similitude,
> In whose conspicuous count'nance, without cloud
> Made visible, th'Almighty Father shines,
> Whom else no Creature can behold.
>
> (3.374–87)

I think that after reading all of *Paradise Lost* a reader coming back to
these lines should understand God's invisibility in the second line as
fundamental, as preceding the glorious brightness he expresses and
not proceeding from it as an effect. We can infer from the last three
lines that, far from hiding God, clouds make him visible, like the
clothes the invisible man wears, since it is only in the Son that God is
visible without clouds. The reference to the brightness of the
seraphim invites the reader to see in this hymn another allusion to the
great chain of being, since there is an implicit comparison of their
brightness with God's. But in addition to the difference between God's
invisibility and his dazzling light, Milton introduces another discontinuity when clouds shade the full blaze. It is this doubly distanced
expression of God that the angels find insufferably bright, and it
appears that Raphael mistakes this tertiary inaccessibility for God's
invisibility. Milton, on the other hand, would see this attenuated
brightness as the top of the great chain of being (or even already

beyond it, since brightest seraphim shade their eyes). Beyond that is God's fundamental inaccessibility. A Miltonic version of the comparative exceeds the superlative of the "brightest Seraphim."

My claim is that the Platonic doctrine that Raphael speaks for is mistaken and that it is this same mistaken doctrine that ultimately tempts the rebels' attempt. The doctrine is mistaken because it regards the forms not as general terms but as super-particulars. I think that Milton's conception of the true God was Gnostic and not Platonic and that the figure Raphael describes is not the God Milton has in mind. Raphael's understanding of God's secrecy and invisibility is pretty tame. He resolves his uncertainty about how to "relate / To human sense th'invisible exploits / Of warring Spirits; how . . . unfold / The secrets of another World" by concluding that they really are not so different from the common knowledge of this world (5.564–69). The hint to Adam indicates his Platonism fairly strongly, with its allusion to the allegory of the cave: "what if Earth / Be but the shadow of Heav'n, and things therein / Each to other like, more than on Earth is thought?" (5.574–76). In books 7 and 8 he thinks of God as guarding only state secrets from the angels, by a sort of divine executive privilege, suppressing what apparently could be revealed. He tells Adam not to inquire too closely about the nature of the universe, "nor let thine own inventions hope / Things not reveal'd, which th'invisible King, / Only Omniscient, hath supprest in Night" (7.121–23). This sounds as though invisibility were an accidental, not an essential, feature of the things that are closest to God. Near the beginning of book 8, Raphael praises God for doing "wisely to conceal" the mechanism of his astronomy "and not divulge / His secrets to be scann'd by them who ought / Rather to admire" (8.73–75). This God comes from Machiavelli, deriving his power not so much from what he keeps to himself as from the fact that he keeps things to himself, which allows him to be the only omniscient one. As a representative of the angels' conception of God, Raphael unwittingly explains how the rebels could have thought themselves capable of replacing him. The angels do not really understand God to be entirely different from themselves. For none of them are secrecy and invisibility inherent attributes of the things they do not know. One gets the feeling that, like Bentley, they would emend "secret" to "sacred" in "the secret top of *Oreb*" (1.6–7) (except that at least Bentley feels there is a possible difference there, which they do not).

Adam and Eve begin with an understanding similar to the angels'. They believe that their inability to see God is a function of their place, and their morning hymn in book 5 conceives of him as being "to *us* invisible" (5.157). They think that were they higher up on the chain, they would be able to see him; thus they praise the angels, "for yee behold him" (161), and Raphael confirms what Milton surely considered an error. Raphael claims that it is the angels' "happy state" to "stand / In sight of God enthron'd" (5.535–36). What does this do but ratify Satan's dream temptation of Eve, with its privileging of visibility? There she was encouraged to equate "high exaltation" with the ability to "*see* / What life the Gods live there, and such live thou" (5.90 and 80–81): thus visibility would mean commensurability—and so susceptibility to being equaled (and, as Satan continues, overthrown). Again, in book 9, Satan's temptation encourages Eve to attempt the clearer sight that Raphael has already told her belongs to the angels:

> Why then was this forbid? Why but to awe,
> Why but to keep ye low and ignorant,
> His worshippers; he knows that in the day
> Ye Eat thereof, your Eyes that seem so clear,
> Yet are but dim, shall perfetly be then
> Op'n'd and clear'd, and ye shall be as Gods,
> Knowing both Good and Evil as they know.
> That ye should be as Gods, since I as Man,
> Internal Man, is but proportion meet.
>
> (9.703–11)

Eve is receptive to Satan's argument here because it is based on the Platonic conception of "proportion meet." Raphael has described the possibility of moving up on the great chain of being; he promised the humans that they could eventually attain the angelic vision that does have sight of God. Satan exploits both Raphael's and Eve's naive notions that God is within the possible reach of sight in order to encourage her to attempt that reach. One of the immediate consequences of Eve's disobedience is a further degradation of her understanding of secrecy and invisibility. She thanks Experience because it "op'n'st Wisdom's way, / And giv'st access, though secret she retire. / And I perhaps am secret; Heav'n is high, / High and remote to see from thence distinct / Each thing on Earth" (9.810–13). Already she senses that eating the fruit does not provide an easy way to heaven, which is high and remote; what momentarily sounds like a claim to godhead—"I perhaps am secret"—immediately reduces to the hope that what she has done will be overlooked. (But the expression of that hope is wonderful: already she's speaking great poetry.)

There is, then, something seriously deficient about the angelic and unfallen conception of God. Empson remarks that book 6 reads like bad science fiction (*Milton's God*, p. 54), which seems a good way of summing up our discomfort with heaven according to Raphael. Therefore, I suggest that the Fall of humanity turns out to be fortunate (to argue that it's not, as Danielson does, is inevitably to prefer God's poetry in book 3 to Milton's) because it enables a much deeper understanding of God. Satan verges on such an understanding when he is closest to Milton, when he is thinking least materially, most poetically, most like an Arian. If the angels are Arians at all, it is in a trivial way; for them God is only unknowable and inaccessible because he is just the other side of knowledge and accessibility. For Adam and Eve, however, the Fall produces a sense of drastic discontinuity between finite intelligences and the unknowable God. This sense of discontinuity is at first primarily negative (as when Adam asks how he will be able henceforth to tolerate the insupportably dazzling sight of God or angel, or when Eve feels that heaven is high and remote), but even in its negative aspect Milton equates discontinuity with poetic power. His dismissal, in his invocation to book 9, of Raphael's account of the war in heaven seems every bit as imperious as Empson's. It is for the "Sad task" of describing the Fall that Milton requests "answerable style" (9.13 and 20); this seems odd at first, since he had shown little anxiety about whether he would be able to ventriloquize a seraphic description of the war in heaven. But he goes on in the invocation to reject poetry about "tilting Furniture" (9.34) and thereby himself voices our half-suppressed embarrassment about the silliness of what's gone on in heaven. Milton is not interested in the standard topics that give

> Heroic name
> To Person or to Poem. Mee of these
> Nor skill'd nor studious, higher Argument
> Remains, sufficient of itself to raise
> That name, unless an age too late, or cold
> Climate, or Years damp my intended wing
> Deprest; and much they may, if all be mine,
> Not Hers who brings it nightly to my Ear.
>
> (9.40–47)

More interesting than the implication that Raphael's narrative is not up to the poetry Milton finally aspires to is the contrast with twilit Eden presented by the opening of book 9. There is more poetic affect in Milton's intense apprehension of his mortality in these lines than in any of the descriptions of the events in heaven. Even the cautious optimism of the last two lines is suffused with a sense of loss. Perhaps he will live to finish the poem, but he will still be susceptible to all the dampening influences of his mortal condition. These lines feel rather like *The Tempest*: the island is magical, but when you leave, every third thought will be of death. I think this passage is so moving because of the contrast between Urania's radiance and Milton's mortal blindness. We get a sense of her radiance but also a sense that the power of that radiance is not a saving but a consoling one. "Nightly" seems to be the key word. For Urania, night is like the nights in paradise before the fall, illumined by the stars, planets, and moon, or like night in heaven: "grateful Twilight (for Night comes not there / In darker veil)" (5.645–46). For Milton, however, it ultimately means the night of his Sonnet 23, forgotten for a moment but returning after his nightly muse has fled. The radiance that illuminates him also intensifies his sense of loss, as when Caliban wakes and cries to sleep.

In the invocation to book 9, Milton both asserts and demonstrates that loss of Eden, the fall into mortality, produces poetic affect. Of course, this is a position that he cannot be comfortable with. One feels that the choiring angels hymning praise to the works of God provide the model of poetry that Milton is least anxious about. But the affect actually derives from the impossibility of sustaining the apparent radiance of that poetry in a fallen condition. For a long time, I think, Milton felt ambivalent about his sense that poetic power is enabled by loss, and at least twice before he tried to dissipate that ambivalence by splitting its antinomies into paired poems: "L'Allegro" / "Il Penseroso" and "On the Morning of Christ's Nativity" / "The Passion."[17] But in *Paradise Lost* he combines celebration and lamentation. This combination reflects Milton's ambivalence about the poetry he writes most powerfully, but this ambivalence also produces the most powerful moments in that poetry. As an evil rhetorician whose language is sublimely intensified in hell, Satan represents the negative side of that ambivalence. The Romantics, however, seem right in thinking that Milton could not avoid, through much of the poem, feeling a strong identity with Satan, an identity that he understood as a real problem: the identification seems to stem from their both having a deeper conception of godliness than does the rest of heaven. This conception seems indissolubly linked to ambivalence. Satan and Milton are both

---

17. One could argue that *Paradise Lost* is the poem that Milton found above his years when he abandoned "The Passion" in 1630. There, too, poetic power is associated with lamentation. In that poem night is the patroness of grief, and so she is a prototype for Urania. Of course Urania herself is not night, even if her visitations are nightly, and this difference is crucial: night for Milton may now be the time of inspiration, but it is not the muse herself; and if the muse should flee, the presence of night will not be consolatory, as it continues to be in "The Passion."

suspicious of the origins of their poetic power, but Satan's final response is to get rid of ambivalence by reifying that origin and by making it either an icon to be rejected (if the icon is God) or worshiped (if it is himself). Milton, on the other hand, had a lot invested in not identifying poetic and iconic thinking. If he calls books the image of God in "Areopagitica" (*Complete Prose*, 2:492), he is very careful to explode the notion that one could call "idols the layman's books" (6:693). Satan cannot sustain the drastically iconoclastic sense that his poetic power springs from something radically unknowable, from unknowability itself. He does not have the negative capability that would enable him to accept ambivalence itself as a condition of power. He does not have the patience that enables a mortal to choose long and begin late and to risk the dissipation of the power of his mortal voice in its own exercise. This is not just another way of saying what the angels say, that his overweening pride made him reject an invisible God who nevertheless should obviously be obeyed. Satan's deep sense that the origin of poetic power is inaccessible far outdoes, in its deep and powerful sublimity, the angels' conceptions of God. But it finally founders, while Milton's does not.

Empson and Bloom see Milton's response to his ambivalence as cutting the Gordian knot by scapegoating Satan and making him despicable (or, more subtly, by recounting how unjust rebellion necessarily makes the highest nobility vile). But *Paradise Lost* seems ultimately to resolve this problem positively too, which is I think, its greatest strength. In giving up Satan it does not give up God or an ambivalent conception of God. Early on, Milton was ambivalent about a poetry based on loss; in *Paradise Lost* he bases his poetry on the very loss that that ambivalence entails, the loss of angelic certainty about the origin of power.

One of Milton's powerful losses was his loss of sight. In the *Second Defense* he responds Platonically. He rejects superficial images but still conceives of them as defective because superficial, not because of anything essential to the image. He claims that the removal of distraction allows him to ignore the simulacra of earth in favor of the apprehension of the radiant image that is truth (*Complete Prose*, 4:589). By asserting the affirmative possibilities of loss, however, he already anticipates the more complex meditations on blindness in *Paradise Lost*. Although, at first, Milton's sense of obscuration is secondary to the divine irradiation planting eyes within him, the later invocations present that obscurity much more powerfully and in turn derive their own power from the power of obscurity. Even in book 3, the apostrophe to light curiously associates that light with darkness, when

Milton says that it "as with a Mantle [did] invest / The rising world of waters dark and deep, / Won from the void and formless infinite" (3.10–12). It is more usual to think of night investing the world with a mantle (as in "The Passion"'s "Befriend me Night, best Patroness of grief, / Over the Pole thy thickest mantle throw" [ll. 29–30]; see also 1.207–8, where night invests the sea); the notion of a mantle of light is somewhat oxymoronic. Obviously the phrase refers to God's illuminating the dark world of waters, but its power comes from our sense that the light is somehow like "the rising world of waters dark and deep." Milton follows this with a comment on his physical blindness: his eyes "roll in vain / To find thy piercing ray, and find no dawn" (3.23–24). The fact that dawn never comes prepares us for the power of his description of his "nightly" wanderings in the lost loci not of God but of inspiration: here the word *nightly* has some of the same charge it will have in book 9. The invocation oscillates between the angelic confidence of the *Second Defense* and the real despair of the blind mortal. I think we are a little surprised by this oscillation, especially when the pendulum swings back without any warning. Milton compares what he wants to believe is his enriched, angelic inner life with the nightingale:

> Then feed on thoughts, that voluntary move
> Harmonious numbers; as the wakeful Bird
> Sings darkling, and in shadiest Covert hid
> Tunes her nocturnal Note. Thus with the Year
> Seasons return, but not to me returns
> Day, or the sweet approach of Ev'n or Morn,
> Or sight of vernal bloom, or Summer's Rose,
> Or flocks, or herds, or human face divine;
> But cloud instead, and ever-during dark
> Surrounds me, from the cheerful ways of men
> Cut off, and for the Book of knowledge fair
> Presented with a universal blanc
> Of Nature's works to me expung'd and ras'd
> And wisdom at one entrance quite shut out.
>
> (3.37–50)

"Thus" seems to promise that Milton will be able to identify himself with the nightingale, but she seems to be more like Urania than like him. For her, nocturnal does not mean blind. In the lines that follow, Milton's use of the cloud to describe the powerful unhappiness that his blindness causes him is interesting. This is not to suggest that God is somehow unhappy in his cloudy isolation but that Milton is equating (even if he retreats to an angelic version of heaven in the subsequent lines) Godlike poetic power with a sense of loss. The specifics of this loss—the exile from the approach of morning and evening and from the sight of flowers and the apprehension of the divine in the human face—anticipate (or reproduce) the lamentations of Eve and Adam in book 11:

> O flow'rs,
> That never will in other Climate grow,
> My early visitation, and my last
> At Ev'n, which I bred up with tender hand
> From the first op'ning bud, and gave ye Names
> . . . .
> This most afflicts me, that departing hence,
> As from his face I shall be hid, depriv'd
> His blessed count'nance; here I could frequent,
> With worship, place by place where he voutsaf'd
> Presence Divine.
>
> (11.273–77; 315–19)

In *Paradise Lost*, then, the origin of real poetic depth is the Fall. Although Adam and Eve had sung angelic hymns in book 4, the power of these hymns is like the power of their lamentations. It comes from our knowledge of their ephemerality. Indeed it comes from a strangely similar knowledge of their own. Eve's beautiful hymn to Adam is partly anachronistic: "With thee conversing I forget all time, / All seasons and thir change; all please alike" (4.639–40). This lyric is moving because we cannot forget time or the near approach of Satan, but it seems faintly odd that Eve expresses any anxiety about time, as though she were mortal. This oddness arises perhaps from the mortal Milton's full investment in this lyric, which is the expression of a mortal wish or a mortal reverie. This investment would explain what may otherwise be an anachronism: Eve's reference to the seasons and their change. The word here cannot help having the resonance that it has in the invocation to book 3, where it means seasons of the year, and the change of seasons that Eve refers to means something more than the change of the hour of the day. This reference is anachronistic, however, because the seasons of the year do not change until earth is tilted on its axis in book 10.

The fact that the Fall is inexorably approaching suffuses these songs with a tinge of sadness. I think this is the reason for a similarly sad irony in book 5, during their morning hymns. There they address Venus as the morning star:

> Fairest of Stars, last in the train of Night,
> If better thou belong not to the dawn,
> Sure pledge of day, that crown'st the smiling Morn
> With thy bright Circlet, praise him in thy Sphere
> While day arises, that sweet hour of Prime.
>
> (5.166–70)

From our perspective, knowing Satan so near at hand, we cannot help thinking of the Lucifer of Isaiah 14. Later in book 5 Raphael will confirm the allusion when he says of Satan, "His count'nance, as the Morning Star that guides / The starry flock, allur'd" the rebel angels (5.708–9; cf. also 689), and in book 7 he will call Satan "*Lucifer . . . / . . .* brighter once amidst the Host / Of Angels, than that Star the Stars among" (7.131–33).

The invocation to book 7 comes close to specifically claiming that the fall—whether from paradise or from political power—is the origin of poetic depth, especially in the way Milton presents himself as like Satan but beyond him:

> More safe I Sing with mortal voice, unchang'd
> To hoarse or mute, though fall'n on evil days,
> On evil days though fall'n, and evil tongues;
> In darkness, and with dangers compast round,
> And solitude.
>
> (7.24–28)

Satan's claim has been that he "brings / A mind not to be chang'd by Place or Time" (1.252–53), but he soon discovers that, in fact, he is changing. Milton, although aware of his mortality, sings "unchang'd." We feel that this claim is not glib, because of the way "hoarse" picks up the sound of "mortal voice." Milton is mortally close to being changed to hoarse or mute, and his assertion that he is still the same in the midst of adversity is more powerful than Satan's, since Satan's immediate response to adversity is the reactive desire for revenge, not the manifestation of poetic power. The word "fall'n" seems important too, especially in its assonance with "mortal." That Milton sings unchanged despite his mortality, his fallen condition (reinforced for him by the Restoration), is a sign of poetic power, a power not available in hell, except occasionally to Satan. Sin's version of Milton's lament here is materialistic (as she is, being a debased allegorical figure); she is agonized at being "with terrors and with clamors compasst round" (2.862). But this power seems unavailable in heaven as well (except, perhaps, to the Son): Abdiel, we know, is secure in the patronage of

God and the good angels, even when "encompass'd round with foes" (5.876), and so his better fight does not seem as good as Milton's.

Paradise Lost explicitly presents a version of the *felix culpa* that justifies reading the poem as about the uneasy conditions of its own aesthetic power. For Milton (and for Satan) loss of Eden or heaven gives rise to a deeper sense of what God's inaccessibility entails than the angels had. For both of these dark figures, this sense is aligned with iconoclasm. But in Eden Adam and Eve are often no better than the angels. Before they fall, they tend to display the same relatively benign idolatry as seems to obtain among the unfallen in heaven.

I have already tried to show that, even before they fell, Adam and Eve were prey to the same idolatrous narcissism that engendered Satan's fall and that it also engenders theirs. Their natural idolatry, however, has more subtle aspects as well. If Milton sometimes associates the urge to name with idolatrous impulses—as though one could name the unknowable and particularize the general—we should feel some suspicion about Adam's first words to God. Adam's response to something he does not understand is to seek to reduce it to the level of his already habitual experience of particulars; one of his first discoveries was that he "readily could name / Whate'er I saw" (8.272–73). Thus, his first confrontation with a vision of the divine leads him to attempt an understanding of it that is qualitatively similar to his understanding of the world around him. Although he worships the "Author of the Universe," he needs to allay his anxieties about how to image him and make him accessible to speech, and so he asks the vision, "O by what Name, for thou / . . . / Surpassest far my naming, how may I / Adore thee[?]" (8.357–60). This scene is especially marked because the biblical allusion is not to Adam but to Moses at the burning bush (Exod. 3:13–14): we are aware of a deeper postlapsarian answer ("I will be") that is evaded in the response to Adam, where Adam's interlocutor ignores the question. The suggestion here is that before the fall the sublime rebuke from the burning bush would have no effect: Adam is awestruck, but his understanding of God is inevitably angelic. For him, God can only be the figure at the highest point of the great chain of being, far surpassing Adam's experience to date but apparently within a reach strenuous enough. He does not possess the more Miltonic conception of God as "above all highth" (3.58).

Our sense of the potential shallowness of paradisal understanding, as compared with the deeper understanding available to mortals, is strongest when Milton depicts the unfallen Adam as knowing no more about death than its name. Satan exploits the ignorance man-

ifested in the first couple's breezy dismissal of the death that they
think they need know no more about; Adam's version of the allegorical monster who's appeared before as "dreadful and deform" (2.706)
is lightly dismissive: "whate'er Death is, / Some dreadful thing no
doubt" (4.425–26). When Satan echoes Adam in his temptation in
book 9, he defuses what might be a consideration powerful enough to
make Eve hesitate with the offhanded "whatever thing Death be"
(9.695); this leaves out even the worry about dreadfulness, since to the
godliness that Eve anticipates, dreadfulness is beneath contempt.
Since the poem is about how death was brought into the world and,
with death, all our woe, it is clear that Milton thought the Edenic
conception of death terribly inadequate, certainly inadequate for the
sublime poetry which loss of Eden made possible. Yet Adam's and
Eve's conception of death in the garden is much like the angels'.
Although the angels understand death as some dreadful thing, and so
do not volunteer to redeem humanity, its dreadfulness dissipates for
them immediately after the Son offers himself:

> on me let Death wreck all his rage;
> Under his gloomy power I shall not long
> Lie vanquisht; thou hast giv'n me to possess
> Life in myself for ever, by thee I live,
> Though now to Death I yield, and am his due
> All that of me can die, yet that debt paid,
> Thou wilt not leave me in the loathsome grave
> His prey, nor suffer my unspotted Soul
> For ever with corruption there to dwell.
>
> (3.241–49)

The self-confidence of this speech mirrors angelic ignorance about
the nature of death. The Son might be referring here to the somewhat clownish allegorical figure of book 2, and indeed the immortals
may be right to hang on to this conception, since death will never
bridge the gap between its own domain and heaven. But the sacrifice
is more than it seems to the angels. Although in heaven he knows his
own immortality, on earth the Son as Milton understands him is
wholly human (whence the lamentations in "The Passion" and "Upon
the Circumcision"). In *Paradise Regained* Jesus knows only by hearsay
and earthly witness that he is the son of God, since he perceives as a
human. That he is human makes the fact that his path will lead
"through many a hard assay even to the death" (1.264), as he puts it, a

much darker experience than its heavenly anticipation.[18] The Son knows that his incarnation will involve the loss of heavenly certitude, which is what makes his sacrifice noble in the first place, instead of the nearly perfunctory gesture it appears in heaven. On this reading, it is this willingness to undergo the experience of uncertainty, this negative capability, that entitles him to the exaltation that God then pronounces. The Son is more godly than the rest of the angels because he is willing to be the conduit of the power of loss, of mortality.

Blanchot sees the proximity of death, the knowledge of mortality, as an encounter with the radically other. Such an encounter is at the root of poetic affect in *Paradise Lost*. The knowledge of mortality becomes knowledge of impersonality, the uncanny intimacy of something absolutely close. The apotropaic gesture of apostrophe which de Man sees as warding off this intimacy is a form of idolatry, of subjectivity, and of subjection. Milton makes us feel the possibility of an alternative to the idolatrous totalization of Platonism when he affirms the positivity of distance over the sterile contiguity of the homogeneous great chain of being. Nothing is closer than distance; its absolute proximity and inextricable embrace render impossible the step back that would open a neutral space and allow distance to be apostrophized; any step back is necessarily an intensification of and nearer approach to distance. The absolute closeness of farness, of the quality of being far away, makes it impossible to master its distance. This absolute proximity of distance opposes what Heidegger the Platonist calls in *Being and Time* "Ent-fernung" (de-severing), in which distance becomes the presence of a plenum holding near and far within a single world.[19] Proximity undoes ontology. When distance becomes absolutely proximate, it cannot be set up and controlled as a unifying idol.

18. See Barbara K. Lewalski's defense of Milton's Arianism: "Milton insists that the entire work of the mediatorial office is undertaken by Christ in his entire person and that no separation or distinction can be made: Christ, he declares, undergoes the birth, circumcision, baptism, temptation, passion, and even the death in his whole person; hence the 'why hast thou forsaken me?'" (*Milton's Brief Epic: The Genre, Meaning and Art of Paradise Regained* [Providence, R.I.: Brown University Press, 1966], p. 154). This whole person may be of two natures, but "for Milton as for Arius it would seem that the divine is in some important way subsumed to the human" (p. 156). She further claims, in an argument congenial to mine, that for Milton kenosis meant "that the Son emptied himself of whatever of divinity he did enjoy as God's image; the form of which he emptied himself could not have been the essence of the Supreme God because that could not have been emptied out, so it could only have been his own essence or nature as the Image of the Father holding all things at the pleasure of the Father" (p. 157).

19. Martin Heidegger, *Being and Time*, trans. John Macquarrie and Edward Robinson (New York: Harper, 1962), pp. 138–39.

Heidegger may be taken as an example of what Milton was not doing. This may seem odd given Heidegger's own meditations on the meaning of death as the origin of meaning, but for Heidegger, death becomes the ultimate idol, the source of all authenticity. I can participate in that authenticity if I serve as a priest at the altar of my own death. From dread comes power, so that Satan would be right to urge Eve to turn the dreadfulness of death into power. For Milton, though, mortality means loss, not loss of one's own power, but loss of other people. Adam already knew the meaning of mortality before he ate the fruit: he knew that Eve would die. His choice for death is not only a gloriously self-destructive (read: Satanic) moment of self-idolatry (which could never issue into the claim "To lose thee were to lose myself)" but also a faithfulness to loss like Antony's or Richard's, even when, or especially when, that faithfulness is not its own recuperation (so that after he loses Eve he decides to lose himself as well).

We know that after eating the apple Adam will behave abominably, even toward Eve; but Adam knows it too, and out of faithfulness to Eve, he will put even that faithfulness mortally at risk. This is faithfulness to what is genuinely unknowable, instead of angelic faithfulness to the easily known allegorical attribute of unknowability. In this way, Adam's faithfulness is the type for Milton's Arian conception of faithfulness to God. For Adam's decision to die on behalf of a fallen mortal is an exact parallel of, if indeed it does not surpass, the Son's.

This is of course an argument against the fallen reader scenario, which would assert that our interpretive skills are on trial in *Paradise Lost*. I agree that they are, but much more so if we are orthodox: the surprise in Adam's sin is its closeness to the actions and motivations of the Son. Thus the extended parallels between Adam and the Son seem important. The Son, as an advocate for humanity, asks the Father, who has just foretold man's first disobedience and punishment,

> shall the Adversary thus obtain
> His end, and frustrate thine, shall he fulfil
> His malice, and thy goodness bring to naught,
> Or proud return though to his heavier doom,
> Yet with revenge accomplish't and to Hell
> Draw after him the whole Race of mankind,
> By him corrupted? or wilt thou thyself
> Abolish thy Creation, and unmake,
> For him, what for thy glory thou hast made?
> So should thy goodness and thy greatness both
> Be question'd and blasphem'd without defense.
>
> (3.156–66)

This advocacy is an instance of the Son's "unexampl'd love" (3.410), but Eve finds Adam providing something close to a second example of it in book 9 when she praises the "glorious trial of exceeding Love, / Illustrious evidence, example high" (9.961–62) of his own commitment to a fallen human being. If Eve's response echoes the angelic response to the Son's self-sacrifice, Adam's theology echoes the Son's:

> Nor can I think that God, Creator wise,
> Though threat'ning, will in earnest so destroy
> Us his prime Creatures, dignifi'd so high,
> Set over all his Works, which in our Fall,
> For us created, needs with us must fail,
> Dependent made; so God shall uncreate,
> Be frustrate, do, undo, and labor lose,
> Not well conceiv'd of God, who though his Power
> Creation could repeat, yet would be loath
> Us to abolish, lest the Adversary
> Triumph and say; Fickle their State whom God
> Most Favors, who can please him long? Mee first
> He ruin'd, now Mankind; whom will he next?
> Matter of scorn, not to be given the Foe.
>
> (9.938–51)

Alastair Fowler, in the notes to the Longman *Paradise Lost*, plays down these parallels and argues that the difference between Adam and the Son is that the Son volunteers himself out of obedience.[20] This interpretation does seem to be the only way to distinguish the sacrifices, but it then seems to leave out any role for the judgment of the umpire conscience (unless conscience meant for Milton something unrecognizable for us today: a faculty which felt more or less at ease as it conceived itself more or less in line with the Father's will, not with its own internal sense of morality. The point is, as Empson has argued, that the predilections of conscience are supposed to be an a priori good.)

The source of these parallel urgings of God to look to his reputation has not, I think, been noticed. It is Exodus 23:12, where Moses counsels God against killing the Israelites: "Wherefore should the Egyptians speak and say, For mischief did he bring them out, to slay them in the mountains and to consume them from the face of the earth? Turn from thy fierce wrath and repent of this evil against thy people." God, of course, has just offered Moses a second people, as

20. *Paradise Lost*, ed. Alastair Fowler (London: Longman, 1971).

Adam supposedly ought to have preferred a second Eve; but God repents after Moses calls him evil. The point of this allusion must be that Milton's theory of good is not voluntaristic (something is not good simply because God willed it). Neither the Son nor Adam, as conceived by Milton, is far from Moses. If Moses is the lowest common denominator, however, then morally good action cannot depend on knowing that you are following God's will (as the Son may be said to know that that's what he's doing, which Fowler supposes the telling distinction from Adam), since Moses does not assume that this is a test of his own faith. So sure is Moses that he is morally right that he says (echoed—an echo also unnoticed—in the passage about the fallen angels losing their names), "Yet now if thou wilt forgive their sin—; and if not, blot me, I pray thee, from the book which thou hast written" (Exod. 32:32). If before his fall Adam echoes the Son, afterward Eve repeats the Son's language. In book 3 the Son offers himself as a sacrifice for humanity:

> Behold mee then, mee for him, life for life
> I offer, on mee let thine anger fall;
> Account mee man; I for his sake will leave
> Thy bosom, and this glory next to thee
> Freely put off, and for him lastly die
> Well pleas'd, on me let Death wreck all his rage.
>   (3.236–41)

In book 10 Eve makes a similar offer:

> both have sinn'd, but thou
> Against God only, I against God and thee,
> And to the place of judgment will return,
> There with my cries importune Heaven, that all
> The sentence from thy head remov'd may light
> On me, sole cause to thee of all this woe,
> Mee mee only just object of his ire.
>   (9.930–36)

The willingness of each to take the blame has more meaning, once they really know what death means, than any accommodation they could have made to each other in Eden: surely Eve's difficult bravery more than makes up for her unfallen ambitiousness.

To persist in immortality, then, is less impressive than remaining unchanged despite one's mortal voice. The Son, Adam and Eve, Milton—all experience the burden of mortality, of a complete estrangement from angelic certitude, and the Son and Adam experience this burden willingly. Faithfulness in the midst of uncertainty is the poem's deepest mystery—faithfulness to a terribly intimate alterity. The radically intimate, radically distant and other being in *Paradise Lost* is God the Father. The language that can speak adequately of him is not known to immortality, and what mortality knows it cannot communicate to the immortals, since what it knows is the impossibility of adequate communication.

The Fall derives from idolatry, is imaged by idolatry, but finally leads to an apprehension that cannot be iconic. Eve eats the fruit in order to aggrandize herself and bows to the tree after she has eaten, but finally she and Adam experience the sense of loss that is the heart of *Paradise Lost*. Adam and Eve relinquish the fugitive and cloistered virtue that was theirs in Eden to bear mortals who, at their best, could produce the type of poetry in *Paradise Lost*.

Every reader must sense that Milton is a better poet than Raphael. Raphael represents the idolatrous angels who adore the letter but do not comprehend the spirit of what they adore. It is illuminating to compare his description of creation with Milton's. In book 7 we get the Urizenic model of creation. Blake was outraged by the notion that the outline of the world should have been determined with "golden Compasses" (7.225), but Raphael admires the workaday dispatch with which the Son and the Holy Ghost go about their business:

> On heav'nly ground they stood, and from the shore
> They view'd the vast immeasurable Abyss
> Outrageous as a Sea, dark, wasteful, wild,
> Up from the bottom turn'd by furious winds
> And surging waves, as Mountains to assault
> Heav'n's highth, and with the Centre mix the Pole.
> Silence, ye troubl'd waves, and thou Deep, peace,
> Said then th'Omnific Word, your discord end.
> . . . .
> Darkness profound
> Cover'd th'Abyss: but on the wat'ry calm
> His brooding wings the Spirit of God outspread,
> And vital virtue infus'd, and vital warmth
> Throughout the fluid Mass, but downward purg'd
> The black tartareous cold Infernal dregs
> Adverse to life; then founded, then conglob'd
> Like things to like, the rest to several place
> Disparted, and between spun out the Air,
> And Earth self-balanc't on her Centre hung.
> (7.210–17, 233–42)

Raphael takes the abyss to be adverse, and in this he understands it as it is usually presented in the poem. Thus for Satan the abyss is so much mire to be slogged through; for the angels, the fact that the Son does not get bogged down in it is a sign of his purity. Adam uses this meaning metaphorically when he cries, "O Conscience, into what Abyss of fears / And horrors hast thou driv'n me; out of which / I find no way, from deep to deeper plung'd!" (10.842–44). The poem opens with a much more profound version of creation, however. Instead of Raphael's alchemical and scientific terminology—"the fluid Mass," the "dregs" "purg'd," "Like things" "conglob'd" "to like"—Milton uses a more poetic language when he addresses the Spirit of God:

> Thou from the first
> Wast present, and with mighty wings outspread
> Dove-like satst brooding on the vast Abyss
> And mad'st it pregnant.
>
> (1.19–23)

It is this version of the abyss as God's element, in the same way that night is Milton's, that Adam will eventually learn, when he understands that his own element is really dust and that his name images not Platonic forms but the formless, the scattered. In his lamentation in book 10 Adam recognizes dust as "our final rest and native home" (10.1085) when he speaks the lines Mary Shelley used as her powerful epigraph: "Did I request thee, Maker, from my Clay / To mould me Man, did I solicit thee / From darkness to promote me?" (10.743–45). The knowledge that "we are dust, / And thither must return and be no more" (11.199) is the knowledge of death that the fruit of the tree instilled. Milton insists on the quality of this knowledge, altering Genesis to have Adam and Eve "know" (but not appreciate) their origin before the Fall. When God climaxes his judgment with the phrase "know thy Birth" before the line from Genesis, "For dust thou art, and shalt to dust return" (10.207–8), there is a strong implication that this knowledge is incommunicable to the immortals. Adam and Eve did not know what this meant, even though they were acquainted with its content, when they were immortal. Knowledge has come to mean something different to them now. The power of the judgment is not available to the unfallen. The judgment is powerful because it reveals the dark nativity of life as being the abyss. The knowledge available to human beings of their natural element produces the poetic affect that Milton associates with godliness. Humans go beyond the fallen angels in this knowledge, since the rebels keep asserting that "in our proper motion we ascend / Up to our native seat" (2.75–76). The rebels reject the apprehension of the abyss that establishes poetic power, and in this refusal of the unknowable they prove themselves as ultimately not like God. Adam's final statement that the Fall was fortunate does not refuse the unknowable. He goes beyond the foreknowledge vouchsafed to Michael when he sees beyond the end of time. Here he at last speaks Milton's words, achieves Milton's insight into the unknowable:

> How soon hath thy prediction, Seer blest,
> Measur'd this transient World, the Race of time,
> Till time stand fixt: beyond is all abyss,
> Eternity, whose end no eye can reach.
>
> (12.553–56)

One of the consequences of my argument is the claim that God does not ever appear in *Paradise Lost*: "whoever was heard or seen was not God." That claim seems to be worth making since it saves God from sounding ridiculous. As I read the poem, the figure of God is an emanation constructed for the dwarfish understandings of the angels. In the "Christian Doctrine" Milton tells us,

It is safest for us to form an image of God in our minds which corresponds to his representation and description of himself in the sacred writings. Admittedly, God is always described or outlined not as he really is but in such a way as will make him conceivable to us. Nevertheless, we ought to form just such a mental image of him as he, in bringing himself within the limits of our understanding, wishes us to form. Indeed he has brought himself down to our level expressly to prevent our being carried beyond the reach of human comprehension, and outside the written authority of scripture, into vague subtleties of speculation. (*Complete Prose*, 6:133–34)

The "safest" way is the way taken by the loyal angels, who are content to form an image of God in their minds. H. R. McCallum uses the injunction in this passage to argue that Milton wants us also to take the safe way out.[21] I agree that part of Milton very much wanted to repress his satanic sense that his idea of God was deeper than that of the Scriptures, but *Paradise Lost* is most powerful when Milton allows that sense full rein. Bloom remarks on the unconventional

---

21. H. R. McCallum, "Milton and Figurative Interpretation of the Bible," *University of Toronto Quarterly* 31 (1962), 397–415.

blasphemy of Milton's conventional claim to be in pursuit of "Things unattempted yet in Prose or Rhyme" (1.16), since one of the prose attempts of the story narrated in *Paradise Lost* is the Bible.[22] Milton at his most powerful refuses the safest way. He calls his song "advent'rous" (1.13), and I think we feel some surprise when Adam gives Eve the same epithet after the Fall (9.921). We can read this more than one way: the angelic reading interprets Milton as casting suspicion on his own enterprise by comparing it with Eve's sin; but more interesting (or adventurous), I think, is the idea that Eve's adventurous deed ultimately results, as Satan has pretended to predict, in enlarging human apprehensions of God.

Milton certainly would not countenance an image of God that went beyond the received images. But the important point is that he doesn't countenance received images either. The extreme Puritanism of his definition of idolatry in the "Christian Doctrine" cuts against an unadventurous literalism: "Idolatry means making or owning an idol for religious purposes, or worshipping it, *whether it be a representation of the true God* or of some false god" (*Complete Prose*, 6:690–91; my emphasis). Milton at his darkest and most powerful—at his most mortal— goes beyond received images, not to another image, but to meditations on loss and exile that share the inessential essence of what the Gnostics, writing against Raphael's hero Plato, called the forefathering abyss.

From the antihierarchical and iconoclastic perspective I have been claiming, Milton's Arminian belief in free will is not really such a surprise, since like the more extreme forms of Calvinism or antinomianism, it rejects the idea that the general will of God should end in a grace whose specificity restricts the play of generosity to a narrow elect. (Although Milton's God concedes that there will be such an elect, they are not the only humans who will find grace [3.183–202].) Milton rejects the ungenerously specifying idea that the wills of individual human beings would actually be predetermined to do good or evil. As I noted above, for Milton salvation was general, and helped by the generosity of God's general grace, individuals could conform or fail to conform to its conditions; for the more standard Puritan line, no specific individual could be worthy of salvation on his or her own, since humans are born in total depravity. Unconditional election, then, is indeed a gift from God, ascribable to his grace; but, like

22. Harold Bloom, *The Breaking of the Vessels* (Chicago: University of Chicago Press, 1982), p. 83.

Milton's general salvation, it has nothing to do with anything specific to the persons to whom God gives this gift.

Miltonic iconoclasm, first of all, rejects the opaque notion of charisma and rejects the incoherent idea (explored in the first part of my Shakespeare chapter) that some consciousnesses could be intrinsically special, sources of generosity without themselves first being radically beneficiary.[23] (It is because by definition there is nothing intrinsically special about the radically beneficiary that Milton rejects Calvinist predestination.) Milton rejects Charles's authority in *Eikonoklastes* because he rejects all claims to charismatic consciousness. In Milton's theology humans are the beneficiaries of the free will—the power of self-origination and self-coincidence—that God grants them and continues to grant through his prevenient grace. That will ought finally to be directed to the generality of God's generosity and not to any specific or created thing. The prevalence of that generality will finally come to the fore when God is no longer conceived as a person, as a specific being or Big Man, but when "God shall be all in all."

God will eventually become or be seen as a general being, indistinguishable from all his beneficiaries: this is even the angel's doctrine in *Paradise Lost*. At the farthest possible remove from this is idolatry: incoherent when directed at specific consciousnesses and even more so when directed at objects without consciousness.

The commandment against idolatry is a commandment against the projection of a god or set of gods without consciousness, and yet, as I argued above, only a god without consciousness can be conceived as an original benefactor and not a beneficiary. When God shall be all in all, one feels, he will become at least a kind of Plotinian unity if not the Gnostic abyss I argued for; it is precisely in this way that he will cease being understood as a person. (As for the Son, his personhood does not pose a problem since for the Arian Milton he does not have the originary and originating ontological status of the Father.) Thus the idol can be seen as parodying some of the features of the radically unknowable God. In the idol, specific and general threaten to come together.

The idol is like the allegorical figure: it is something without interiority, something whose otherness is the otherness that lacks interiority or the receptive passivity of consciousness. Yet allegorical fig-

23. I use the theological term *charisma* advisedly here, since my argument is that Satan rejects the Son's charisma, and also the Father's, in *Paradise Lost* and that this is a kind of iconoclasm.

ures always have an apparent consciousness, an artifical intelligence. Perhaps Milton's Plotinian or unknowable and Gnostic God can be distinguished from an idol through the counterintuitive claim that the idol has consciousness (a consciousness without passivity) and that God does not. Idols and allegorical figures are utterly public, utterly engaged in public interactions. Their being consists entirely in their social existence. All that they lack of consciousness is its passivity. This would mean, however, that they lack the capacity to become part of a preterite community, "the community of those who have no community."

From another point of view, however, the idol or image can be seen not as a kind of fully public participator in life free from the extreme passivity that is the vanishing residue of consciousness. Rather, if the fact that it is not a subject is apprehended, it can be seen as something purely residualized, an image and not a presence. This is the fact that I think Milton urges with regard to the image of God in *Paradise Lost*, for this kind of image is tied up with the mortality of consciousness. As Blanchot writes, the remains of the dead become for us pure images, pure resemblances, resembling nothing. The dead person is both here and nowhere, having become only an image. "Man is made in his image," he writes,

> this is what the strangeness of the dead body's resemblance teaches us. But the formula must also be understood this way: *man is unmade in his own image*. The image has nothing to do with signification, sense, such as they are implied by the existence of the world, the effort of truth, the law and the light of day. The *image* of an object not only is not the sense of that object and not only does not aid in any understanding of it, but tends to withdraw it from the world in maintaining it in the immobility of a resemblance which has nothing to resemble.[24]

Worship, or idolatry—as I argue Satan partly understood—is not the proper response to an image when the image has nothing to do with the world but has rather become an "anonymous, sightless, and impersonal resemblance" (*L'espace littéraire*, p. 355) which undoes the world. Worship seeks to naturalize under the sign of power a relationship that is not a relationship but an apprehension of the proximity of alterity.[25]

24. Maurice Blanchot, *L'espace littéraire* (Paris: Gallimard, 1955), p. 354.
25. Thus Blanchot sees idolatry as an impatiently literal response to the image, but one which can come undone: "Cette exigence d'un dénouement prématuré est le principe de la figuration, elle engendre l'*image* ou si l'on veut l'idole, et la malédiction qui s'y attache est celle qui s'attache à l'idolâtrie. L'homme veut l'unité tout de suite, il la

I think that *Paradise Lost* is a meditation on these two different conceptions of the image. It rejects the former as the same kind of meretriciousness that can be found in pagan epics. As to the latter conception, Milton's meditations seem to me close to Blanchot's. In Emmanuel Levinas's related formulation, the face of the other is the face of God. In *Paradise Lost* this comes out, I think, as the idea that the image of the human is an image of the God who has no proper image (although the Son is the image he cultivates for the angels). The image of the human then resembles nothing in the world. The fallen Adam bitterly rails against Eve that she was "supernumerary" (10.887)—an excess that led to his utter loss. But he moves from this bitterness to his earlier and more noble sense that she is not an excessive object productive of loss but is herself the human image of loss. Images, when regarded purely as images, undo themselves as presences and finally undo even the presence of the image. Adam and Eve turn out also to be here and nowhere: images of mortality and also mortal images, images of a God who can't be imaged, least of all as an immortal radiance. Regina Schwartz writes of *Paradise Lost* as moving from shadowy type not to truth but to shadowy type, and I think that in Milton as in Herbert and Shakespeare, bounty gives way to extremity, to a residualized language that is the language of poetry and not of power.[26] As in Shakespeare, authority for Milton depends on

---

veut dans la séparation même, il se la représente, et cette représentation, image de l'unité, reconstitue aussitôt l'élément de la dispersion où il se perd de plus en plus, car l'image, en tant qu'image, ne peut jamais être atteinte, et elle lui dérobe, en outre, l'unité dont elle est l'image, elle l'en sépare en se rendant inaccessible et en la rendant inaccessible" (ibid., pp. 92–93; This demand for a premature denouement is the principle of figuration; it engenders the *image* or if you prefer the idol, and the malediction which attaches to it is the malediction which attaches to idolatry. Man wants unity right away, he wants it within separation itself, he represents it to himself, and this representation, image of unity, immediately reconstitutes the element of dispersal where he becomes more and more lost; for the image, insofar as it is an image, can never be attained, and it dispossesses him, besides, of the unity of which it is the image, it separates him from that unity by making itself inaccessible and by making unity inaccessible).

26. Regina Schwartz, "From Shadowy Types to Shadowy Types: The Unendings of *Paradise Lost*," *Milton Studies* 24 (1988), 123–39. This essay is in many ways in concord with mine. Schwartz argues that "to speak of types at all is to encode particulars with the blueprint of another master-narrative: the Bible." She also argues that this reference to authority, to what I would call the authority of the public or general, is undone by Milton, who replaces fulfillment with perpetual deferral: "Summary conclusions that continue, and so do not summarize or conclude; moments of enlightenment that turn out to be veiled after all: Milton has foiled all of the classic features of typology, and he has used typology to do it. The shadowy types allude to a truth he withdraws, and the prefigurations to a fulfillment he obviates" (p. 133). Just such a shadowy type would the Blanchotian image recall, as another passage from Blanchot might indicate: "L'image,

privileged visibility, but beyond that visibility, and beyond that authority, is the language of unreality—the unreality of the image, of Calliope, for example. This is a language of irremediable loss. For the image in Milton might be said to be invisible and ungraspable, just as the face of the other is invisible, and if you are a being who can see it, you too are doomed to invisibility.

The image makes for a general undoing of generality. In the real world, Peirce would argue, there are no images since all images participate in ontology directly: the world is made up of signs, and signs have the substantial being of reality. Idols too have this reality. The Blanchotian image, however, has no such substance, and thus it is finally related to the literary, which becomes an uncanny image precisely because it rejects all images. Blanchot describes what I think

---

d'après l'analyse commune, est après l'objet: elle en est la suite; nous voyons, puis nous imaginons. Après l'objet viendrait l'image. «Après» signifie qu'il faut d'abord que la chose s'éloigne pour se laisser ressaisir. Mais cet éloignement n'est pas le simple changement de place d'un mobile qui demeurerait, cependant, le même. L'éloignement est ici au coeur de la chose. La chose était là, que nous saisissions dans le mouvement vivant d'une action compréhensive,—et, devenue image, instantanément la voilà devenue l'insaisissable, l'inactuelle, l'impassible, non pas la même chose éloignée, mais cette chose comme éloignement, la présente dans son absence, la saisissable parce qu'insaisissable, apparaissant en tant que disparue, le retour de ce qui ne revient pas, le coeur étrange du lointain comme vie et coeur unique de la chose" (*L'espace littéraire*, p. 347; The image, according to the normal analysis, is after the object: it follows on the object; we see, then we imagine. After the object would come the image. 'After' means that first the thing must become distant in order to become graspable. But this distancing is not the simple change in place of something moveable which would nevertheless remain the same. Distancing is here at the heart of the thing. The thing was there; we grasped it in the living movement of a comprehensive action—and, become image, suddenly behold it become the ungraspable, the unactual, the impossible, not the same thing distanced, but that thing as distancing, the present in its absence, the graspable because ungraspable, appearing insofar as it has disappeared, the return which does not come again, the strange heart of the far away as the life and unique heart of the thing). This might almost be a reading of Milton's Sonnet 23. Herman Rapaport's interesting book undertakes a far more Derridean account of Milton than mine (*Milton and the Postmodern* [Lincoln: University of Nebraska Press, 1983]). But naturally there are significant overlaps between Derrida and Blanchot, especially since Blanchot is Derrida's strong precursor. In this regard Rapaport is interested in the idea of simulacra without origin, which bear some resemblance to Blanchot's comments on the image and to Schwartz's account of shadowy types ungrounded in a truth finally present. Milton has lately received some other deconstructive readings, readings which bear a family resemblance to mine: see Herbert Marks, "The Blotted Book," in *Remembering Milton*, pp. 211–33; Jonathan Goldberg, *Voice Terminal Echo: Postmodernism and English Renaissance Texts* (New York: Methuen, 1986), pp. 124–58; Catherine Belsey, *John Milton: Language, Gender, Power* (New York: Blackwell, 1988); and, earlier, the structuralist reading of Donald Bouchard's *Milton: A Structural Reading* (Montreal: McGill-Queens University Press, 1974), for example. But I wish to eschew the Derridean categories, since I am interested not in linguistic undecidability but in what I am calling preterite affect.

happens in *Paradise Lost* as well, and in any system where authority seeks a place in language and not in presence:

> Poetry is commonly thought to be a language that, more than any other, appropriates images. It is probable that there is here an allusion to a much more essential transformation: the poem isn't a poem because it includes a certain number of figures, of metaphors, of comparisons. On the contrary: the particular characteristic of the poem is that nothing makes for an image in it. So what we are seeking must be expressed differently: isn't it the case that language as a whole becomes, in literature, an image, not a language which would contain images or which would describe reality in figures, but which would be its own image, an image of language—and not a language in images—or again an imaginary language, a language which no one speaks, that is to say which is spoken from its own absence, just as the image appears upon the absence of the thing, a language which addresses itself also to the shadow of events, not to their reality, just because the words which express them are not signs, but images, images of words and words where things become images? (*L'espace littéraire*, p. 28n)

Wittgenstein asks, "What makes my image of him an image of *him*?" and cautions, "Not its looking like him." What moors the image to the object is the general realm of language games in which they both participate. A crown in chess is the image of the king because we recognize not a resemblance but the image's use in the game. That the pawn looks something like the bishop does not make the pawn an image of the bishop. An image that resembles him is an image of *him* if there is a language game in which someone intends to (make a move in a language game, a move which will) refer to him. Resemblance alone will not connect the two. Resemblance or the image is instead the residue of the icon when it has lost all its virtues, projected or real. This space of loss, of the depletion or exhaustion of effectivity or even of being in the world, is literary space.

Index

Library of Congress Cataloging-in-Publication Data

Flesch, William, 1956–
   Generosity and the limits of authority : Shakespeare, Herbert, Milton / William
Flesch.
      p.   cm.
   Includes bibliographical references and index.
   ISBN 0-8014-2642-1
   1. English literature—Early modern, 1500–1700—History and
criticism.   2. Generosity in literature.   3. Shakespeare, William, 1564–1616—
Criticism and interpretation.   4. Herbert, George, 1593–1633—Criticism and
interpretation.   5. Milton, John, 1608–1674—Criticism and interpretation.
6. Authority in literature.   I. Title.
PR428.G45F58   1992
820.9'353—dc20   92-52753